The Selected Works of Cyril Connolly

Volume One: The Modern Movement

by the same author

The Rock Pool (1936)

Enemies of Promise (1938)

The Unquiet Grave (1944)

The Condemned Playground (1945)

The Missing Diplomats (1952)

Ideas and Places (1953)

Les Pavillons (1962)

Previous Convictions (1963)

The Modern Movement (1965)

The Evening Colonnade (1973)

A Romantic Friendship (1975)

Journal and Memoir (1983)

Shade Those Laurels (1990)

The Selected Works of Cyril Connolly

Volume One: The Modern Movement

CYRIL CONNOLLY

Edited and with an Introduction by Matthew Connolly
Foreword by William Boyd

PICADOR

For my family

First published 2002 by Picador
an imprint of Pan Macmillan Ltd
Pan Macmillan, 20 New Wharf Road, London N1 9RR
Basingstoke and Oxford
Associated companies throughout the world
www.panmacmillan.com

ISBN 0 330 48169 X

1 3 5 7 9 8 6 4 2

A CIP catalogue record for this book is available
from the British Library.

Typeset by SX Composing DTP, Rayleigh, Essex
Printed and bound in Great Britain by
Mackays of Chatham plc, Chatham, Kent

Contents

Acknowledgements

Thanks to my mother for encouraging this project; Peter Straus for his enthusiasm; everyone at Picador, especially Pete Ouvry for his consistent care; William Boyd for the foreword; Deborah Rogers, my father's agent; Jeremy Lewis, ahead of me at every turn; the London Library, for having lots of books; Colindale for long, happy days of microfilm; Bella for lending her flat; Mary for the quote; and anybody interested enough to read this.

Matthew Connolly

The Summing Up by W. Somerset Maugham. Extract reprinted by permission of A. P. Watt Ltd on behalf of the Royal Literary Fund.
Death in the Afternoon by Ernest Hemingway, published by Jonathan Cape. Extracts reprinted by permission of The Random House Group Ltd.
The Cantos, and 'The Garrett' from *Selected Poems*, by Ezra Pound. Extracts reprinted by permission of Faber and Faber Ltd.
'As I walked out one evening', 'A Summer Night', 'Who's Who' and 'Marginalia' from *Collected Poems*; 'Spain', 'I see it often since you've been away' and 'The latest ferrule has now tapped the curb' from *The English Auden*; and 'Birthday Poem' from *Look, Stranger!*, by W. H. Auden. Extracts reprinted by permission of Faber and Faber Ltd.
The Dog Beneath the Skin by W. H. Auden and Christopher Isherwood. Extract reprinted by permission of Faber and Faber Ltd.
'The Love Song of J. Alfred Prufrock', 'Preludes I and IV' and 'A Dedication to My Wife' from *Collected Poems 1909–1962*, and 'Song to the Opherian' from *The Waste Land Facsimile*, by T. S. Eliot. Extracts reprinted by permission of Faber and Faber Ltd.

'The Conflict' by C. Day Lewis. Extract reprinted by permission of PFD on behalf of the Estate of C. Day Lewis.
Another Time by W. H. Auden. Extract reprinted by permission of Faber and Faber Ltd.
Extracts from *Ulysses – Anna Livia Plurabelle; Work in Progress/ Finnegans Wake* reproduced with the permission of the Estate of James Joyce © Copyright, the Estate of James Joyce.

Foreword

In early 1945 Evelyn Waugh was languishing in Yugoslavia, bored and dispirited, waiting for the war to end. He had recently completed *Brideshead Revisited*, the most important novel of his career, when Nancy Mitford sent him a copy of *The Unquiet Grave* by Cyril Connolly. Waugh read and reread Connolly's book and scribbled his reactions on the margins. The marginalia are extensive, full of insight and full of self-delusion. Waugh used the opportunity both to excoriate and to analyse his old acquaintance ('friend' is too loaded a word for their complex relationship) and the comments he made on the book are fascinating, not just for what they say about Connolly but also for the light they throw on Waugh himself.

For Waugh was obsessed with Connolly: fascinated and irritated by him; alternately admiring and contemptuous; secretly envious and publicly derisive. These are a set of contrasting reactions easily understood by Connolly fans (amongst whom I count myself among the most ardent) because you cannot read Cyril Connolly for very long without wanting to acquire – and then developing – a relationship with the personality of the man himself. This is rarely the case with readers and writers. Everyone is curious (I'm deeply curious about the character of Evelyn Waugh, for example) but the dislocation between the mind that creates and the man who suffers (in T. S. Eliot's phrase) is usually happily observed. My admiration of Waugh's novels is not diluted by his rebarbative personality. But with Connolly there is a marked difference and the difference is that the artist and the man are so conjoined and intermingled that you cannot savour the one without the other and vice versa. Connolly famously declared that it was the 'true function' of a writer to try and produce a masterpiece 'and that no other task is of any consequence'. Whatever the veracity of this claim there's no doubt that one of the great frustrations of his life was that he himself so conspicuously failed to live up to his own stern injunction. Yet the more one reads and the more one learns about him perhaps the fairest conclusion to arrive at is that Cyril Connolly's greatest memorial – his particular masterpiece – is precisely that conjunction of life and work: that both how he lived (1903–1974) and what work he produced form a unique and lasting whole. To invert the old saying: in Connolly's case we cannot see the trees for the wood. It's the wood – whole and entire – that interests us and not so much the individual oaks and elms.

This may seem harsh but, while almost everything Connolly wrote was stylish and intelligent, informed and passionate, there is no one book, or sequence of writings, that one can hold up as unequivocally excellent or fully achieved. The famous parodies are clever but finally lightweight and ephemeral; the millions of words of literary criticism and journalism suffer from the built-in obsolescence that undermines all journalism, however fine. *Enemies of Promise*, that precocious memoir, is good – but patchy. *The Unquiet Grave* is maddeningly flawed – pretentious, self-serving, arch – as well as achingly honest and true. *The Rock Pool* (Connolly's one novel) is an interesting failure – and so on. Yet the sum of his uneven parts add up to something formidable. He's a writer for all seasons, for all readers. Waugh sneered at his amateur psychoanalysing. 'We love only once,' Connolly wrote, 'and on how that first great love affair shapes itself depends the pattern of our lives.' 'Nonsense,' Waugh mocked in the margin. But there was never a truer comment made about his own life and situation and perhaps it pained him to see Connolly hitting a personal nail so squarely on the head.

Thus one's reading and relish of Connolly's work is shaped and conditioned by what one knows of the man himself to a degree not shared by any other writers. More will be derived, for example, from reading the prefaces to the monthly issues of *Horizon* (which magazine he edited from 1939 to 1950) if you know about the history of *Horizon*, Connolly's editorial lifestyle, his love affairs, the animosities and gossip that surrounded that period of London cultural life.* *The Rock Pool* – self-conscious, straining for effect – becomes far less unwieldy once you know the background to its composition and who the thinly disguised characters are based on, and so forth.

This is not to denigrate or diminish Connolly's skill as a writer and literary journalist. I first came across his work during the late 1960s and early '70s when he was writing a weekly book review for the *Sunday Times*. At school and university I read Connolly's weekly review religiously, whatever the subject, with – at that time – no insider knowledge about the man. What stimulated me was, I think, his enthusiasm. This was no dry, jaded don routinely turning out his 800 words, no embittered hack assailing grander reputations for the sake of a weekend's frisson. Though I now know the drudgery of the weekly review caused him intense pain it never seemed to come through in the writing. He could pick and choose, of course, and the books he wrote about reflected his passions – French literature, the Classics, the Augustans, the great Modernists – and his passion was contagious. From the reviews I moved on to *The Unquiet Grave* and was completely captivated by it. This 'word cycle', a loosely yoked collection of *pensées*, lengthy quotations, reflections on literature and autobiography, in many ways earns all of Waugh's strictures – snobbish, fey, posturing, self-pitying – yet I can think of few better evocations of intellectual melancholy, if I can put it that way, of the dissatisfactions inherent in a life nurtured by and charged with European culture: of individual human insufficiency confronted by the great artistic ideals and achievements. Connolly is no Montaigne, he has none of his calm, resigned sagacity (though Montaigne is one of the presiding spirits of the book), but Connolly captures something ineffably present in the human spirit. And as he roves through world literature trying to pin down these emotions he does so with a candour and a kind of gloomy relish that is very easy to

* Essential accompaniment to these volumes therefore includes Jeremy Lewis's unrivalled *Cyril Connolly, a Life*; Michael Sheldon's excellent book on the Horizon years, *Friends of Promise*, Barbara Skelton's hilarious memoir of life with Cyril – *Tears Before Bedtime* – and David Pryce-Jones's *Cyril Connolly: Journal and Memoir*. There are others but these form an ideal starter pack.

identify with (particularly when you are young: it is a perfect book for the young, would-be *littérateur*). We have all felt like this, have reached to art for solace and found only more despair, but only Connolly could be so unashamedly candid about it and make a virtue of his inadequacy.

This honesty, try as he might to disguise it, surfaces again and again in his writings and I think is what makes him perennially modern. Connolly is always confessing his failures one way or another, and like all great confessors (Rousseau and Boswell spring to mind as real Connolly precursors and fellow-spirits) we are both appalled by what they tell us and at the same time drawn to them. We're all human – all too human – but not all of us will admit to it in print. The vicarious thrill and recognition we take in confessional writings is one of the great literary pleasures and is nowhere more evident than in Connolly's *London Journal*. Here we have the essence of the young Cyril, just down from Oxford, out of pocket, out of love, fretting and dissatisfied. I think the *London Journal* deserves its place alongside *The Unquiet Grave* and *Enemies of Promise* as representing the best of Connolly. One regrets that this fragment is all we have (it seems Connolly was more of a note-book-jotter than a journal-keeper). On the evidence of these few pages he could have been our modern Boswell; and how wonderful it would have been to have Connolly's *journal intime* to set alongside Virginia Woolf's diaries – fascinating, yet highly contrived and self-conscious, written, unlike Connolly's, with both eyes firmly fixed on posterity.

Connolly earns my further affection by being the great self-appointed anti-Bloomsbury figure. He drew up the battle lines himself early in life, placing himself in Chelsea ('that leafy tranquil cultivated *spielraum* . . . where I worked and wandered') precisely to counter what he saw as the desiccated fastidiousness, the preciosity, the snobbism and the cliquishness of Bloomsbury. Chelsea, by contrast, was more open to Europe, grubbier, sexier, more rackety, more worldly and hedonistic. It was not simply a question of the new generation rejecting the values of the older, he saw instead a real opposition: of contrasting lifestyles, of political and cultural values, of attitudes to art. And it was an opposition that he maintained all his life: there was always in his life not just a love of European culture (especially that of France and Spain) but also a love of beauty, of women, of alcohol and food, of sea and sunbathing, of idleness and travel. Connolly is one of the great evokers of place and of pleasure: whether he is talking about a meal of a rough red wine and *steak frites*, or wandering through Lisbon or Rome looking at architecture, one feels through his words the physical relish he takes in the experience. He makes you want to do the same things and derive the same intense enjoyment as he does. When he writes that he wants to live in France, somewhere in a magic circle embracing the Dordogne, Quercy, the Aveyron and the Gers, in a 'golden classical house, three stories high with *œil de bœf* windows looking out over water . . . [with] a terrace for winter, a great tree for summer and a lawn for games; a wooden hill behind and a river below, then a sheltered garden indulgent to fig and nectarine . . .' you respond, instinctively, 'How true, that's exactly where I want to live and how I want to live as well.' In a curious way he is both a great and dangerous role model: most of us share, to one degree or another, Connolly's prodigious appetites, both venal and exalted, and most of us share, to one degree or another, Connolly's failings, both petty and debilitating. This small, podgy, balding, pug-faced, funny, gossipy, lazy, clever, cowardly, hedonistic, fractious, difficult man somehow manages to enshrine in his work and life everything that we aspire to, and that intellectually ennobles us, and all that is weak and worst in us as well.

I think this explains both the fascination and repulsion that Waugh felt. Physically and temperamentally they were not far apart: both small, egotistical, selfish, stout and unhandsome. Waugh took the opposite route to Connolly and studiously and desperately reinvented himself as a parodic Tory squire cum reactionary man of letters. It is a facile over-simplification, but Waugh decided to live a lie while Connolly remained true to himself – however flawed or inadequate that self happened to be. Both men were consumed with self-loathing: both of them, Waugh said, were 'always tired, always bored, always hurt, always hating'. Waugh became the rich and acclaimed novelist, with a large family, living in a country house; Connolly was always the indigent, the hard-up journalist scraping a living but, somehow, seeming to attract a succession of beautiful women prepared to put up with him. Waugh's life appears superficially the more successful and achieved and yet, for all his endless moaning, Connolly seems far and away the happier man. The secret, I think, was in his resolute secularity and worldliness: he did not seek solace in spirituality (as Waugh did), instead he took both simple and intelligent pleasure in what the world offered, whether it came in the shape of a building, a marsupial, the company of friends, a fine claret, a train journey, a cigar, a sunny terrace, a beautiful woman, a good book, a Georgian teapot or a painting. That relish of life and its potential joys (and the sense of their fragility and transience) permeates his work and gives it its enduring value – and, I suspect, for I never met him, permeated the man as well. There is a wonderful passage in the *London Journal* that, I believe, sums up the essence of the Cyril Connolly appeal. It was written in 1929. Unhappy in love, paranoid, fed up with London and duplicitous friends, the young Cyril Connolly flees to Paris for consolation and takes a room at the Hôtel de la Louisiane on the Left Bank:

> Hôtel de la Louisiane
>
> . . . I have a room for 400 francs a month and at last I will be living within my own and other people's income. I am tired of acquaintances and tired of friends unless they're intelligent, tired also of extrovert unbookish life. Me for good talk, wet evenings, intimacy, *vins rouges en carafe*, reading, relative solitude, street worship, exploration of the least known *arrondissements*, shopgazing, alley sloping, café crawling, Seine loafing, and plenty of writing from the table by this my window where I can watch the streets light up . . . I am for the intricacy of Europe, the discrete and many folded strata of the old world, the past, the North, the world of ideas. I am for the Hôtel de la Louisiane.

Yes, yes! you cry spontaneously, when you read this. So am I. I'm for all this too. I'm for the life of the Hôtel de la Louisiane. And this, in the end, also explains why we are for Cyril Connolly.

William Boyd. Chelsea, October 2000

Introduction

'One of the penalties of parenthood is to have our love life explained by our children.' So my father wrote in 1971 (beginning a review of a book on Pound by his daughter, Mary de Rachewiltz). Happily, if he had any fears that either of his own children would do the same, they were unfounded. Instead, it is a great pleasure to be able to draw attention back to his writing. It is a lot better than mine, so I shall be brief in explaining my selection.

Volume I, *The Modern Movement*, comprises various critical essays and reviews largely concerned with modern writing and authors, and begins, ironically, with his farewell to novel-reviewing at the early age of twenty-five. He returns to novels after a couple of examples of his reviews in non-literary fields (although he does bring writers into his exhibition review – notably Waugh, characterizing the relationship between them that William Boyd describes in his Foreword). In the brevity of his film-reviewing career he was following the example of his friend John Betjeman, who had foresworn the practice in 1935.*

The first section of Volume I is dominated by *Enemies of Promise* – or by half of it, as I have disobeyed my father's instructions by detaching the autobiographical section (with the excuse that it does appear later, in Volume II). The other book that features in this volume is *The Modern Movement*, which also lends its title, but due to limited space it has been abbreviated to the list of '100 Key Books' and the overview essays.

My father's discussion of modern writers leads on to his passion for collecting their first editions, culminating in the Texas exhibition

* Betjeman's account of this is reprinted in *Coming Home*, ed. Candida Lycett Green, 1997.

alluded to in the earlier piece 'Apotheosis in Austin', in which Waugh taunts him from beyond the (Unquiet) grave.*

The last section of this volume is centred upon his time as editor of the magazine *Horizon* (1939–50), when attention was focused on the writer's role in war, politics and society: the issue of a living wage for writers is raised in *The Cost of Letters*.† The volume concludes with a later post-mortem of '*la littérature engagée*' and a piece addressing the nostalgia for *Horizon*.

The final issue of *Horizon* included his famously gloomy, but also prophetic, pronouncement: 'It is closing time in the gardens of the West and from now on an artist will be judged only by the resonance of his solitude or the quality of his despair.' This deserves to be included in any Connolly anthology, so I quote it here. That was the hard part of making this selection: deciding what to omit. His reviews were looked forward to by many each week, and even at this distance every one of them seems to contain one brilliant line at the very least. Looking through them all, it is clear that he couldn't be accused of laziness, although that is the charge he levelled against himself. Even if he is sometimes coasting along, stylistically he remains far ahead of the pack.

Matthew Connolly

* A full account of Waugh's commentary was given by Alan Bell in the *Spectator*, 7 March 1987.

† The replies to this from other authors were reprinted and updated in a book of the same name in 1998, with an introduction by Alain de Botton.

Ninety Years of Novel-Reviewing

(1929)

The reviewing of novels is the white man's grave of journalism; it corresponds, in letters, to building bridges in some impossible tropical climate. The work is gruelling, unhealthy, and ill-paid, and for each scant clearing made wearily among the springing vegetation the jungle overnight encroaches twice as far. A novel-reviewer is too old at thirty; early retirement is inevitable, 'les femmes soignent ces infirmes féroces au retour des pays chauds', and their later writings all exhibit a bitter and splenetic brilliance whose secret is only learnt in the ravages on the liver made by their terrible school. What a hard-boiled, what a Congo quality informs their soured romanticism! Invalided out only in February, my memory is still fresh with the last burgeoning of prolific and uniform shrubs and bushes. Those leathery weeds, so hard to kill, at first attract through the beauty of their flowers – the blurb or puff 'splurging', as a botanist has described it, 'its gross trumpet out of the gaudy wrapper'. Wiry, yet insipid, characterless, though bright, these first-flowering blooms of Girtonia or Ballioli are more oppressive in their profusion, most reviewers will agree, than the forest giants, the Galsworthys and Walpoleworthys, whose creeper-clad trunks defy attempts to fell them.

An unpleasant sight in the jungle is the reviewer who goes native. Instead of fighting the vegetation, he succumbs to it, and, running perpetually from flower to flower, he welcomes each with cries of 'genius!' 'What grace, what irony and distinction, what passionate sincerity!' he exclaims as the beaming masterpieces reproduce themselves rapidly, and only from the banned amorphophallus, 'unpleasant, dreary, difficult, un-English', he turns away his eyes.

Another sight for the cynic is the arrival of the tenderfoot who comes fresh from the university and determined, 'above all, to be just – to judge every book on its merits – not to be led astray by the airs and graces of writing, the temptations to score off a book in reviewing, but primarily to try and help the author while advising the reader as well'. 'The great thing,' he begins, 'is never to forget one's standards – and never to grow stale.' I remember very well sitting round the camp fire one night when Tenderfoot and 'Goo-Goo' (who was then going native) were 'doing' a book. The date escapes me, but it should be easily traceable, for I remember there was some talk of the *Mercury* falling off, and the *Criterion* getting dull.

'This book,' said Goo-Goo, 'has genius, and not only is it a work of genius – of passionate intellectual sincerity and emotional directness – but it comes very near to being the best novel of the month, or at least of the latter part of it.'

'Although I would willingly give an earnest,' interrupted the Tenderfoot, 'that this is Miss Bumfiddle's first novel, she seems to be a writer of very delicate intention, and has brought to a difficult subject a restraint, a distinction, that, to my thinking, makes *Goosegrass or Cleavers* remarkable not only as a novel, which, if not of the very first order (remember my standards), does at least attempt to state the series of reactions which a young woman of keener sensibility and more vulnerable perception than the common must inevitably receive in the conflict between genius – I use the word in all circumspection – and what, for want of a better definition, we must call life. I should like, however, to suggest to Miss Bumfiddle, in all fairness—'

'*Goosegrass or Cleavers*,' broke in Goo-Goo, beaming tipsily, 'is modern, as the name implies – as modern as Matisse or Murasaki. It is bold, and confronts the critic in all the perishable flamework of youth – of post-war youth burning fitfully in all its incandescent ardour. Take the scene where Alimony leaves her parents:

> Midway between springsummer and summerautumn falls the old-fashioned month of August-come-July – season of gross yellow moons,

brown grass, and lousy yearnings. Alimony lay awake counting the slats of the blind that seemed to scab viciously across the rich broth of evening sunlight like the splayed fingers of a crucified neargod, a flayed Marsyas. She hated bed by daylight. Through the windows came the noise of the party and her parents' voices. 'Now try and rush the red down to the next hoop – with luck you might perhaps push her through it. O dear! You should have poked her more.' 'But I did poke her.' Alimony cringed involuntarily. To think she ever would be one with the ungainly old – and yet to-morrow was her birthday! It was hot, stifling – out in the fields perhaps. . . . She opened the introduction to a novel beside her. 'A short while ago a friend of mine put into my hands an object which I had little difficulty in recognizing – Sir James Buchan and Mr. John Barrie, whom I consulted, soon confirmed me. "Yes," they said, "it is a book, but only identifiable as such by a few discriminating people."' Idly she turned the pages. 'Girt slough of cloud lay cast upon the jannock mere. Weaver, be th'art there – weaver, I'm drained with love of you among the drule scrobs, though in the village they call me a hard woman.' 'Ah, to write – to write like that,' thought Alimony – 'to write like Mary Webb. But how, without experience? Out in the fields perhaps.' . . . She rose and collected a few scattered belongings. Tiptoeing down the stairs, she saw it was not yet past seven. Suddenly she imagined herself tiptoeing through life, a broken stalk embalmed of this day's roses – like her own equivocal youth, now cast behind for ever. 'Alimony! go back to bed.' It was her mother. Something in Alimony seemed to snap. She turned, her face transfigured. 'For crap's sake leave me alone, mother. I will not be run by people; all my life people have been trying to run me and all my life I've been escaping them. I damn will continue to. I guess my life is my own, even if it is a mess, isn't it? And you presume to speak to me when I have to listen to you and Poppa fighting on the lawn like a pair of alley cats. Hell and all it gripes me so I guess I could upchuck.' 'Dearest mine o' mine, my own ownest, my octopet.' 'Oh, go sit on a tack, Mother – can't you see I've had enough of it?' She flung out, past the front door, with its friendly knocker, on to the gravel, by the dining-room windows. She turned to look through them. Her birthday presents were there for the morning; on the table was the solemn cake with its eleven candles. The click of croquet balls sounded faint on the lawn. 'Weaver,' she sighed again; and something told her the old Alimony was dying – would be dead, perhaps, before the night was past – before even the moon of metroland had risen on the filling stations.

'A strong book,' resumed Goo-Goo. 'This is no work for those who prefer—'

'One has to be on one's guard, of course,' said Tenderfoot, 'against being too sympathetic to a writer simply because she provides a restatement of one's own problems.'

'One of the few modern masterpieces,' continued the other, 'a book for the library rather than the linen room – for those who like to find, between a Bradshaw and breviary, between a gold and a glister, a modern-ancient trifle that will fulfil Milton's definition of the novel as something slow, sinuous, and sexy. A work, in fact, a work of— But be it not mine to deface our lovely currency by stressing that most distressful word. Simply I will say – slowly, sinuously, but not, I hope, sexily, "Welcome, Miss Bumfiddle! welcome, Alimony!"'

And yet, looking back on those evenings when the fates of so many unreadable books, and so many more unread ones, were brilliantly decided, I can't help feeling regret and tenderness rather than relief at being free of them. It is easy to forget the nerve-strain and the nausea, the cynical hopelessness with which we strove to quench the indefatigable authors. There is something so clean and surprising about a parcel of review copies that one cannot but feel pleasure in opening them. The sense of getting something for nothing, though short-lived, is pleasant while it lasts, and the early expectations one had of discovering a new writer are perhaps less keen a pleasure than one's later hopes of being able to discredit an old one. The real fault of English fiction is that it has ceased to be readable. If novels were only this, it would matter much less that they were bad. American writers are readable; in general, a second-rate American book carries a reader along with it. He may resent this afterwards, but it is desirable at the time. The English novel doesn't, and never will so long as it consists either of arranged emotional autobiography or a carefully detached description of stupid people to show that the author is too clever to be clever. But I am getting into my stride again. Meanwhile a new generation of novel-reviewers is growing up, and this thought brings me to the real tragedy of reviewing – to that ironical and irrevocable law of poetic justice which ennobles the humdrum work and allows the broken journalist to feel in his very ruin something of the divine. For all the novels that he scotches the novel will in time scotch him; like the King at Nemi, the slayer shall himself be slain. Brave and agile, the reviewer enters the ring. He rushes blindly at the red wrappers. He disembowels a few old hacks. But his onsets eventually grow futile, his weapons are blunted, his words are stale. He may go under nobly, a Croker facing his Keats; he may simply wear out in praising or abusing – (it matters not which) – the never-ceasing flow of second-rate and worthy productions – but eventually the jungle claims him.

What advice, then, would I give to someone forced – for no one could be willing – to become a reviewer? Firstly, never praise; praise dates you. In reviewing a book you like, write for the author; in reviewing any other, write for the public. Read the books you review, but you should need only to skim a page to settle if they are worth reviewing. Never touch novels written by your friends. Remember that the object of the critic is to revenge himself on the creator, and his method must depend on whether the book is good or bad, whether he dare condemn it himself or must lie quiet and let it blow over. Every good reviewer has a subject. He specializes in that subject on which he has not been able to write a book, and his aim is to see that no one else does. He stands behind the ticket-queue of fame, banging his rivals on the head as they bend low before the guichet. When he has laid out enough he becomes an authority, which is more than they will. And had I stood the climate, this was what I might have been! The problem of the retiring age has long bewildered economists. Wandering, as I now do, among other finished critics, broken in health and temper by the rigours of the service, or the censure of authors, publishers, and public, I can't help wondering, in the shabby watering-places, the *petits trous pas chers* near Portsmouth or the Riviera that the retired inhabit, if we are really down and out. Can a reviewer come back? Is he too old at twenty-five? Could he find a place, with younger men, in the front lines where they stem the advance of autumn novels – and die in harness? I know it is foolish to dream, to think on these possibilities. I should face facts as bravely as I once faced fiction.

miser Cyrille desinas ineptire
et quod vides perisse perditum ducas—

And yet these secret heartburns are only human. The other day, languishing among the back numbers in a French hotel, I received a letter from New York which almost gave me hope again. 'When,' demanded the writer – 'when will you tell the public that Mr. Compton Mackenzie, in his last three novels, has not only recaptured the prose style of Congreve, but also Congreve's attitude to life?' 'When,' I breathed – and there were tears in my eyes – 'when shall I?'

The Movies
(1939)

At half-past ten or eleven in the morning the services are held, the congregation file silently into their places, speech is out of order, though in some temples they are handed a glass of warm champagne and a dry cigar. After the ceremony the unwilling worshippers drift away, and the film critics have witnessed another trade show.

Shipyard Sally was my first glimpse of Gracie Fields, and is an easy way of getting to see the best-known artiste in the Empire, the woman who will be to the soldiers of the next war what Clara Butt, Violet Loraine, and Britannia herself were to the last. I found her very interesting, an actress with three selves, London, Lancashire, and Imperial. The Imperial Gracie Fields sings in a powerful, rather sharp, but absolutely official voice, the Songs that Made England. Her 'Annie Laurie' is like the *Mauretania* or the cover of *Punch* or the Needles, something you may or may not like, but which it would be impossible to imagine different. I am sure her 'Land of Hope and Glory' is equally correct. The Lancashire Gracie Fields is disingenuous. It is curious how in real life the women who are good pals, who seem full of pluck and Hemingway mateyness, always make everyone very unhappy, and the 'jannock' side of our Gracie suggests the aggressive and even the acquisitive instincts. But the London Miss Fields is an accomplished comic actress who comes on as an agreeable surprise; and there are mysterious glimpses of a gaunt and rather grim woman who isn't pretty and doesn't care. *Shipyard Sally* is one of the usual English messes, a miserably unreal story, in which the script can never make up its mind if it is a musical comedy or a Powerful Drama. Like much English humour, it is in execrable taste. This English humour is really a synonym for fear, fear of life, fear of death, fear of anti-fascism, fear of sentiment, intelligence, sex, a cosy English fear of anything and everything; there is plenty of fear in this film, and a large dose of snobbery. Baby food for knowing babies. Horrible. Why do rich artists allow themselves to be seen in this kind of picture? There should be a special letter B after every film with a Butler in it. Then we should be warned.

These English films I find growing more sinister, they are a kind of decadence, not romantic *fin de siècle* decadence, but a drooling softening of the brain in a still majestic carcase. The people who write them and produce them, who act in them and go to see them, who have lost all respect for, and knowledge of, the workings of the head or heart, seem an omen, part of the writing on the wall.

The best films are those which are mature and adult. England seems capable of making these only in documentaries, America makes many more, but the sense of maturity is confined to the relations between men and men, or men and nature. Only in France does the heart come into its own in the screen.

Retour à l'aube is an excellent film. It stars Danielle Darrieux as she should be, not in an historical role, but as a simple young comic actress of remarkable depth. Her face, with that look of a plump northern French wit and sadness is Renaissance, like a Clouet, or a song of Ronsard; her voice is delicious, her acting admirable. In this film she is the wife of the stationmaster in a Hungarian village, but is swept from her geese and melons to the delights of Budapest. She misses the evening train – the missing of trains should almost be censored from the film, as too strong meat for nervous people, especially when the missing of one makes, as in this case, the difference between virtue and vice, innocence and disillusion. She stays on for one night in which she sees enough of male cupidity, lust, disloyalty, and cruelty (including a Vice Squad whose faces seem infected by every attribute of the class they are paid to suppress) to last a lifetime. This film has dignity and poetry, it is ethically correct (we even sympathise with the husband waiting at home), and there are moments, as when Danielle Darrieux sings a peasant song, drunk in her first night-club, that give one hope for the cinema as Art again. There is nothing outstanding in the direction or photography of the picture, it is based on true values, human, dramatic, and aesthetic, and on the old conception of Comedy which the English have lost.

The Hardys Ride High is a homely piece of work, appallingly sentimental, but interesting. Interesting because it treats seriously, though without depth, an ethical problem, and because it is very American. The problem is whether riches make for happiness, and we see Mickey Rooney, to whom I give credit for being most of the time intentionally tiresome, Pa, and Mother inheriting two million dollars and a marble palace in Detroit. What happens is what you would expect to happen, but there is satisfaction in seeing the problem solved without recourse to arms. The scene where Mickey Rooney is almost seduced by an enormous chorus girl is, because supposed to be comic, genuinely repulsive, and there are some loose ends which indicate cutting. A mild entertainment for those who like lovable folk and horse sense, and yet with something more, for Rooney is one of the few actors at his age, and behind the outrageously typical small-town family is someone with a shrewd knowledge of psychology.

The Rich Bride at the Forum is an enthralling piece of Russian incompetence. As propaganda it is grotesque, as photography negligible, as musical comedy non-existent. The screen seems often in total darkness, through which glimmer an occasional tractor, the Black earth and teeming mothers of Ukraine. I thought for a long time it was a parody, but no, it is the genuine Russian article and quite modern. Except for the worship of the Tractor it reminds one of 1907, very early slapstick, a hero and heroine running much too fast, a man chasing another for comic relief, and cries of 'Tractor', 'Thunder', 'The Corn', 'Quick the Tractor' – which end in a prize-giving ceremony under Stalin's portrait. To one a bicycle, to another a banner, to some more a certificate, for good work on the Collective Farm. A more imbecile production than could have been made thirty years ago in the Middle West round the arrival of a T-model.

~

This month's *March of Time* is a history of the films in the form of a series of shots from the earliest times to the present day. It is a great pity it is not much longer, because the subject is fascinating, and once galloped through like this, will be less likely to be done again with the proper attention. As a synopsis of what should be spread out over several performances *The March of Time* is extremely entertaining. We see the first silent kisses (more passionate than those of today), the origins of Charlie Chaplin, *The Birth of a Nation*, Al Jolson yowling away in Sonny Bwah, Greta Garbo, and the harrowing shot from *All Quiet on the Western Front* of the hand reaching for the butterfly, and the Great Moment ('she must have been a very little Queen') from *Cavalcade*. The history, in fact, of gigantic technical improvement aided by considerably less improvement in acting, and none at all in ideas about what films are for. Or perhaps just a little, because the glimpse of *Zola* is a cut above the one of Rudolf Valentino dancing the tango in the *Four Horsemen*, and today, as well as Zola, we have Fred Astaire. How they had to overact in those silent films! What mouthing grimaces and scuttling feet – and what memories they recall. And those of us who are old enough to remember Silent Films, who were dazzled by *Caligari* or *A Woman of Paris* will be disturbed to find how bits of *The March of Time* which now seem comic once wrung our hearts. That Tango, for example, once implied visions of a wildly exciting existence which was characterised in the early Twenties by the expression *low life*. It went with pictures of Quais and brothels, with the aesthetic conception of the Underworld, a world more real and more exciting than the one we lived in, a land of promise for the non-political young Bourgeois. And those who booed and broke tables at the first night of *Le Sacre* could not have been more disappointed than I, one evening in Berlin, at the première of Sonny Bwah.

I have now visited cinemas for five weeks during which I have seen several hundred people killed, and listened to a great many jokes I could not laugh at. I have really enjoyed one film, *Retour à l'aube*, and somewhat enjoyed *Hostages*. *The March of Time* has also given me pleasure. It seems to me that all the materials are here for a great art, the money, the time, the technique, the necessity, and the artists. What is lacking is any conception of what a work of art ought to be. I shall be glad not to go to any more films for a while; either they are too morbid or I am, and they seem to me to point no moral except that the human race is not yet old enough to manage firearms, or handle money or attack the simplest question of human relations. Getting into difficulties? Then introduce the Atlantic fleet, some elephants, a regal butler, and the Syrup of Figs man. Guns, butlers, duchesses, dogs. Here you see a pig being skinned alive – not a very cheerful noise is it – but we all need shaving brushes, and here you see a very close shave indeed – a Chinese execution!

Henry Lamb
(1932–3)

To be pitchforked into art criticism without either the knowledge or the taste that distinguishes an art critic is a frightening thing. Like a new boy who arrives in the middle of a term, one adopts a brazen attitude, secretly keeping one's ears open for the jargon of the older boys, then timidly experimenting in the new slang. To this end I have bought *Words wanted in connection with Art*, by Roger Fry. Art, artist, artifact, author, beauty, blütezeit, œuvre (to be anglicized as 'oover'), impasto, pompier . . . They are all words I want and soon I hope to be able to show you some of them.

What are one's first impressions on visiting the Leicester Galleries? That Mr Lamb is a fashionable painter, an academic painter, an English painter. Does this mean he is a bad painter? At first sight, yes; but the moment one examines his work this is contradicted, for within these limitations it is very much alive. Modern painting rushes along like an express, at every stop a few artists are set down and disappear into the landscape, occasionally they pace disconsolately down the line, sometimes they are content with their destination. At one of these wayside platforms remains Mr Lamb – a rebel, but destined obviously to be a rebel academician. Just as a virus can only remain alive in a carefully prepared gelatine so the mild, but genuine, heterodoxy of Mr Lamb is exactly preserved in the conservative environment in which he paints. He resembles those outspoken, free-minded, self-contemptuous young diplomats who are such good company while kicking against the pricks, and so dull when they have freed themselves and vanished into journalism. Mr Lamb should exhibit constantly and perversely in the Academy and enjoy the distinction of being the best thing there.

The portraits were the draw of the exhibition. They are the work of a fashionable painter still unfashionably critical of his sitters. Mr Evelyn Waugh, for instance, what a fascinating likeness! He sits with a mug of beer and a pipe, wearing a red tie and a green sweater and gazing truculently at the observer. A man confidently unsure of himself, always half-burning what he has half-adored.

Mr David Garnett (gold flake for him!) suggests another type, the *Paysan de Paris*, the brilliant clod. He seems to have asked somebody a poser in an inn; he has the bumpkin look, not uncommon in Bloomsbury, as of a shrewd yokel who has just given a London gentleman the wrong directions and received a large tip.

Mr Lamb is a painter of integrity, charming in sketches, delicate in landscapes, mischievous in portraits; it is my misfortune not to appreciate him at his true worth. He suggests the poetry of Edmund Blunden, which I am not up to either, but he surely suggests it more than in that older period when he painted so ably Mr Lytton Strachey: so vividly the roofs of Poole.

New Novels
(1929–35)

To review some novels again after a lapse of several years might be an alarming experience. In any other branch of activity there would be new technique to master, new names to learn, new rivals to study. One would be out of date, superannuated. But that is not the way with English fiction. Naturally reviewing has seen changes. One misses Walter Pater's appreciations in the *Guardian*, and, of course, poor Churton Collins. But otherwise, they are all there, the familiar faces; the novels are the same, the writers are the same, the same lovers hold hands on the front of the cover, and the men who were boys when I was a boy endorse each other inside the jacket.

When first given novels to review I was told of the two golden rules for this kind of journalism. Never to use 'I', and always to link the books up by some common denominator, to bind them, in the kitchen sense, into a well-rounded article by a liaison of generalities. It seems high time both these rules should be broken. A mere veto on one personal pronoun is not going to stop a reviewer talking about himself; and since novel-reviewing is so much a matter of individual preference, it seems absurd to disclaim the fact. The second rule, by which books are grouped by their subject instead of being classed by their merit, is a direct cause of the lack of standards in estimating modern fiction. How often has one read (or written) 'four out of these six books deal with the only child (though of different ages and sexes). Ever since Oedipus the only child has occupied a peculiar position' . . . a thousand words follow . . . 'The remaining two books, *The Waves* and *Once Aboard the Lugger*, are both about the sea.'

One of the difficulties of reviewing novels is that of grading them.

An ambitious failure by a serious artist is obviously something quite different from an accomplished pot-boiler, yet in reviewing, the one is whole-heartedly blackened because it does not come off; the other, because it is good of its kind, praised beyond due measure. Novels should really be classified by letters, an alpha double minus then, like *Tender is the Night*, would still be a cut above a beta plus, like *The Captain Hates the Sea*; yet this is too academic a notification. Highbrow, middlebrow and lowbrow would be more suitable if all three were not terms of abuse, nor can one classify novelists as first and second growths, nor multiply the stroke of a writer by his bore.

We have a whole school of second-rate English fiction. At this moment there must be numberless young men searching through the *Oxford Book of English Verse* for appropriate chapter headings, grave young women pondering over the best pseudonyms to give their friends. Like caterpillars infected by the ichneumon fly, these stripling manuscripts browse and fatten on the green food of their author's emotional experience, but, sleeker and longer though they grow, the invisible worm is gnawing them within. Soon they will enter their bright seven-and-sixpenny chrysalis, but by then, alas, they will be dead.

When a writer is born among the Chatto islanders in the little-known Gollancz archipelago a dirge is sung over his cradle: 'May he be dowered with the gift of unpresentability – some antisocial tic, drink, drugs, unbuttoning, or a too great readiness to proceed to the extremes of malice; may he never support a family nor accept a regular income from a publisher nor join an advertising agency; may his personal appearance early be disfigured by the clot of age and his bones cast unhonoured over the flimsy countryside.' Anthropologists will pardon this rough translation.

Having mentioned a few don'ts for novelists a fortnight ago, it was not surprising to meet a novelist who had been concocting a few don'ts for reviewers. One objection raised to me was that the reviewer has too much power, he can dismiss in a line a book that it has taken six months to write, and he can even admit, in certain papers, that he has not read it. This is based on a misconception, for during six months the novelist has spent on his novel, the reviewer has to read about a hundred and eighty novels, and they must all be taken into account, and their effect on him, when the one line of superior criticism comes to be written. He may even have already read and reviewed several novels exactly like the one in question. As to whether he will have read the book there is much difference of opinion. There is a fiction that reviewers always read the books they review, and that to catch them out in ignorance of something in the book is to utterly discredit them. This dates from the time when learned books were reviewed by learned men, and to make a mistake was to prove your ignorance. But novels are not learned books, if they are bad on one page they will seldom be good on the next, and to have missed out something in the middle will not make much difference to one's appreciation of the book, as if it was a long unbroken train of mathematical argument. A novel-reviewer is a high-class taster, he rolls a few pages of a novel round his mouth, spits them out, and waits for the famous aftertaste to crown his enjoyment of the flavour and the bouquet. If all three are absent he does not continue to swill the remainder of the bottle. In practice, however, he can always put up a good fight about any novel, for there is a way of reading with one's eyes fixed on the page and one's fingers automatically turning them over that does not exclude a delightful procession of images from passing behind the retina; winning lottery tickets, eccentric wills, old Palladian houses going for a song, adoring young admirers, warm beaches meticulously lapped by a tepid sea, southern capitals, and spirit voices that cry 'but surely, Connolly, you with your millions . . .' Reviewers have too much power, indeed; when even an unfriendly one-line review is immediately wiped out by a paean of praise from another paper! Perhaps they have power in so much that a novelist who has been unfavourably reviewed has little chance of getting the verdict reversed, though sometimes they can do much to mitigate it. If you can remember a review of Mr Jarrard Tickell's *See How They Run* in these pages, you will agree it was unappreciative, yet he has scored neatly by inserting, in a full-page advertisement of the book in a news magazine, 'the Daily So-and-So praised it, the Evening Such-and-Such was enthusiastic, the NEW STATESMAN AND NATION devoted a column to quotation.' If only Mr Tickell could write as well as he can advertise! No, reviewing is a whole-time job with a half-time salary, a job in which one's best work is always submerged in the criticism of someone else's, where all triumphs are ephemeral and only the drudgery is permanent, and where nothing is secure or certain except the certainty of turning into a hack . . . as one leaves the pile, tired with the feeling of obscure guilt that comes after a day spent in this thankless task of drowning other people's kittens.

Enemies of Promise
(1938/49)

Part One: Predicament

1 *The Next Ten Years*

This is the time of year when wars break out and when a broken glass betrays the woodland to the vindictive sun. Already the forest fires have accounted for a thousand hectares of the Var. We fight them by starting little manageable blazes which burn a strip to ashes before the main conflagration has had time to arrive. These flames in turn must be extinguished and isolated by setting fire to other and still more obedient strips till the last cinders expire in the garden where I am writing.

It is after lunch (omelette, Vichy, peaches) on a sultry day. Here is the plane tree with the table underneath it; a gramophone is playing in the next room. I always try to write in the afternoon for I have just enough Irish blood to be afraid of the Irish temperament. The literary form it takes, known as the 'Celtic twilight', consists of an addiction to melancholy and to an exaggerated use of words, and such good Irish writers as there have been exorcize the demon by disciplining themselves to an alien and stricter culture. Yeats translated Greek, while Joyce, Synge, and George Moore fled to Paris. For myself I find Augustan Latin and Augustan English the best correctives. But they do not at all times function well and when I write after dark the shades of evening scatter their purple through my prose. Then why not write in the morning? Unfortunately in my case there is never very much of the morning, and it is curious that although I do not despise people who go to bed earlier than I, almost everyone is impatient with me for not getting up. I may be working in bed on a wet morning and they have nothing to do yet they cannot conceal their feelings of superiority and ill-will.

But between the dissipated bedridden morning and the dangerous night fall the cicada hours of afternoon so pregnant in their tedium and these I now have free for the problem that is obsessing me.

THE NEXT TEN YEARS

1 What will have happened to the world in ten years' time?

2 To me? To my friends?

3 To the books they write?

Above all to the books – for, to put it another way, I have one ambition – to write a book that will hold good for ten years afterwards. And of how many is that true today? I make it ten years because for ten years I have written about books, and because I can say, and this is the gravest warning, that in a short time the writing of books, especially works of the imagination which last that long, will be an extinct art. Contemporary books do not keep. The quality in them which makes for their success is the first to go; they turn overnight. Therefore one must look for some quality which improves with time. The short-lived success of a book may be the fault of the reader, for newspapers, libraries, book societies, broadcasting, and the cinema have vitiated the art of reading. But the books of which I am thinking have all been read once, and have all seemed good to discriminating readers. They go bad just the same.

Suppose we were describing English literature in 1928. We would mention Lawrence, Huxley, Moore, Joyce, Yeats, Virginia Woolf, and Lytton Strachey. If clever we would add Eliot, Wyndham Lewis, Firbank, Norman Douglas, and, if solid, Maugham, Bennett, Shaw, Wells, Galsworthy, Kipling. Of these Strachey, Galsworthy, Bennett, Lawrence, Moore, Firbank are dead and also out of fashion. They are as if they had never been. Suppose new manuscripts were discovered, a

Five Towns by Bennett, a *Forsyte* by Galsworthy, even another novel by Lawrence, it would be a nightmare. We can account for this prejudice as a natural reaction from the work of yesterday to that of today, but much of it is unnatural because during their lifetime these writers were unnaturally praised. Since their booms, the reputations of Shaw, Joyce, Firbank, and Huxley and many others have declined; in fact, of the eminent writers of ten years ago, only the fame of Eliot, Yeats, Maugham, and Forster has increased. And the young writers of ten years ago are also stringing out.

My own predicament is – how to live another ten years.

Living primarily means keeping alive. The predicament is economical. How to get enough to eat? I assume however that most people who read this will have made some kind of adjustment, in fact I am writing for my fellow bourgeois. A writer has no greater pleasure than to reach people; nobody dislikes isolation more than an artist, a difficult artist most of all – but he must reach them by fair means – if he flatters them, if he screams at them, begs from them, lectures them or plays confidence tricks on them, he will appeal only to the worthless elements, and it is they who will throw him over. Meanwhile the way I write and the things I like to write about make no appeal to the working class nor can I make any bridge to them till they are ready for it. So I greet you, my educated fellow bourgeois, whose interests and whose doubts I share.

Another way to keep alive is not to get killed. That is a political question. The official policy by which we are not to get killed is by keeping out of war, but in order to keep out of war it is necessary to avoid the role of the good Samaritan; we have to pass by on the other side.

To have to dispense with their ideals and thus support a cynical policy in which they do not believe is a humiliating position for idealists. They therefore cannot be said to remain spiritually alive and this necessity of choosing between the perils of war and physical extermination and the dangers of an ostrich peace and spiritual stagnation, between physical death and moral death, is another predicament.

Since at present our own expectation of life is so insecure, the one way to make certain of living another ten years is to do work which will survive so long. For the best work explodes with a delayed impact. There is E. M. Forster, who has only produced two books since the last war, yet he is alive because his other books, which are from twenty to thirty years old, are gaining ground among intelligent readers. Their pollen fertilizes a new generation. There are reasons for this. To begin with, the novels of Forster state the general conflict which is localized in the political conflict of today. His themes are the breaking down of barriers: between white and black, between class and class, between man and woman, between art and life. 'Only connect . . .', the motto of *Howards End*, might be the lesson of all his work. His heroes and heroines, with their self-discipline, their warm hearts, their horror of shams and false emotion, of intellectual exclusiveness on the moral plane and of property, money, authority, social and family ties on the material one, are the precursors of the left-wing young people of today; he can be used by them as a take-off in whatever direction they would develop. Thus the parable form of Forster's novels may survive the pamphlet form of Shaw's plays, despite their vigorous thinking, because Forster is an artist and Shaw is not. Much of his art consists in the plainness of his writing for he is certain of the truth of his convictions and the force of his emotions. It is the writer who is not so sure what to say or how he feels who is apt to overwrite either to conceal his ignorance or to come unexpectedly on an answer. Similarly it is the novelist who finds it hard to create character who indulges in fine writing. This unemphatic, even style of Forster's makes him easy to re-read, for it contains nothing of which one can get tired except sprightliness. But there is another reason why the work of Forster remains fresh. His style has not been imitated.

What kills a literary reputation is inflation. The advertising, publicity and enthusiasm which a book generates – in a word its success – imply a reaction against it. The element of inflation in a writer's success, the extent to which it has been forced, is something that has to be written off. One can fool the public about a book but the public will store up resentment in proportion to its folly. The public can be fooled deliberately by advertising and publicity or it can be fooled by accident, by the writer fooling himself. If we look at the book pages of the Sunday papers we can see the fooling of the public going on, inflation at work. A word like genius is used so many times that eventually the sentence 'Jenkins has genius. *Cauliflower Ear* is immense!' becomes true because he has as much genius and is as immense as are the other writers who have been praised there. It is the words that suffer for in the inflation they have lost their meaning. The public at first suffers too but in the end it ceases to care and so new words have to be dragged out of retirement and forced to suggest merit. Often the public is taken in by a book because, although bad, it is topical, its up-to-dateness passes as originality, its ideas seem important because they are 'in the air'. *The Bridge of San Luis Rey*, *Dusty Answer*, *Decline and Fall*, *Brave New World*, *The Postman Always Rings Twice*, *The Fountain*, *Good-bye, Mr Chips* are examples of books which had a success quite out of proportion to their undoubted merit and which now reacts unfavourably on their authors, because the overexcitable public who read those books have been fooled. None of the authors expected their books to become bestsellers but, without knowing it, they had hit upon the contemporary chemical combination of illusion with disillusion which makes books sell.

But it is also possible to write a good book and for it to be imitated and for those imitations to have more success than the original so that when the vogue which they have created and surfeited is past they drag the good book down with them. This is what has happened to Hemingway who made certain pointillist discoveries in style which have almost led to his undoing. So much depends on style, this factor of which we are growing more and more suspicious, that although the tendency of criticism is to explain a writer either in terms of his sexual experience or his economic background, I still believe his technique remains the soundest base for a diagnosis, that it should be possible to learn as much about an author's income and sex-life from one paragraph of his writing as from his cheque stubs and his love-letters, and that one should also be able to learn how well he writes, and who are his influences. Critics who ignore style are liable to lump good and bad writers together in support of preconceived theories.

An expert should be able to tell a carpet by one skein of it; a vintage by rinsing a glassful round his mouth. Applied to prose there is one advantage attached to this method – a passage taken from its context is isolated from the rest of a book, and cannot depend on the goodwill which the author has cleverly established with his reader. This is important, for in all the books which become bestsellers and then flop, this salesmanship exists. The author has fooled the reader by winning him over at the beginning, and so establishing a favourable atmosphere for putting across his inferior article – for making him accept false sentiment, bad writing, or unreal situations. To write a bestseller is to set oneself a problem in seduction. A book of this kind is a confidence trick. The reader is given a cigar and a glass of brandy and asked to put his feet up and listen. The author then tells him the tale. The most favourable atmosphere is a stall at a theatre, and consequently of all things which enjoy contemporary success that which obtains it with least merit is the average play.

A great writer creates a world of his own and his readers are proud to live in it. A lesser writer may entice them in for a moment, but soon he will watch them filing out.

But darkness falls, frogs croak, the martins bank and whistle over the terrace and the slanting hours during which I can be entrusted with a pen grow threatening with night.

2 *The Mandarin Dialect*

Before continuing with our diagnosis it becomes necessary to have a definition of style. It is a word that is beginning to sound horrible, a quality which no good writer should possess. Stephen Spender can even brashly say of Henry James:

As always with great aestheticians there is a certain vulgarity in his work, and this vulgarity found its expression in violence. It is vulgarity of a kind that we never find in the work of coarser writers like Fielding, Smollett and Lawrence, but which we always are conscious of in writers like Flaubert, or Jane Austen, or Wilde.

The dictionary defines style as the 'collective characteristics of the writing or diction or artistic expression or way of presenting things or decorative methods proper to a person or school or period or subject, manner of exhibiting these characteristics'. This suggests a confusion since the word means both the collective characteristics and the manner of exhibiting them, and perhaps this confusion may account for the distaste in which the topic is held. For a surprising number of people today would agree in principle with Spender, or would argue that the best writers have no style. Style to them seems something artificial, a kind of ranting or of preening. 'The best writing, like the best-dressed man', as Samuel Butler said, is sober, subdued, and inconspicuous.

In point of fact there is no such thing as writing without style. Style is not a manner of writing, it is a relationship; the relation in art between form and content. Every writer has a certain capacity for thinking and feeling and this capacity is never quite the same as any other's. It is a capacity which can be appreciated and for its measurement there exist certain terms. We talk of a writer's integrity, of his parts or his powers, meaning the mental force at his disposal. But in drawing from these resources the writer is guided by another consideration; that of his subject. Milton's prose style, for example, is utterly unlike his verse. Not because one is prose and the other poetry; it reveals a quite different set of qualities. The Milton of *Paradise Lost* is an aloof and dignified pontiff who makes no attempt to enter into a relationship with the reader, whose language exhibits a classical lack of detail, whose blank verse is restrained, and whose sublime sentences, often ending in the middle of a line, suggest the voice of a man who talks to himself trailing off into silence. The Milton of the pamphlets is out to persuade the reader and confute his enemy, the style is forceful, repetitive and prolix; he bludgeons away at his opponent until he is quite certain that there is no life left in him, the magnificent language is remarkable for detailed exuberance and masculine vitality. The same distinction can be made between the prose and verse style of Marvell. The style of these writers varies with their subject and with the form chosen. One might say that the style of a writer is conditioned by his conception of the reader, and that it varies according to whether he is writing for himself, or for his friends, his teachers or his God, for an educated upper class, a wanting-to-be-educated lower class or a hostile jury. This trait is less noticeable in writers who live in a settled age as they soon establish a relationship with a reader whom they can depend on and he, usually a man of the same age, tastes, education, and income, remains beside them all their life. Style then is the relation between what a writer wants to say; his subject – and himself – or the powers which he has: between the form of his subject and the content of his parts.

Style is manifest in language. The vocabulary of a writer is his currency but it is a paper currency and its value depends on the reserves of mind and heart which back it. The perfect use of language is that in which every word carries the meaning that it is intended to, no less and no more. In this verbal exchange Fleet Street is a kind of Bucket Shop which unloads words on the public for less than they are worth and in consequence the more honest literary bankers, who try to use their words to mean what they say, who are always 'good for' the expressions they employ, find their currency constantly depreciating. There was a time when this was not so, a moment in the history of language when words expressed what they meant and when it was impossible to write badly. This time I think was at the end of the seventeenth and the beginning of the eighteenth century, when the metaphysical conceits of the one were going out and before the classic tyranny of the other was established. To write badly at that time would involve a perversion of language, to write naturally was a certain way of writing well. Dryden, Rochester, Congreve, Swift, Gay, Defoe, belong to this period and some of its freshness is still found in the *Lives of the Poets* and in the letters of Gray and Walpole. It is a period which is ended by the work of two great Alterers, Addison and Pope.

Addison was responsible for many of the evils from which English prose has since suffered. He made prose artful and whimsical, he made it sonorous when sonority was not needed, affected when it did not require affectation; he enjoined the essay on us so that countless small boys are at this moment busy setting down their views on Travel, the Great Man, Courage, Gardening, Capital Punishment, to wind up with a quotation from Bacon. For though essay-writing was an occasional activity of Bacon, Walton, and Evelyn, Addison turned it into an industry. He was the first to write for the entertainment of the middle classes, the new great power in the reign of Anne. He wrote as a gentleman (Sir Roger is the perfect gentleman), he emphasized his gentle irony, his gentle melancholy, his gentle inanity. He was the apologist for the New Bourgeoisie who writes playfully and apologetically about nothing, casting a smoke screen over its activities to make it seem harmless, genial, and sensitive in its non-acquisitive moments; he anticipated Lamb and Emerson, Stevenson, *Punch* and the professional humorists, the delicious middlers, the fourth leaders, the memoirs of cabinet ministers, the orations of business magnates and of chiefs of police. He was the first Man of Letters. Addison had the misuse of an extensive vocabulary and so was able to invalidate a great number of words and expressions; the quality of his mind was inferior to the language which he used to express it.

> I am one, you must know, who am looked upon as a Humanist in Gardening. I have several Acres about my House, which I call my Garden, and which a skilful Gardener would not know what to call. It is a Confusion of Kitchen and Parterre, Orchard and Flower Garden, which lie so mixt and interwoven with one another, that if a Foreigner who had seen nothing of our Country should be conveyed into my Garden at his first landing, he would look upon it as a natural Wilderness, and one of the uncultivated Parts of our Country. My flowers grow up in several Parts of the Garden in the Greatest

> Luxuriancy and Profusion. I am so far from being fond of any particular one, by reason of its Rarity, that if I meet with any one in a Field which please me, I give it a place in my Garden . . . I have always thought a Kitchen-garden a more pleasant sight than the finest Orangerie, or artificial Green-house [etc.].

Notice the presentation of the author (whose mind is also a *jardin anglais*); he is eccentric, unpractical, untidy but glories in it and implies superiority over the foreigner, he prefers home-grown vegetables to exotic fruits and in short flatters the Little Man and also the city Soames Forsytes of his day. The court jester with his cap and bells is now succeeded by the upper middle class with his 'awkward-squad' incompetence, his armchair, carpet slippers, and gardening gloves.*

I shall christen this style the Mandarin, since it is beloved by literary pundits, by those who would make the written word as unlike as possible to the spoken one. It is the style of all those writers whose tendency is to make their language convey more than they mean or more than they feel, it is the style of most artists and all humbugs and one which is always menaced by a puritan opposition. To know which faction we should belong to at a given moment is to know how to write with best effect and it is to assist those who are not committed by their temperament to one party alone, the grand or the bald, the decorative or the functional, the baroque or the streamlined that the following chapters are written.

Here are two more examples by Lamb and Keats of its misuse.

> (I) My attachments are all local, purely local. I have no passion (or have had none since I was in love, and then it was the spurious engendering of poetry and books) to groves and vallies. The rooms where I was born, the furniture which has followed me about (like a faithful dog, only exceeding him in knowledge) wherever I have moved

* 'For these reasons there are not more useful Members in a Commonwealth than Merchants. They knit Mankind together in a mutual Intercourse of good Offices, distribute the gifts of Nature, find Work for the Poor, add Wealth to the Rich, and Magnificence to the great.' Compare Addison's attitude to the Merchants with Congreve's, for whom a decade earlier they were comic cuckolds.

– old chairs, old tables, streets, squares, where I have sunned myself, my old school – these are my mistresses.

(II) I had an idea that a man might pass a very pleasant life in this manner. Let him on a certain day read a certain page of full Poesy or distilled Prose, and let him wander with it, and muse upon it, and reflect from it, and bring home to it, and prophesy upon it, and dream upon it, until it becomes stale – but when will it do so? Never! When Man has arrived at a certain ripeness in intellect any one grand and spiritual passage serves him as a starting-post towards all the two and thirty Palaces. How happy is such a voyage of conception, what delicious diligent indolence! A doze upon a sofa does not hinder it, and a nap upon Clover engenders ethereal finger-pointing. The prattle of a child gives it wings . . . [etc., etc.].

Notice how untrue these sentiments are. Lamb's old school is not a mistress, nor is an old bookcase. The bookcase has to be packed up and put on a van when it moves; to compare it to a faithful dog is to suggest that Lamb is beloved even by his furniture. The delicious middlers probably believe it, for Essayists must be lovable, it is part of their role.

'Until it becomes stale – but when will it do so? Never!' Now, Keats is lying. 'I am often hard put to it not to think that never fares a Man so far afield as when he is anchored to his own Armchair!' One could turn this stuff out almost fast enough to keep up with the anthologies. 'The Man', 'your Man', always occurs in these essayists. (Addison: 'There is nothing in the World that pleases a Man in Love so much as your Nightingale.')

Here are two recent examples (also from the *Oxford Book of English Prose*). The authors are Compton Mackenzie and Rupert Brooke.

(I) Some four and twenty miles from Curtain Wells on the Great West Road is a tangle of briers among whose blossoms an old damask rose is sometimes visible. If the curious traveller should pause and examine this fragrant wilderness, he will plainly perceive the remains of an ancient garden, and if he be of an imaginative character of mind will readily recall the legend of the Sleeping Beauty in her mouldering

> palace; for some enchantment still enthralls the spot, so that he who bravely dares the thorns is well rewarded with pensive dreams, and, as he lingers a while gathering the flowers or watching their petals flutter to the green shadows beneath, will haply see elusive Beauty hurry past. *The Basket of Roses* was the fairest dearest inn down all that billowy London Road . . .

Heigh ho! Georgian prose! Notice the words, especially the adverbs which do not aid but weaken the description, serving only to preserve the architecture of the sentence. They are Addison's legacy. A catalogue of flowers follows. I will begin at flower thirty-five.

> There was Venus' Looking-glass and Flower of Bristol, and Apple of Love and Blue Helmets and Herb Paris and Campion and Love in a Mist and Ladies' Laces and Sweet Sultans or Turkey Cornflowers, Gillyflower Carnations (Ruffling Rob of Westminster amongst them) with Dittany and Sops in Wine and Floramer, Widow Wail and Bergamot, True Thyme and Gilded Thyme, Good Night at Noon and Flower de Luce, Golden Mouse-Ear, Prince's Feathers, Pinks and deep red Damask Roses.
>
> It was a very wonderful garden indeed.
>
> (II) He was immensely surprised to perceive that the actual earth of England held for him a quality which he found in A—— and in a friend's honour, and scarcely anywhere else, a quality which, if he'd ever been sentimental enough to use the word, he'd have called 'holiness'. His astonishment grew as the full flood of 'England' swept him on from thought to thought. He felt the triumphant helplessness of a lover. Grey, uneven little fields, and small, ancient hedges rushed before him, wild flowers, elms, and beeches. Gentleness, sedate houses of red brick, proudly unassuming, a countryside of rambling hills and friendly copses. He seemed to be raised high, looking down on a landscape compounded of the western view from the Cotswolds, and the Weald, and the high land in Wiltshire, and the Midlands seen from the hills above Princes Risborough. And all this to the accompaniment of tunes heard long ago, an intolerable number of them being hymns.

'England has declared war,' he says to himself, 'what had Rupert Brooke better feel about it?' His equipment is not equal to the strain and his language betrays the fact by what might be described as the 'Worthington touch'. 'If he'd ever been sentimental he'd have called it "holiness",' i.e. he calls it holiness. 'Triumphant helplessness of a lover' has no meaning. It is a try-on. 'Little, small, grey, uneven, ancient, sedate, red, rambling, friendly, unassuming' – true escapist Georgian adjectives. They might all be applied to the womb.

Pope as an Alterer is a very different case. He is one of the great poets of all time and the injury he did to English verse consisted in setting it a standard to which it could not live up. He drove lyricism out except from isolated artists like Burns and Blake, and left his successors the task of continuing in a form which he had already perfected, and for which they had neither the invention nor the ear.

A waving glow the blooming beds display
Blushing in bright diversities of day

After this plenty poetry had become by the time of the Romantics barren and pompous, once again the content of the poetical mind was unequal to the form. The first Romantics, Wordsworth, Southey, and Coleridge, therefore, set themselves to write simply, to entice poetry away from the notion of the Grand Style and the Proper Subject; their language was monosyllabic, plebeian, their subjects personal or everyday. They wore their own hair.

3 *The Challenge to the Mandarins*

The quality of mind of a writer may be improved the more he feels or thinks or, without effort, the more he reads and as he grows surer of this quality so is he the better able to make experiments in technique or towards a simplification of it even to its apparent abandonment and the expression of strong emotion or deep thought in ordinary language. The great speeches in *Lear* and *Samson Agonistes* do not seem revolutionary to us because we do not recognize them as superb and daring manipulations of the obvious. Any poet of talent could write: 'The multitudinous seas incarnadine' or 'Bid Amaranthus all his beauty shed', but only a master could get away with 'I pray you undo this button', or Lear's quintuple 'Never'.

Style is a relation between form and content. Where the content is less than the form, where the author pretends to emotion which he does not feel, the language will seem flamboyant. The more ignorant a writer feels, the more artificial becomes his style. A writer who thinks himself cleverer than his readers writes simply (often too simply), while one who fears they may be cleverer than he will make use of mystification: an author arrives at a good style when his language performs what is required of it without shyness.

The Mandarin style at its best yields the richest and most complex expression of the English language. It is the diction of Donne, Browne, Addison, Johnson, Gibbon, de Quincey, Landor, Carlyle, and Ruskin as opposed to that of Bunyan, Dryden, Locke, Defoe, Cowper, Cobbett, Hazlitt, Southey, and Newman. It is characterized by long sentences with many dependent clauses, by the use of the subjunctive and conditional, by exclamations and interjections, quotations, allusions, metaphors, long images, Latin terminology, subtlety, and conceits. Its cardinal assumption is that neither the writer nor the reader is in a hurry, that both are in possession of a classical education and a private income. It is Ciceronian English.

The last great exponents of the Mandarin style were Walter Pater and Henry James who, although they wrote sentences which were able to express the subtlest inflections of sensibility and meaning, at the worst grew prisoners of their style, committed to a tyranny of euphonious nothings. Such writers, the devotees of the long sentence, end by having to force everything into its framework, because habit has made it impossible for them to express themselves in any other way. They are like those birds that weave intricate nests in which they are as content to hatch out a pebble as an egg. But the case of Henry James is sadder still, for his best writing, that found in his later books, charged with all the wisdom and feeling of his long life, went unappreciated. As he reminded Gosse, he remained 'insurmountably unsaleable', and of his collected edition of 1908 he could say, like Ozymandias, 'Look on my *works* ye mortals and despair.'

The reason for this failure of James to reach an audience lay in the change that had come over the reading public, a change to which he could not adapt himself. The early books of James appeared as three-volume novels which sold at thirty-one and sixpence. They reached a small leisured collection of people for whom reading a book – usually aloud – was one of the few diversions of our northern winters. The longer a book could be made to last the better, and it was the duty of the author to spin it out. But books grew cheaper, and reading them ceased to be a luxury; the reading public multiplied and demanded less exacting entertainment; the struggle between literature and journalism began. Literature is the art of writing something that will be read twice, journalism what will be grasped at once, and they require separate techniques. There can be no delayed impact in journalism, no subtlety, no embellishment, no assumption of a luxury reader and since the pace of journalism waxed faster than that of literature, literature found itself in a predicament. It could react against journalism and become an esoteric art depending on the sympathy of a few, or learn from journalism and compete with it. Poetry, which could not learn from journalism, ran away and so we find from the nineties to the last war desolate stretches with no poets able to make a living and few receiving any attention from the public. The stage is held by journalist-poets like Kipling and Masefield, while Hopkins, Yeats, Bridges, de la Mare, Munro, and a few others blossom in neglect.

Prose, with the exception of Conrad who tried to pep up the grand style, began to imitate journalism and the result was the 'modern movement'; a reformist but not a revolutionary attack on the Mandarin style which was to supply us with the idiom of our age. Shaw, Butler, and Wells attacked it from the journalistic side – George Moore, Gissing, and Somerset Maugham, admirers of French realism, of the Goncourts, Zola, Maupassant, from the aesthetic.

Only Wilde belonged to the other camp, and the style he created was his own variation of the introspective essayist:

> On that little hill by the city of Florence, where the lovers of Giorgione are lying, it is always the solstice of noon, of noon made so languorous by summer suns that hardly can the slim naked girl dip into the marble tank the round bubble of clear glass, and the long fingers of the lute-players rest idly upon the cords. It is twilight also for the dancing nymphs whom Corot set free among the silver poplars of France. In eternal twilight they move, those frail diaphanous figures, whose tremulous white feet seem not to touch the dew-drenched grass they tread on.

Notice the amount of 'romantic' words, now well-known hacks, 'solstice, languorous, eternal, frail, diaphanous, tremulous', which help to date the passage, while Shaw, who was the same age, was then writing:

> This is the true joy in life, the being used for a purpose recognized by yourself as a mighty one; the being thoroughly worn out before you are thrown on the scrapheap; the being a force of Nature instead of a feverish selfish little clod of ailments and grievances complaining that the world will not devote itself to making you happy. And also the only real tragedy in life is the being used by personally minded men for purposes which you recognize to be base. All the rest is at worst mere misfortune or mortality; this alone is misery, slavery, hell on earth; and the revolt against it is the only force that offers a man's work to the poor artist, whom our personally minded rich people would so willingly employ as pander, buffoon, beauty monger, sentimentalizer, and the like.

This sentence with its boisterous sentiments and creaking gerunds might have been written today. It is not a question of subject. The beauty of the Giorgione picture is just as alive as a sense of social injustice. Giorgione is not Sir Alma Tadema. But while the first passage is dead, constructed out of false sentiment and faulty linguistic material, the second is in the idiom of our time. For the idiom of our time is journalistic and the secret of journalism is to write the way people talk. The best journalism is the conversation of a great talker. It need not consist of what people say but it should include nothing which cannot be said. The Shaw passage could be talked; the Wilde passage would hardly stand recitation.

Moore also was not to remain a realist for long – but Moore, after his *Esther Waters* period, carried on his warfare against the Mandarin style from another position. In his *Ave, Salve, Vale* books he describes the Irish rebellion against the official literary language.

> Alas, the efforts of the uneducated to teach the educated would be made in vain; for the English language is perishing and it is natural that it should perish with the race; race and grammatical sense go together. The English have striven and done a great deal in the world; the English are a tired race and their weariness betrays itself in the language, and the most decadent of all are the educated classes.

He perceived, however, the increasing unreality of Anglo-Irish, of Yeats and Synge filling their notebooks with scraps of Tinkers' dialogue which could be used only in plays, and in plays only about tinkers, and instead he moulded for himself a simplified prose in which he could describe pictures, books, people, places, and complex sensations – yet always maintain an unassuming unsophisticated equality with the reader.

> The artist should keep himself free from all creed, from all dogma, from all opinion. As he accepts the opinions of others he loses his talent, all his feelings and ideas must be his own.
>
> I never knew a writer yet who took the smallest pains with his style and was at the same time readable. Plato's having had seventy shies at one sentence is quite enough to explain to me why I dislike him.
>
> Men like Newman and R. L. Stevenson seem to have taken pains to acquire what they called a style as a preliminary measure – as something that they had to form before their writings could be of any value. I should like to put it on record that I never took the smallest

pains with my style, have never thought about it, and do not know or want to know whether it is a style at all, or whether it is not, as I believe and hope, just common, simple straightforwardness. I cannot conceive how any man can take thought for his style without loss to himself and his readers.

Here in the colloquial English of 1897 is Samuel Butler attacking the Mandarin style. The musing introspective attitude of Pater and of Wilde's essays, is replaced by one more social and argumentative.* This *arguing* style (as opposed to the soliloquy) is typical of the new relationship with the reader which is to sweep over the twentieth century and dominate journalism and advertising. It may be described as *you*-writing from the fact that there is a constant tendency to harangue the reader in the second person. It is a buttonholing approach. The Addison manner on the other hand, has degenerated into whimsical *we*-writing. 'We have the best goods. We like quality. We're funny that way', is one sort of advertising. 'You realize the inconveniences of inadequate plumbing. Then why not of inadequate underclothing?' is the other.

Meanwhile, Wells, also, was not inactive (though it was not till 1915 that he attacked Henry James in *Boon*, a bogus autobiography). Henry James, in two magnificent letters (Vol. II, pp. 503–8, of his letters), answers Wells's criticism.

Wells wrote:

To you literature, like painting, is an end, to us literature is a means, it has a use. Your view was, I felt, altogether too prominent in the world of criticism and I assailed it in lines of harsh antagonism. I had rather be called a journalist than an artist, that is the essence of it, and there was no antagonist possible than yourself.

James replied that his view can hardly be so prominent or it would be reflected in the circulation of his books.

* 'Mr Walter Pater's style is, to me, like the face of some old woman who has been to Madam Rachel and had herself enamelled. The bloom is nothing but powder and paint and the odour is cherry blossom. Mr Matthew Arnold's odour is as the faint sickliness of hawthorn.' – Butler.

> But I have no view of life and literature, I maintain, other than that our form of the latter (the novel) in especial is admirable exactly by its range and variety, its plasticity and liberality, its fairly living on the sincere and shifting experience of the individual practitioner . . . Of course for myself I live, live intensely and am fed by life, and my value, whatever it be, is in my own kind of expression of that . . . Meanwhile I absolutely dissent from the claim that there are any differences whatever in the amenability to art of forms of literature aesthetically determined, and hold your distinction between a form that is (like) painting and a form that is (like) architecture for wholly null and void. There is no sense in which architecture is aesthetically 'for use' that doesn't leave any other art whatever exactly as much so; and so far from that of literature being irrelevant to the literary report upon life, and to its being made as interesting as possible, I regard it as relevant in a degree that leaves everything else behind. It is art that *makes* life, makes interest, makes importance, for our consideration and application of these things, and I know of no substitute whatever for the force and beauty of its process. If I were Boon I should say that any pretence of such a substitute is helpless and hopeless humbug; but I wouldn't be Boon for the world, and am only yours faithfully, Henry James.

The justification for Wells's attack must lie in the defence it provoked, for these two majestic letters from the dying giant form a creed which he might not otherwise have left us. One is reminded of a small boy teasing an elephant which gets up with a noble bewilderment, gives him one look, and shambles away.

We are not concerned here with the people who prefer to be journalists rather than artists, but with those who have tried to make journalism into an art, and already it is possible to define the opponents of the Mandarin style, all those who tried to break it up into something simpler and terser, destroying its ornamentation, attacking its rhythms and giving us instead the idiom of today. Thus Moore's new language is somewhat lyrical, for his standards are aesthetic. Norman Douglas is intellectual, with a strong imaginative side. Maugham is also imaginative, though play-writing interferes with his literary development, but

Butler, Shaw, Wells, Bennett, write as plainly as they can. If Henry James could have given up all hope of being read, had abandoned novels and written but a few magnificent pages about ideas that stirred him, he might have been happier and had greater influence. But he was obsessed with the novel to the neglect even of his long short stories; he still considered the novel the supreme art form, as it had been for Turgenev, Balzac, and Flaubert. So he continued to write novels which came into competition with the journalistic novels of Wells and Bennett or the speeded-up Jamesian of Conrad, rather than take refuge in the strongholds of the leisurely style – memoirs, autobiography, books of criticism – or else venture out into the experimental forms of the short story. The younger writers whom he patronized – Rupert Brooke, Compton Mackenzie, and Hugh Walpole* – were more remarkable for talent, personal charm and conventionality than for the 'beginning late and long choosing' of genius, the crabwise approach to perfection.

4 *The Modern Movement*

Meanwhile Butler's dictum 'a man's style in any art should be like his dress – it should attract as little attention as possible' reigned supreme, though only since Brummell had this stranglehold of convention been applied to what we wear.

> Here, on these remote uplands, I prefer to turn my back on the green undulations of Massa and Sorrento, of Vesuvius and Naples, Ischia and Phlegaean fields: all these regions are trite and familiar. I prefer to gaze towards the mysterious south, the mountains of Basilicata, and the fabled headland Licosa, where Leucosia, sister-siren of Parthenope, lies buried. At this height the sea's horizon soars into the firmament smooth as a sheet of sapphire, and the eye never wearies of watching those pearly lines and spirals that crawl upon its surface, the paths of

* It is interesting to speculate on the effect Henry James might have had on, say, E. M. Forster, Virginia Woolf, and Lytton Strachey had he bestowed on them the loving criticism which he lavished on his more personable disciples.

> silver-footed Thetis – a restful prospect, with dim suggestions of love and affinity for this encircling element that reach back, for aught we know, to primeval days of Ascidian-life. There is a note of impotence in the sea's wintry storms, for it can but rage against its prison bars or drown a few sailormen, an ignoble business: true grandeur is only in its luminous calm.

This is a good example of the reformed Mandarin. It is leisurely but not too leisurely, the syntax is easy, the thought simple, the vocabulary humdrum. The use of classical names takes for granted a reader who will accept this coin. The intellectual attitude is evident in the author's genial patronage of Nature and his calm analysis. It is readable, good-mannered, and seems today a little flat, for the coins mean less to us, and yet it is redeemed by the lovely image of the patterns on the sea from a height – if we know who Thetis is. It comes from Norman Douglas's *Siren Land* (1911).

> The poor little wife coloured at this, and, drawing her handkerchief from her pocket, shed a few tears. No one noticed her. Evie was scowling like an angry boy. The two men were gradually assuming the manner of the committee room. They were both at their best when serving on committees. They did not make the mistake of handling human affairs in the bulk, but disposed of them item by item, sharply. Calligraphy was the item before them now, and on it they turned their well-trained brains. Charles, after a little demur, accepted the writing as genuine, and they passed on to the next point. It is the best, perhaps the only way, of dodging emotion. They were the average human article, and had they considered the note as a whole it would have driven them miserable, or mad. Considered item by item, the emotional content was minimized, and all went forward smoothly. The clock ticked, the coals blazed higher, and contended with the white radiance that poured in through the windows. Unnoticed, the sun occupied his sky, and the shadows of the tree stems, extraordinarily solid, fell like trenches of purple across the frosted lawn. It was a glorious winter morning. Evie's fox terrier, who had passed for white, was only a dirty

grey dog now, so intense was the purity that surrounded him. He was discredited, but the blackbirds that he was chasing glowed with Arabian darkness, for all the conventional colouring of life had been altered. Inside, the clock struck ten with a rich and confident note. Other clocks confirmed it, and the discussion moved towards its close.

To follow it is unnecessary. It is rather a moment when the commentator should step forward. Ought the Wilcoxes to have offered their home to Margaret? I think not. The appeal was too flimsy.

This is a passage from E. M. Forster's *Howards End* (1910) and shows a great departure from the writing of the nineteenth century. Extreme simplicity, the absence of relative and conjunctive clauses, an everyday choice of words (Arabian darkness is the one romanticism, for darkness in Arabia can be no different from anywhere else) constitute a more revolutionary break from the Mandarin style than any we have yet quoted. Twenty-two short sentences follow. How remote it is from James, Meredith, Conrad, Walter Pater, whom one cannot imagine interpolating themselves into a novel to ask a question, and answer 'I think not'! From a passage like this derives much of the diction, the handling of emotional situations and the attitude to the reader of such writers as Virginia Woolf, Katherine Mansfield, David Garnett, Elizabeth Bowen.

The hardest task in modern criticism is to find out who were the true innovators. Forster I think was one. Novels like *The Longest Journey* and *Howards End* established a point of view, a technique, and an attitude to the reader that were to be followed for the next thirty years by the psychological novelists. Intellectual rebels against the grand style, such as Norman Douglas, who still wrote for Oxford and Cambridge graduates, for educated men, were not reformists. Forster wrote for men and women, chiefly women, of a larger though still cultured public, and evolved a more radically simplified, disintegrated, and colloquial form of art.

Now we are coming on the tracks of the writers of 1927–8. They are going to be judged by the contents of their minds and the form of their books and by what they make of them. From their failures and their successes we shall endeavour to learn how in the future to avoid failure, and so create that great book which will last a round ten years. This list forms the next stage in their pursuit.

SOME BOOKS IN THE MODERN MOVEMENT: 1900–1922

1900 Dreiser, *Sister Carrie*; *Oxford Book of English Verse*.

1901 Gissing, *By the Ionian Sea*.

1902 James, *The Wings of the Dove*; Yeats, *The Celtic Twilight*; Maugham, *Mrs Craddock*; Belloc, *The Path to Rome*.

1903 Butler, *Way of all Flesh*; Gissing, *Private Papers of Henry Rycroft*; James, *The Ambassadors*.

1904 Baron Corvo, *Hadrian VII*.

1905 Wilde, *De Profundis*; Forster, *Where Angels Fear to Tread*; Firbank, *Odette D'Antrevernes*; James, *The Golden Bowl*; H. G. Wells, *Kipps*.

1906 Galsworthy, *The Man of Property*.

1907 Forster, *The Longest Journey*; Beardsley, *Venus and Tannhäuser*; Gosse, *Father and Son*; James, *The American Scene*; Joyce, *Chamber Music*.

1908 Conrad, *A Set of Six*; Forster, *A Room with a View*.

1909 Stein, *Three Lives*; Beerbohm, *And Even Now*.

1910 Forster, *Howards End*; Bennett, *Old Wives' Tale*; Wedgwood, *Shadow of a Titan*; Saki's Stories; Wells, *Mr Polly*; Shaw, *Plays Pleasant and Unpleasant*.

1911 Beerbohm, *Zuleika Dobson*; Douglas, *Siren Land*; Lawrence, *The White Peacock*; Moore, *Ave*; Lytton Strachey, *Landmarks in French Literature*; Lowes Dickinson, *A Modern Symposium*;

Hugh Walpole, *Mr Perrin and Mr Traill.*

1912 Douglas, *Fountains in the Sand*; Samuel Butler, *Notebooks*; Beerbohm, *Christmas Garland*; Moore, *Salve*; Forster, *Celestial Omnibus*; Stephens, *Crock of Gold*; *Georgian Poetry* (*to 1918*).

1913 Conrad, *Chance*; Lawrence, *Sons and Lovers*; Mansfield, *In a German Pension.*

1914 Wyndham Lewis, *Blast*; Moore, *Vale*; Imagists' *Anthology* (Aldington, H. D., Pound, etc.); Monro, *Children of Love*; James Joyce, *Dubliners*; Compton Mackenzie, *Sinister Street.*

1915 Douglas, *Old Calabria*; Firbank, *Vainglory*; Somerset Maugham, *Of Human Bondage*; *Catholic Anthology* (includes Eliot's *Prufrock*); Virginia Woolf, *The Voyage Out*; Brooke, *1914*, etc.; D. H. Lawrence, *The Rainbow.*

1916 Moore, *The Brook Kerith*; Firbank, *Inclinations*; Joyce, *A Portrait of the Artist*; *Ulysses* starts in the *Little Review.*

1917 Douglas, *South Wind*; Eliot, *Prufrock*; *Wheels* (includes the Sitwells); Firbank, *Caprice.*

1918 Strachey, *Eminent Victorians*; Lewis, *Tarr*; Pearsall Smith, *Trivia*; Bridges, *The Poems of Gerard Manley Hopkins* and *The Spirit of Man*; Waley, *170 Chinese Poems.*

1919 Cabell, *Jurgen*; Firbank, *Valmouth*; Maugham, *The Moon and Sixpence*; Daisy Ashford, *The Young Visiters*; Barbellion, *Diary of a Disappointed Man*; [Anderson, *Winesburg-Ohio*]; Beerbohm, *Seven Men.*

1920 Huxley, *Limbo* and *Leda*; Eliot, *The Sacred Wood*; Wilfred Owen, *Poems*; Henry James, *Letters.*

1921 Huxley, *Crome Yellow*; Strachey, *Queen Victoria*; Virginia Woolf, *Monday or Tuesday, Poems of To-day.*

1922 Housman, *Last Poems*; Mansfield, *The Garden Party*; Garnett, *Lady Into Fox*; Strachey, *Books and Characters*; Beerbohm, *Rossetti and His Circle*; Yeats, *Later Poems*; Gerhardi, *Futility*; Galsworthy, *Forsyte Saga*; James Joyce, *Ulysses*; Virginia Woolf, *Jacob's Room*.

Not all of these books are of equal significance but they reveal how long ago most of our well-known writers began, how they overlap, how thick the field was before the Armistice. There will be several new names to talk about on our way to 1928.

I shall not group writers under movements, for the reason that between the nineties and the present day they scarcely exist. I recognize a complicating trend or inflation in the nineties, a simplifying one of deflation (realism, Georgian poetry) that followed. Then a further complicating process (Bloomsbury) and a further deflation (Hemingway), and I find the simplest guide the words used by writers themselves and the purposes for which they are employed. One faith unites all the writers discussed (with the exception of Shaw and Wells); whether realists, intellectuals, or imaginative writers, from Pater to Joyce they believed in the importance of their art, in the sanctity of the artist and in his sense of vocation. They were all inmates of the Ivory Tower.

An 'ivory tower' is a vague image and those who adopt it may take advantage of the vagueness. The image was taken by Flaubert from Alfred de Vigny and all who accept it are to some extent his pupils; if they do not admire *Bouvard*, they admit *Bovary*; if they reject *Bovary* they will recognize the *Letters*, *Salammbô*, the *Tentation*, or the *Éducation Sentimentale*.

We write in the language of Dryden and Addison, of Milton and Shakespeare, but the intellectual world we inhabit is that of Flaubert and Baudelaire; it is to them, and not to their English contemporaries that we owe our conception of modern life. The artist who accepts the religion of the Ivory Tower, that is of an art whose reward is perfection and where perfection can be attained only by a separation of standards from those of the non-artist, is led to adopt one of four roles: the High

Priest (Mallarmé, Joyce, Yeats), the Dandy (Firbank, Beerbohm, Moore), the Incorruptible Observer (Maugham, Maupassant), or the Detached Philosopher (Strachey, Anatole France). What he will not be is a Fighter or a Helper.

The tradition of dandyism is purer in France. Baudelaire was obsessed with *'l'éternel supériorité du Dandy'* as were Nerval, Laforgue, D'Aurevilly. When the wit and lyricism are shallow the resulting dandyism will have a popular success – and we get Noel Coward and Paul Morand – when deep, we find the most delicate achievements of conscious art. Meanwhile there are one or two more contributions to the idiom of our time to be considered.

The period 1900–1914 was that of the Dublin School – Yeats, Moore, Joyce, Synge, and Stephens. The sentiment of these writers was anti-English; they found the Mandarin style the language of their oppressors for they were sufficiently interested in the National Movement to consider themselves oppressed. For them England was the Philistine and since they could not use Gaelic, their aim was to discover what blend of Anglo-Irish and French would give them an explosive that would knock the pundits of London off their padded chairs. All had lived in Paris, and all had absorbed French culture. Moore kept strictly to it, using his Irish background as an excuse for spiteful criticism and ponderous ancestor-worship, but always preferring simple and racy expressions and unforced sentences as the basis of his style. Yeats was engrossed in his mysticism and Gaelic legends; the French influence is more apparent in his verse-forms, and in his cryptic utterances, sanctioned by Mallarmé. Synge went on from Villon to pick up peasant talk on the Aran islands and twine it into plays.

> It isn't that I haven't prayed for you, Bartley, to the Almighty God. It isn't that I haven't said prayers in the dark till you wouldn't know what I'd be saying, but it's a great rest I'll have now, and it's time surely. It's a great rest I'll have now, and great sleeping in the long nights after Samhain, if it's only a bit of wet flour we do have to eat, and maybe a fish that would be stinking.

There could be no clearer example than this of the extent of that insurrection against the prose of the capital which was the Celtic movement.

James Stephens's *The Crock of Gold* was an attempt to reconcile Classical mythology with Celtic. It proved that the Irish could beat the English at whimsy and produce a rival to *The Wind in the Willows* and *Peter Pan*.

Of much greater importance are *Dubliners* and *A Portrait of the Artist*. These books are written in a reformed Mandarin, influenced by French Realism. The style is not as unconventional as Yeats's or Synge's, or even as Moore's, and fits in more with the English of Maugham (*Of Human Bondage*) and of the Lawrence of *Sons and Lovers*. The favourite epithet of all these writers at that time was 'grey'.

(I) The park trees were heavy with rain and rain fell still and even in the lake, lying grey like a shield. A game of swans flew there and the water and the shore beneath were fouled with their green-white slime. They embraced softly impelled by the grey rainy light, the shield-like witnessing lake, the swans. – Joyce, *Portrait of the Artist*.

(II) The day broke grey and dull. The clouds hung heavily, and there was a rawness in the air that suggested snow. A woman servant came into the room in which a child was sleeping, and drew the curtains. – *Of Human Bondage*, opening paragraph.

(III) I stood watching the shadowy fish slide through the gloom of the mill-pond. They were grey, descendants of the silvery things that had darted away from the monks in the young days when the valley was lusty. The whole place was gathered in the musing of old age. The thick-piled trees on the far shore were too dark and sober to dally with the sun; the weeds stood crowded and motionless. – Lawrence, *The White Peacock*.

1914–15 were important years in the Modern Movement. Besides *Dubliners*, Joyce's first prose book, we have *Of Human Bondage*, the first poems of Eliot, Firbank's *Vainglory*, Lawrence's *Rainbow*, Douglas's *Old Calabria* and Virginia Woolf's *Voyage Out*. Wyndham Lewis edits *Blast*. The most serious artists among them continued to produce throughout the war. Joyce wrote *A Portrait of the Artist* and *Ulysses*. From his rooms in Oxford, Firbank let slip a novel a year. In 1918 Lytton Strachey, a conscientious objector, was able to launch *Eminent Victorians* on a war-weary world. Moore produced *The Brook Kerith* and Douglas *South Wind*, perhaps their two greatest books, Huxley appears in two slim volumes of poetry, Eliot in *Prufrock*, while the Sitwells emerge in *Wheels*; Lewis writes *Tarr*, and Pearsall Smith publishes *Trivia* in unashamed Mandarinese. 1914 was also the year of an important bad book, *Sinister Street*. It is a work of inflation, important because it is the first of a long line of bad books, the novels of adolescence, autobiographical, romantic, which squandered the vocabulary of love and literary appreciation and played into the hands of the Levellers and Literary Puritans.

Three years afterwards came *South Wind*, a book which, although one now recognizes in it reiterations and longueurs, remains a flower of the intellectual school, a book that was to reform for a while Compton Mackenzie and which stated for the first time the predicament (when anxious to be successful in love or at making a living) of the Petrouchka of the twenties, the Clever Young Man. The plight of Dedalus in revolt against the Jesuits is too particular; Michael Fane of *Sinister Street* is a born success; it is Denis of *South Wind*, pursuing the Italian chambermaid and cut out by the rough young scientist, who is the hero of *South Wind* and the years that follow, the Oxford Boy, the miserable young man on the flying trapeze.

5 *Anatomy of Dandyism*

Dandies in literature have often begun by making fun of the Mandarin style, for it is the enemy of their qualities of wit and lyricism, though in the end they come round to it. Dandyism is capitalist, for the Dandy surrounds himself with beautiful things and decorative people and remains deaf to the call of social justice. As a wit he makes fun of seriousness, as a lyricist he exists to celebrate things as they are, not to change them. Moore's *Confessions of a Young Man* is a typical dandy book but one finds much dandyism in Wilde and some in Saki who, however, adulterated his Wilde to suit the *Morning Post* and to procure the immediate impact of journalism. In his work the reactionary implication of dandyism is very clear.

Of the young men of these years (1914–18) Firbank, Eliot, and Huxley, the three most prominent, were dandies. Firbank followed Beardsley and Apollinaire, Eliot followed Laforgue, Huxley, Eliot and Firbank. They were intellectuals, but in his writing Firbank took pains to conceal the fact and so can best be taken as an example of the type. He harked back to the dandyism of the seventeenth century; his play *The Princess Zoubaroff* is based on Congreve and among his few allusions are one to the Memoirs of Grammont and another to the acting of Betterton. He was an impressionist; his sentences are hit or miss attempts to suggest a type of character or conversation, or to paint a landscape in a few brush strokes. When something bored him, he left it out (a device which might have improved the quality of innumerable novelists). Firbank is not epigrammatic, he is not easily quotable, his object was to cast a sheen of wit over his writing. Like all dandies, like Horace, Tibullus, Rochester, Congreve, Horace Walpole, and the youthful Beckford, like Watteau and Guardi, he was obsessed with the beauty of the moment, and not the beauty only, but the problem of recording that beauty, for with one false touch the description becomes ponderous and overloaded and takes on that unreal but sickly quality often found in modern paganism. Firbank, like Degas, was aware of this and, like Degas, he used pastel.

What is his contribution to modern literature? To what extent can we profit from him if we wish to write well ourselves?

One thing which we recognize not to have kept in him is an element of sexuality. Firbank was homosexual, which is not a factor of importance in the assessment of a writer's style, but he was of the breed with a permanent giggle and the result is a naughtiness in his books, a sniggering about priests and choirboys, nuns and flagellation, highbrows and ostlers which shocks us because it does not come off. It is meant to be a joke but it actually betrays the author, his inhibitions and his longings and it is his capacity for not betraying himself that is the secret of his art. It is this element which looks back to the nineties, to Beardsley and Corvo, when so much more looks forward. For the 'queen' or homosexual capon, being usually a parasite on society, a person with an inherited income and no occupation, can criticize that society only in jest. When goaded by wars and slumps it will become unfriendly and any criticism, however frivolous, will seem impertinent. Firbank, like most dandies, disliked the bourgeoisie, idealized the aristocracy and treated the lower classes as his brothel.

It is customary to assume that Firbank was frivolous because frivolity was his only medium of self-expression. In fact he was no less serious than Congreve or Horace Walpole but he recognized frivolity as the most insolent refinement of satire. The things Firbank hated were the moral vices of the bourgeoisie, stupidity, hypocrisy, pretentiousness, greed, and the eye on the main chance. What distinguishes the characters he writes about is their unworldliness and he believed that the most unworldly people are those who are born with everything. It was a complete vagueness about money, a warm erratic unjudging heart, a muddled goodness, an instinctive elegant disorder that he loved. The quality common to his characters is their impulsiveness; their virtue lies in their unawareness of evil. Where they are ambitious, their ambitions are preposterous. To be perpetuated by a stained-glass window, to shine in the highest circles of Cuna-Cuna, to go to Athens, to be a great tragic actress and yet to remain unconscious of the difficulty of attaining these ends, was what appealed to him. Whom he disliked were the schemers, the Becky Sharps, the Babbitts. Here is Mrs Sixsmith, thinking of her dead friend, Sally.

> Those final palatial houses, she reflected, must be full of wealth . . . old Caroline plate and gorgeous green Limoges: Sally indeed had proved it! The day she had opened her heart in the Café Royal she had spoken of a massive tureen *too heavy even to hold.*
>
> Mrs Sixsmith's eyes grew big.

Or:

> And now a brief lull, as a brake containing various delegates and 'representatives of English Culture' rolled by at a stately trot – Lady Alexander, E. V. Lucas, Robert Hichens, Clutton Brock, etc. – the ensemble, the very apotheosis of the worn-out *cliché*.

For what he hated was vulgarity and vulgarity of writing as much as vulgarity of the heart. Indeed, the writers with the most exquisite choice of words, those who take pains to avoid the outworn and the obvious to achieve distinction of phrasing, are equally susceptible to the fine points of the human heart. The world to Congreve is a sink out of which a few young people manage to drag themselves, to Horace Walpole an arena which friendship alone makes tolerable. They are strongly conscious of good and evil. 'To write simply,' explains Maugham, 'is as difficult as to be good.' Perhaps one requires the other. For Dandies are perfectionists and Perfectionism involves disappointment and from the disappointments is built up the idea of an elect, of a few human beings gifted with distinction of mind and heart heaving themselves up from the general mud-bath. Some are kept up for a few years by their beauty, breeding or charm, but all those without moral qualities and a courageous intelligence are bound to flop back.

'Now that the ache of life with its fevers, passions, doubts, its routine, vulgarity and boredom was over, his serene unclouded face was a marvelment to behold. Very great distinction and sweetness was visible there together with much nobility and love, all magnified and commingled,' writes Firbank of the death-mask of Cardinal Pirelli and it was the last sentence but two he ever wrote; his most serious, though not his most successful, for he is nervous of his own seriousness and suddenly produces a word, 'marvelment', out of his old 1890 past to reassure him. But it is the sentence of an ascetic, as must be all those who are dandies in the fullest sense.

The lesson one can learn from Firbank is that of inconsequence. There is the vein which he tapped and which has not yet been fully exploited.

His method was to write in dialogue, and to omit what would not fit in. Narrative prose as opposed to dialogue is used only for vignettes of places or descriptions of characters when they first appear. It is the most brisk and readable form of writing, making demands on the reader's intelligence but none on his eye or ear: and it is to Firbank that we owe the conception of dialogue – not as a set-piece in the texture of the novel, as are the conversations of Wilde and Meredith – but as the fabric itself. A book by Firbank is in the nature of a play where passages of descriptive prose correspond to stage directions.

As a prose writer Firbank did not have a large or an interesting vocabulary and his work is full of spelling mistakes, but he wrote with a horror of the cliché and with a regard for the words he used, achieving the freshness he needed by grammatical inversion, and by experiments in order. He also applied impressionism with startling results.

> The mists had fallen from the hills, revealing old woods wrapped in the blue doom of Summer.

> Boats with crimson spouts, to wit, steamers, dotted the skyline far away, and barques with sails like the wings of butterflies, borne by an idle breeze, were winging more than one ineligible young mariner back to the prose of the shore.

> It was the Feast night. In the grey spleen of evening through the dusty lanes towards Mediavilla, country-society flocked.

Do they come off? On the whole yes, much better than his overloaded passages in *Cardinal Pirelli* and *Santal*, for it is one of the weaknesses of the dandy's position that the seriousness on which it is based must at all costs be concealed. The preoccupation of the dandy is with the moment.

> Every moment some form grows perfect in hand or face; some tone on the hills or the sea is choicer than the rest; some mood or passion or insight or intellectual excitement is irresistibly real and attractive for us – for that moment only. Not the fruit of experience, but experience

> itself, is the end. A counted number of pulses only is given to us of a variegated dramatic life. How may we see in them all that is to be seen in them by the finest senses? How shall we pass most swiftly from point to point, and be present always at the focus where the greatest number of vital forces unite in their purest energy? To burn always with this hard gemlike flame, to maintain this ecstasy is success in life . . . Not to discriminate every moment some passionate attitude in those about us, and in the brilliancy of their gifts some tragic dividing of forces on their ways, is, on this short day of frost and sun, to sleep before evening.

So wrote Pater, calling an art-for-art's sake muezzin to the faithful from the topmost turret of the ivory tower. By leaving out the more affected 'any stirring of the senses, strange dyes, strange colours, and curious odours, or work of the artist's hands, or the face of one's friend' it becomes one of the great passages of Mandarin writing, and as a text concentrates as much on the moment in personal relations, on the ethical moment as on the sensual one. Henry James spent his life in 'discriminating passionate attitudes and tragic divisions in those about him' as thoroughly as Wilde investigated his own moods or Moore and Yeats and Joyce waited for 'some tone on the hills or the sea'. Pater, when he realized its implications, suppressed the passage which is but the philosophy of the refractory pupil of Socrates, Aristippus of Cyrene, who believed happiness to be the sum of particular pleasures and golden moments and not, as Epicurus, a prolonged intermediary state between ecstasy and pain.

The artistic fault of the Cyrenaic philosophy is a tendency to fake these golden moments, inevitable when they are regarded as the only ones worth living for; the artist becomes like the medium who has to produce a psychic experience to earn her money, and the result is that he leans too heavily on the moment, and so produces that effect of satiety which runs, for instance, through the translations of Mackail. Similarly if we examine the kind of poetry that we read and appreciate when we are unhappy, we soon find that it is not the best kind or, if the best, that we appreciate it for the wrong reasons, we overemphasize it to make it support a weight which it was not intended to bear. The perfectionists, the art-for-art's sakers, finding or believing life to be intolerable except for art's perfection, by the very violence of their homage can render art imperfect. This was the danger of Firbank's growing seriousness, it is a danger which besets all lyric poets, dandies and ephemerids although it is a danger which by emotional awareness and technical discipline they can often avoid.

At the moment Dandyism in its extreme form, Perfectionism, is on the increase, for Perfectionists, like the hermits of the *Thebaid*, take refuge from the world in private salvation. I have known many perfectionists, all of whom are remarkable for the intense stripping process which they carry out. Their lives are balloons from which more and more ballast has to be cast; they never have more than one suitcase, wear no pyjamas or underclothes, travel constantly and are the mystics of our time '*pressés de trouver le lieu et la formule*'. An element of guilt and expiation in their activity awakens distrust in the complacent herd and certainly perfection has a bleaching, deathwishful quality. But it is so seldom attained that a little respect for it would do no harm to its detractors.

It will be seen then that dandyism, despite its roots in the *status quo* and its tendency to pessimism, is a tenable position – since any position which can be shown to produce good writing is tenable – for as long as the writer can count on a natural constitutional gaiety to inform his lyricism. When that disappears, as in Housman, the wit becomes bitter, the lyricism morbid. It is therefore suitable to young writers or to those with plenty of money. They have their roots in manure but the orchid blooms the richer for it, until ultimately the bloom dies down, and the manure is left. Tibullus, Rochester, Watteau, and Leopardi – the greatest perfectionist of them all – died before this could happen. Congreve retired; Walpole and Beckford became ancestor-worshipping and reactionary antiquarians; only Horace and Degas, obedient always to the discipline of their art and intellectually agile, arrogant and tough, remained perfectionists to the last. Had he lived, Firbank would not have written worse, he would have written differently.

[NOTE: The debt of Firbank to Beardsley's *Under the hill* is not here sufficiently stressed. It is the archetype of sophisticated butterfly impressionism in our tongue. Firbank perhaps was never quite so witty, vicious or well-informed as the adolescent of genius; however he was more radiantly preposterous, a humorist of wider calibre.]

6 *A Beast in View*

I have taken Firbank as the type of the writer dandy but what has been said of him is also true of the early Eliot and the early Huxley. Eliot is the purest of the three, for a lyric poet works in a more distilled medium than narrative prose.

> Let us go then, you and I,
> When the evening is spread out against the sky . . .
> Let us go, through certain half-deserted streets . . .

I have often wondered what it must have felt like to discover these opening lines of *Prufrock* in *Blast* or the *Catholic Anthology* in 1914–15 with the Rupert Brooke poems, Kitchener's Army, and *Business as Usual* everywhere. Would we have recognized that new, sane, melancholy, light-hearted, and fastidious voice?

> There will be time, there will be time
> To prepare a face to meet the faces that you meet;
> There will be time to murder and create.

Surely we would have noticed it, would have 'lingered in the chambers of the sea' and experienced that exquisite sensation, the apprehension of the first sure masterful flight of a great contemporary writer. But how few of us did!

What can one learn from Eliot? Not to be ashamed of borrowing and to assimilate what we borrow. Yet his influence on young writers is disconcerting; Auden, I think, is the one young poet to survive it. The reason I believe is that Eliot, the purest artist and most austere critic in England today, is yet a writer whose background is unfamiliar – the least like anyone else's. He is an American expatriate who is escaping from a far more refined and cultivated, though perfectly barren society, than any he can find here – in other words, he is not running away from a rough America to a cultured England but from an overpolite and civilized humanism to the bellyworld of post-war London. As a result his poetry is a struggle to break down inhibitions in himself by which the coarser Englishman is not troubled and his solution, the Anglo-Catholic church, one that makes small appeal to his imitators.

Yet in spite of this he is a master; he has created for us a world of his own. There are places where I miss Firbank, in Knightsbridge or Rome, going over some Balkan palace or in an autumnal cathedral city; there are remarks one overhears or whole scenes between simple, fatuous, complacent people when one recognizes that the artist who could best have done them justice is no more. But there exists a whole mood for whose expression we must thank Eliot, the mood is dissatisfaction and despondency, of barrenness and futility – the noon-day devil, the afternoon impotence which is curiously unpoetical and which no one else has been able so adequately to render into verse.

The idea of futility is an important concept in the twenties and dominates the poetry of Eliot (up to *Ash Wednesday*), the novels of Huxley (to *Point Counter Point*), and much of the work of Lawrence, Hemingway, and Joyce. It is an extension of the ivory tower attitude which arises from a disbelief in action and in the putting of moral slogans into action, engendered by the First World War. Thus Henry James and the authors who were killed in the war had no such experience, it was left to those who survived beyond 1917 to make the discovery.

> Behold, behold, the goal in sight
> Spread thy fans and wing thy flight

sings Janus, in Dryden's *Secular Masque*, and Venus adds:

> Calms appear when storms are past
> Love will have his hour at last,

but the chorus is not taken in:

All, all of a piece throughout:
Thy chase had a beast in view;
Thy wars brought nothing about;
Thy lovers were all untrue.
'Tis well an old age is out,
And time to begin a new.

And that might well have been the device of the writers of the early twenties.

I have said that futilitarianism is an extension of the philosophy of the Ivory Tower, because no writer of that group pretended that art was futile; it is the men of action who do that. Behind the concept of futility is a passionate belief in art, coupled with a contempt for the subjects about which art is made. This puts too great a strain on technique, for even Flaubert in *Bouvard and Pécuchet*, the Baedeker of futility, has not been able to avoid unintentionally boring the reader. But the novelists of the 1920s were not Flaubert's equals in construction. They knew that they had been 'had' and they were in a hurry to tell the world about it. Those who had been fooled most were the young men who had fought and survived the war; the literature of that time in consequence is predominantly masculine, revolving round a theme which may be called 'The Clever Young Man and the Dirty Deal'. When I search for the most representative work of the period, I am inclined to choose *Petrouchka*, for though pre-war the ballet expresses the situation with clarity. The people at the fair are the audience whom Petrouchka, the introspective young masochist, wishes to win over; the Magician who controls him is Fate, that cruel deity of the Housman poems, or the Vile Old Man, the general, the father too old to fight, gleefully sacrificing his son. Petrouchka's problem is how to keep alive, and have a successful love affair, and his rival, the Moor, is the hated man of action, the accomplished womanizer who has not been to Balliol and has nothing of Hamlet in him, but in whom vulgarity triumphs. This situation or relationship has a way of turning up in many books.

Characteristics of the Clever Young Men and their Dirty Deals

AUTHOR	MAN	PLACE OF EDUCATION	NATURE OF PREDICAMENT	SOLUTION
Douglas	Denis, *South Wind*	Oxford	Inability to seduce a woman. Rival, young scientist. Father, Keith.	Acquires virility and self-respect instead by assisting drunken pseudo-father to sober up.
Huxley	Denis, *Crome Yellow*	Oxford	Inability to seduce a woman. Rivals, painter and rich young peer. Father, Scogan.	Flight to London ('and what on earth was he going to do in London when he got there?').
Huxley	Chelifer, Gumbril, Quarles	Oxford	Inability to seduce a woman. Rivals, all their friends. Father, Cardan, etc.	Expatriation (Mantua), the picture gallery and the reading-room.
Eliot	Alfred Prufrock	?	General indecision and fear of experience. Rival, Sweeney. Runs away from women.	Polite resignation.
Joyce	Stephen Dedalus	Clongowes	Superiority to vulgar surroundings, yet at mercy of them. Rival, Buck Mulligan. Father, Bloom.	'Silence, exile and cunning.' Expatriation, discovery of pseudo-father (Bloom).
Hemingway	Jake, *The Sun Also Rises*	?	War wound, hence inability to seduce a woman, general aroma of diffused alcoholism. Rivals, boxer, bull-fighter, etc.	Trout-fishing, drink, the Catholic Church.

The father-chorus in these books is not malignant, rather it is wistful and friendly; in some books of the period he is a priest. The lesson we can learn from this school is the danger of allowing those literary vices, cleverness and self-pity, to come up too often for air. It was, however, the clever young men who were the first to see the vanity of the war and the greater vanity of the peace. They could not settle down to boring jobs and unprofitable careers with pre-war patience and their cleverness seemed a liability rather than an asset. Besides women did not like it. Nor were they yet sure whether they liked women, for they were still romantic enough to be appalled by the distinction between love and lust and to find the inevitable transition degrading.

Such a state of war between intellect and the sense, unless a genuine truce is made between them, can only end unhappily. Either the sense conquers the mind and we get the erudite sensualist, the Keith of *South Wind*, the Cardan of *Those Barren Leaves* with his consciousness of wasted opportunities, or the mind is triumphant and we have what Huxley became, a moralist and a puritan. I have considered him in his early works as a dandy for it is only in them that he is an artist and in them that his irony and lyricism are unadulterated. *Leda*, *Limbo*, *Crome Yellow*, and the stories of *Little Mexican* belong to this period, *Antic Hay* begins another.

I quote him often because he is the most typical of a generation, typical in his promise, his erudition, his cynicism, and in his peculiar brand of prolific sterility.

7 *The New Mandarins*

It is as difficult to foretell the weather in a language as in the skies, and as urgent. In our case the problem is to find out what sort of writing at this moment at the end of the thirties is likely to last. We have seen that there are two styles which it is convenient to describe as the realist, or vernacular, the style of rebels, journalists, common-sense addicts, and unromantic observers of human destiny – and the Mandarin, the artificial style of men of letters or of those in authority who make letters their sparetime occupation.

The lyrical or dandy style matures with age into the Mandarin.

As in party government, there is an interaction between these two styles; each will seem in or out of office at a given moment; when one style is in abeyance it will receive new blood and be thrust forward, when the other is at the height of its success it will wither away. The panjandrums of the nineteenth century, Ruskin, Arnold, Pater, Meredith, Henry James, Swinburne, Conrad, give way to the realists, Gissing, Butler, Moore, Maugham, Bennett, Wells, and Shaw. It was now their turn to be driven from the temple. It was in 1906, I think, that the disheartened Conservative party, after being trounced in the general election, were elated by an attack made on their victors by young F. E. Smith. In the same year, in the pages of a dull review, another gifted young man, also a dark horse, was attacking the successful literary doctrine of the day, and the day's most eminent critic.

> The study of Sir Thomas Browne, Mr Grosse says, 'encouraged Johnson, and with him a whole school of rhetorical writers in the eighteenth century, to avoid circumlocution by the invention of superfluous words, learned but pedantic, in which darkness was concentrated without being dispelled'. Such is Mr Grosse's account of the influence of Browne and Johnson upon the later eighteenth-century writers of prose. But to dismiss Johnson's influence as something altogether deplorable is surely to misunderstand the whole drift of the great revolution which he brought about in English letters. The characteristics of the pre-Johnsonian prose style – the style which Dryden first established and Swift brought to perfection – are obvious enough. Its advantages are those of clarity and force; but its faults, which, of course, are unimportant in the work of a great master, become glaring in that of the second-rate practitioner. The prose of Locke, for instance, or of Bishop Butler, suffers, in spite of its clarity and vigour, from grave defects. It is very flat and very loose; it has no formal beauty, no elegance, no balance, no trace of the deliberation of art. Johnson, there can be no doubt, determined to remedy these evils

by giving a new mould to the texture of English prose; and he went back for a model to Sir Thomas Browne . . . With the *Christian Morals* to guide him, Dr Johnson set about the transformation of the prose of his time. He decorated, he pruned, he balanced; he hung garlands; he draped robes; and he ended by converting the Doric order of Swift into the Corinthian order of Gibbon . . . Attacks of this kind – attacks upon the elaboration and classicism of Browne's style are difficult to reply to, because they must seem, to anyone who holds a contrary opinion, to betray such a total lack of sympathy with the subject as to make argument almost impossible . . . The truth is that there is a great gulf fixed between those who naturally dislike the ornate, and those who naturally love it. There is no remedy; and to attempt to ignore this fact only emphasizes it the more . . . Browne's 'brushwork' is certainly unequalled in English literature, except by the very greatest masters of sophisticated art, such as Pope and Shakespeare; it is the inspiration of sheer technique.

It was not till 1918, however, that the author, Lytton Strachey, became well known with *Eminent Victorians*.

Eminent Victorians is a revolutionary book. Through what at first sight seemed only biographical essays – on Arnold, Florence Nightingale, General Gordon and Cardinal Manning, dead for half a century – the author contrived to attack and undermine all that was most cherished in the morality of today. The public-school system, public service, philanthropy, the army, the empire, the Church, all were questioned in these sleek periods and skulking behind them, authority itself, the nature of the will, the hypocrisy by which good men climb and cling to power were in their turn examined and exposed. *Eminent Victorians* is the work of a great anarch, a revolutionary text-book on bourgeois society written in the language through which the bourgeois ear could be lulled and beguiled, the Mandarin style. And the bourgeois responded with fascination to the music, like seals to the Eriskay love-lilt. At first the suave tones brought nothing but pleasure: this was the civilization they had been fighting to save: here were the restored humanities, the accent of the 'studious cloister of Trinity': too late they understood that four Victorian idols had been knocked off their pedestals in such a way that they have never been replaced, or deemed in any manner replaceable. And after they had dismissed the book as 'clever, but unsound', worse was to follow, a questioning of the values the Victorians stood for and all reflected from the eyes of their own demobilized and disillusioned children.

The trial of Oscar Wilde was responsible for a flight from aestheticism which had lasted twenty years. He had himself done much to discredit it by the vulgar and insincere element which he had introduced; his conviction was the climax. From that moment the Philistine triumphed and although there were still poets and critics who loved beauty, who were in fact romantic, their romanticism was forced to be hearty. Hence the cult of beer and Sussex, of walking and simplicity which ended with Masefield, Brooke, Squire, and Gould; hence the leanest years in the history of English verse and the manly criticism of Quiller-Couch and Walter Raleigh. It was left to Lytton Strachey to lay the ghost of Reading Gaol, to proclaim '*un peu faiblesse pour ce qui est beau – voilà mon défaut*', and so make nonconformity again permissible.

With the success which his first two books gained him, Strachey's bitterness disappeared, he became a lion and settled down to a quiet life of private pleasure. His gifts appear, as with all fine critics, when he is able to love and to admire and for this reason he is at his best when writing about the eighteenth century. As a critic he is admirable, as a biographer he is slightly vulgar. In his second book, *Queen Victoria*, his insurrectionary movement expired, he could not dislike Melbourne or Disraeli, or such a human bundle as his subject. By *Elizabeth and Essex* his style has become an elaborate experiment in cliché which, though rising to fine passages, contains not a little of the sniggering we have commented on in Firbank. It is his first book (*Eminent Victorians*), so admirably argued and constructed, original, polished, and daring, to which we can profitably return together with his essays and criticism. There is much to be learnt from his gifts, from his intellectual pride, his forceful phrasing, his love of beauty and gesture, his grasp of character;

'he is not dead but sleepeth' and one day these gifts will be rescued from the neglect into which, by his spectacular success, they were too soon precipitated.

Another Mandarin to emerge from his retreat in 1918 was Pearsall-Smith whose *Trivia* was the preliminary bombardment in a long attack which is not yet exhausted against puritanism in English letters. His anthology of English prose (1919) which omits Dryden and devotes only twelve pages to the eighteenth century from Addison to Lamb, concentrating entirely on fine writing and the purple patch, continued the onslaught. He is with Professor Mackail the last of the old Mandarins, of the men of the eighties, and the most intransigent.

Meanwhile a new Mandarin was taking over the novel. In 1915 Virginia Woolf published *The Voyage Out*. This was followed by *Night and Day*, *Monday or Tuesday* (1921), *Jacob's Room* (1922), *Mrs Dalloway* (1925), *To the Lighthouse* (1927) and *Orlando* (1928), one of the books in which, like *Elizabeth and Essex* or *Point Counter Point*, the new Mandarin movement of the twenties culminates.

Virginia Woolf seemed to have the worst defect of the Mandarin style, the ability to spin cocoons of language out of nothing. The history of her literary style has been that of a form at first simple, growing more and more elaborate, the content lagging far behind, then catching up, till, after the falseness of *Orlando*, she produced a masterpiece in *The Waves*.

Her early novels were not written in an elaborate style. Her most significant book is *Monday or Tuesday* (1921) and demonstrates the rule that Mandarin prose is the product of those who in their youth were poets. In short it is romantic prose. Not all poets were romantic prose writers (e.g. Dryden) but most romantic prose writers have attempted poetry.

The development of Virginia Woolf is the development of this lyrical feeling away from E. M. Forster, with his artlessness and simple, poetical, colloquial style, into patterns of her own. The reveries of a central character came more and more to dominate her books. In *The Waves* she abandoned the convention of the central figure and described a group of friends, as children, as young people and finally in late middle age. In a series of tableaux are contrasted the mystery of childhood, the promise of youth, the brilliance of maturity and the complex, unmarketable richness of age. If *The Years* seems an impressionist gallery with many canvases, landscapes, portraits, and conversation pieces, then *The Waves* is a group of five or six huge panels which celebrate the dignity of human life and the passage of time. It is one of the books which comes nearest to stating the mystery of life and so, in a sense, nearest to solving it.

In *Mr Bennett and Mrs Brown*, Virginia Woolf attacked Bennett, Wells, and Galsworthy for their materialism, for the doctrine of realism which they had made all powerful in the 1900s.

For Mandarin prose is romantic prose and realism is the doctrine of the vernacular opposed to it. Thus among the new Mandarins of the twenties were several who began as poets; besides Virginia Woolf and Lytton Strachey, it included the work of the Sitwells with their flowery periods and predilection for highly coloured and sophisticated settings.

But the greatest Mandarin was Proust who has become so familiar as almost to rank as an English writer. He exhibits, beyond all others, the defect of the Mandarin style; the failure of the writer's intellectual or emotional content to fill the elaborate frame which his talent plans for it. The honeycombs continue to develop but fewer and fewer pollen-bags are emptied into them. There are many great passages where the complexity is worthy of the emotion expended on it, where very subtle and difficult truths are presented in language that could only express them if difficult and subtle.

Notwithstanding, now that the element of novelty and cult-snobbery has worn off, much of Proust, as of his master Ruskin, must stand condemned. He is often repetitive and feeble; the emotions of envy, jealousy, lust, and snobbishness around which his book is built, though they generate an enormous impetus, are incapable of sustaining it through twenty or thirty volumes; Swann's jealousy of Odette is enough without Proust's jealousy of Albertine, Saint-Loup's of Rachel and Charlus's of Morel and if the emotions repeat themselves, so also do the stories, the situations, the comments, parentheses and clichés. Proust will remain a great writer, but his titles to fame may have to be considered. His hatred and contempt for the life of action suited the war-weary and disillusioned generation he wrote for, his own snobbery offered them both a philosophy and a remunerative career, he believed also in art for art's sake. He was in no sense a new writer although it was the illusion of novelty which contributed so much to his success. His models are pre-war, his artists are taken from the *haute bourgeoisie*, they are members, like his politicians and men of science, of the terrifying class which ruled in France and which corresponded to the Forsytes in England; his nobility are of the same period, so are his operas, his dinner-parties; it is the world of the Dreyfus Case, the Victorian world. He was modern enough to attack the values of this world but he had nothing to put in their place, for their values were his own, those of the narrator of the book who spends his life in going to parties and watching snobs behave but is never a snob himself.

In short, although he is preoccupied with time, his world is static because in all the movements of his book there is no movement of ideas. 'Everything changes,' he seems to say, 'and I am the historian of that change', but what in fact he declares is that nothing changes except the small social set which he admired in his youth and which fell to pieces. How did they change? They grew older and went out less or got mixed up in anti-social love affairs or lost their money or died – but nothing else changed for him. There was a new face with an old title in a box at the opera – but the title and the box are always there, coveted and prized by the ruling class of six or seven countries; there are no new ideas, no revolution in wisdom, no reversals of taste, nobody to declare that they never want to see an opera again.

Proust was a reactionary writer so steeped in the lore of the high society which he envied in the nineties and with such a nostalgia for the emotions of his own childhood, he was so much the introspective masochist that he admitted no change in his world beyond the inescapable evidence of old age that confronted him. The aim of his book was to revive his past and he discovered that by remembering everything that had happened, and by relying on intuitive visions produced by familiar smells and noises, such a revival was possible. And where he failed to revive it, his style, that blend of unselective curiosity with interminable qualification, would carry on like a lumbering, overcrowded, escaped tram that nobody can stop.

Proust lives rather through his extrovert satirical scenes, his balls and dinner-parties, the great ironical spectacle of the vanity of human wishes displayed by the Baron de Charlus and the Duchesse de Guermantes and through the delightful pictures which he provides of the countryside and his neighbours, the plain of Chartres, the coast, the quiet streets which Swann climbed in the Faubourg St Germain. Where his egocentric masturbatory self-analysis begins to function and his anxiety neurosis about his grandmother or Albertine, love or jealousy, comes into play, then all is tedious and unreal, like that asthma which his psychiatrist said he was unwilling to cure since something more unpleasant would be bound to take its place.

There are two more of these new Mandarins worth examining. We have seen that Aldous Huxley is a writer particularly accessible to the spirit of his time and by the middle twenties his period of dandyism was over. The influence of Mallarmé and Prufrock waned and he set himself to moralize on the flux around him. Witty, serious, observant, well read, sensitive, and intelligent, there can have been few young writers as gifted as Huxley – as can be seen from his early stories, *Happily Ever-After*, *Richard Greenow*, *Little Mexican*, *Young Archimedes*, or *The Gioconda Smile*.

Yet he had the misfortune to suffer from what he considered, quoting Buddha, to be the deadliest of mortal sins, unawareness, for he was both unaware of his own nature as a writer and of the temptations into which he was falling. His nature was a very English one, that of the divided man, the lover of beauty and pleasure dominated by the puritan conscience. At first his dichotomy is apparent in his treatment of love. Love means everything to him but sex – and sex, although he is obsessed by it, is disgusting. The conflict is extended to become a warfare between the senses on one side and the intellect, generously moralizing in the moment of victory, on the other until Huxley the intellectual pulls the lower self along like a man pulling a dog by a leash; there are glimpses of other dogs, lamp-posts, green grass, trousers and tree-trunks; then comes a jerk, 'eyes look your last' and a scientific platitude.

It is a question whether anyone so at war with himself can be a novelist, for to the novelist a complete integration is necessary; the proper medium for the split-man is the *Journal Intime* or the *Dialogue. Ends and Means* owes its success to being a complete break with the novel for as a novelist, apart from being at war with himself, Huxley was hampered by his inability to create character or see a character except in an intellectual way.

The greatness of a novelist like Tolstoy is that he creates characters who being real creations are able to think and behave unlike themselves, to be false to type. Proust also had some of this greatness, and in English, Thackeray. But weaker novelists can only sling a few traits on to the characters they are depicting and then hold them there. 'You can't miss So-and-so,' they explain, 'he stammers and now look, here he comes – "What's you name?" "S-s-s-so-and-s-s-s-so." There you see, what did I tell you!' Nearly all English novels are written to this prescription. Huxley suffers from the intellectual's difficulty of communicating with the people around him except through the intellect. In consequence the only people he can write about at length are those with whom he can carry on an intellectual discussion.

But the consequences of Huxley's *artistic* unawareness are more serious. He is a defaulting financier of the written word, and nobody since Chesterton has so squandered his gifts. A contract to produce two books a year forced him to vitiate that keen sense of words with which he started and as he had less to say, so, by a process which we have noticed, he took longer in which to say it. For such a writer who had to turn out 200,000 words a year, the Mandarin style was indispensable.

By dinner-time it was already a Story – *the latest addition* to Mary Amberley's *repertory*. The *latest*, and as good, it seemed to Antony's

> *critically attentive ear*, as the *finest classics of the collection*. Ever since *he received her invitation*, he now realized, *his curiosity had been tinged* with a *certain vindictive hope* that she would have *altered for the worse, either relatively in his own* knowledgeable *eyes, or else absolutely* by reason of the *passage of these twelve long years*; would have degenerated from what she was, or what he had imagined her to be, at the time when he had loved her. Discreditably enough, *as he now admitted to himself, it was with a touch of disappointment* that he had found her *hardly changed from the Mary Amberley of his memories*. She was forty-three. *But her body was almost as slim as ever, and she moved with all the old swift agility*. With *something more than the old agility indeed*; for he had noticed that she was now agile on purpose, that she acted the part of one who is *carried away by a youthful impulse* to break into quick and violent motion – acted it, moreover, in circumstances where the impulse could not, if natural, possibly have been felt.
>
> After a lonely dinner – for Helen was keeping to her room on *the plea of a headache* – Gerry went up to sit with Mrs Amberley. He was *particularly charming that evening*, and so *affectionately solicitous that Mary forgot* all her *accumulated grounds* of complaint and *fell in love* with him *all over again*, and for *another set of reasons* – not because he was so *handsome, so easily and insolently dominating*, such a ruthless and *accomplished lover*, but because he was *kind, thoughtful, and affectionate*, was everything, *in a word*, she had previously known he wasn't.

I quote these as examples of Huxley's writing, of the muse's revenge, but they also show the influence of Proust in all its flatulence. Thus, although the clichés I have italicized are examples of the lack of distinction in Huxley's writing, as is the use of unnecessary adverbs or the dogged repetition, the determination to hit the nail on the head and then hit it on the head and then hit it on the head, that vulgarity with which we are familiar, yet there is also here the Proustian note: '. . . either relatively . . . or else absolutely . . . what she was, or what he had imagined her to be', etc. It is fake analysis and fatigued introspection, a frequent combination in Mandarinism at its worst.

The last and strangest arrival among these new Mandarins was Joyce. *Work in Progress* is a Mandarin book which demands, and demands in vain, complete leisure, the widest education and devoted patience from the reader who wishes to understand it. It could not be more remote from colloquial English, from the spoken word. But on his way there Joyce had experimented with both styles. Thus *Dubliners* and *A Portrait of the Artist* are in reformed or anti-Mandarin, and belong to the early years of Joyce's Irish rebellion against the academic pundits and the literature of the ruling class, while the value of *Ulysses* and its importance to this analysis of the trends in English prose lies in the mixture of styles to be found there. In *Ulysses*, Joyce, a sensitive stylist, is trying to make his mind up as to the side he will take in the battle of the books. Thus we have in the passages where Stephen Dedalus holds the stage the Anglo-Irish lyrical mixture that we find in the *Portrait of the Artist*. But whenever Bloom is on the scene the language becomes the demotic journalese in vogue where people like Bloom foregather, and corresponds to the French of Céline who in his *Voyage au bout de la nuit* creates a Bloom-like character. In the two long reveries, that of Mrs Bloom and the Cyclopean Nameless One, the style is petty bourgeois, almost proletarian; in the Lying-in hospital and the strange penultimate chapter highly Mandarin.

The quality common to the Mandarins was inflation either of language or imagination or of both and it was this inflation which made inevitable a reaction against them. For their success was enormous. In the history of literature there can have been few books more talked and written about; few names more mentioned than those of Proust, Joyce, Lytton Strachey, Virginia Woolf, the Sitwells and Paul Valéry. Their moment was propitious. After the post-war disillusion they offered a religion of beauty, a cult of words, of meanings understood only by the initiated at a time when people were craving such initiations.

The world had lived too long under martial law to desire a socialized form of art, for human beings in the mass had proved but a union of slaughterers. There was more hope and interest in extreme individuality. This romantic restatement of the individual was of value to the younger generation since it enabled them to inflate their own lives and gave them a depth and importance which they otherwise lacked. Soon the universities were flooded with emotional dud cheques, stumers on the bank of experience forged in the name of Swann or Dedalus, Monsieur Teste or Mrs Dalloway. Proustians developed a wool-winding technique in friendship, an indefatigable egotism in affairs of the heart, combined with a lively social ambition. Valérians made it clear that everything was a little more difficult than it seemed and then more difficult again. The Dedalus young men were defeatist, proud and twisted, their rudeness was justified by the impact of some ancestral curse; the Waste Landers were more miserable still while the young Huxleys found relief in epigrams and bawdy erudition.

> Oh yes, decidedly
> Having a sense of humour and a past
> One will amuse oneself, decidedly . . .

The Gidian immoralists were perverse and moody, the Stracheyites wore fringes and hooted with a dying pejorative fall, the Virginians were impulsive, the Mansfieldians very simple and 'back-to-childhood', the Sitwellians went to the ballet in white ties and began their sentences with lingering sibilance: 'I must say I do definitely think . . .' It was the golden age of Bloomsbury under the last long shadow of the Ivory Tower, a romantic, affected, and defeatist epoch; action was discredited, it had caused the war; 'And as for goodness – listen to Freud. Truth? but what about Einstein? History? Have you read the *Decline of the West*? Nothing remains but beauty. Have you read Waley's *170 Chinese Poems*? Beauty – and, of course, one's intellectual integrity and personal relations.'

I have not dealt at length with these authors because I am assuming that the reader for whom this is written, the artist in his search for a relative immortality, will know the most important book about them: Edmund Wilson's *Axel's Castle* (Scribner's, 1931), which includes essays on Yeats, Valéry, Eliot, Proust, Joyce, and Gertrude Stein. His summing up is against them, in so far as it is against their cult of the individual which he feels they have carried to such lengths as to exhaust it for a long time to come, but it is a summing up which also states everything that can be said in their favour when allowance for what I have termed 'inflation' has been made. Here is the last paragraph:

> The writers with whom I have here been concerned have not only, then, given us works of literature which, for intensity, brilliance, and boldness as well as for an architectural genius, an intellectual mastery of their materials, rare among their Romantic predecessors, are probably comparable to the work of any time. Though it is true that they have tended to overemphasize the importance of the individual, that they have been preoccupied with introspection sometimes almost to the point of insanity, that they have endeavoured to discourage their readers, not only with politics, but with action of any kind – they have yet succeeded in effecting in literature a revolution analogous to that which has taken place in science and philosophy: they have broken out of the old mechanistic routine, they have disintegrated the old materialism, and they have revealed to the imagination a new flexibility and freedom. And though we are aware in them of things that are dying – the whole belle-lettristic tradition of Renaissance culture perhaps, compelled to specialize more and more, more and more driven in on itself, as industrialism and democratic education have come to press it closer and closer – they none the less break down the walls of the present and wake us to the hope and exaltation of the untried, unsuspected possibilities of human thought and art.

On this verdict we will leave them.

8 *The New Vernacular*

The mass attack on the new Mandarins was launched in the late twenties. By that time these had squandered their cultural inheritance, for their inflationary period coincided with the Boom and their adversaries were to come into their own with the Slump. In spite of their apparent success and publicity, the three great Mandarin books of 1928, *Orlando*, *Elizabeth and Essex*, *Point Counter Point*, were disappointing; they were not, except in America, popular successes and met also with considerable highbrow opposition.

This opposition may be said to have formed in three quarters. One quarter was that of the old realists, the remainder of those young men who had rejected Pater, Swinburne, Meredith, and James. Of these Moore was too ill-read to be a good critic, Bennett too successful for he was anxious to conceal by his indiscriminate welcome to novelty the poverty of his own exhausted impulse; the opinion of Galsworthy, Shaw, Wells, Kipling was no longer of value in matters of art. It remained for Somerset Maugham, after his long excursion as a playwright, to return as the champion of 'lucidity, euphony, simplicity, and the story with a beginning, a middle and an end', the doctrines of his French masters.

The second quarter was Paris which held in the attack on the new Mandarins the line taken by Dublin against their predecessors thirty years before. It was here that conspirators met in Sylvia Beach's little bookshop where *Ulysses* lay stacked like dynamite in a revolutionary cellar and then scattered down the Rue de l'Odéon on the missions assigned to them. Here Gertrude Stein had launched her attacks on English culture by rinsing the English vocabulary, by a process of constant repetition, of all accretions of meaning and association. The prose style of Ezra Pound was hardly academic, and Joyce also, till he became the Mandarin of *Work in Progress*, remained a king over the water for those who were discontented with the court of Bloomsbury. James Joyce, ambered in the Rue de Grenelle, and Gertrude Stein were the exiled royalties round whom centred the plots against Virginia Woolf and Lytton Strachey.

Any estimate of Miss Stein must largely depend on the pleasure derivable from her creations, but she applied to the writing of English as early as 1909 (*Three Lives*) a method which was to have far-reaching results. It was a simplification, an attack on order and meaning in favour of sound but of sound which in itself generated a new precision. Two young men were to be influenced by it, Sherwood Anderson and Ernest Hemingway, who each took Gertrude Stein's method and added to it his own quality of readability. The paper *Transition* was the court gazette of these kings in exile.

The third quarter in which opposition to the Mandarins arose was that of their contemporaries, Lawrence and Lewis. Lawrence, as the early lyricism of his pre-war books evaporated, became a master of the colloquial style. Though his work is marred by carelessness, repetition, and want of ear and a tendency to preach and rant which ill-health accentuated, it is always vigorous, thoughtful and alive, the enemy of elaboration and artifice, of moral hypocrisy and verbal falseness. The poems in *Pansies* and *Nettles* are examples of the vernacular style at its best, as is the satire in his later books and stories such as *Lady Chatterley*. Around Lawrence centred Middleton Murry and his wife, Katharine Mansfield, who said in her diary that the greatest pleasure she had received from her stories was that they had given pleasure to the printer who set them up, and also several younger writers of whom Richard Aldington, who also had one foot in Paris, and Robert Graves were the most important. A friend of Lawrence, though more influenced by George Moore, was David Garnett whose *Lady Into Fox* and *Sailor's Return* were excellent anti-Mandarin books, combining something of the dandyism of Eliot and Firbank with a rustic basis, a fantasy logically worked out in language as simple as Defoe's.

The most dangerous enemy of the new Mandarins was Wyndham Lewis who after his realistic novel *Tarr* (1918) was preparing his onslaught on the citadels of literary culture; on the one hand Stein's simplicity and Joyce's complexity were to be attacked, with Hemingway, Faulkner, and all other derivatives, while in England Bloomsbury was to tremble, Lawrence to be chastised for his worship of the black sun of the solar plexus, and the Sitwells to be exterminated by an assassination five hundred pages long. Roy Campbell, in *The Georgiad*, brought up the rear. Since Lewis's style is that of a painter turned writer, it is difficult of analysis, being strongly marked by the visual quality of his imagination. His early books are full of fine onsets and satires and descriptions written in a technique of his own while his later ones are more colloquial or what he would call 'informal'.

To estimate his work is not easy. *The Art of Being Ruled*, *Time and Western Man*, *The Childermass*, *The Enemy*, and *The Apes of God* contain some of the most vigorous satire, original description and profound criticism produced by the twentieth century; Lewis was unique in being a philosophical critic, who, attacking the modern conception of 'time', was able to illustrate the workings of that conception by ranging up and down the whole of contemporary literature from the best poetry to the best seller, the best seller to the lowest kind of journalism or jazz.

As a constructive critic however he has little to offer, a belief in reason as opposed to metaphysical or sexual mysticism, a belief in western civilization, in the physical world, in the comic aspect of love, in the external approach to things (describing people via their personal appearance) and in the value of humour and satire. All this is not negligible, but it is not on a scale with the world he has set out to destroy or with his machinery of destruction.

What Lewis believes in most is himself and the measure he applies to his contemporaries is how far they differ from that yardstick and how far they stand in his way. His criticism also suffers from a lack of proportion. He will attack a writer on philosophical or moral grounds and then as violently for the most superficial and frivolous of errors; or he will turn from rending an important writer to maul an obscure and inconsiderable hack. He is like a maddened elephant which, careering through a village, sometimes leans against a house and carelessly demolishes the most compact masonry, trumpeting defiance to the inhabitants within, sometimes pursues a dog or a chicken or stops to uproot a shrub or bang a piece of corrugated iron. His writing can be redundant and slovenly, his dialogue is often dull, his novels begin with scenes worthy of a great master and gradually lose themselves in unplanned verbosity. His last volume of criticism, *Men Without Art*, while containing brilliant glimpses of his mind, is unexpectedly trivial and often bullying and unfair. His later books are ragged and his style has become somewhat unbuttoned. From an article of his in the Fascist quarterly, *British Union*, one gets the impression that it is because he is writing now for a new class of reader, the petty bourgeois, the philistine small tradesman, the Fascist under-dog.

What is necessary for Lewis is that some of his admirers or he himself should make an omnibus Lewis, an anthology of his best thought and finest passages, applying to his work the selection and compression which in the spate of his original creation have been wanting.

To go further it is necessary to bring the production chart up to date and I have added after some of the more extreme examples the letters (M) or (V) according as to whether they are written in the Mandarin, or Vernacular or Colloquial style.

1923 Mansfield, *The Dove's Nest* (V); Huxley, *Antic Hay* (M); Firbank, *The Flower Beneath the Foot* (Dandy); Hemingway, *In Our Time* (V); Willa Cather, *A Lost Lady*; Elizabeth Bowen, *Encounters*; Eliot, *The Waste Land*.

1924 Mansfield, *Something Childish* (V); Huxley, *Little Mexican*; Firbank, *Prancing Nigger*; Forster, *Passage to India*; Garnett, *Man in the Zoo* (V); Edith Sitwell, *The Sleeping Beauty* (M); Osbert Sitwell, *Triple Fugue* (M).

1925 Huxley, *Those Barren Leaves* (M); Dreiser, *American Tragedy* (V); Eliot, *Poems* (M); Compton-Burnett, *Pastors and Masters*; Garnett, *Sailor's Return* (V); Fitzgerald, *The Great Gatsby*; Loos, *Gentlemen Prefer Blondes* (V); Woolf, *Mrs Dalloway* (M); Day Lewis, *Beechen Vigil*; Noel Coward, *The Vortex* (V); Geoffrey Scott, *Portrait of Zelide* (M).

1926 Huxley, *Two or Three Graces* (M); Hemingway, *Torrents of Spring* (V); Quennell, *Poems* (M); Lawrence, *Plumed Serpent*; Baring, *Daphne Adeane* (V); Cather, *My Mortal Enemy* (V); Fowler, *Modern English Usage*; V. Woolf, *To the Lighthouse* (M); Maugham, *The Casuarina Tree* (V).

1927 Bowen, *The Hotel* (M); Lehmann, *Dusty Answer* (M); Hemingway, *The Sun Also Rises* (V), *Men Without Women* (V); Lewis, *The Wild Body*, *Time and Western Man*, *The Lion and the Fox*; Mackenzie, *Vestal Fires*; Wilder, *Bridge of San Luis Rey* (M); Westcott, *The Grandmothers* (M).

1928 Sassoon, *Memoirs of a Fox-hunting Man*; Woolf, *Orlando* (M); Lawrence, *Lady Chatterley's Lover* (V); Nicholson, *Some People*; Edwards, *Winter Sonata* (V); Waugh, *Decline and Fall* (V); Isherwood, *All the Conspirators* (V); Lewis, *The Childermass*; Mackenzie, *Extraordinary Women*; Strachey, *Elizabeth and Essex* (M); Huxley, *Point Counter Point* (M); E. Sackville-West, *Mandrake Over the Water-Carrier* (M).

1929 Compton-Burnett, *Brothers and Sisters*; H. Green, *Living* (V); W. Faulkner, *The Sound and the Fury* (M); Hemingway, *Farewell to Arms* (V); Lawrence, *Pansies* (V); Joyce, *Fragments of Work in Progress* (M); Quennell, *Baudelaire and the Symbolists* (M); Graves, *Goodbye to All That* (V); Aldington, *Death of a Hero* (V).

1930 Kafka, *The Castle*; Dashiell Hammett, *Maltese Falcon* (V); O. Sitwell, *Dumb Animal* (M); Maugham, *Cakes and Ale* (V), *The Gentleman in the Parlour*; W. H. Auden, *Poems*; T. S. Eliot, *Ash Wednesday* (M); Evelyn Waugh, *Vile Bodies* (V); Spender, *Twenty Poems*; Lewis, *The Apes of God*.

1931 V. Woolf, *The Waves* (M); Roy Campbell, *The Georgiad* (V); A. Powell, *Afternoon Men* (V); Edmund Wilson, *Axel's Castle*.

1932 W. H. Auden, *The Orators*.

There are, we know, many kinds of vernacular; the colloquial language of Hemingway is different from the colloquial language of Maurice Baring yet each believes in informality and simplicity, they never use a word that they would not in conversation – words like 'nay', 'notwithstanding', 'pullulating', 'mephitic', 'sublunary', 'Babylon', 'lest', 'corpulent', 'futurity', 'ecstasy', etc.

The outstanding writer of the new vernacular is Hemingway and he was aided by the talkies as were realists a generation before by journalism. The talking picture popularized the vocabulary with which Hemingway wrote and enabled him to use slang words in the knowledge that they were getting every day less obscure, he surf-rode into fame on the wave of popular American culture. Here, taken from *Death in the Afternoon*, is a spat between him and a Mandarin which is in itself a defence of the new style:

> Mr Aldous Huxley writing in an essay entitled *Foreheads Villainous Law* commences: 'In [naming a book by this writer] Mr. H. ventures, once, to name an Old Master. There is a phrase, quite admirably expressive' [here Mr Huxley inserts a compliment], 'a single phrase, no more, about "the bitter nail-holes" of Mantegna's Christ; then quickly, quickly, appalled by his own temerity, the author passes on (as Mrs Gaskell might hastily have passed on, if she had somehow been betrayed into mentioning a water-closet) passes on, shamefacedly, to speak once more of Lower Things.
>
> 'There was a time, not so long ago, when the stupid and uneducated aspired to be thought intelligent and cultured. The current of aspiration has changed its direction. It is not at all uncommon now to find intelligent and cultured people doing their best to feign stupidity and to conceal the fact that they have received an education' – and more; more in Mr Huxley's best educated vein which is a highly educated vein indeed.
>
> What about that, you say? Mr Huxley scores there, all right, all right. What have you to say to that? Let me answer truly. On reading that in Mr Huxley's book I obtained a copy of the volume he refers to and looked through it and could not find the quotation he mentions. It may be there, but I did not have the patience nor the interest to find it, since the book was finished, and nothing to be done. It sounds very much like the sort of thing one tries to remove in going over the manuscript. I believe it is more than a question of the simulation or avoidance of the

appearance of culture. When writing a novel a writer should create living people; people, not characters. A *character* is a caricature. If a writer can make people live there may be no great characters in his book, but it is possible that his book will remain as a whole; as an entity; as a novel. If the people the writer is making talk of old masters; of music; of modern painting; of letters; of science; then they should talk of those subjects in the novel. If they do not talk of those subjects and the writer makes them talk of them he is a faker, and if he talks about them himself to show how much he knows, then he is showing off. No matter how good a phrase or a simile he may have, if he puts it in where it is not absolutely necessary and irreplaceable, he is spoiling his work for egotism. Prose is architecture, not interior decoration, and the Baroque is over. For a writer to put his own intellectual musings, which he might sell for a low price as essays, into the mouths of artificially constructed characters, which are more remunerative when issued as people in a novel, is good economics, perhaps, but does not make literature. People in a novel, not skilfully constructed *characters*, must be projected from the writer's assimilated experience, from his knowledge, from his head, from his heart, and from all there is of him. If he ever has luck as well as seriousness and gets them out entire they will have more than one dimension and they will last a long time. A good writer should know as near everything as possible. Naturally he will not. A great enough writer seems to be born with knowledge. But he really is not; he has only been born with a quicker ratio to the passage of time than other men and without conscious application, and with an intelligence to accept or reject what is already presented as knowledge. There are some things which cannot be learned quickly, and time, which is all we have, must be paid heavily for their acquiring. They are the very simplest things and because it takes a man's life to know them the little new that each man gets from life is very costly and the only heritage he has to leave. Every novel which is truly written contributes to the total of knowledge which is there at the disposal of the next writer who comes, but the next writer must pay, always, a certain nominal percentage in experience to be able to understand and assimilate what is available as his birthright and what he must, in turn,

> take his departure from. If a writer of prose knows enough about what he is writing about he may omit things that he knows and the reader, if the writer is writing truly enough, will have a feeling of those things as strongly as though the writer had stated them. The dignity of movement of an iceberg is due to only one-eighth of it being above water. A writer who omits things because he does not know them only makes hollow places in his writing. A writer who appreciates the seriousness of writing so little that he is anxious to make people see he is formally educated, cultured or well-bred, is merely a popinjay. And this too, remember: a serious writer is not to be confounded with a solemn writer. A serious writer may be a hawk or a buzzard or even a popinjay, but a solemn writer is always a bloody owl.

The passage is an excellent example of Hemingway's style; notice the clumsy, facetious get-away, the admirable relation in the central passage between the language used and the thought to be conveyed, the polemical anti-climax at the end, and notice also the slovenliness of such a phrase as 'if a writer of prose knows enough about what he is writing about he may omit things that he knows'. Like most writers of the thirties Hemingway seems terrified to blot a line.

Hemingway's difficulties as a writer arise from the limitations of realism. His style, derived from Huck Finn, Stein, Anderson with perhaps a dash of Firbank, is the antithesis of fine writing. It is a style in which the body talks rather than the mind, one admirable for rendering emotions: love, fear, joy of battle, despair, sexual appetite, but impoverished for intellectual purposes. Hemingway is fortunate in possessing a physique which is at home in the world of boxing, bull-fighting and big game shooting, fields closed to most writers and especially to Mandarins; he is supreme in the domain of violence and his opportunity will be to write the great book (and there have been no signs of one so far) about the Spanish war. Hemingway's tragedy as an artist is that he has not had the versatility to run away fast enough from his imitators. The talkies that facilitated his success brought on a flood of talkie-novels, the trick of being tough, the knack of writing entirely in dialogue interrupted only by a few sentimental landscapes caught on and with each bad copy the prestige of the original was affected. A Picasso would have done something different; Hemingway could only indulge in invective against his critics – and do it again. His colleagues in American realism, Dos Passos, O'Hara, Caldwell, have found the same difficulties and the Hemingway style is now confined to sporting journalists on the daily papers, advertising men with literary ambitions, cinema critics, and the writers of thrillers. The first you-man sentence of the *Portrait of the Artist*, 'when you wet the bed first it is warm, then it gets cold', a sentence intended to represent the simple body-conscious needs of early childhood, after dominating fiction for years, would seem to have had its day.

Lewis has attacked Hemingway for being a 'dumb ox', for choosing stupid inarticulate heroes who are the passive victims of circumstance rather than active and intelligent masters of their fate. Yet at the period at which Hemingway wrote his best books it was necessary to be a dumb ox. It was the only way to escape from Chelsea's Apes of God and from Bloomsbury's Sacred Geese.

The most resolute and coherent of the opponents of fine writing has been Somerset Maugham although his hostility arises, he tell us, from his incapacity.

> I discovered my limitations and it seemed to me that the only sensible thing was to aim at what excellence I could within them. I knew that I had no lyrical quality, I had a small vocabulary and no efforts that I could make to enlarge it much availed me. I had little gift of metaphors; the original and striking simile seldom occurred to me. Poetic flights and the great imaginative sweep were beyond my powers . . . I knew that I should never write as well as I could wish, but I thought with pains I could arrive at writing as well as my natural defects allowed. On taking thought it seemed to me that I must aim at lucidity, simplicity and euphony. I have put these three qualities in the order of the importance I assigned to them.

Maugham (I am quoting from *The Summing Up*, though some of the arguments there are to be found in earlier books) then goes on to criticize Ruskin and Sir Thomas Browne with justice and to attack the influence of King James's Bible on English prose.

> Ever since, English prose has had to struggle against the tendency to luxuriance. When from time to time the spirit of the language has reasserted itself, as it did with Dryden and the writers of Queen Anne, it was only to be submerged once more by the pomposities of Gibbon and Dr Johnson. When English prose recovered simplicity with Hazlitt, the Shelley of the letters, and Charles Lamb at his best, it lost it again with de Quincey, Carlyle, Meredith, and Walter Pater . . .
>
> For to write good prose is an affair of good manners. It is, unlike verse, a civil art . . . Poetry is baroque. I cannot but feel that the prose writers of the baroque period, the authors of King James's Bible, Sir Thomas Browne, Glanville, were poets who had lost their way. Prose is a rococo art. It needs taste rather than power, decorúm rather than inspiration and vigour rather than grandeur . . . It is not an accident that the best prose was written when rococo, with its elegance and moderation, attained its greatest excellence. For rococo was evolved when baroque had become declamatory, and the world, tired of the stupendous, asked for restraint. It was the natural expression of persons who valued a civilized life. Humour, tolerance, and horse-sense made the great tragic issues that had preoccupied the first half of the seventeenth century seem excessive. The world was a more comfortable place to live in and perhaps for the first time in centuries the cultivated classes could sit back and enjoy their leisure. It has been said that good prose should resemble the conversation of a well-bred man. Conversation is only possible when men's minds are free from pressing anxieties. Their lives must be reasonably secure and they must have no grave concern about their souls. They must attach importance to the refinements of civilization. They must value courtesy; they must pay attention to their persons (and have we not also been told that good prose should be like the clothes of a well-dressed man, appropriate but unobtrusive?). They must fear to bore, they must be neither flippant, nor solemn, but always apt; and they must look upon 'enthusiasm' with

> a critical glance. This is a soil very suitable for prose. It is not to be wondered at that it gave a fitting opportunity for the appearance of the best writer of prose that our modern world has seen, Voltaire . . . The writers of English, perhaps owing to the poetic nature of the language, have seldom reached the excellence that seems to have come so naturally to him . . . If you could write lucidly, simply, euphoniously and yet with liveliness you would write perfectly; you would write like Voltaire.

I have quoted this passage because it is a typical defence of vernacular prose, as also of much literary wish-fulfilment. Maugham thinks with pleasure of the civilized and wealthy society of the eighteenth century, he has made his own life wealthy and civilized and therefore would like to believe that the prose of the eighteenth century is the best. But supposing a new age of 'great tragic issues' is now in being, then a prose of humour, tolerance, and horse-sense will seem frivolous and archaic! And what writer could have been more lucid and simple, more admired by Maugham than Swift who, living in the heart of that courteous and cultivated age, contrived to go mad in it? Nor is the prose of Blake so negligible. Incidentally the defects of the colloquial style are well illustrated in this passage. The vocabulary is flat. 'Sit back and enjoy', 'pressing anxieties', 'reasonably secure', 'grave concern', 'critical glance', 'fitting opportunity', 'it is not to be wondered at', while not yet officially clichés, are phrases so tarnished as to be on the way to them. They come from the vocabulary of political journalism; from the atmosphere where words deteriorate faster than in any other and the defect of the colloquial style, the breathlessness, the agitated dullness of the sentence which is too short for both eye and ear, becomes apparent. The phrases rattle like peas being shelled into a tin, the full stops bring the reader up short, the effect, owing to the absence of any relative clauses, is of reading a list of aphorisms and the best aphorists, even La Rochefoucauld, can be read only for a few pages. Again, the language of the Bible is more plain than complicated; its bad influence on English style has been in the direction of archaistic simplicity and is apparent in a writer like Kipling. It is no accident, as Maugham would say, that he goes on to praise American literature, ignorant, he claims, of the Authorized Version, and to flatter American writers, galvanized by their journalism.

This concludes the case for the vernacular style. There remains one other argument often heard in its favour. 'If culture is to survive it must survive through the masses; if it cannot be made acceptable to them there is no one else who will be prepared to guarantee it, since the liberal capitalist society who protected it will not be in a position to do so after another slump and a war. Much that is subtle in literature and life will have to be sacrificed if they are to survive at all; consequently it is necessary for literature to approach its future custodians in a language they will understand.'

The old world is a sinking ship, to get a place in the boats that are pushing off from it not money nor leisure, the essayist's elegance nor the pedant's erudition will avail; the sailors are not impressed by courtesy or attention to one's person, nor even by good clothes and the conversation of a well-bred man; we cannot take our armchair with us. Nothing will admit us but realism and sincerity, an honest appeal in downright English. As far back as 1847 Tennyson said that the two great social questions impending in England were the 'housing and education of the poor man before making him our master, and the higher education of women' and as the time for making him our master grows nearer, so his education becomes more necessary since on it depend the cultural values which he will choose to preserve.

For this reason left-wing writers have tended to write in the colloquial style while the Mandarins, the wizards and prose charmers remain as supporters of the existing dispensation. In England the ablest exponents of the colloquial style among the young writers are Christopher Isherwood and George Orwell, both left-wing and both, at the present level of current English, superlatively readable. Here is an experiment:

> The first sound in the mornings was the clumping of the mill-girls' clogs down the cobbled street. Earlier than that, I suppose, there were factory

whistles which I was never awake to hear. There were generally four of us in the bedroom, and a beastly place it was with the defiled impermanent look of rooms that are not serving their rightful purpose. One afternoon, early in October, I was invited to black coffee at Fritz Wendel's flat. Fritz always invited you to 'black coffee' with emphasis on the black. He was very proud of his coffee. People used to say it was the strongest in Berlin. Fritz himself was dressed in his usual coffee-party costume – a thick white yachting sweater and very light blue yachting trousers. You know how it is there early in Havana, with the bums still asleep against the walls of the buildings; before even the ice waggons come by with ice for the bars? Well we came across the square from the dock to the Pearl of San Francisco to get coffee. My bed was in the right-hand corner on the side nearest the door. There was another bed across the foot of it and jammed hard against it (it had to be in that position to allow the door to open), so that I had to sleep with my legs doubled up; if I straightened them out I kicked the occupant of the other bed in the small of the back. He was an elderly man named Mr Reilly. He greeted me with his full-lipped luscious smile.

'Lo, Chris!'

'Hullo, Fritz. How are you?'

'Fine.' He bent over the coffee-machine, his sleek black hair unplastering itself from the scalp and falling in richly scented locks over his eyes. 'This darn thing doesn't go,' he added.

We sat down and one of them came over.

'Well,' he said.

'I can't do it,' I told him. 'I'd like to do it as a favour. But I told you last night I couldn't.'

'You can name your own price.'

'It isn't that. I can't do it. That's all. How's business?' I asked.

'Lousy and terrible.' Fritz grinned richly.

Luckily he had to go to work at five in the morning so I could uncoil my legs and have a couple of hours' proper sleep after he was gone.

This passage is formed by adding to the first three sentences of Orwell's *Road to Wigan Pier* the first five sentences of Isherwood's

Sally Bowles and then the first two sentences of Hemingway's *To Have and Have Not*. I have woven the beginning of the three stories a little further. Next three sentences by Orwell, then dialogue by Isherwood to 'added', by Hemingway to 'That's all', by Isherwood to 'richly' and last sentence by Orwell again. The reader can now go on with whichever book he likes best, Orwell and his bed, Fritz and his coffee, or Harry Morgan and Havana. As Pearsall Smith says of modern writers: 'The diction, the run of phrase of each of them seems quite undistinguishable from that of the others, each of whose pages might have been written by any one of his fellows.'

This, then, is the penalty of writing for the masses. As the writer goes out to meet them half-way he is joined by other writers going out to meet them half-way and they merge into the same creature – the talkie journalist, the advertising, lecturing, popular novelist.

The process is complicated by the fact that the masses, whom a cultured writer may generously write for, are at the moment overlapped by the middle-class best-seller-making public and so a venal element is introduced.

According to Gide, a good writer should navigate against the current; the practitioners in the new vernacular are swimming with it; the familiarities of the advertisements in the morning paper, the matey leaders in the *Daily Express*, the blather of the film critics, the wise-cracks of newsreel commentators, the know-all autobiographies of political reporters, the thrillers and 'teccies, the personal confessions, that *I was a so-and-so*, and *Storm over such-and-such*, the gossip-writers who play Jesus at twenty-five pounds a week, the straight-from-the-shoulder men, the middlebrow novelists of the shove-halfpenny school, are all swimming with it too. For a moment the canoe of an Orwell or an Isherwood bobs up, then it is hustled away by floating rubbish, and a spate of newspaper pulp.

It is interesting to notice the conflict between the two ways of writing in Auden. In the ballads he has lately been writing, excellent of their kind, he has attempted to reduce poetry to a record of simple and universal experience expressed in colloquial language.

O plunge your hands in water
Plunge them in up to the wrist
Stare, stare in the basin
And wonder what you've missed.

The glacier knocks in the cupboard
The desert sighs in the bed,
And the crack in the tea-cup opens
A lane to the land of the dead.

At the same time the bulk of his poetry has always remained private and esoteric.

9 *The Cool Element of Prose*

It is now time to express an opinion on the battle between the styles. I do not say that one is better than the other; there is much to admire in both; what I have claimed is a relationship between them, a perpetual action and reaction; the realists had it their way in the years before the war; from 1918 to 1928, the period of Joyce, Proust, Valéry, Strachey, Woolf, the Sitwells, and Aldous Huxley, the new Mandarins ruled supreme, while from 1928 to 1938 the new realists have predominated. The deflationary activities of the Cambridge critics (Richards, Leavis) have replaced the inflationism of Bloomsbury. But we have now had ten years of this new realism; ten years in which it has grown more popular and more tyrannical. Its vocabulary, never rich, has been worn away by the attrition of success; its exponents have been wearied by the enormity of their imitators.

It is possible to bring forward other causes for the silence or the deterioration of a writer than the weaknesses of his literary creed and the other causes are as likely to be correct. All we can say of the realists of the last ten years, is that nothing in their technique seems to have insured them against the disastrously short term of the writer's life. Realism, simplicity, the colloquial style, would appear to have triumphed everywhere at the moment – yet where are their triumphant professors? With the exception of Isherwood among the young and Maugham among the old their prestige is already fading. The movement has passed out of their hands and sunk to a wider and more anonymous stratum, to the offices, the studios and the novelists' week-end cottages where is produced the great bulk of present-day commercial writing.

I have discussed the situation with Isherwood, whom I regard as a hope of English fiction, and I have suggested how dangerous that fatal readability of his might become. The first person singular of the German stories, Herr Christoph, or Herr Issyvoo, is the most persuasive of literary salesmen – one moment's reading with him and one is tobogganing through the book, another second and one has bought it – but he is persuasive because he is so insinuatingly bland and anonymous, nothing rouses him, nothing shocks him. While secretly despising us he could not at the same time be more tolerant; his manners are charming and he is somehow on our side against the characters – confidential as, when playing with children, one child older or less animal than the rest will suddenly attach itself to the grown-ups and discuss its former playmates.

Now for this a price has to be paid; Herr Issyvoo is not a dumb ox, for he is not condemned to the solidarity with his characters and with their background to which Hemingway is bound by his conception of art, but he is much less subtle, intelligent, and articulate than he might be. In the little knitted skein from the three books it will be remembered that not only was the language almost identical and the pace the same but the three 'I's' of Isherwood, Orwell and Hemingway were also interchangeable; three colourless reporters.

In Isherwood's earlier *The Memorial*, however, there is no first person. The hero is a character who is more favoured than the others, and in the Berlin diary (*New Writing*, No. 3) the first person singular, unhampered by the conventions of fiction, at once postulates a higher level of culture and intelligence, and possesses a richer vocabulary. In conversation, Isherwood, while admitting the limitations of the style he had adopted, expressed his belief in construction as the way out of the difficulty. The writer must conform to the language which is understood by the greatest number of people, to the vernacular, but his talents as a novelist will appear in the exactness of his observation, the justice of his situations and in the construction of his book. It is an interesting theory, for construction has for long been the weak point in modern novels. It is the construction that renders outstanding *The Memorial*, *Passage to India*, and *Cakes and Ale*.

But will the construction, however rigid and faultless, of future books, if they are written in what will by then be an even more impoverished realist vocabulary, contribute enough to set those books apart from the copies made by the ever-growing school of imitators? At present it is impossible to tell; the path is beset by dangers; it is fortunate that Isherwood, who possesses the mastery of form, the imaginative content of a true novelist, is able to see them.

The most convincing attack on the realism of the thirties was made by Pearsall Smith in his pamphlet on *Fine Writing* (reprinted in *Reperusals*, 1936). A Mandarin of the generation of the eighties, an admirer of Pater and Jowett and a friend of Henry James, he represents not a reaction against the new realism, but the old Adam, the precious original sinner, against whom the later realists took action. He, in return, attacks their austerity:

> May it be accounted for by the fact that the spirit of Puritanism, having been banished from the province of moral conduct, has found a refuge among the arts? Do these critics of the art of writing, like certain critics of other arts, occupy themselves with the craft of literary composition because they think it wrong? . . . I shall make to our modern critics, especially of the Cambridge school, a few suggestions which are not amiable, and are perhaps unfair. The disconcerting fact may first be pointed out that if you write badly about good writing, however profound may be your convictions or emphatic your expression of them, your style has a tiresome trick of whispering, 'Don't listen,' in your reader's ears. And it is possible also to suggest that the promulgation of new-fangled aesthetic dogmas in unwieldy sentences may be

> accounted for – not perhaps unspitefully – by a certain deficiency in aesthetic sensibility; as being due to a lack of that delicate, unreasoned, prompt delight in all the varied and subtle manifestations in which beauty may enchant us.

He goes on to suggest that economic causes are also responsible:

> Are not the authors who earn their livings by their pens, and those who, by what some regard as a social injustice, have been more or less freed from this necessity – are not these two classes of authors in a sort of natural opposition to each other? He who writes at his leisure, with the desire to master his difficult art, can hardly help envying the profits of the money-making authors, since his own work at least till years, and often many years, have passed, has no appreciable market value. Unsaleability seems to be the hall-mark, in modern times, of quality in writing.

Puritanism in other people we admire is austerity in ourselves, yet there is much truth in Pearsall Smith's accusation. Writing is a more impure art than music or painting. It is an art, but it is also the medium in which many millions of inartistic people express themselves, describe their work, sell their goods, justify their conduct, propagate their ideas. It is the vehicle of all business and propaganda. Since it is hard to paint or to compose without a certain affection for painting or music, the commercial element – advertisers, illustrators – is recognizable and in a minority, nor do music and painting appeal to the scientific temperament.

But writing does. It is an art in which the few who practise it for its own sake are being always resented and jostled through its many galleries by the majority who do not. And the deadliest of these are the scientific investigators, clever young men who have themselves failed as artists and who bring only a passionate sterility and a dark, wide-focusing resentment to their examination of creative art. The aim of much of this destructive criticism, though not as yet publicly avowed, is entirely to eliminate the individual style, to banish imaginative beauty and formal art from writing. Prose will not only be as unassuming as good clothes, but as uniform as bad ones. For there is no use in

Maugham arguing that a writer to be distinct from others must heighten his colloquial modern style by reading Newman and Hazlitt; he is by now, if he is like any other modern writer, moving too fast and such authors will seem to him, if he has the patience to read them, so occupied with unreal problems and so contaminated by a leisurely attitude to life as to be hardly less archaic than their stylistic rivals, Lamb, Ruskin, Pater, Matthew Arnold. The remedy is proposed too late.

The one way by which a cure can be undertaken is to persuade such writers to re-read their own books or those contemporary books which, up to a year ago, they most admired. Then, however jauntily they may protest – 'Well, it was what the public wanted at the time – it was in me and it had to come out; it means no more to me now than my old toe-nails – and hell, who wants to read the same book twice, anyway,' a doubt will have arisen.

On the other hand Maugham expresses a truth when he says that much writing of the kind he dislikes is the work of 'Poets who have lost their way'. The defect of Mandarin writing is not that it is poetical or imaginative prose, but that much of it is not prose, but bad poetry. It is a fact of importance that the prose of true poets is firm and muscular. Landor, Coleridge, Shelley, Donne, Shakespeare, Milton, Dryden, Blake, Hopkins, Yeats, Eliot, Gray, Cowper, to name but a few, could write admirable prose – for poetry is a more precise art than prose and to write it implies qualities which prove valuable in the 'other harmony'.

The poetry of prose writers on the other hand is unworthy of them and very often they will have become prose writers only after the failure of a slim volume of verse. Since the decay of the Romantic Movement poetry has gone through a bad patch and severe discipline has been necessary to those who write it; consequently others who start out with only facility, sensibility, and a lyrical outlook, rather than undergo the hardships of the training, have allowed their poetical feeling to relax in prose. The result has been to inflate and romanticize prose in its turn and thus to bring about a philistine, puritan, and pedestrian reaction. The Tough Guy, of whose company we are now growing tired, is the inevitable offspring of the androgynous Orlando. There is no reason why prose should not be poetical provided that the poetry in it is assimilated to the medium and that its rhythms follow the structure of prose and not of verse – it is the undisciplined, undigested, unassimilated poetry written often in unconscious blank verse and bearing no relation to the construction, if any, of the book, which has discredited 'fine writing'.

At the moment the vernacular is triumphant. Damon Runyon sweeps the land. The You-men are everywhere victorious.

That is the situation. Is there any hope? Is there a possibility of a new kind of prose developing out of a synthesis of Orlando and the Tough Guy? Will the strong writers of the colloquial school heighten the form of their work or can the Formalists deepen their content? We must look to the poets for a lead, for there are signs that from them is coming a revival of imaginative prose. I like to detect a foreshadowing of it in Landor's description of the lioness with her young, which appears, like an oasis, in Richards's *Principles of Literary Criticism*.

> On perceiving the countryman, she drew up her feet gently, and squared her mouth, and rounded her eyes, slumberous with content, and they looked, he said, like sea-grottoes, obscurely green, interminably deep, at once awakening fear and stilling and suppressing it.

Such a phrase belongs to the real texture of prose, a texture now rarely seen, where syntax and a rich vocabulary are woven in a pattern to match the thought of the maker.

> I know that I am I, living in a small way in a temperate zone, blaming father, jealous of son, confined to a few acts often repeated, easily attracted to a limited class of physique, yet envying the simple life of the gut, desiring the certainty of the breast or prison, happiest sawing wood, only knowledge of the real disturbances in the general law of the dream; the quick blood fretting against the slowness of the hope; a unit of life, needing water and salt, that looks for a sign.

> From the immense bat-shadow of home; from the removal of land-

marks, from appeals for love and from the comfortable words of the devil, from all opinions and personal ties; from pity and shame; and from the wish to instruct . . . in the moment of vision; in the hour of applause; in the place of defeat; and in the hour of desertion, O Holmes, Deliver us.

These two quotations from *The Orators* (W. H. Auden; Faber, 1932) show imaginative prose coming to life again by way of a young poet influenced by Rimbaud and the Prayer Book. And when the language comes to life, it ceases to be an imitation. The prose of Spender is also unusual and in his critical book, *The Destructive Element*, he makes a study of that great Mandarin, Henry James, which must affect the values of any contemporary who reads it, since he has restated for his generation the relationship between writing and ethics. The revival of the poetical drama and the Group Theatre gives writers like Eliot, Auden, Isherwood, and MacNeice opportunities for declamatory and non-commercial prose.

Other glimpses of a revival in imaginative writing may be found in George Barker's *Janus* (Faber, 1935), Hugh Sykes-Davies's *Petron* (Dent), David Jones's *In Parenthesis* (Faber), Djuna Barnes's *Night Wood* (Faber), Henry Miller's *Tropic of Cancer* (Obelisk Press), and Henry Green's remarkable novel *Living* (Dent).*

One further question is raised by Maugham. 'I have never much patience', he states, 'with the writers who claim from the reader an effort to understand their meaning.' This is an abject surrender for it is part of the tragedy of modern literature that the author, anxious to avoid mystifying the reader, is afraid to demand of him any exertions. 'Don't be afraid of me,' he exclaims, 'I write exactly as I talk – no, better still – exactly as you talk.' Imagine Cézanne painting or Beethoven composing 'exactly as he talked'! The only way to write is to consider the reader to be the author's equal; to treat him otherwise is to set a value

*Readers who find the lioness quotation stirs them, like the memory of something of which they have been long deprived, may amuse themselves by searching for this quality in modern prose, this combination of imagination and accuracy into magic, and they will be fortunate if they can discover a single example.

on illiteracy and so all that results from Maugham's condescension to a reader from whom he expects no effort is a latent hostility to him as of some great chef waiting on a hungry Australian. As Richards says of the poet: 'It is hard and, in fact, impossible, to deny him his natural and necessary resources on the ground that a majority of his readers will not understand. This is not his fault but the fault of the social structure.'

At the present time, for a book to be produced with any hope of lasting half a generation, of outliving a dog or a car, of surviving the lease of a house or the life of a bottle of champagne, it must be written against the current, in a prose that makes demands both on the resources of our language and the intelligence of the reader. From the Mandarins it must borrow art and patience, the striving for perfection, the horror of clichés, the creative delight in the material, in the possibilities of the long sentence and the splendour and subtlety of the composed phrase.

From the Mandarins, on the other hand, the new writer will take warning not to capitalize indolence and egotism nor to burden a sober and delicate language with exhibitionism. There will be no false hesitation and woolly profundities, no mystifying, no Proustian onanism. He will distrust the armchair clowns, the easy philosophers, the prose charmers. He will not show off his small defects, his preferences or his belongings, his cat, his pipe, his carpet slippers, bad memory, clumsiness with machinery, absent-mindedness, propensity for losing things, or his ignorance of business and of everything which might make the reader think he wrote for money. There will be no whimsy, no allusiveness, archaism, pedantic usages, no false colloquialisms or sham lyrical outbursts; there will be no 'verily' and 'verity', no 'when all is said and done', no 'to my way of thinking', 'hardly of my own choosing', 'I may be very stupid but', and no 'if it be a sin to be half in love with the old days then I must aver', there will be no false relationship between art and experience; none of those dodges by which the sedentary man of letters is enabled to write about women, fighting, dancing, drink, by switching over to a prepared set of literary substitutes called Venus, Mars, Bacchus, and Terpsichore. References to infinity, to the remoteness of the stars and planets, the littleness of man, the charm of dead civilizations, to Babylon and Troy, 'on whose mouldering citadel lies the lizard like a thing of green bronze' will be suspect. The adventurers 'among their books', the explorer who never leaves his desk, will be required to live within their imagination's income.

From the realists, the puritans, the colloquial writers and talkie-novelists there is also much that he will take and much that he will leave. The cursive style, the agreeable manners, the precise and poetical impact of Forster's diction, the lucidity of Maugham, last of the great professional writers, the timing of Hemingway, the smooth cutting edge of Isherwood, the indignation of Lawrence, the honesty of Orwell, these will be necessary and the touch of those few journalists who give to every word in their limited vocabulary its current topical value. But above all it is construction that can be learnt from the realists, that discipline in the conception and execution of a book, that planning which gives simply written things the power to endure, the constant pruning without which the imagination like a tea-rose reverts to the wilderness.

He will not borrow from the realists, or from their imitators, the flatness of style, the homogeneity of outlook, the fear of eccentricity, the reporter's horror of distinction, the distrust of beauty, the cult of a violence and starkness that is masochistic. Nor will he adopt the victory mentality of those left-wing writers who imagine themselves already to be the idols of a conquering proletariat and who give their laws in simple matter-of-fact hard-hitting English to a non-existent congregation. That time is not yet; the artist today is in the position of a patient Mahomet towards whom the great art-hating mountain of the British public must eventually sidle.

This would seem the state of our literature. The battle between the schools I think has been proved to exist, but as with all civil wars, there are places where and moments when the fight rages with greater violence than at others. I have concentrated on those writers in the forefront of that battle, and any criticism I have made of them is intended only to relate them to it. Thus to call Proust a bad influence is not to deny that he is a great writer, but rather to consider his work in terms of what can be learnt from it today. It is the privilege of living in the twentieth century that one can take both sides in such controversies.

What I claim is that there continue action and reaction between these styles, and that necessary though it were and victorious as it may appear, the colloquial style of the last few years is doomed and dying. Style, as I have tried to show, is a relationship between a writer's mastery of form and his intellectual or emotional content. Mastery of form has lately been held, with some reason, to conceal a poverty of content but this is not inevitably so and for too long writers have had to prove their sincerity by going before the public in sackcloth and ashes or rather in a fifty-shilling suit and a celluloid collar. Now has come the moment when the penance is complete and when they may return to their old habit. It is no more a question of taking sides about one way or another of writing, but a question of timing, for the you-man writing of he-men authors is going out and the form must be enriched again. Our language is a sulky and inconstant beauty and at any given moment it is important to know what liberties she will permit. Now all seems favourable. Experiment and adventure are indicated, the boom of the twenties has been paid for by the slump of the thirties; let us try then to break the vicious circle by returning to a controlled expenditure, a balanced literary budget, a reasoned extravagance.

Part Two: The Charlock's Shade (1938/49)

The Strongest Poison ever known Came from Caesar's Laurel Crown.

BLAKE

10 *The Blighted Rye*

We have seen how closely the style of a book may affect its expectation of life, passing through a charnel house in which we have observed the death and decomposition of many works confident ten years ago of longevity, hailed as masterpieces of their period and now equal in decay. A few only present an air of health and claim some immunity from the venom of time. It is necessary now to analyse the conditions which govern the high rate of mortality among contemporary writers, to enter a region 'where the thin harvest waves its wither'd ears . . .', a sombre but, to those for whom it is not yet too late, a bracing territory.

> There thistles stretch their prickly arms afar,
> And to the ragged infant threaten war;
> There Poppies nodding, mock the hope of toil,
> There the blue Bugloss paints the sterile soil;
> Hardy and high, above the slender sheaf,
> The slimy Mallow waves her silky leaf;
> O'er the young shoot the Charlock throws a shade,
> And clasping Tares cling round the sickly blade;
> With mingled tints the rocky coasts abound,
> And a sad splendour vainly shines around.

Let the 'thin harvest' be the achievement of young authors, the 'wither'd ears' their books, then the 'militant thistles' represent politics, the 'nodding poppies' day-dreams, conversation, drink, and other narcotics, the 'blue Bugloss' is the clarion call of journalism, the 'slimy mallow' that of worldly success, the 'charlock' is sex with its obsessions, and the 'clasping tares' are the ties of duty and domesticity. The 'mingled tints' are the varieties of talent which appear; the 'sad splendour' is that of their vanished promise. These enemies of literature, these parasites on genius we must examine in detail; they are blights from which no writer is immune.

Before making further use of Crabbe's description of the heath with its convenient symbols we must answer a question sometimes put by certain literary die-hards, old cats who sit purring over the mouseholes of talent in wait for what comes out. 'Is this age', they pretend to ask, 'really more unfavourable to writers than any other? Have not writers always had the greatest difficulty in surviving? Indeed, their path today seems made much easier than it was, to give an example, for myself!' The answer, if they wanted an answer, is yes. Yes, because a writer needs money more than in the ivory tower decade since he can no longer live in a cottage in the country meditating a blank verse historical drama and still get the best out of himself. Yes, because he is more tempted today than at any other time by those remunerative substitutes for good writing: journalism, reviewing, advertising, broadcasting, and the cinema, but most of all because a writer today can have no confidence in posterity and therefore is inclined to lack the strongest inducement to good work: the desire for survival.

For it is clear that 'posterity' even to Samuel Butler,* writing in the last century, meant the reading public of the next few hundred years while since then the uncertainties of fame have so increased that Maugham confines it to two generations. A writer must grow used to the idea that culture as we know it may disappear and remain lost for ever or till it is excavated, a thousand years hence, from a new Herculaneum. Horace's boast of immortality, his '*non omnis moriar*', anticipated neither the hostility of the Church nor the ignorance of the Dark Ages. Of the two thousand years of posthumous life, a thousand slid by in a coma. One has but to consider the dearth of writers in Italy and Germany, the extinction of the cultural activity of the Weimar republic or the war waged by those countries against the intelligentsia of Spain to perceive how ephemeral are the securest literary reputations, the most flourishing movements. At any moment the schools of Athens may be closed, the libraries burnt, the teachers exterminated, the language suppressed. Any posthumous fame or the existence of any posterity capable of appreciating the arts we care for, can be guaranteed only by fighting for it, and for many who fight there will be no stake in the future but a name on a war-memorial.

*'All books die sooner or later but that will not hinder an author from trying to give his book as long a life as he can get for it . . . Any man who wishes his work to stand will sacrifice a good deal of his immediate audience for the sake of being attractive to a much larger number of people later on. Briefly the world resolves itself into two great classes – those who hold that honour after death is better worth having than any honour a man can get and know anything about, and those who doubt this; to my mind those who hold this and hold it firmly, are the only people worth thinking about.'

The love of posthumous fame is a common psychological substitute for the love of perfection, even as the love of perfection may prove a projection into the world of art of a sense of guilt. Thus astrologers find this love of perfection in those born under the sign of Virgo; it is to the artist as virginity to the nun and this love of purification they declare confined to those born between the end of August and the end of September. A writer should not be too conscious of such abstractions as perfection and posterity, 'the cackle of the unborn about the grave', he should be above a flirtation with time, determined only to restore to the world in a form worthy of his powers something of what he has taken out of it. He must be a helping writer, who tells us what he sees through his periscope, or there will be no writers and no readers left.

Otherwise Butler has stated the problem clearly. What ruins young writers is over-production. The need for money is what causes over-production; therefore writers must have private incomes. As he put it 'No gold, no holy ghost.' Genius is independent of money, but the world will always destroy it if it can. A writer, then, to avoid over-production, unless he acquires a private income, must either learn to make more money from his books or to earn money in other ways congenial to the writing of them.

To make more money from a book it is necessary either to pot-boil, to give way to the taste of the reading public at the expense of the judgement of the author, or to find technical ways of improving sales. Other ways of earning money and still finding time to write consist of journalism, teaching, advertising, the Civil Service, and the family business. Journalism will be discussed separately. Of the other remedies, teaching provides long holidays and the work is not such as to make inroads on the creative imagination, but not many people can teach or enjoy teaching and, in spite of the long holidays, the work seems to make any enlargement of the writer's experience awkward and unwelcome. Of the dons at Oxford and Cambridge remarkably few attain literary eminence and the best known among them are writers who have mixed in the world outside the universities. This is even more true of schoolmasters. Nor is the Civil Service the Parnassus which it became in the nineties; its talent would seem to have run dry with Humbert Wolfe. Since being a civil servant is a static, arid, and parasitic occupation, it is unlikely that anyone who is content with it will possess the imagination that creates or the talent which will mature and ripen.

Most unsatisfactory is advertising for there is something about copy-writing which so resembles the composition of lyric poetry as to replace the process. When in order to satisfy a corset manufacturer in search of a slogan, a writer has to think of the rousing or the lapidary phrase, the assonance of vowels and consonants, the condensation of thought, the inflections of delicate meaning at his disposal, he will be in no mood to write anything else. The family business, if we have such a family and if it does no business, is the best way out.

An outside job is harmful to a writer in proportion as it approximates to his vocation. Thus reviewing poetry is the worst profession for a poet, while broadcasting, advertising, journalism or lecturing all pluck feathers from the blue bird of inspiration and cast them on the wind. Living at home, on the other hand, confines the writer's experience to the family circle; rich marriages do not usually go with congenial tastes or a mutual love of the literary life and patrons are capricious and hard to come by; besides, a relationship with one in these days is open to imputation.

It is curious that while the brief flowering and quick extinction of modern talent is everywhere so apparent, yet little should have been written on the subject. Our two sages, Pearsall Smith and Maugham, croak their warnings but there is no sign that they are regarded.

> As soon as any glimmering of talent, any freshness or originality, makes its appearance, it is immediately noted and exploited [Pearsall Smith, *Prospects of Literature* (Hogarth Press, 1927)]. Editors of the weekly and even of the daily papers seize upon it; they have acquired, one may almost say of them, the habits of cannibals or ogres; they suck the brains of young writers, and then replace them by a new bevy of adolescent talent. Publishers also compete nowadays with editors in

> killing the goose whose golden eggs they live on. As soon as a young author makes a success his publisher urges him to repeat it at once; other publishers are eager to win his patronage, and he is not infrequently offered a fixed income on the condition that he shall regularly provide one or two volumes a year. It would be invidious to mention names, but in following the careers of the more recent writers whose first books have charmed me, I almost invariably find that their earliest publications, or at least earliest successes, are their best achievements; their promise ripens to no fulfilment; each subsequent work tends to be a feeble replica and fainter echo of the first.

Maugham is more inclined to blame the talent that is so easily exhausted, and which he calls 'the natural creativity of youth'.

> One of the tragedies of the arts is the spectacle of the vast numbers of persons who have been misled by this passing fertility to devote their lives to the effort of creation. Their invention deserts them as they grow older, and they are faced with the long years before them in which unfitted by now for a more humdrum calling, they harass their wearied brain to beat out material it is incapable of giving them. They are lucky when, with what bitterness we know, they can make a living in ways, like journalism or teaching, that are allied to the arts.

The causes are interlocking. The trouble is that authors are not paid enough. If three hundred pounds were the normal advance on a book instead of fifty, a writer could take his time over it and refuse other work; that it is not is due to the intermediate profits and expenses of book production, and to the indifference of the reading public which is growing more impatient with books as it becomes more dependent on magazines. *The Reader's Digest* and its fellows will soon read the books for him.

The torpor of the reading public conditions the publisher; parsimonious to authors who fail to dispel that torpor, he is exacting and impatient with those who have succeeded. When publishers vacillate (and as repressed sadists are supposed to become policemen or butchers so those with an irrational fear of life become publishers), the second villain, the editor, steps in – even Tennyson complained of him. 'All the magazines and daily newspapers, which pounce upon everything they can get hold of, demoralize literature. This age gives an author no time to mature his work.'

11 *The Blue Bugloss*

Let us now tackle the problem of journalism – deadliest of the weeds on Crabbe's Heath – in its relation to literature. We have suggested that journalism must obtain its full impact on the first reading, while literature can achieve its effect on a second, being intended for an interested and not an indifferent public. Consequently the main difference between them is one of texture. Journalism is loose, intimate, simple, and striking; literature formal and compact, not simple and not immediately striking in its effects. Carelessness is not fatal to journalism nor are clichés, for the eye rests lightly on them. But what is intended to be read once can seldom be read more than once; a journalist has to accept the fact that his work, by its very todayness, is excluded from any share in tomorrow. Nothing dates like a sense of actuality than which there is nothing in journalism more valuable. A writer who takes up journalism abandons the slow tempo of literature for a faster one and the change will do him harm. By degrees the flippancy of journalism will become a habit and the pleasures of being paid on the nail, and more especially of being praised on the nail, grow indispensable. And yet of the admirable journalism that has appeared in the literary weeklies, how little bears reprinting, how little even has been reprinted! The monthly and quarterly papers approximate more to literature and permit subjects to be treated at greater length, but they are few indeed! For brevity is all-important; it is the two-thousand-word look which betrays journalism, which makes the reader hurry on when he opens a volume of criticism and finds it to consist of jerky and disjointed essays: 'The Prose of Keats', 'Beddoes Revisited', 'The English Hexameter', 'Hazlitt's Aunt', 'After Expressionism What?', 'Miss Austen's Nephew', all with the fatal asterisk directing the reader to the title of some book once reviewed.

There are certain people who benefit from journalism. They are easily recognized and fall into two classes. The first are amateur writers who, through lack of a public or through not having to consider a public, are verbose and obscure, who have acquired so many mannerisms or private meanings for the words they use or who employ such leisurely constructions that an editor alone, since they will not listen to their friends, can impatiently cure them. The other class who benefit are those well-stored minds who suffer from psychological sloth, and who can only reveal their treasures in short articles for quick returns. But this class includes few young writers and these would soon succumb to the atmosphere breathed with such impunity by a Hazlitt or by a wise old literary stager.

There is one other fortunate class: those who are masters of a literary style which so resembles journalism that they can make the transition from one tempo to the other without effort. Readers of *Abinger Harvest* by E. M. Forster will have found that there is about those essays nothing ephemeral since they are in the language of E. M. Forster the novelist. His literary style is cursive and no concession has to be made. The styles overlap; the tempos coincide. This is also true of Lytton Strachey who imposed his literary style on his editors. There are several writers in the same position as Forster. The danger for them is that, if their journalism is literature, so is their literature journalism and Hemingway, for example, appears unable to distinguish between them, which accounts for the unevenness of such books as *Green Hills of Africa* or *Death in the Afternoon.*

Maugham detects another evil in journalism besides the vulgarization of a writer's style.

> There is an impersonality in a newspaper that insensibly affects the writer. People who write much for the press seem to lose the faculty of seeing things for themselves; they see them from a generalized standpoint, vividly often, sometimes with hectic brightness, yet never with

that idiosyncrasy which may give only a partial picture of the facts, but is suffused by the personality of the observer. The press, in fact, kills the individuality of those who write for it.

Journalism for most writers means reviewing.

Let Walter Savage Shelleyblake be a young author. Let his book be called *Vernal Aires*. Soon will come the delicious summons from the literary editor of *The Blue Bugloss*. 'Dear Shelleyblake, I was so interested to meet you the other night and have a chance to tell you what I think of *Vernal Aires*. I have been wondering if you would like to try your hand at a little reviewing for us. We are looking for someone to do the Nonesuch *Boswell*, and your name cropped up.'

The Nonesuch *Boswell* alone is worth four guineas, and soon a signed review, 'Expatriate from Auchinleck' by Walter Savage Shelleyblake, appears in the literary supplement of *The Blue Bugloss*. It is full of ideas and Mr Vampire, the editor, bestows on it his praise. The next book which Shelleyblake reviews, on Erasmus Darwin, is not quite so good but his article 'Swansong at Lichfield', is considered 'extremely bright'. Suddenly his name appears under a pile of tomes of travel; the secrets of Maya jungles, Kenya game-wardens, and ricocheting American ladies are probed by him. In a year's time he will have qualified as a maid-of-all-work and be promoted to reviewing novels. It is promotion because the novel review is a regular feature, because more people read them and because publishers 'care'. If he is complimentary and quotable he will be immortalized on the dust wrapper and find his name in print on the advertisements. And eight to ten novels a fortnight, sold as review copies, add to his wage.

Certain facts must now be stated. However much Mr Vampire admired *Vernal Aires* and however fond he is of Walter Shelleyblake, he is, before anything else, an editor. He is concerned with *The Blue Bugloss* and whether each number is bright enough to paint the sterile soil. In so far as he is developing in Walter latent gifts – competence, a turn for satire, lucidity, polish – his interests coincide; but they can never be identical, and the use Walter makes of these gifts is not his own concern but Mr Vampire's. The competition for the best books, the Nonesuch *Boswells*, is fierce; Mr Vampire is often lucky to get one of them himself and so if Shelleyblake is anxious to write several thousand words on the influence of Horace on English poetry or the psychological reasons for the retirement of Congreve, he will have to go on being anxious and hurry up with his copy on *Backstairs and Petticoats* (a chronicle of famous Royal Mistresses), or six more autobiographies, headed by *Fifty Years Down Under*.

Myself a lazy, irresolute person, overvain and overmodest, unsure in my judgements and unable to finish what I have begun, I have profited from journalism, owing to the admirable manipulation of my manager and trainer. Yet even so I would say to Shelleyblake, who clearly does not belong to the Hazlitt group, that any other way of making money would be better, that reviewing is a whole-time job with a half-time salary, a job in which the best in him is generally expended on the mediocre in others. A good review is only remembered for a fortnight; a reviewer has always to make his reputation afresh nor will he find time for private reading or writing, for he is too busy reading other people's books and this will disincline him to read when he is not working. The sight of his friends' books accumulating depresses him and he knows that, besides losing the time to write books of his own, he is also losing the energy and the application, frittering it away on tripe and discovering that it is his flashiest efforts which receive most praise.

There are not more than four or five posts in reviewing that carry with them money, freedom, and dignity, whose holders can inherit the mantle of Arnold and Sainte-Beuve, so that the most Shelleyblake can expect is that, by reading two books a day and writing for three papers, he may make about four hundred a year. During this time he will incur the hostility of authors, the envy of other reviewers, and the distrust of his friends against whose books he will seem invariably prejudiced; the public will view him with indifference or accept him as an eccentric on whom they will launch their views and their manuscripts while old friends will greet him with, 'Are you writing anything now?' – 'apart of course from your articles,' they will add. 'I read you – but I don't say I agree with you,' will be another approach, to which, 'I know you, but I don't say I like you,' is the correct answer.

No, if Walter Shelleyblake must be a journalist, there is but one chance for him. He must declare war on his employers and so manoeuvre them that he never reviews a bad book, never reviews more than one at a time and never writes a review that cannot be reprinted, i.e. that is not of some length and on a subject of permanent value. He will know that the bad books he reads are like hours on a sundial, *vulnerant omnes, ultima necat*, all wound, the last one mortally, neither will he spend himself on cheap subjects, nor put down his whole view of life in a footnote, for he will write only about what interests him. And whatever happens to him (and there are no pensions for literary hacks), he must realize that he is not indispensable.

> Brightness falls from the air,
> Queens have died young and fair . . .

but not *The Blue Bugloss* and Mr Vampire and his new young men will be perfectly able to get on without him.

12 *The Thistles*

At the moment politics, the thistles

> . . . that stretch their prickly arms afar,
> And to the ragged infant threaten war

are more dangerous to young writers than journalism. They are dangerous because writers now feel that politics are necessary to them, without having learnt yet how best to be political.

Indifference to politics among artists has always been associated with a feeling of impotence. Thus those great non-politicals, the ivory-tower dwellers, flourished helpless under the second Empire or in the Paris of 1870 after defeat in the Franco-Prussian war. English writers, in the late

Victorian age, were equally helpless; only Kipling, who celebrated the jingoism and imperialism of the ruling class and the materialism of the time, and Shaw, who attacked them, obtained a political foothold. The 'nineties' were a reaction of artists against a political world which they abhorred but could not alter. William Morris alone of the Victorian writers combined poetry with socialism, while Tennyson's conception of the role of the poet as the supreme Endorser of new achievement in material progress was so forbidding as to deter young writers from taking any interest in such subjects. This widespread indifference to politics crystallized into a theory that politics were harmful, that they were not artistic material of the first order, that an artist could not be a politician. Politics belonged to that realm of action which Proust and Strachey had discredited. A belief in action indicated a belief in progress, a belief in progress was Victorian and ridiculous.

Yet if we look at writers through the ages we see that they have always been political. Greek poets were political, they championed democracy or defended oligarchs and tyrants according to their sentiment. Pindar was political as were Aeschylus and Euripides, Plato and Aristotle, Catullus and Cicero, Virgil and Horace. Dante was engrossed in politics as were most of the artists of the Renaissance. Nobody told Byron he would be a better writer if he did not attempt *The Vision of Judgement* or Wordsworth not to bother with *Toussaint l'Ouverture*; Swift was not considered to have cheapened himself by *The Drapier Letters* or *The Conduct of the Allies*, nor Dryden to have let down poetry by *Absalom and Architophel*. To deny politics to a writer is to deny him part of his humanity. But even from a list of political writers we can deduce that there are periods in the history of a country when writers are more political, or more writers are political than at others. They are not the periods of greatest political tension, they are those in which authors can do most, can be listened to, can be important, can influence people and get their own way. Thus Roman poets ceased to be political after the Empire because they were powerless. A writer during the age of Augustus could not play the part of Catullus or Cicero. Writers flourish in a state of political flux, on the eve of the crisis, rather than in the crisis itself; it is before a war or a revolution that they are listened to and come into their own and it was because they were disillusioned at their impotence during the war that so many became indifferent to political issues after the peace.

It is clear that we are living now in a transition period as suited to political writing as were the days of Ship Money or the reign of Queen Anne. Writers can still change history by their pleading, and one who is not political neglects the vital intellectual issues of his time and disdains his material. He is not powerless, like the Symbolists of 1870, the aesthetes of the eighties and nineties, the beer-and-chivalry addicts of the nineteen hundreds or the demobilized Georgian poet on his chicken farm. He is not a victim of his time but a person who can alter it, though if he does not, he may soon find himself victimized. By ignoring the present he condones the future. He has to be political to integrate himself and he must go on being political to protect himself. Today the forces of life and progress are ranging on one side, those of reaction and death on the other. We are having to choose between democracy and Fascism, and Fascism is the enemy of art. It is not a question of relative freedom; there are no artists in Fascist countries. We are not dealing with an Augustus who will discover his Horace and his Virgil, but with Attila or Hulaku, destroyers of European culture whose poets can contribute only battlecries and sentimental drinking songs. Capitalism in decline, as in our own country, is not much wiser as a patron than Fascism. Stagnation, fear, violence and opportunism, the characteristics of capitalism preparing for the fray, are no background for a writer and there is a seediness, an ebb of life, a philosophy of taking rather than giving, a bitterness and brutality about right-wing writers now which was absent in those of other days, in seventeenth-century Churchmen or eighteenth-century Tories. There is no longer a Prince Rupert, a Dr Johnson, a Wellington, Disraeli, or Newman, on the reactionary side.

We have seen that writers are politically-minded when they are able to accomplish something; that these periods are those of change, on the eve of revolutions and civil wars and before the resort to arms takes matters out of their control, and we have seen that we are in such a period now, and that unless writers do all they can it will be too late; war will break out and the moment be past when the eloquence of the artist can influence the destiny of humanity.

If political writing is no more than the exercise of the instinct of self-preservation, there can be no reason for classing 'politics' among the weeds that stifle writers. But there are dangers about being political of which writers are unaware and so seldom avoid. Thus being political is apt to become a whole time job.

> Today the expending of powers
> On the flat ephemeral pamphlet and the boring meeting,

writes Auden, though copies of his pamphlets are excessively rare. Canvassing, making speeches, and pamphleteering are not the best medium for sensitive writers. They involve much time and trouble and can be better performed by someone else. To command a listening senate, however, is a secret ambition of many writers and it is easy to justify it – to be 'thankful that my words can be any comfort to these poor men', etc. The truth is that oratory is a coarser art than writing and that to become addicted to it is to substitute the ruses of the platform for the integrity of the pen. Neither is a writer improved by sitting on committees and cultivating the chairmanities.

Another effect of becoming too political is that such activity leads to disillusion. Thus writers become disheartened by the vulgarity of politicians. They find it hard to realize that the militants and executives of a movement may be narrow-minded, envious, ambitious, and ungrateful, yet their cause remains fundamentally just and right. Their political judgement is often unsound for they refuse to allow for the slow motions of public opinion; they are disheartened by personal rebuffs and bored by drudgery. Defeatism is their occupational disease.

Politicians, on their side, can be unappreciative. Their favourite arts are those which are enjoyed in relaxation: light music or Mickey Mouse, the *Oxford Book of English Verse*, Edgar Wallace, Wodehouse, Webb. They do not like art to be exacting and difficult; they may envy the artists who collaborate with them because they do not understand their success, but with their idealism and their tender consciences they seem to them priggish and patronizing. The enmities of highbrow and lowbrow, man of action and man of thought, classical side and modern side are not yet buried and reappear, over the ephemeral pamphlet or at the boring meeting, in unexpected forms.

In what way then should a writer be political? How can he make best use of his weapons?

Firstly, by satire. This is a satirical age and among the vast reading public the power of an artist to awaken ridicule has never been so great. To make the enemies of freedom look silly, to write like Low's cartoons or like

> I met murder on the way,
> He wore the mask of Castlereagh,

is the duty of any who can.

Then, if he is intelligent, he can analyse situations, draw attention to tendencies, expose contradictions and help his more active colleagues by cultivating lucidity, profundity, and detachment. And lastly, he can help to contribute the idealism without which any movement fails. He must, in his serious writing, avoid propaganda and the presence in his work of lumps of unassimilated political material.* Like the termites who chew up the food for the fighters his role is to digest the experience

*It is objectionable because it introduces into the form a lower level of workmanship, that of the pamphlet or the tract, and an imperfect fusion with the creative process. Propaganda is betrayed by an air of naïveté, as in, 'Tomorrow he would canvas as he had never canvassed before,' and 'I had met the insidious power of Ann and defeated it, and now there was a splendid synthesis forming inside me,' or 'He was an admirable man and I felt warmed and happy when I looked at him. At Oxford he got up and stretched. I think he had read every word of the *Daily Worker* in eighty minutes since we had left Paddington.' Those are from a very young author. Here is an example from Upward:

'"There will be a time of harshness and bitter struggle, but out of it will come flowers; splendour and joy will come back to the world. And life will be better than it has ever been in the world's history."

'"How soon can I join the workers' movement?"

'". . . You can join some time within the next few days."

'"I don't want to wait."'

This passage in a thoughtful novel brings a whiff of the Salvation Army. Right-wing propaganda, however, can be detected by an appeal to the reader to be 'realistic'.

they bring him. For this reason the poets are the best political writers for they have the best digestions, and can absorb their material. A poem like *Locksley Hall*, which has been so distilled, remains an alive and contemporary piece of thought.

> I myself must mix with action, lest I wither in despair.
> What is that which I should turn to, lighting upon days like these?
> Every door is barred with gold, and opens but to golden keys,
> Every gate is thronged with suitors, all the markets overflow.
> I have but an angry fancy: what is that which I should do?

And so we find the best modern political writing in such a book as Spender's *Trial of a Judge* or a poem like Day Lewis's:

> Yet living here,
> As one between two massing powers I live,
> Whom neutrality cannot save
> Nor occupation cheer.

The novelists who feel their responsibilities are also searching for something deeper and more universal than superficial realism and are finding it in the allegory. A story of Isherwood's like *The Novaks* shows how political reality can inform and deepen, can be informed and deepened, by private experiences; and Spender's *Cousins* and his *Burning Cactus* are also excellent illustrations. To strike deep and keep general should be the maxim of the political artist, and he should avoid describing any experience that he has not first integrated and made part of him. He must take pains with his vocabulary for political writing is honeycombed with clichés; having been deadened to their meaning by oratory, politicians have no feeling for words; a phrase which seems healthy at night will be on the sick-list by morning. There is a tendency for left-wing journalists to criticize left-wing poets for being obscure which is dangerous and stupid. The public are not expected to understand the formulas from which are evolved a new explosive or a geodetic aeroplane. The poet is a chemist and there is more pure revolutionary propaganda in a line of Blake than in all *The Rights of Man*.

But if he wishes to be respected by politicians, to be treated as an ally to whom a certain eccentricity is permitted, a writer must let them alone and refrain from taking sides in political quarrels. There is a general left-wing position which has never been defined but which permits a working agreement with the parties, as they now stand, and which is well suited to a writer. To abandon this general position is safe for a militant journalist; for an artist, it may lead to a damaging retreat. There is so much side-choosing, heresy-hunting, witch-burning, and shadow-cabinet-making among the parties of the left, so much victory mentality among people for whom victory is most uncertain, that caution in a writer should be welcome. It is no time to quarrel with our own side.

I will conclude this excursion among the Thistles by quoting two points of view of left-wing writers, both Communists, Upward and Stephen Spender. Upward, I find, is too logical for the times, his pronouncement on the only possible way for a writer to live is reminiscent of Tolstoy's socialist analysis of art which proved that Hugo's *Les Misérables* and Harriet Stowe's *Uncle Tom's Cabin* were the two great books of the nineteenth century. Spender lacks the narrowness and aridity of Marxist critics.

> A writer today who wishes to produce the best work that he is capable of producing, must first of all become a socialist in his practical life, must go over to the progressive side of the class conflict . . . He must be told frankly that joining the workers' movement does mean giving less time to imaginative writing, but that unless he joins it his writing will become increasingly false, worthless as literature. Going over to socialism may prevent him, but failing to go over *must* prevent him from writing a good book (*The Mind in Chains*).

What is meant by 'going over'? Upward thinks it must mean the abandonment of the bourgeois life and immersion in the work of the socialist parties. I do not think so. I think a writer 'goes over' when he has a moment of conviction that his future is bound up with that of the working classes. Once he has felt this his behaviour will inevitably alter.

Often it will be recognized only by external symptoms, a disinclination to wear a hat or a stiff collar, an inability to be rude to waiters or taxi-drivers or to be polite to young men of his own age with rolled umbrellas, bowler hats and 'Mayfair men' moustaches, or to tolerate the repressive measures of his class. He is like a caterpillar whose skin dulls and whose appetite leaves it before becoming a chrysalis. Often a writer is unable to go over. He approaches the barrier, shies, and runs away. Such writers will externalize their feelings and satirize those who have made the transition, who have jumped off the slowly moving train for the one which they believe leads towards life and the future. The angriest are the most frightened. But these fears can be surmounted by a moment of vision. It may be practical, a glimpse of the power of the writer in the socialist state or of his impotence in a capitalist one, going in perhaps, like Turgenev, sixty-first at a fashionable dinner, or it may be a mystical feeling of release and emancipation. It is too early yet to say whether writers have done anything for Spain, but it is clear that Spain has done an immense amount for writers, since many have had that experience there and have come back with their fear changed to love, isolation to union, and indifference to action.

> This is a time then when anyone who is anxious to avert a protracted world war will have to work very hard to undermine the whole system of armed alliances. If we hope to go on existing, if we want a dog's chance of the right to breathe, to go on being able to write, it seems that we have got to make some choice outside the private entanglements of our personal life. We have got to try somehow to understand that objective life moving down on us like a glacier, but which after all, is essentially not a glacier but an historic process, the life of people like ourselves, and therefore our 'proper study'.

> Ultimately, however interested the writer may be as a person, as an artist he has got to be indifferent to all but what is objectively true. The road the future will tread may be the road of Communism, but the road of the artist will always be some way infinitely more difficult than one which is laid down in front of him.

These two quotations are from Stephen Spender's *Destructive Element*, and express a point of view that is sometimes forgotten. Political writing is dangerous writing, it deals not in words, but in words that affect lives, and is a weapon that should be entrusted only to those qualified to use it. Thus a burst of felicitous militancy with the pen may send three young men to be killed in Spain; for whose deaths the author is responsible. If human beings have any right they have the right to know what they are dying for. 'Better live an hour as a lion than a lifetime as a lamb' is stencilled all over Italy – but supposing one is a lamb?

There is one last warning that must be given. In Blake's words, 'The eagle never lost so much time as when it submitted to learn from the crow' – and if we look back at the political activities of artists, however necessary and satisfying they may have seemed at the time, now that time is past it is not by them they are remembered. Milton's poetry is read more than the *Areopagitica*. Marvell's pamphlets are read not at all, the political poems of Shelley and Byron are not preferred to their lyrics, the Houyhnhnms are more familiar to us than the *Conduct of the Allies*, *Robinson Crusoe* means more than the *True Born Englishman*, *The Lotus Eaters* than *Locksley Hall*. The writers who were most political in the last war are not the most famous. Zola too was more political than Flaubert, Lamartine than Baudelaire, and the truth is that the value of political experience to a writer's art is indirect. Not Milton's polemical prose is the justification of his political life, but his character of Satan, his great assemblages in Hell. And this is true today, so that a writer whose stomach cannot assimilate with genius the starch and acid of contemporary politics had better turn down his plate.

13 *The Poppies*

Let us now glance at the poppies, at the danger which is becoming known as 'escapism'. This is not a significant word, for in itself escaping cannot be right or wrong nor worthy of comment until we know from what danger the escapist is fleeing and whether flight is his best method of preservation. Escaping from a concentration camp or a burning building is admirable, escaping from responsibility, like the patient who wrote to his psychiatrist that he was 'only happy when he had cast off every shred of human dignity' is sometimes not. We are all destroyed through that first escapist, Eve, and saved by the second who built an ark. The word is generally employed by realists to beat romantics with; thus it was 'escapist' to live at Tossa or Torre Molinos till 1936, when the centre of actuality shifted, and Sir Peter Chalmers-Mitchell, who had retired to end his days in the sun, found himself, for a few hours in Malaga, in the intenser glare of History.*

It is vain to accuse people of escaping from contemporary reality. Time is not uniform for all of us, neither is our imagination's food nor our artistic material. We cannot all do our best work with the sun in our eyes. There is but one crime; to escape from our talent, to abort that growth which, ripening and maturing, must be the justification of the demands we make on society.

At present the realities are life and death, peace and war, fascism and democracy; we are in a world which may soon become unfit for human beings to live in. A writer must decide at what remove from this conflagration he can produce his best work and be careful to keep there. Often a writer who is escaping from his own talent, from the hound of heaven, will run into what appears to be reality and, like a fox bolting

*Expatriation is often beneficial, as a stage in which the writer cuts adrift from irritating influences. It is a mistake to expect good work from expatriates for it is not what they do that matters but what they are not doing. It gives them a breathing-space in which to free themselves from commercialism, family and racial ties or from the 'gentleman complex' which attacks public school and university writers, just as the spectre of their 'family business' haunts American ones. Only occasionally does a writer create a work out of his expatriation; Hemingway's *The Sun Also Rises* is such an exception. (Henry James was not an expatriate in so far as he repatriated himself as an Englishman – he exchanged American Society for international society and then settled down as an English man of letters.) It is important however to distinguish between the flight of the expatriate which is an essential desire for simplification, for the cutting of ties, the writer 'finding' himself in the hotel bedroom or the café on the harbour and the brisker trajectory of the travel addict, trying not to find but to lose himself in the intoxication of motion. 'How narrow is the line', as Nicolson wrote of Byron's last journey, 'which separates an adventure from an ordeal, and escape from exile.'

into a farm kitchen, will seek sanctuary from his pursuers in group activities outside. And after a time the hounds will be called off, the pursuit weaken – a signal that the Muses no longer wish to avail themselves of his potentialities. Thus among the hardest workers in political parties will be found, like Rimbaud at Harar, those whom the God has forsaken.

The old-fashioned boltholes of writers who do not wish to undertake the responsibility of creating a work of art are no longer so easy of access. Drink is available and there are still artists who drink to excess out of the consciousness of wasted ability, for drunkenness is a substitute for art; it is in itself a low form of creation. But it is not drink which is the temptation, since that is but a symptom of the desire for self-forgetfulness, as is also the case with drugs which play small part in the literary life in England, though among French writers opium has made much headway.

The harmless activities of day-dreaming and conversation are more insidious. Day-dreaming bears a specious resemblance to the workings of the creative imagination. It is in fact a substitute for it and one in which all difficulties are shelved, all problems ignored, a short cut ending in a blank wall. This is even more true of conversation; a good talker can talk away the substance of twenty books in as many evenings. He will describe the central idea of the book he means to write until it revolts him.

As journalism brings in quicker returns than literature so the profits of conversation are more immediate than those of journalism. By the silence which he commands, the luxury of his décor, and by the glow from the selected company who have been asked to meet him, a good talker is paid almost before he opens his mouth. The only happy talkers are dandies who extract pleasure from the very perishability of their material and who would not be able to tolerate the isolation of all other forms of composition; for most good talkers, when they have run down, are miserable; they know that they have betrayed themselves, that they have taken material which should have a life of its own, to dispense it in noises upon the air.

Than good conversation nothing is sooner forgotten and those who remember it do so unconsciously and reproduce it as their own. Coleridge, Swinburne, Wilde, Harry Melville, Vernon Lee – not much survives now of the conversation of these mighty-mouthed international geysers. They were at the mercy of a few indolent, forgetful, and envious listeners. If we try to record the spoken word of one of these chrysostoms it becomes apparent that thirty per cent of their talk is a series of reassuring and persuasive qualifications, a buttonholing of the listener; it is the ardour of the talker's wooing which convinces the audience of the splendour of his talk. This is not true of talkers of the old school like Bernard Berenson who use their golden tongues for denunciation, but modern conversationalists make too free a use of the glad eye. They are apologetic, not only because they monopolize and individualize in an age opposed to these things, but because they are taking part in a ceremony of self-wastage and their audience knows it.

Sometimes when in flight from the demands of talent, from the bite of the gadfly, writers will seek refuge in gentility, in ancestor-worship, or by becoming members of an unliterary sporting class. They will breed bulldogs, hunt, shoot, attend race-meetings, and try to lose contact with all other writers except those whose guilt is of equal standing. This instinct to hide themselves in a world where books are unheard of in no way resembles the artist's desire for '*luxe, calme, et volupté*', for a lavish, ostentatious life, but is a particularly English affliction, and it is no exaggeration to say that nearly every English author since Byron and Shelley has been hamstrung by respectability and been prevented by snobbery and moral cowardice from attaining his full dimensions. It is this blight of insular gentility which accounts for the difference between Dickens, Thackeray, Arnold, Tennyson, Pater and Tolstoy, Flaubert, Rimbaud, Baudelaire, Gide; it is the distinction between being a good fellow or growing up.

There remains one other major escape, religion. It is not so common now for writers to join a church. I know two Anglo-Catholic and one Roman Catholic convert among my contemporaries. All three are people of exceptional sensibility, poetically-minded writers for whom the ugliness of materialism is a source of horror. Are they escaping from their talent or from conditions which would have rendered impossible the use of it? We must wait and see. Religious faith involves the surrender of the intellect but not of the sensibility, which under its protection may long continue to develop. Yet for an intellectual, joining a church implies regression, it is a putting on of blinkers, a hiding under the skirts of one of the great reactionary political forces of the world and the poet drawn to the confessional by the smell of incense finds himself defending the garotte and Franco's Moors. Art becomes a means not an end to the churchman as to the politician. Churches are the retreat of artists with aesthetic appreciation, delicate humour, ethical sensibility, and a sense of spiritual reality, who lack the inquiring mind, the constructive intellectual fearlessness which is the historic factor in western civilization and which has now moved far onwards from religion.

But in vain we discuss the nature of the poppies which put writers to sleep or try to restrict their use. Since those who are escaping from their talent employ them, let us find out why they are escaping. Many are in flight for psychological reasons which belong to their childhood and with which this book is not competent to deal. But in authors who have dried up, who have put their hobby before their vocation, who now are doing well in the city or who collect first editions or old dust-wrappers, who run chicken-farms or set and solve Greek cross-word puzzles, who write detective stories or who have transferred their sensibility to cheese and old claret, there is one fact in common. They have all been promising.

Promise! Fatal word, half-bribe and half-threat, round whose exact meaning centred many tearful childhood interviews. 'But you promised you wouldn't', 'But *that* wasn't a promise', 'Yes it was – you haven't kept your promise', till the meaning expands and the burden of the oath under which we grew up becomes the burden of expectation which we can never fulfil. 'Blossom and blossom and promise of blossom, but never a fruit' – the cry first heard in the nursery is taken up by the schoolmaster, the friendly aunt, the doting grandmother, the inverted bachelor uncle. Dons with long reproachful faces will utter it and the friends of dons; the shapes and simulacrums which our parents have taken, the father-substitutes and mother-types which we have projected will accuse us and all await our ritual suicide. Whom the gods wish to destroy they first call promising.

Young writers if they are to mature require a period of between three and seven years in which to live down their promise. Promise is like the medieval hangman who, after settling the noose, pushed his victim off the platform and jumped on his back, his weight acting as a drop while his jockeying arms prevented the unfortunate from loosening the rope. When he judged him dead he dropped to the ground. Promise is that dark spider with which many writers are now wrestling in obscurity and silence. Occasionally they win and the load of other people's wish-fulfilments is cast off; they produce a book; more often after a struggle for breath they are stifled for ever. Let us listen in to them for a moment, poor wretches, on whom the executioner calls in the small hours.

Two o'clock. You won't accomplish anything now. Do you remember all the things you wanted to be? How Granny loved you! How we pinched and scraped to keep you at Oxford – and then those horrible bills! They killed Granny, you know, though we didn't tell you at the time. Now you're old enough to know. It wasn't that she minded the money – it was the thought you could ever do anything dishonourable. You did promise, you remember? That you could give all those bad cheques! Your father never got over it. Oh, we were all so proud of you. How could you, how could you, how could you!

Three o'clock. 'We always hoped you'd write. A serious book, I mean. We can't count the kind of stuff you're doing now. I know a high academic degree is not always the true justification for three years here. There are many people whose careers after leaving college bring us more distinction than anything they achieve while they are up. We take a long view. But I think you'll agree we were very patient with you and I doubt if the stuff you are turning out now will prove we were right. Still we must be tolerant. I had hoped great things for you and I dare say I was rather silly. Anyhow I shall always be glad to hear from you.'

Why didn't you write to him? He would so have loved a letter. He often spoke of you before he died. I may say he was deeply hurt at what he considered, rightly or wrongly, your ingratitude. He had been fond of you in spite of everything. If you'd even troubled to send him a postcard! Why didn't you? Why didn't you? Why didn't you?

Four o'clock. Teeth hurt? I don't envy you at forty. Just as you're going to sleep you give a kind of twitch all over and wake up! H'm – a kind of noise like a clock makes before it strikes goes off at the back of your nose? That's bad! Your heart seems to miss a beat and you sit right up in bed with a jerk? Your blood beats too fast? Your mind races along? You can't breathe properly? Your bladder troubles you? A kind of dull aching pain somewhere in the side? You think it must be the spleen? H'm – And a sharp searing pain in the oesophagus? That all? Oh yes – and a feeling like someone blowing up a balloon at the back of the nose? I wonder if you have some near relative or great friend whom I could talk to, just to check up on your family history. Your mother? Good. Well, Mr Shelleyblake, if you don't mind waiting in here I think I'll try and get right through on the phone to her.

Five o'clock. *How old are you!* H'm, I see. Just about halfway. And you've done precisely what? H'm. Well, I must be off. Another patient. Sleep well, see you tomorrow, same time, same place.

~

Sloth in writers is always a symptom of an acute inner conflict, especially that laziness which renders them incapable of doing the thing which they are most looking forward to. The conflict may or may not end in disaster, but their silence is better than the overproduction which must so end and slothful writers such as Johnson, Coleridge, Greville, in spite of the nodding poppies of conversation, morphia, and horse-racing, have more to their credit than Macaulay, Trollope, or Scott. To accuse writers of being idle is a mark of envy or stupidity – La Fontaine slept continually and scarcely ever opened his mouth; Baudelaire, according to Dr Laforgue, feared to perfect his work because he feared the incest with his mother which was his perfect fulfilment. Perfectionists are notoriously lazy and all true artistic indolence is deeply neurotic; a pain not a pleasure.

14 *The Charlock's Shade*

Sex, the charlock's shade, is no more the danger that it was and seldom do we meet with a syphilitic Baudelaire, squandering his fortune and ruining his health for a coloured mistress; the temptations of artists today are group-temptations in which the Cynaras and the Jeanne Duvals play little part. However for a writer to be too fond of women is not uncommon and the result may be found that they make crippling demands on his time and his money, especially if they set their hearts on his popular success. The charlock or wild mustard throws a more baleful shade on the young shoot when it is the love that dare not speak its name.

Many writers have been homosexual or gone through a homosexual period and, although from a literary standpoint it is enriching, they must grasp the limitations of homosexuality and plan production accordingly. Thus a male homosexual, if cut off by his attitude from experience with women, will have a certain difficulty in depicting them. This is not of consequence if he is, for example, a critic or a poet who works at that intense and sublimated level at which passion is general and the object of such passion without importance. But many writers are neither poets nor critics, and for novelists, short-story writers, and playwrights, difficulties arise. Thus homosexual novelists who are able to create mother-types and social mother-types (hostesses) and occasionally sister-types (heroines) have trouble with normal women and may often make them out worse or better than they are. They are forced to describe things they know little about because so much of life is concerned with them. Courtship, marriage, childbearing, and adultery play a major part in existence, a knowledge of the relations between men and women is essential to a novelist, and a comparison of, say,

War and Peace with novels written by less normal authors will show how few acquire it. The heroine of *War and Peace*, Natasha, is a delightful creature, but she is capable of leaving her hero and running away with a man whom she does not love, after a single meeting, because he looked at her in a certain way. But she remains delightful because Tolstoy continues to find her lovable for being human. If Natasha had been one of Proust's heroines he would have turned her into a monster, she would have been analysed till nothing remained of her but lust and self-interest.

Nor is Proust's system of giving the male characters in his life girls' names and putting them as girls into his novel satisfactory. Their real sex protrudes and they have no plausible relationships with other characters in the books (Albertine is unreal when she confronts Charlus or Swann or the Duchesse de Guermantes; there is an ambiguous cloud over her relations with the author), and they are incapable of child-bearing, home-making, husband-cheering, or any of the drabber functions of woman. There is no solution for these problems. Nothing, for example, will make the two amorous young girls in *The Importance of Being Earnest* either young or amorous. The homosexual writer, until we can change society, must construct his books so as to avoid situations where a knowledge of such women is required, just as stammerers avoid certain words and substitute others. Otherwise the equipment of the homosexual writer: combativeness, curiosity, egotism, intuition, and adaptability, is greatly to be envied.

The clasping tares of domesticity represent the opposite danger, and these too have grown less formidable. The harried author who sits in a garret surrounded by screaming children, with duns at the door and a sick wife nagging from the bed, is a thing of the past. But there remains some substance in the vision. The initial difficulty is in the sensitive writer's inability to live alone. The more he is alone the more he falls in love, if he falls in love he is almost certain to marry, if he marries he is apt to take a house and have children, if he has a house and children he needs more money, must do uncongenial work and so deny himself the freedom which may have inspired him.

The homosexual is unable to treat of a section of the life of human beings but in return he is free from the limitations of that life. He is apt to have a private income, he renews himself by travel, he has time for old friends and for the making of new ones and as he grows old remains isolated, free from responsibilities and ties and if he has been able to break free from the parasitism which is the weakness of homosexuals, he is detached. If he has joined the creative class, he is likely to become, like Gide, the 'lonely old artist-man' that Henry James called himself.

In recent times the balance of literary success late in life is in favour of the childless writer. Children dissipate the longing for immortality which is the compensation of the childless writer's work. But it is not only a question of children or no children, there is a moment when the cult of home and happiness becomes harmful and domestic happiness one of those escapes from talent which we have deplored, for it replaces that necessary unhappiness without which writers perish. A writer is in danger of allowing his talent to dull who lets more than a year go past without finding himself in his rightful place of composition, the small single unluxurious 'retreat' of the twentieth century, the hotel bedroom.

The fertility of the writer is often counterchecked by the happiness of the man. Each does not want the same thing, and where their desires conflict, the writer-self will be the one to suffer. The 'animal serenity', the 'broad human touch' which Maugham envies in great writers, in Tolstoy and perhaps in Thackeray and Dickens, can only be obtained by a series of experiences which have extinguished the lesser artists who have attempted them. As far as one can infer from observation it is a mistake for writers to marry young, especially for them to have children young; early marriage and paternity are a remedy for loneliness and unhappiness that set up a counter irritation. Writers choose wives, not for their money or for their appreciation of art but for their beauty, and a baby is even less capable of seeing the artist's point of view. As Tennyson put it –

> O love, we two shall go no longer
> To lands of summer across the sea;

So dear a life your arms enfold
Whose crying is a cry for gold.

Thus there would seem little to choose between the tares and the charlock. The homosexual avoids domesticity, he pays a price but pays it with his eyes open, the normal author walks into a trap. Most young writers are weak and know little about their weaknesses or their predicaments. They make a rush for the solution which promises them an immediate advantage and are not apprehensive of its after-effects. If they find the years when they come to London after the cosiness of the university unendurable then they marry the first person whom they can. They work hard to make money, grow torpid with domesticity, and their writing falls off. After seven years or so they often divorce and their talent is given another chance which (it depends on how they marry again) may or may not be taken.

In general it may be assumed that a writer who is not prepared to be lonely in his youth must if he is to succeed face loneliness in his middle age. The hotel bedroom awaits him. If, as Dr Johnson said, a man who is not married is only half a man, so a man who is very much married is only half a writer. Marriage can succeed for an artist only where there is enough money to save him from taking on uncongenial work and a wife who is intelligent and unselfish enough to understand and respect the working of the unfriendly cycle of the creative imagination. She will know at what point domestic happiness begins to cloy, where love, tidiness, rent, rates, clothes, entertaining, and rings at the doorbell should stop, and will recognize that there is no more sombre enemy of good art than the pram in the hall.

Some critics encourage a mystical belief in talent. They hold that in the nature of things it must come to fruition, that 'if it is in you it's bound to come out', that true genius can neither be depressed by illness or poverty nor destroyed by success or failure. They go so far as to claim that people die at the right time, that Keats and Shelley had nothing more to say, that Marlowe, or André Chénier met their violent deaths at the appropriate moment. This fatuous romantic fatalism is based on an optimistic nature and a refusal to face facts. If Milton had been drowned like Lycidas, there would have been people to say that he would never have written anything else. But talent is something which grows and which does not ripen except in the right kind of soil and climate. It can be neglected or cultivated and will flower or die down. To suppose that artists will muddle through without encouragement and without money because in the past there have been exceptions is to assume that salmon will find their way to the top of a river to spawn in spite of barrages and pollution. 'If it's in you it's bound to come out' is a wish-fulfilment. More often it stays in and goes bad.

Fewer counsels and more money is what every artist must demand from society and it is the idiocy of society in refusing these demands, except to servile and indifferent performers, which is largely responsible for the present line up of artists against that society.* Capitalism is expelling the artist as Spain expelled her Jews or France her Huguenots and the effects will soon be apparent; the French nobles who had Voltaire flogged acted with similar foresight.

15 *The Slimy Mallows*

Of all the enemies of literature, success is the most insidious. The guides whom we have quoted, whose warnings come through to us from various parts of the field, are unanimous against this danger. Pearsall Smith quotes Trollope. 'Success is a poison that should only be taken late in life, then only in small doses.' Maugham writes:

> The common idea that success spoils people by making them vain,

*I should like to see the custom introduced of readers who are pleased with a book sending the author some small cash token: anything between half-a-crown and a hundred pounds. Authors would then receive what their publishers give them as a flat rate and their 'tips' from the grateful readers in addition, in the same way that waiters receive a wage from their employers and also get what the customer leaves on the plate. Not more than a hundred pounds – that would be bad for my character – not less than half-a-crown – that would do no good to yours.

egotistic, and self-complacent is erroneous; on the contrary it makes them, for the most part, humble, tolerant, and kind. Failure makes people bitter and cruel. Success improves the character of a man, it does not always improve the character of an author.

Success for a writer is of three kinds, social, professional, or popular. All three bring money but in none of them is money all important. Success is bad for a writer because it cuts him off from his roots, raises his standard of living and so leads to overproduction, lowers his standard of criticism and encourages the germ of its opposite, failure.

Social success was the variety which most appealed to writers up to the Slump, for social success, besides gratifying the snobbery which is inherent in romantic natures, also provided them with delightful conditions, with the freedom and protection of large country houses.

There are writers for whom such success is beneficial, who find there is the material they need and the leisure to absorb it; their public is also found among the world of fashion. Thus if Proust had been a social failure, if Pope had never been asked to a ball nor Henry James presented to a duchess, *The Rape of the Lock*, *Le Côté de Guermantes*, *The Ambassadors*, could never have been written. It is clear that a social success benefits some writers and is bad for others; it is because we envy it more than other success that we denounce it so often. Writers are helped by it if they are dandies or lyricists; if they have suffered from poverty to the extent of being warped or weakened rather than braced or steadied by it; if they are homosexuals who need a frame to expand on, a beanstalk to climb up or the kind of backing which will impress and so free them from the domination of middle-class parents; it is good for satirists and playwrights, priests and poets. Congreve, Gay, Wilde were all the better for 'being taken up' for they were whisked away to the field best suited for the flowering of their gifts, nor would Donne and Jeremy Taylor have written great prose had they delivered their wonderful sermons to a slum parish. It must be remembered that in fashionable society can be found warmhearted people of delicate sensibility who form permanent friendships with artists which afford them ease and encouragement for the rest of their lives and provide them with sanctuary. Lady Suffolk's friendship with Pope, Lord Sheffield's with Gibbon, Horace Walpole's for Gray, Lady Gregory's for Yeats, Lady Cunard's for George Moore acted as conservatories where the artist's talents ripened at a suitable temperature, neither forced too quickly, nor exposed to the rigours of the Grub Street winter. That Milton or Blake or Keats or Hopkins did not require such friendships does not discredit those who do.

> Blest be the great for those they take away
> And those they leave me. . . .

But apart from these especial intimacies or from such a comfortable greenhouse as Holland House, there is little to be derived from an indiscriminating indulgence in fashionable society. That society is hard-hearted, easily bored and will exact from a writer either a succession of masterpieces or a slavish industry in providing amusement at its own level, while he in his turn acquires an appetite for external values, which, besides being hard to gratify, creates professional hostility and excludes him from a larger world in which he might be happily employed. The people for whom social success is most dangerous are the realists who have no place among such unreality, the militants whose weapons rust in that atmosphere or writers like Bennett who have already found their material, and can only deteriorate when transplanted.* The best that can happen for a writer is to be taken up very late or very early, when either old enough to take its measure, or so young that when dropped by society he has all life before him. Married writers in particular are tormented by the contrast between the world where they dine and the world in which they wake up for breakfast, nor

*Thus a writer not intended for social success was Swift, and it is interesting to notice what snobbish intoxication, what unpleasant vanity creep into the *Journal to Stella* at the height of his 'swingboat' or fashionable period. Johnson's comments on Addison's marriage to Lady Warwick may also be considered: 'The marriage, if uncontradicted report can be credited, made no addition to his happiness, it neither found them nor made them equal . . . It is certain that Addison has left behind him no encouragement of ambitious love.'

are the relations between writers' wives and worldly hostesses renowned for cordiality.

Unfortunately the danger is past. Fashionable society is no longer a temptation as when it maintained a cultural standard. The singing birds nest no more in the great country houses; our Henry Jameses and Robert Brownings of today are not met roaring for lunch in Belgrave Square. 'Cliveden's proud alcove' has no Pope to sing in it. Maugham has shown that it is possible to possess and not be possessed by society, Forster that it is quite easy to do without it altogether, while Moore has summed it up: 'Well-mannered people do not think sincerely, their minds are full of evasions and subterfuges . . . To be aristocratic in Art one must avoid polite society.' A young writer must be careful not to pay the world more attention than it gives him, he may satirize it but is not advised to celebrate it, nor become its champion, for the moribund will turn on their defenders.*

Professional success, the regard of fellow-artists and would-be artists, is a true delight, for it is absurd to assume that good writers cannot be famous in their lifetime. There have always been a few thousand judges of good literature, and these judges have recognized talent however unusual and uncontemporary, even as they have accorded to masterpieces of the past an appreciation independent of fashion. Thus nobody could be more forgotten than the poet Campbell yet the other day John Betjeman pointed out three lines from the Battle of the Baltic which he admired.

> . . . When each gun
> From its adamantine lips
> Spread a death-shade round the ships
> Like a hurricane eclipse
> Of the sun.

Yet Tennyson, according to Palgrave, singled out the 'death-shade'

*When suffering from social envy of other writers there is only one cure – to work. Whatever consideration they are enjoying may then come your way and in any case by working you are doing what they would most envy you.

for praise when he was compiling the *Golden Treasury*, even as he admired Marvell's *To His Coy Mistress* or Cowper's *Poplars*, poems outside the general range of Victorian sensibility. These celebrators of the unfashionable best are the custodians of taste, the bodyguard of talent, like Maurice Baring who has kept alive, in *Have You Anything to Declare*, French poetry that would be lost to English readers were it not for his impartial ear. In similar fashion Strachey wrote about Racine, Pearsall Smith about Sainte-Beuve and Madame de Sévigné, writers who tend to be ignored owing to the cult of more violent sensations, while Diderot, St Evremond, Shenstone, and Cowper have all of late received sensitive homage.

If a professional success is painful in that it arouses the envy of the ex-artists, a popular success is fatal. Much has been written on the subject; I will try to summarize.

Success is a kind of moving staircase, from which an artist, once on, has great difficulty in getting off, for whether he goes on writing well or not, he is carried upwards, encouraged by publicity, by fan-mail, by the tributes of critics and publishers and by the friendly clubmanship of his new companions. The fan-mail gives the writer a sense of a mission. 'Well, if I have made them forget their troubles for a moment, my stuff may be some good.' Publicity also seems innocuous since once a writer is 'news' he continues to be so independently of his own wishes; besides it helps to sell his books. As for the critics' habit of praising a first book and damning a second, that can be put down to a personal grievance. 'I regard every attack', a writer once told me, 'as worth about sixpence a word.'

A popular success may depend on the entertainment value of a writer or his political quality or his human touch. Those with the human touch never recover; their sense of mission grows overwhelming. Neither harsh reviews, the contempt of equals, nor the indifference of superiors can affect those who have once tapped the great heart of suffering humanity and found out what a goldmine it is. Writers who have a political success may keep their heads, for they may soon experience a political disappointment.

I myself had that experience. I went three times to Spain. The first time I returned with enthusiasm and wrote an enthusiastic and popular article. The second time I came back less hopeful but still militant and fire-eating and my articles were still successful. The third time I returned with a hopeless premonition of defeat; all I was certain of was the weakness of the Aragon front, the dissension (which broke out in the May fighting) among the Catalans and the enormous difficulties which faced the Government in procuring food and material for war. Knowing Spanish (unlike the other fire-eaters) I had the misfortune to receive many confidences from people who already showed a personal weariness of the war. I came back with a septic throat, and the feeling that we experience when we see a tired fox crossing a field with the hounds and the port-faced huntsmen pounding after it. I could either conceal this feeling and try to write another fire-eater, or say nothing at all, or tell the truth. I thought the readers of my paper had the right to know the truth as I saw it and so I wrote a depressing article, recording the points of view of different people I had met and adding my own reflections. It was the time when Malaga and Bilbao fell and the article made me immensely unpopular. I had been unpopular before for saying *Journey's End* was a bad play and for criticizing the deification of Housman, but literary unpopularity was very different from the political kind, from being called a coward, a Fascist, a stabber-in-the-back, etc., and grateful to my escapism, I fled abroad. It is a mistake to exceed the artist's role and become political investigator.

The entertainer, on the other hand, suffers from no criticism whatever. No one has told P. G. Wodehouse which is his best book or his worst, what are his faults or how he should improve them. The fate of the entertainer is simply to go on till he wakes up one morning to find himself obscure.

For every admirer whom a writer gains by any means except the legitimate quality of his art he will gain an enemy. He will be an unconscious enemy, one who feels uneasiness at seeing the writer's name in the publisher's advertisements, who turns the other way from his picture in the Tube, one of those who voted against Aristides because he was tired of hearing him called 'the just'.

Every admirer is a potential enemy. No one can make us hate ourselves like an admirer – '*de lire la secrète horreur du dévouement dans des yeux*' – nor is the admiration ever pure. It may be *us* they wish to meet but it's themselves they want to talk about.

Popular success is a palace built for a writer by publishers, journalists, admirers, and professional reputation makers, in which a silent army of termites, rats, dry rot, and death-watch beetles are tunnelling away, till, at the very moment of completion, it is ready to fall down. The one hope for a writer is that although his enemies are often unseen they are seldom unheard. He must listen for the death-watch, listen for the faint toc-toc, the critic's truth sharpened by envy, the embarrassed praise of a sincere friend, the silence of gifted contemporaries, the implications of the dog in the manger, the visitor in the small hours. He must dismiss the builders and contractors, elude the fans with an assumed name and dark glasses, force his way off the moving staircase, subject everything he writes to a supreme critical court. Would it amuse Horace or Milton or Swift or Leopardi? Could it be read to Flaubert? Would it be chosen by the Infallible Worm, by the discriminating palates of the dead?

To refuse all publicity which does not arise from the quality of his work, to beware of giving his name to causes, to ration his public appearances, to consider his standards and the curve of development which he feels latent within him, yet not to indulge in gestures which are hostile to success when it comes, must be the aim of a writer.

Failure is a poison like success. Where a choice is offered, prefer the alkaline.

There is a kind of behaviour which is particularly dangerous on the moving staircase – the attempt to ascend it in groups of four and five who lend a hand to each other and dislodge other climbers from the steps. It is natural that writers should make friends with their contemporaries of talent and express a mutual admiration but it leads inevitably to a succession of services rendered, and however much the writers who help each other may deserve it, if they too frequently proclaim their gratitude they will arouse the envy of those who stand on their own feet, who succeed without collaboration. Words like 'log-rolling' and 'back-scratching' are soon whispered and the death-watch ticks the louder. Such writers must remember that they write for the reader – the most unloved person in the world. No jokes must be made which can't be explained to him, no relationships mentioned in which he is not asked to share. His capacity for being hurt, for feeling slighted and excluded, for imagining that he is being patronized, is infinite. And his capacity for revenge.

Success is most poisonous in America. According to Van Wyck Brooks, 'The blighted career, the arrested career, the diverted career are, with us, the rule. The chronic state of our literature is that of a youthful promise which is never redeemed.' He calls American literature 'one long list of spiritual casualties'. Hemingway gives an account of the diseases of American authors which is worth comparing with our own analysis of spiritual tares.

> We do not have great writers. Something happens to our good writers at a certain age.
>
> You see we make our writers into something very strange, we destroy them in many ways. First economically. They make money. It is only by hazard that a writer makes money, although good books always make money eventually. Then our writers when they have made some money increase their standard of living and they are caught. They have to write to keep up their establishments, their wives, and so on, and they write slop. It is slop not on purpose but because it is hurried. Because they write when there is nothing to say or when there is no water in the well. Because they are ambitious. Then once they have betrayed themselves, they justify it and you get worse slop. Or else they read the critics. If they believe the critics when they say they are great then they must believe them when they say they are rotten and they lose confidence. At present we have two good writers who cannot write because they have lost confidence, through reading critics. If they wrote, sometimes it would be good and sometimes not so good and sometimes it would be

> quite bad, but the good would get out. But they have read the critics, and they must write masterpieces. The masterpieces the critics said they wrote. They weren't masterpieces of course. They were just quite good books. So now they cannot write at all. The critics have made them impotent.*

It is not authors only who are killed by criticism but critics as well; they seem, like scorpions, able to destroy themselves with their own venom. But Hemingway's point is well made. The praise from a critic is inflated by hope as often as his censure is distorted by envy, since his longing for perfection or his desire to be a John the Baptist may drive him prematurely to recognize a Messiah and his disappointment thereby become correspondingly aggravated. Also, as Desmond MacCarthy has remarked, there comes a moment when every clever young man prefers to display his cleverness by exposing a writer's faults rather than proclaiming his virtues. That moment is most apt to occur in the early thirties which is a bad time all round both for creators and critics, or it may occur when the critic is in his early thirties and the writer in his early forties. Butler said an author should write only for people between twenty and thirty as nobody read or changed their opinions after that. Those are the years when the artists are promising and the admirers full of admiration; by the time the artist has ceased to be promising and become a good writer, the admirer is a critic whose judgements are flavoured by his own self-hatred or who, taking the author as a symbol of his own youth, refers all his later books back to his earliest. When an admirer says, 'Ah, yes! But if only he would write another *Prufrock!*' he means, 'If only I was as young as when I first read *Prufrock*.' The sour smell of the early thirties hangs over most literary controversy.

The shock, for an intelligent writer, of discovering for the first time that there are people younger than himself who think him stupid is severe. Especially if he is at an age (thirty-five to forty-two) when his self-confidence is easily shaken. The seventh lustre is such a period, a menopause for artists, a serious change of life. It is the transition from

*Scott Fitzgerald? Thornton Wilder? Glenway Westcott? John O'Hara?

being a young writer, from being potentially Byron, Shelley, Keats, to becoming a stayer, a Wordsworth, a Coleridge, a Landor. It would seem that genius is of two kinds, one of which blazes up in youth and dies down, while the other matures, like Milton's or Goethe's, through long choosing, putting out new branches every seven years. The artist has to decide on the nature of his own or he may find himself exhausted by the sprint of youth and unfitted for the marathon of middle age. A great many writers die between those years; some like Hart Crane, Harry Crosby, Philip Heseltine commit suicide; others succumb to pneumonia and drink or have nervous breakdowns. Others become specialists in the arts or in hobbies verging on the arts. Writers turn painters or painters writers or renew themselves through someone from whom they can obtain self-confidence and encouragement and a vicarious youth. Eventually, though critics are unfriendly, creation difficult and the future monotonous or uncertain, a new position is established and the young writer of promise becomes a master in his prime, one who can pass into old age as a sage, a prophet or a venerated, carefree and disreputable figure.

But English criticism, unless it proceeds from the indiscriminate malice of rotting ambition, is unfair only in that it is overkind – for a critic is subject to temptations of his own. Through praising their books, he gets to know more and more authors personally and once he has met them finds it embarrassing to alter his opinion. Critics in England do not accept bribes but one day they discover that in a sense their whole life is an accepted bribe, a fabric of compromises based on personal relationships, and then it is in vain to remember that, like James's old man of letters, 'our doubt is our passion, and our passion is our task'.

16 *Outlook Unsettled*

Such are the dangers and present temptations of writers. What consolations can be offered them? What positive advice will procure for a new book a decade of life and assure its author a patent from oblivion for another ten years? We have seen that realism, simplicity, the familiar attitude to the reader are likely to grow stale, that imagination, formality, subtlety, controlled by an awareness of the times we live in, are due to return. We can also learn something of the forms which have vitality and are assured of a future. Many writers who have no feeling for the live or the dead form still attempt those which are doomed to failure. The record of literature is that of great writers who perfect a form, imitators who bring into disrepute that perfection, and a new artist arising to perfect another.

Thus *Paradise Lost* dislocated the English language for a hundred years for it became impossible to write blank verse which was not an imitation of Milton. Ultimately Cowper broke away and after him Wordsworth and Tennyson. Since then poets have been trying to escape from Tennyson by returning to the blank verse of the Elizabethans. Coming after Milton, Pope was the first poet to elude blank verse and bring to perfection a new form, the couplet, and this couplet in its turn paralysed the poets of the eighteenth century till it was adapted by Crabbe and Byron. Blake and Collins meanwhile had broken free from the couplet and made possible the rebellion of the romantics who can be said to have held their own until *The Waste Land*.

A writer has to construct his shell, like the caddis worm, from the débris of the past, and, once there, despite the jostling of contemporaries, is safe till a younger generation dispossesses him or until the vicissitudes of taste crumble it about him. He may attempt a new form or he may revive an old one. But the revival, if it is to succeed, must not be too premature.

Which forms are available at the moment? The novel, the play, the poem, the article, the short story, the biography, and the autobiography seem the most fertile.

From the novel, dominant literary form of the last hundred years, has emerged a succession of masterpieces. But there have been a number of bad novels and from them certain facts can be deduced. Firstly, that bad novels do not last; there is no point, therefore, in writing one unless it comes up to championship standard. And the novel is not a suitable form for young writers. The best novels (of Stendhal, Flaubert, Proust, James, etc.) are written from early middle age onwards. It is unsuitable because the construction of a long book is exacting for the young, whose novels generally begin well and go off and who lack staying power, and because to write a novel an author must have experience of people as they are, and have resolved the contradictions in his own nature; he must be integrated, a machine for observation.

Young writers force upon real people the standards, motives, and behaviour which appeal to them in books; they are split men, at war with themselves, and uncertain of their philosophy. I know of admirable young novelists but their development was difficult, for they began as lyricists or satirists; even *Wuthering Heights* is not so much a novel as a lyric of sublimated eroticism. The satire of Evelyn Waugh in his early books was derived from his ignorance of life. He found cruel things funny because he did not understand them and he was able to communicate that fun. But the predicament of the humorist is that his sensibility, if it should go on developing, causes him to find things less and less amusing, 'for all our wit and reading do but bring us to a truer sense of sorrow'. The English humorist must therefore either cease to be funny and thereby lose his entertainment status, or abandon his integrity and, aesthetically stunted, continue to give his public what it wants. For this reason humorists are not happy men. Like Beachcomber or Saki or Thurber they burn while Rome fiddles, or, like P. G. Wodehouse, repeat themselves with profitable resignation.

The short story and the long short story are more fruitful. The short story avoids routine, it is the most fluid and experimental of forms, as Elizabeth Bowen says:

> Peaks of common experience soar past an altitude line into poetry. There is also a level immediately below this, on which life is being more and more constantly lived, at which emotion crystallizes, from which a fairly wide view is at command. This level the short story is likely to make its own.

The long short story is one of the most rewarding and yet neglected forms in literature whose abandonment is solely due to the animosity of publishers. While short stories can be published in magazines and then in book form and so be paid for twice, long short stories of from twenty to fifty thousand words can be published nowhere. Yet *The Aspern Papers*, *Sylvie*, *Candide*, *The Alien Corn*, *A Lost Lady*, and *Death in Venice* show to what perfection it can be brought, and *Sylvie* and *Daisy Miller* prove it an ideal medium for youthful creation.

The play is another form whose revival seems possible, the length is right for young authors, the technical difficulties can be solved by good advice. There are in particular two forms of drama which can be reclaimed by art: the English comedy and the revue. The prose comedy of manners is one of the finest creations of English literature, the perfection of our native dandyism. In Congreve the English language reaches the farthest point to which it can be pushed in the direction of stylized, colloquial, contemporary elegance. It is the polished, racy talk of men in periwigs, with muffs and long waistcoats. From that moment people were to shorten their wigs and subdue their clothing, to begin the retreat to bald heads, sock-suspenders, and undistinguished diction. The tragedy of Congreve was that, although a young man, his mission was to bring an old form to perfection and then see it into its grave.

We know very little about Congreve. His predicament was that he belonged to the past; the form he perfected, the comedy of manners, belonged in spirit to the reign of Charles II, and was haunted by that prince of dandies Wilmot, Earl of Rochester. Rochester had already been taken by Etherege as the hero of his charming *Man of Mode* and it was his habit of joking confidentially, almost wistfully, with his servant which, satirized here, established the favourite relationship of hard-up young master and wily, doting valet which has been a feature of the English comedy down to Jeeves. But what appealed to contemporary writers in Rochester was his mixture of gaiety and dignity, of the personal integrity of a man true to his own thought and feeling with the disregard of all law and convention of the nobleman and the rake. Such a hero is profoundly antipathetic to a bourgeois society, in which he is a kind of enviable outlaw; he can only exist round a court. His tradition retarded Congreve as much as that of Oscar Wilde and the nineties retarded many young writers of the 1920s. How typical of the most classical dandyism, for instance, was his reserve. 'He is comparatively reserved; but you find something in that restraint which is more agreeable than the utmost exertion of talent in others' – (Waller). Congreve must have felt an obsession for a man of an earlier generation so like what he himself would have wished to be, just as even Pope felt a certain nostalgia for the small-scale 'little England' quality of Charles II's court. The diction of his heroes closely resembles that which Etherege attributed to Rochester; one of Rochester's most favoured mistresses was a prominent member of Congreve's cast and Gosse mentions that Congreve bought a portrait of him. The Restoration comedy, after all, belonged to the Restoration, yet by a paradox it attained perfection in the 1690s. *The Way of the World* appeared in 1700 and was a failure. There is a rumour that Congreve went on the stage in a fury and told the audience he would never write anything for them again. Certainly he must have been conscious that he had put the best of his genius into it. What he could not have been conscious of in his disappointment was that the audience of 1700 had changed; the merchants of the reign of Anne, the Whigs, the new middle class would not stand for situations in which extravagant sons ruined selfish and bestial old fathers, duped their humdrum creditors, seduced the wives of aldermen, made fun of country squires, got up in the afternoon and went out to see who they could pick up in the park after supper. London was becoming less and less like the Rome of Terence. It was a serious city. In the same year Addison's pompous *Cato* had a stupendous success.

There is room now for a revival of comedy. We have no dandyism of the Left. A play which is politically and socially true of its time and which yet achieves the elegance of *Love for Love* or the beginning of *The Importance of Being Earnest* would be secure of a future. Another likely form is the intelligent revue because short satirical sketches are easily written by young writers and because a revue which flattered the intelligence of the audience would present an element of surprise. Most creative writing today is Left in sentiment. It would gain by conquering those fields of comedy which are still feebly defended by Toryism in retreat, by dukes and butlers and people who think the word Epstein a joke in itself, by men of pleasure turned sour and baby blimps just cutting their water-wings.

The long article has a future, especially in the form of the critical essay, the analysis of times and tendencies, and the skilled 'reportage'. But articles which cannot be reprinted are not worth writing.

Poetry is highly explosive, but no poet since Eliot can but perceive the extreme difficulty of writing good poetry. The moment a poet forgets this, he will be superseded by a writer of prose. We have one poet of genius in Auden, who is able to write prolifically, carelessly, and exquisitely, nor does he seem to have to pay any price for his inspiration. It is as if he worked under the influence of some mysterious drug which presents him with a private version, a mastery of form and of vocabulary.

But poets have to keep in training. Poetry, to stand out, must be a double distillation of life that goes deeper than prose. It must be brandy as compared to wine, otherwise consumers will get their poetry from short stories and novels. This distillation of experience can be achieved only by a writer who maintains his sensibility and integrity at a high pitch and concentrates on the quality of his production. He must examine the meaning, weight, force, pace, and implication of a word, he must calculate the impact of each line on the reader, know what concessions can be made to sound or sense, and deliver the finished poem only after a drastic trial. Otherwise prose will catch up on him. As things stand, inspiration is not enough, dreams have had their day, lucky shots miss the target. A poet, with the exception of mysterious water-fluent tea-drinking Auden, must be a highly conscious technical expert. Poetry is an instrument of precision. That is why societies in return must respect him as they respect scientists or all who have made greater sacrifices in their interest than they themselves care to. The poet is susceptible to the temptations which we have described by reason of his sensibility and we must not bully him.

'Popular, popular, unpopular,
You're no poet,' the critic cried.
'Why?' said the poet. 'You're unpopular!'
Then they cried at the turn of the tide,
'You're no poet!' 'Why?' 'You're popular!'
Pop-gun: popular and unpopular.*

A lyric poet has the advantage over a prose-writer that he is entrusted with the experience of the ages; he is not a political conscript nor can he be accused of escapism if he confines himself to celebrating the changing seasons, memories of childhood, love, or beauty. The tyranny of form to which he is subject is compensated by his free access to material. Literary history goes to prove that lyrical poetry is the medium which more than any other defies time. Didactic poetry becomes unreadable; epics are pillaged for a few similes; plays quarried for the songs in them; novels and essays crumble or ossify; but ten minutes' extra thought on the choice of a word or the position of a stress may make in the lyric a difference of a thousand years. There is no age or period at which great lyric poetry cannot be written. It is possible to argue that Homer and Virgil today would have written in prose, that Shakespeare would have written novels – but Sappho, even after the international situation had been explained to her, would have remained true to verse.

One of the colophons of literature, one of those great writers who put full stop to a form of art, was Marcel Proust. The form whose consummation he brought about was the autobiographical novel. *The Way of All Flesh*, *Of Human Bondage*, *A Portrait of the Artist* preceded it; after 1922 they could not have been written, and such autobiographical novels as appear now are not by great writers. They are the green shoots which continue to put forth from a tree that has been cut down.

The result of the flight of all but the most obstinate from this dying form has been a return of emphasis to the autobiography which has an advantage over the novel in that it demands no fictional gifts from the

*Not Lawrence: Tennyson.

writer and a disadvantage in that it permits no alibis; the characters are not imaginary and the hero is the one character with whom the author dare find fault. An interesting contribution was Harold Nicolson's *Some People*, which, disguised as short stories, is an autobiography where each episode represents a hurdle taken by the author on his way to maturity. Cowley's *Exile's Return* is another example of the planned autobiography (the one kind now worth writing), and in England I find it a temptation not to mention Orwell and Isherwood again. Closely related to reportage-autobiography is ideology-autobiography, in which an author looks back on himself in relation to the ideas of his time, a classic example of which is *The Education of Henry Adams*. There is room for many planned books of this sort by writers who can analyse themselves in relation to their environment and avoid padding, but all journalism must be kept out – so must the ideology, for the faults of these books are already apparent.*

To write well and to go on writing well depends on our sense of reality. There is such a thing as literary health and so far we have considered only literary diseases. If a writer is not writing as well as he would like to or as often as he would wish, he should give himself an examination. Is he satisfied with his reality? Is he '*dans le vrai*'? If not, when and how has he departed from it? Reality is a shifting thing. I take it to mean the nature of things as they are and as they will be. It is life and the future, however unpleasant, and not death and the past, however desirable. What people want to happen is real if it can be willed to happen, and there are realities of the imagination – such as the belief in a future life or in a perfectible human society – which transcend

*'A man scurried through the Chancellery. He moved too fast for me to get a glimpse of him – but I just discerned an ulster and a soft felt hat. "That fellow's scared," I muttered. "You bet he is," said Jeff Post. "It's Schuschnigg (Schacht – Stresemann)." It was the only time I saw him till I followed his coffin down the Siegenallee.' Or (ideological): 'All that year Lenin was drinking café crèmes in Geneva. Trotsky was growing a beard, Kautsky was writing "one step forward, two steps backward"; the Tennessee soapboilers' strike was repressed after twenty-nine days. Jaurès was fighting a municipal election but, obsessed with sex and education, my development was still experiencing a bourgeois time-lag of some two thousand years. I might have been talking with survivors of the 1905 revolution. I preferred to study Plato, Picasso, and Proust.'

at times the physical realities of death and annihilation. But for a professional writer it involves the realities of his time, the ideas and the actions which are changing the world and shaping history. The most real thing for a writer is the life of the spirit, the growth or curve of vision within him of which he is the custodian, selecting the experiences propitious to its development, protecting it from those unfavourable. When he fails to do this something seems to rot; he becomes angry, frightened, and unhappy, suffering from what Swift called 'that desiderium which of all things makes life most uneasy'.

The spiritual reality of the artist may come into conflict with the historical reality of his time and true to his own reality, he may even have to sacrifice himself by his opposition to the external world and so find that no life but premature death is required of him. There is no mysticism in this. We create the world in which we live; if that world becomes unfit for human life, it is because we tire of our responsibility. Genius is important in creating that world and therefore will be among the first things to suffer. There are destructive elements – war, plague, earthquake, cancer, and the dictator's firing squad are among them – which take no account of the unfinished masterpiece or the child in the womb. They are real and their reality must never be under-estimated but there remains a reality of will and spirit by which within the unchanging limitations of time and death they can be controlled.*

Having satisfied himself of how he stands in relation to his time and whether his talent is receiving proper nourishment, an ailing writer will inquire about those other sources of creative happiness: health, sex, and money.

The health of a writer should not be too good, and perfect only in

*The Spanish poet Lorca was shot because he fell into the power of an element which detested spiritual reality. Yet Lorca fell into those hands because he lived in Granada. Had he lived in Barcelona or Madrid he would be alive today like Sender or Alberti. But he lived in reactionary Granada, a city of the past, of gipsies and bull-fighters and priests, and he made his best poems about bull-fighters and gipsies. That element in him which sought the past, which drew him to the medievalism of Andalusia, contained the seed of his own death, placing him, who was no friend to priests or feudal chiefs, in a city where the past would one day come to life, and prove deadly.

those periods of convalescence when he is not writing. Rude health, as the name implies, is averse to culture and demands either physical relief or direct action for its bursting energy. Action to the healthy man seems so desirable that literary creation is felt to be shaming and is postponed till action has engendered fatigue which is then transmitted to the reader. Also, in 'this England where nobody is well', the healthy writer is communicating with a hostile audience. Most readers live in London; they are run-down, querulous, constipated, soot-ridden, stained with asphalt and nicotine and, as a result of sitting all day on a chair in a box and eating too fast, slightly mad sufferers from indigestion. Except on holiday an author should not be fitter than his public or too well for reading and meditation. The relationship of an author with his reader is the barometer of his aesthetic health. If he flatters or patronizes, is hostile or pleading, then something is amiss with him.

A preoccupation with sex is a substitute for artistic creation; a writer works best in an interval from an unhappy love-affair, or after his happiness has been secured by one more fortunate. So far as we can generalize it would seem that the welling up of the desire for artistic creation precedes a love-affair. Women are not an inspiration of the artist but a consequence of that inspiration. An artist, when his talent is uncoiling, has the desirability of any object fulfilling its function but he also enjoys a certain clearheadedness. His habits become moderate, he drinks less because drink has no longer a psychological appeal. He does not lack confidence, he lives contentedly within his income and he sees love and friendship as delightful things but without their glamour. It is after creation, in the elation of success or the gloom of failure, that love becomes essential.

Solvency is an essential. A writer suffering from financial difficulties is good only for short-term work, and will leave all else unfinished. And if he has too much money, unless he has had it all his life, he will spend it, which is also a substitute for creation. Every writer should, before embarking, find some way however dishonest of procuring with the minimum of effort, about four hundred a year. Otherwise he must become a popular success or be miserable. Success he will take in his stride for fewer writers are marred by it than are discouraged by failure. It is wholesome magic.

> Gently dip, but not too deep
> For fear you make the golden beard to weep.

Failure on the other hand is infectious. The world is full of charming failures (for all charming people have something to conceal, usually their total dependence on the appreciation of others) and unless a writer is quite ruthless with these amiable footlers, they will drag him down with them. More dangerous are those who are not charming – the trapped foxes who bite the hand that would set them free and worst of all the Kibitzers, the embittered circle of scoffing onlookers –

> The common rout
> That, wandering loose about,
> Grow up and perish as the summer fly
> Heads without name, no more remembered.

It is by a blend of lively curiosity and intelligent selfishness that the artists who wish to mature late, who feel too old to die, the Goethes, Tolstoys, Voltaires, Titians, and Verdis, reach a fruitful senescence. They cannot afford to associate with those who are burning themselves up or preparing for a tragedy or whom melancholy has marked for her own. Not for them the accident-prone, the friends in whom the desire for self-destruction keeps blistering out in broken legs or threatening them in anxiety-neuroses. Not for them the drumming finger, the close-cropt nail, the chewed glasses, the pause on the threshold, the wandering eye, or the repeated 'um' and 'er'.

We create the world in which we live and the artist plays a dominant role in that creation. By extension he can live in any world which he has created. At present, some artists are creating a militant, others a pacifist world, and it is not artists only who are creating worlds, but capitalists and dictators. There is doubt about which world is best as there is doubt about which world will triumph. If a Fascist world wins we may expect a black-out of art as under Attila. A Communist world may make experiments in intolerance and then grow tired of them. Or nothing may happen during our lifetimes and a few drops of patronage still be wrung from a barren capitalism. Honours will be conferred on the adroit, smart luncheon parties given, medals awarded. Or a world revolution may establish conditions in which artists will through their own merit reach the public from whom they have been isolated.

Within his talent it is the duty of a writer to devote his energy to the search for truth, the truth that is always being clouded over by romantic words and ideas or obscured by actions and motives dictated by interest and fear. In the love of truth which leads to a knowledge of it lies not only the hope of humanity but its safety. Deep down we feel that, as every human being has a right to air and water, so has he a right to food, clothing, light, heat, work, education, love, and leisure. Ultimately we know the world will be run, its resources exploited and its efforts synchronized on this assumption. A writer can help to liberate that knowledge and to unmask those pretenders which accompany all human plans for improvement: the love of power and money, the short-sighted acquisitive passions, the legacies of injustice and ignorance, the tiger instinct for fighting, the ape-like desire to go with the crowd. A writer must be a lie-detector who exposes the fallacies in words and ideals before half the world is killed for them. It may even be necessary for the poet to erect a bomb-proof ivory tower from which he can continue to celebrate the beauty which the rest of mankind will be too guilty, hungry, angry, or arid to remember. There is room in the arts besides the militant novelists and journalists for the 'necessary lovers', but the success worshippers, those for whom life is a Perpetual Party, a buffet where one swigs, if fortunate in the draw, for eighty years and then grudgingly makes room, are as out of favour as those who justify abuses as our Christian burden 'in this Vale of Tears'. The artist of today must bear a wound – '*cette blessure*', according to Gide, '*qu'il ne faut pas laisser se cicatriser, mais qui doit demeurer toujours douleureuse et saignante, cette blessure au contact de l'affreuse réalité.*'*

*'That wound which we must never allow to heal but which must always remain painful and bleeding, the gash made by contact with hideous reality.'

No Peace for Elephants
(1953)

A reviewer should have no feelings, only judgment and his judgment should recognise no values other than literary. Until a machine is invented which can vamp out a criticism of a book, he should try to be that machine. Sometimes, however, his feelings intervene and where no literary element is present to distract him they may even boil over.

Herr Oberjohann is, or was, since no biographical details are provided after 1938, a German explorer, intrepid, resourceful, who because of his 'passion for animals', obtained employment with various dealers, notably Hagenbeck and went out to stock his zoos and circuses. 'Not content with capturing animals, Oberjohann was always intent on studying their behaviour and psychology, on understanding them and making himself understood by them.' *Wild Elephant Chase** describes the cream of four years of hardship and adventure in the Lake Chad region, where, he was told, the largest elephants in Africa were to be found, tormented by insects but secure in their impregnable swamps from man.

When Herr Oberjohann arrived, like Tribulat-Bonhomet the swan-killer, in his home-made leather suit, with his guns and beaters and whip and pipe, the herd numbered about two hundred. For the next four years the animals were to know no peace while Herr Oberjohann dogged their footsteps, examined their droppings and abducted nineteen small calves, all of whom died, their grief-stricken mothers going mad or being shot, together with any adult animals who allowed him to approach them. In addition he conducted some experiments to

*By Heinrich Oberjohann (Dobson).

prove that baby elephants who were impregnated with his scent were trampled to death by their mothers. We can therefore estimate that he reduced the herd by about fifty during the four years in which he 'understood' them.

Occasionally he permits a crocodile tear to water his home-made buckskin:

> I looked over at the dying cow; she was bleeding profusely and a big patch of the water in front of her was coloured a deep blood-red. . . . Now the sounds from the cow grew. She was talking in her own tongue, the elephant language. I wished I could understand what she was saying. It was an uncanny sound and it got under my skin, for it was through my own brutality, my crime against nature, that this elephant mother lay dying. I longed to escape. I refused to remain any longer as witness to this tragic scene. I wondered whether the people back home, whether Carlo Hagenbeck himself, had any idea of the unspeakable tragedy which is involved in robbing a fellow creature of its freedom.

In the next chapter he has quite recovered:

> I fired; the leading elephant went down on his knees. One of the cows, refusing to be frightened off by the death of her companion, rushed wildly ahead. . . . I fired again. The cow collapsed. Now I turned my attention to the baby elephants.

Mindful of the casualties of Hiroshima, we proudly call this the Atomic Age but future historians may look back on this century as the time when man finally exterminated everything larger than himself and ceased to be a trustee for the older forms of life on his planet: whales, basking-sharks, dugongs and manatees, sea-lions, sea-leopards and sea-elephants, walruses and polar-bears, giraffes – and elephants. Capable of living to a hundred, of kissing, of combining together, of thinking ahead and endowed with extrasensory perception or telepathy, their continued existence is clearly intolerable.

Perhaps the French authorities of the Chad region could take them under their control, perhaps the four Powers who control tropical Africa could pool the remaining herds in a safety zone as in the Belgian Congo. Meanwhile we can do little but hamper Herr Oberjohann's further exercises in 'understanding' by omitting to read a book in which so much fascinating elephant lore is purchased at such fearful cost by a man who, knowing he is doing wrong, is yet unwilling to stop.

A Cato of the Campus
(1957)

Sometimes I am reproached for reviewing yet another work on Georgian tongue-scrapers or the culture of the custard-apple.

I will confess a secret: it is not just that I care for such things; I feel it is also my duty to protect my little flock of readers, for while they are puzzling over these aberrations some really dreadful book-about-books-about-books of the kind which drove me to despair when I was myself an editor may be blowing harmlessly over their heads to bury its nose in the mud.

I seldom review novels because I think the best novels should be the gratification of those whose task it is to peruse the worst, but I continue to read them; books about the novel, however, I often find suspect. They are of no help to the novelist and usually represent some young professor's deplorable attempt to launch his thesis or swell his curriculum. One digs out some text – 'The modern novel is the bankrupt blood-bank of Western civilisation' – and starts fitting the novelists into the blood-groups, with Henry James as the original plasma. It is essential to deal with the same writers as rival professors, but also to redistribute the praise and blame among them, and to lead out at least one dark horse. Attack Maugham, Huxley, Greene, Waugh by the way – honour Ford Madox Ford; reverence Conrad, for in a few years we shall all have to read him. Footnotes for the women writers; disparagement and wonder for Lawrence, lip-service to Leavis, a hem and a haw for Hemingway and Hawthorne, and I wish you all the best.

What distinguishes Professor McCormick* from other practitioners

* *Catastrophe and Imagination* by John McCormick.

of this genre is his attack on myself. As I trundled through his consistently vigorous, logical and felicitous chapters (each one of which, if submitted to me at *Horizon*, would certainly have been passed on with a recommendation to the editor of *New Writing* or vice versa), I began to be flattered by the many references to myself. Imagine my bewilderment when I found a whole section at the end devoted to castigating the vice of 'Cyrillism' – my ears have not so burned since I was awarded alligator status in the *Moscow Encyclopaedia*:

> This ironically adolescent atmosphere created an attitude which I think of as Cyrillism – a mixture of scornful sentimentality, repressed intellectual cleverness, flippancy, and subtle complicated snobberies. Cyrillism is not of the slightest importance to the art of the novel, though in pervading minor novelists it must affect the potentialities of the art; it is of great importance in the economics of English publishing, reviewing, and in the dōling out of official largesse. . . . While Cyrillism has made an appearance in America, having been introduced by English expatriates, it is not the problem that is in England.

Don't be too sure, professor . . .

I am also responsible for something called the 'Firbank–Connolly sort of writing' which 'carries the cachet of intellectualism without being intellectual; it is made up of attitudes that answer to our apparent need for snobbery of some description' and I find that 'all the Sitwells, Cyril Connolly, William Sansom and Angus Wilson; and in America, Truman Capote, Tennessee Williams, Paul Bowles and Frederick Buechner' are locked in the same cell.

'This group,' the Professor writes elsewhere, 'the American Ronald Firbanks' are 'belated decadents' who 'gravitate to extreme situations and inflate extremity with giggling gusto to the point where it becomes ridiculous and nauseating'. And this time he cites, as well as Capote, Williams and Buechner, Gore Vidal and Carson McCullers.

Here, by way of contrast, is an example of McCormickism:

> 'M. Merieau-Ponty has said: "Because we are in the world, we are condemned to meaning".*' In terms of the novel, meaning translates, I suspect, into 'reality', not photographic reality, of course, but the reality which emerges when mind and imagination combine to organise experience into a communicable entity. The difficulty with Scott is that finally his mind is uninteresting.'
>
> *Herbert Spiegelberg, 'French Existentialism: its social philosophies', *Kenyon Review*, XVI No. 3, Summer 1954, p. 459.

Now the Cyrillist, poor hack, would only have space to say, 'The difficulty with Scott is that finally his mind is uninteresting' (it is not the least of Professor McCormick's difficulties either); and the remark, in brute isolation, would smack, quite unfairly, of 'repressed intellectual cleverness'. I should like to give one or two more examples. One, of the method by which the professors invent a situation in order to make room for their categories:

> The catastrophe brought into modern society a sense of urgency and a new tempo; it made for a new consciousness of self and of the place of the self in society; it created an atmosphere in which the loss of old certainties, the presence of new anxieties, and the thrusting forward of public issues combined to isolate man from man and group from group. The novelist promptly discovered that new techniques were required to express the new fragmentation of society . . .

I used to produce this ideogram about the Renaissance when I was at school, and lead on to Montaigne and Rabelais; the Professor uses it for the First World War.

My last extract shows the real danger of McCormickism; the Ceremony of the Mare's Nest, or Elevation of the Dark Horse:

> *A Step to Silence* (1952) and *The Retreat* (1953) are better novels than anything of Virginia Woolf or D. H. Lawrence, for example; they are the product of great literary energy whose sensibility is in the finest sense contemporary. Newby has learned creation of character from Dickens and perhaps from Dostoievski: he has learned pace, movement

> and a method of seeing from, I suspect, Conrad. His prose is clear with our twentieth-century kind of clarity. . . . His uniqueness rests in his conception of how human beings react upon one another; it is here that Newby's contemporary sensibility exercises its effect.

Surely Mr P. H. Newby deserves better than that?

As a critic, Professor McCormick is omnivorous; he has read every imaginable novel and regurgitates them all, particularly Fitzgerald, Hemingway, and Faulkner, very palatably; his classifications are intelligent, though I detect a pro-Minnessotan and anti-British bias, however slight. If only . . . but there is largesse to distribute, a position at the British Council to fill, subtle snobberies to dream up, a report from Sofia (in Cyrillic script), still another book on Georgian tongue-scrapers coming in . . . if only he would write a novel himself.

Deductions from Detectives
(1931)

Mash – a kind of bran mash, a great packing case of bran with here an arm and there an ear – a weapon or a corpse sticking out of it – that, I suppose, is all that survives in the mind from the detective stories we have read. And yet, in a hundred years our thrillers will have become text-books of social history and regarded as the most authentic chronicles of how we lived.

For the detective story is the only kind of book now written in which every detail must be right; nobody cares in fiction, even in biography, what cigarettes, what make of car the hero uses, or where he gets his clothes, but in the compression of the detective story where every touch must add something to our knowledge of the characters, their walk in life, their propensities for crime, such incidents become of extreme importance, they must render an accurate delineation of the business of living. How Philo Vance's Régie Turc cigarettes betray his European culture snobbery! He is in detective fiction the only remaining superior person. And Lord Peter Wimsey, how we wince each time he says, 'Have a Sobranje'; here surely he betrays his feminine creator, may she soon alter it to 'have a Balkan'. And motor cars, a course of detection passes us through a regular Olympia. For to be car conscious is to be aware of one more efficient and infallible way of summing people up quickly. Let us consider in this light the position of some of our detectives.

Lord Peter Wimsey	50 h.p. Daimler double six.
Bull Dog Drummond	Bentley, open.
Petersen (villain)	Mercedes-Benz, supercharged tourer.
Lakington (villain)	cream-coloured Rolls-Royce.

Colonel Antony Gethryn	16-cyl. 'surbaissé' Voisin.
Colonel Gore	Buick roadster.
Father Brown	none.

Notice how absolutely right Wimsey is – a Rolls-Royce is vulgar, a Daimler correct but for a detective too slow. There remains the enormous 12-cylinder Daimler capable of 100 miles an hour. And how natural for Il Drummond to be a 'Bentley Boy', it suggests at once someone brave but oafish, a 'cheery soul'. Mercedes, Hispano, Isottas and all foreign cars in racing trim are the villain's share in motoring; the long, black, wicked-looking Voisin of Gethryn indicates only that he is in secret service. Colonel Gore has made just enough money to get out of the Morris ruck in which flounder all Scotland Yard detectives and those of the brilliant amateurs who occasionally allude to the 'old bus'. Sir Clinton Driffield is a few rungs higher up the same ladder. Already, you see, a classification seems possible. We may take certain types – Wimsey, the aristocrat, the Duke's brother, the *gratin* of London Society but with fashionable democratic leanings. He collects first editions, and though he prefers 1915 to 1911 Burgundy, he is a judge of wine. Otherwise he is impeccable and, in any social dilemma, uncertain whether to recognise or let oneself be recognised, one asks, 'What would Wimsey do?'

The Drummond, in spite of 'my cousin Stavely', is not so much an aristocrat as the flower of a fashionable military world of baronets and younger sons. 'A sportsman and a gentleman, and the combination of the two is an unbeatable product.' Though they are utterly dissimilar and antipathetic, they lead a similar kind of life, attended by ex-batmen valets in bachelor flats in Mayfair. The Drummond's is in Half Moon Street and Wimsey's overlooks Green Park: even perhaps they may have met, Wimsey leaving the chemist in Piccadilly on some errand for his mother just as the Bull Dog, with Ted Jerningham (only son of Sir Patrick Jerningham, of Jerningham Hall) and Algy and the rest of the lads enter to settle their last night's hangover with the usual morning draught.

Otherwise they are poles apart, true heirs of Court and Country Party. The Drummond is for beer and whisky, a pipe smoker, a national hero, his head, as Mr Raymond Mortimer has written, should be engraved on the reverse of our coinage. Phyllis, his wife, is blade straight and steel true. He is not afraid to send her alone to Le Touquet. Wimsey is relatively decadent, a detective only to forget an unhappy love affair and then to fall for a murderess and afterwards chuck her! In Paris Wimsey stays at the Meurice, Petersen at the Bristol (it's quieter), while the Drummond, whose French is better than he will admit, puts up at the Ritz and dines a few doors down the street, at Maxim's.

Of the others, Gethryn, Driffield, Gore represent three different levels in the same 'milieu'. Gethryn is an urbane soldier, rich, with a lovely wife and a house in Knightsbridge, but essentially a military man, the kind you hear saying how much better printed the English translation of Proust is, at smart luncheon parties. He visits in great country houses. Sir Clinton Driffield is a country bore, a person of position, pompous, humourless, and grim. Colonel Gore is the saddest case of all. His people were once very well known in the West Country, he was a famous polo player in a crack regiment – but they lost everything, and he could never consequently tell his adorable 'Pickles' how much he cared about her. He went off to Central Africa . . . she married another man and finally teased him, from being estate agent and secretary to a golf club, into setting up as a private detective. But everyone has been very decent, they remember the old days, and he still gets an occasional chukka.

In the next group are all the Scotland Yard detectives, Inspectors French, Frost, Parker, Wilson, Pointer, etc. They are plain people. I like French and Pointer the best, Wilson the least. But enough of them.

Apart from a few freaks like Thorndike, Poirot, and Father Brown, there is one more distinct group – the bright young things. It consists of Government officials, like Egerton, or clever products of the universities who are drifting simultaneously into detection and journalism. There is Ronald Knox's appalling hero and the more typical Roger Sheringham, who sometimes lunches besides Wimsey at Isola Bella, but like the Drummond keeps a cask of 4X Ale. He is the only one who is reticent. The rest are no longer great gentlemen, nor even well off. They are bumptious exhibitionist Rugby-and-Balliol Broadcasting young men, virile male virgins, inquisitive, middlebrow, opportunist. They wear rough clothes, interesting ties and Bloomsbury black hats. They shovel poor Colonel Gore off the pavement and laugh at Beau Drummond's Three Nuns profile framed in the window of the 'Junior Sports Club'. They find Wimsey effeminate: 'Young puppies', murmurs Sir Clinton uneasily, as they make little Oxford jokes on the steps of the London Library till Professor Thorndike finds some difficulty in getting through. I prefer even American women like Madam Storey and Lynn Macdonald to these new English sleuths who are taking murder away from country houses and millionaires' mansions and planting it in Boulestin's, the Russian Ballet, or the Zoo.

And this brings me to the second great virtue of detective stories, they are the last repository of our passion for the countryside. I used, in my ancient integrity, to despise both bridge and detective stories; the one, I would say, killed conversation and the other poetry, or the desire to read it. Alas, conversation kills itself and bridge is often the only way to prop it up, for then the strain is taken off talking which becomes easier and more candid for ceasing to be the main attraction. This, too, is what the detective story has done for verse. Living in the south of France I began to pine for the English winter; in vain I turned to Georgian poets and lyric novelists of our unproductive soil. I experienced a kind of nausea; the language hackneyed and outworn, did not convey the sense; the sense, where conveyed, seemed exaggerated and mawkish. I took to buying all the English books I could and discovered Freeman Wills Croft. Suddenly I realised that here was the ideal medium for describing scenery. Here were books where the stress was taken off the countryside (which then seemed to spring up like trodden grass), and conveyed to the events which took place in it; where local colour was useful as well as beautiful; where Grantchester was not an overworked sentimental symbol, but a place whose loveliness was enhanced because it was accidental, like the metaphors of *Paradise Lost*, or the landscapes in *Tales of the Hall*. And so I treated my homesickness, walking with Inspector French round the Mumbles, gazing down winter estuaries, making innumerable railway journeys, exploring Rochester with Thorndike, going with Mr Fletcher to country towns till I could find my way in any of them to the Doctor's pleasant Georgian house, the rectory, the spinster's cottage, the eccentric lawyer's office. There was the inn parlour where I asked a few apparently harmless questions, and finally the dingy room where the inquest was held.

And the country houses, the great parks dripping in the autumn weather, the brilliant company, the rooms I have slept in, finding my way from the map on the first page. Those awkward scenes when the guests are solemnly assembled and informed of the tragedy – how seldom have I been allowed to stay till Monday morning! I prefer the station hotels, the country inns where rustic curiosity is allowed to triumph over politeness. And the meals! The fare of every detective is as carefully delineated as his suspicions; the chops, the steaks, the birds I have shared with them, the Yquem of Wimsey, Inspector French's claret at the Plymouth hotel, the Drummond's tankards, Gore's whisky, Sir Clinton's port. Stray landscapes emerge from the débris, a charming account of the Island of Porquerolles, Gore on the Mendips, Wimsey up in Galloway, Inspector French at Bordeaux and sailing down a hidden gum-scented forest river in the Landes. Even Sherlock Holmes, whose methods of detection are now hopelessly out of style, intolerably primitive, unfair and *vieux jeu*, is becoming what I have prophesied for Wimsey, Bull Dog, Sheringham and Kitchen's *Death of my Aunt*, a period piece, a social document. We read him for Baker Street, for those *fin de siècle* fogs from which emerged the clopping of clients' hansoms, for the tiaras, the crowns, the incognitos, the landladies, for all the paraphernalia of the nineties in which Holmes himself, the syringe implacably pressed to the bare arm, murmuring, the fiddle beside him, *l'homme c'est rien, l'œuvre c'est tout*, is so much the British figurehead that he deserves at least a drop scene in *Cavalcade*. So in time to come will little booklets appear, and someone yet unborn will investigate where Wimsey loved and deliver the Romanes lecture on 'Sapper's women'.

Lastly, it can be said for detective novels that they are the most advanced, the nearest approach to pure form of any work produced today. While the novel grows more and more sprawling, dragging from incident to incident, volume to volume, weltering in emotions, the typical unplanned exuberant Romantic achievement, so its sister the detective story grows ever more classical, as the characters, the scene, the actions are more strictly compelled by the writer's rigid subordination to plot. And the plot also, how increasingly severe are the laws which govern it. No longer may the detective keep evidence to himself nor may any highly esoteric branch of knowledge be exploited for the crime. The alibi, for instance, is more often the central problem than the crime itself, for it is a problem that can only be constructed by human ingenuity, without appeal to rare poisons, witch-doctors, etc., and only by human ingenuity can it be solved. At the moment the problem is one of combining an intricate crime, as dry as a Torquemada cross-word puzzle, with the most entertaining psychology possible, the vividest and most malicious presentation of character. Of course, something has to be sacrificed for sophistication, and in this case it is the element of horror. A corpse has to be supplied in ingenious circumstances at a very early stage in the book. The reader is now hardened to all forms of killing, nor will he wait till the middle chapter for the crime, although the delay provides the author with a chance to shock the reader by first making him really attached to the murdered man. In America, too much is made of both horror and psychology. Van Dine tries to create suspense by frequent killings, Rufus King almost achieves it and in the 'psychological' novels of Kay Strahan and Mary Rinehart two-thirds of the book is sometimes over before the crime. The detective story, in fact, is the 'trobar clus', the 'chant royale' or 'double ballade' of contemporary literature, as exacting as the sonnet but with none of the sonnet's subject-matter's romantic concessions to the Moi Haissable. But inside the formal shell – the accepted stages of the plot – the detective story, unlike any other form of literature, alone assumes an increasing intelligence in the reader from year to year. It is wholly progressive, presupposing even more acumen in the critics; the only art which writes increasingly up to its readers and not increasingly down; to a connoisseur no story before *Trent's Last Case* is readable; and every one since that year, if you have a palate, can be unhesitatingly dated. The English in fact are supreme in detective stories and have been ever since *The Moonstone*. They are our ablest, our most authentic British export. I hope I have shown what harm we do to them by reading them in bulk and refusing to believe that the sediment they leave, the residuum, the interior mush of error and surfeit from all these books that we send ourselves to sleep with, may one day prove valuable.

The Private Eye
(1953–62)

An American writer once explained to me his conception of the underworld, it was the only true world, the realm of natural, spontaneous feeling and action whose values were loyalty, courage and intensity of living and whose opponents the police, the rich, 'society' as we call it were, by comparison, half alive and therefore all the more envious of the values of the freedom-lovers whom they set out to destroy.

The American private detective is now an established figure in modern myth. Poor, celibate, despised by the public, suspected by the police, loyal only to his client and his code, he moves in a world of money, murder, morons and nymphomania, a cigarette in his mouth, just keeping his head above water and his body out of gaol or bed. He has no hobbies, no friends, no home, no memories, no past and no future, he lives in the present – 'twenty-five dollars a day and expenses' – and for that we know he will be insulted, betrayed and beaten up, but never quite killed or arrested, while the blondes thicken and the corpses accumulate in his antechamber. If he is a success he will be played by Humphrey Bogart and analysed by international sociologists with a puff on his jacket from Mr. Auden and Mr. Somerset Maugham.

Mr. Raymond Chandler's Marlowe is now the champion, having defeated Mr. Dashiell Hammett's Sam Spade. 'His powerful books,' writes Mr. Auden, 'should be read and judged, not as escape literature, but as works of art.' And very bad works of art they are.

> 'Hell, what was eating me? I killed a cigarette and took another sheet of paper. This time I'd play it straight and cut down on the blondes. 'Dashiell Hammett,' I wrote, 'old father, old artificer, twenty years

a-going, silent upon a peak in the Beverley Wiltshire. Connolly billed him once with Hemingway in the sleazy Thirties. Now they're all gone except Perry Mason and how many a tired tycoon or pushed politician knows the name of the guy who grows him? Erle Stanley Gardiner, alias A. A. Fair.' I killed another cigarette. This one wasn't going too well either. I crumpled the page up and tossed it behind the radiator; the analysts or the blondes could fight for it one day. Raymond Chandler, I wrote again, fifteen letters – Philip Marlowe, thirteen – but the syllables tallied. Have you noticed how many novelists reproduce the exact amount of syllables in their pseudonyms and those of their characters – Malachi Mulligan = Oliver Gogarty and so on.

Reading these king-size authors how can you help a little of their style rubbing off on you? I pressed the buzzer – not the dummy one – and my secretary freezed in. You can always tell a good secretary: she'll play it just one short of sex-appeal because she knows it'll mean another sort of job for her if she ever holes the putt.

'Kill those stubs, Miss Mouse, and don't look so easy on the private eye. This is Mr Connolly, a limey critic who can't get Philip Marlowe out of his dandruff. He's come out West to scrape some Brown Windsor off his old school tie.'

'Mr Marlowe's not got much use for critics, Mr Connolly, he'll last and they won't.'

'Yeah – he'll last – like the snow on Ben Leavis.' I took the pin out of that one, counted five, and lobbed it back.

'Go put yourself in orbit, Mr Connolly.'

'Miss Mouse!'

'Scram, beat it, achieve absence, get missing, crawl back under your oxygen tent, gum a "not wanted on voyage" sticker on your trap and report to the purser. Fade out.'

The crack seemed almost airborne for a moment, then it heaved a deep sigh that sounded like P. G. Wodehouse and went for a Burton.

The recipe which Mr. Chandler employs is to take a central erotic situation and then mount it like a jewel in a setting of murders. There are no rules: the reader is not expected to solve a puzzle but to career over a switchback of violent sensations. The titles of these books, *The Big Sleep*, *Farewell My Lovely*, *The High Window*, *The Lady in the Lake*, convey the erotic character, the Love–Death motive – and there is at least one wholesome and one attractive but abnormal woman in each novel.

We have to accept certain specifications, that there is a kind of beauty which drives men mad, that most people will do anything for money, that every possible vice and even eccentricity exists within ten miles of Los Angeles, that guns are as interesting as cars and cars nearly as interesting as people and people almost as important as their clothes, and that wisecracks are the dog language of introduction – and if we accept all this we can enjoy a long thrilling afternoon dodging the bullets.

But these are not works of art because they have no internal composition; the three kinds of characters – crooks, cops and blondes – are without reality, they exist only through action, through violence, they cannot cook a meal or write a letter or read a book. The spotlight, the private eye, moves from scene to scene, crime to crime, whisky to whisky, crack to crack – but if every murdered person in all four novels had been the slayer instead of the slain nobody would give a damn.

Who does exist then? Only Marlowe. He plays chess with himself, goes to bed, gets up, smokes a pipe, likes whisky, lives on sandwiches, is permanently tall, dark and handsome. He is perhaps interested to see how much punishment he can take or how much excitement he can cram into twenty-four hours, but he is principally a moralist whose aims are the regeneration of young women and the reform of the police.

> 'All right,' I went on heavily, 'will you take her away? Somewhere far off from here where they can handle her type, where they will keep guns and knives and fancy drinks away from her? Hell, she might even get herself cured, you know. It's been done.' (*The Big Sleep*.)
>
> 'I said (to the detectives) "Until you guys own your own souls you don't own mine. Until you guys can be trusted every time and always,

> in all times and conditions, to seek the truth out and find it and let the chips fall where they may – until that time comes I have a right to listen to my conscience, and protect my client the best way I can."'
>
> (*The High Window*)

Although the core of Mr. Chandler's novels is romantic and erotic the detail is photographic in its realism. As well as a ballistics expert and an institutional psychiatrist, the writer of crime stories must be something of a fashion expert and interior decorator. I like best that description of the Waste Land which always crops up in these books. 'Bunker Hill is old town, lost town, shabby town, crook town,' etc.

Let us say that for the eternal adolescent who likes a warm and vivid underworld served up with intelligent comment and accurate make-believe, with torture, rape and murder controlled by wit, decency and good taste, neither nauseating nor grotesque, Mr. Chandler hits exactly the spot.

There is also a lyrical vein which comes out in the love interest, in the careful descriptions of Californian landscape and *louche* urban backdrops.

Structurally, Chandler was honest, intelligent, modest, confident that he could do one thing well and aware that that was not enough; like Dashiell Hammett he saw that the 'private eye' (the perfect Bogart role) incarnated this rootless individualism of modern man, at war with criminals yet distrusted by authority.

On Englishmen Who Write American

(1949)

Let us go back for about thirty years. Imagine trying to deliver a lecture in 1918 on the influence of American literature on Kipling, Hardy, Shaw, Yeats, Conrad, Bennett, Galsworthy or George Moore. It would be a very short lecture. And now to go back twenty years, let us picture the lecture being given about 1928 – the influence of American literature on Forster and Eliot, Joyce, Lawrence, Huxley, Virginia Woolf, Lytton Strachey, Wyndham Lewis and the Sitwells – it would be a very much longer lecture, but on the whole the fort is still being held. Lawrence has written a book on American literature, and Virginia Woolf (in 1925) an essay on American fiction in praise of Sinclair Lewis, Sherwood Anderson, Ring Lardner and Willa Cather. But if we substitute the influence of French literature for American in both these imaginary lectures we see how much more significant the subject would become.

Now let us bring the lecture up to date and present it on the influence of America on Auden, Spender, Isherwood, Waugh, Graham Greene, Aldous Huxley, Elizabeth Bowen, T. S. Eliot and the Sitwells. Auden and Isherwood are American citizens, Huxley a permanent resident, Spender more often there than not, Waugh indebted to it for his most brilliant *tour de force*, Eliot considerably less expatriate than he used to be and the Sitwells welcomed visitors. Maugham, an active English writer since the Eighteen Nineties, was writing in *The Razor's Edge* almost as an American. In fact, the fort has collapsed and the difficulty now would be to name any major English writers who were not deeply influenced by America. Dylan Thomas with Edith Sitwell and one or two esoteric poets are the only ones I can think of.

In 1925 Virginia Woolf had not yet perceived what was happening. She saw with great clearness only the negative aspect – the cessation of English influence on America. 'The English tradition is formed upon a little country: its centre is an old house with many rooms each crammed with objects and crowded with people who know each other intimately, whose manners, thoughts and speech are ruled all the time, if unconsciously, by the spirit of the past. But in America there is baseball instead of society; instead of the old landscape which has moved men to emotion for endless summers and springs, a new land, its tin cans, its prairies, its cornfields, flung disorderly about like a mosaic of incongruous pieces waiting order at the artist's hands; while the people are equally diversified into fragments of many nationalities.' But it is the old house with many rooms which is going to fall. The tin cans are on their way over.

If we glance at the writers of before 1914, at Hardy, Kipling, Conrad, Galsworthy, Bennett, Wells and so on, we see that they have in common a certain traditional *gravitas*, a dignity and sense of the high seriousness of life. This noble and tragic feeling, in which stoicism, patriotism and a sense of public duty were blended with a respect for art, formed the climate of these British writers at the height of their influence. They inevitably reflected the material greatness of the country to which they belonged. This is the sceptre which has passed and if we can understand this we can see how America has really come to influence Britain.

Our British climate was out of date, our Roman *gravitas* was not enough for a world which was becoming obsessed with the problem of despair. And with our senatorial writers went out the senatorial style. The young veterans of the 1914 war found it pompous, and besides, life was much worse than that. Hemingway and Faulkner, Dos Passos and Cummings, brought something new to the language. Something vivid, fresh, cynical and masculine. *The Sun Also Rises* and *A Farewell to Arms* were enormously surprising to those who read them as they came out.

Everything was much worse than one had been told, but the knowledge, expressed in this new contemporary idiom, brought a kind of liberation. The pessimism, the gravity, the doubt, the stoicism and humanism of the giants of the first quarter of a century were somehow bolstered up by Christianity, even in the most unchristian of these writers, and they were so respectable and so successful besides; what could they know of the utter futility and absurdity and misery of life which seemed to us almost an American discovery? Virginia Woolf and E. M. Forster appeared to glimpse it and then to withdraw into their Bloomsbury fastness of private virtue and personal relations, into the pleasantest private sitting room of the old English Heartbreak-Horseback family mansion, there to spin *Orlando* and *Abinger Harvest*. Eliot gave a lead in *The Waste Land*, but was soon set apart by his conversion; Huxley also could not long bear the spectacle.

Meanwhile, the American film and the American thriller infiltrated into our popular culture and the American film meant the gangster film. Between-war Europe was gangster crazy because the gangster represented the anarchic adolescent conception of liberty which civilization in time of peace has perforce to stifle, because the police-and-gangster relationship reflects the decay of society, and because the trapped gangster who aimlessly butchers friend and foe alike is a symbol of the cruelty and lack of meaning of life itself.

The healthy Anglo-Saxon nineteenth-century materialist humanism of 90 per cent of American culture may in short be said to have had no influence at all. When we do lose our writers altogether to America, it is to Greenwich Village, Fire Island or the Californian desert, not to the salons of Park Avenue or the drawing rooms of Beacon Hill. 'When necessity is associated with horror and freedom with boredom,' Auden opens *The Age of Anxiety*, 'then it looks good to the bar business.'

Gangsters and Prohibition, Violence and Drink and the consequent self-examination to which they lead, these formed undoubtedly the American contribution – and still do. On the whole, very few English writers have been actively influenced by the style of Hemingway or Dos Passos or Faulkner, though one can detect an immense amount of Hemingway in English journalism, but the climate and subject-matter of these writers have made a deep impression.

And American humour has had an even more devastating influence than American despair, probably because it is, through its sense of the absurd, so close to despair. James Thurber, Charles Addams, Dorothy Parker or Peter Arno work with a savagery which reduces the mild Georgian breed of English humorist to silence rather than to emulation.

One would like to see, since the war, a reassertion of an English supremacy, a style, an energy, a sense of values, but I do not think we are any nearer to it. In France the bracing and pessimistic existentialist philosophy supplies a perfect ideological background to American fiction. Faulkner, Caldwell and Steinbeck are household words, Sartre is a kind of Franco-American figure; the American novel, supreme expression of the American attitude to life, moves instantly into the fabric of the French philosophical anecdotal essay which is the expression of their outlook, like an ostrich egg descending the gullet of a python. The German occupation made the French 'mad' in the American sense and brought them nearer to the American 'madness' than to the British good-tempered fortitude.

I have just read two books which have a bearing on this point: one is *The Naked and the Dead*, a truly formidable experiment in the American *gravitas* which in this country met with an idiotic campaign launched by the *Sunday Times*, London, for repression. Now this book has the great fault of trying to paint a fresco in which every face carries, as it were, its whole life-story plain for the reader, instead of concentrating on the central composition and sketching in the others – but what an astonishing performance for a young man of twenty-five and what a triumph for an attitude to life which places such enormous emphasis on the drabbest detail and the humblest individual, which struggles to adjust the balance between the cruelty and futility of war and its passionate and absorbing interest! Cut by about a third it could have been a great book; no one here has done anything like it.

The other book is Paul Bowles' first novel, *The Sheltering Sky*. Here we are very nearly back at Hemingway's *The Sun Also Rises* (which is where we came in): the meanderings of a pair of hard-drinking leisured Americans and a nymphomaniac wife over an existentialist Africa. (A sheik corresponds to the young bull-fighter.) But what a change! The characters in the Hemingway story are adults viewed by an adolescent; Bowles' characters talk of their adolescence; but in the courage and intelligence of their despair they are fully grown up. They carry the isolation and loneliness of human beings, even those whose ties are closest, a stage further than any American writer hitherto; it is that rare thing, a first novel which gets better and better as it goes on and whose finest effects of writing seem always reserved for the next page.

If we compare the adventures of Brett and Jake with those of Kit and Port we see how enormously the expatriate theme has, in the last twenty years, increased in scope and horror. The last mystery still remains man, but we seem to know a little more about that part of man in which the mystery resides, to know better how to look.

To present these researches in the guise of fiction and in a language slightly ahead of its time seems to be the achievement of American literature, even as it points out where England, perhaps too sharply divided into aristocracy and common man, each class smugly self-supporting, has fallen behind.

Passion, pride, loneliness, anger and a preoccupation with the condition of man are the artistic virtues which are least encouraged in that 'old house with many rooms, each crammed with objects and crowded with people who know each other intimately', and now converted by the all-embracing state into twice as many flats – whose occupants practise what the editor of the *Observer*, writing of our essayists, proudly calls 'that decent mid-browed tolerance and gentle gusto which the narrow and severe English intellectuals despise as trivial and the American craver of toughness rejects as too sickly.'

The Modern Movement (1965)

The Modern Movement began as a revolt against the bourgeois in France, the Victorians in England, the puritanism and materialism of America. The modern spirit was a combination of certain intellectual qualities inherited from the Enlightenment: lucidity, irony, scepticism, intellectual curiosity, combined with the passionate intensity and enhanced sensibility of the Romantics, their rebellion and sense of technical experiment, their awareness of living in a tragic age. The crucial generation, the generation which reconciled these opposites, was that of Baudelaire, Flaubert, and Dostoievsky (born in 1821), of Whitman, Melville and Ruskin (b. 1819), of Edmond de Goncourt and Matthew Arnold (1822), to which one might add Renan (1823), Turgenev (1818), and Courbet (1819), to complete the picture. All these artists, we feel, have something which reaches out to our own age although so much of them belongs to the past, all are difficult to pin down, to analyse, to put into categories, because of the duality in their own natures resulting from their inheritance of critical intelligence and exploring sensibility.

One sees this inheritance stemming from Voltaire and d'Holbach on the one side, Rousseau and Diderot on the other, with Stendhal and Constant, Chateaubriand and Chénier widening the breach – (Daudet called Flaubert '*le confluent de Chateaubriand avec Balzac*') – but in this welter of precursors one cannot at any time point and say: 'This is the Modern Movement.' Flaubert died in 1880, the year in which Apollinaire was born, only a year or two before Pound, Picasso, and E. M. Forster saw the light and six years after Somerset Maugham. 1880 seems to me the point at which the Modern Movement can be diagnosed as an event which is still modern to us, more modern than many of us, not something put away in the moth-balls of history. So I have taken it as a point of departure though both Baudelaire and Flaubert reach into it through the power of their posthumous works, the Letters which, in Flaubert's case, constituted the bible of Art for Art's Sake, his explosive anti-bourgeois satire, *Bouvard et Pécuchet* (1881), and Baudelaire's two devastating journals which were not published till 1887.

Flaubert and Baudelaire: our two fallen fathers, ruined, destroyed, tragic yet each a beacon light glowing for posterity, Baudelaire's fitfully from his mother's home at Honfleur, Flaubert's unbrokenly from his house at Croisset, illuminating the two banks of the Seine, the water-way to Paris, Trouville, Deauville, Honfleur, Rouen. . . . (Flaubert's grandmother's family was called Cambremer!) The Misses Colliers whom he adored on the beach, his '*fantômes de Trouville*', were the original '*jeunes filles en fleurs*' though, like Baudelaire, he preferred exotic women.

Born in the same year, with six letters of their names in common, achieving fame within a year (1856–7) with two masterpieces, *Madame Bovary* and *Les Fleurs du Mal*, both of which were prosecuted, Flaubert with a mother who would never let go of him, Baudelaire with a mother of whom he would never let go ('You have no right to re-marry with a son like me'), they would seem to entangle and yet they probably met only once or twice at Madame Sabatier's.

After the novelist had praised *Les Fleurs du Mal* – '*Ah, vous comprenez l'embêtement de l'existence, vous! Vous pouvez vous vanter de cela sans orgueil*' – Baudelaire invited Flaubert to his mother's at Honfleur, but nothing came of it.

In 1858 the Goncourts coined the word 'Modernity'* while Gautier, to whom *Les Fleurs du Mal* was dedicated and who also adored Flaubert, '*un grand génie, tous ses livres des chefs d'œuvre*', contributed out of his lifetime of glorious hackery the celebrated phrase which

* But Littré cites Gautier for the word a few years later.

belongs to the Movement, '*Toute ma valeur . . . c'est que je suis un homme pour qui le monde visible existe.*'

Although Flaubert influenced many writers of the golden age of the Modern Movement, particularly Conrad (who began *Nostromo* on the end papers of his *Education sentimentale*), Joyce and Pound, he was accepted only with reservations by Proust and Valéry and has not exercised the magic of Baudelaire on succeeding generations. There is a starkness about the poet's intelligence as in the phrase he used to his mother to describe his love affair with the half-caste Jeanne Duvall:

'*Cela a duré assez longtemps mais enfin c'est fini*',

which might have been his comment on his own life. After being for many years the private literary property of Arthur Symons he has emerged to be reinterpreted by Sartre and magnificently translated by Robert Lowell.

> Only when we drink poison are we well –
> We want, this fire so burns our brain tissue,
> To drown in the abyss – heaven or hell,
> Who cares? Through the unknown, we'll find the *new*.

The Seventies were the decade of Verlaine and Zola, of the beginnings of Henry James and Tolstoy, of Meredith and Swinburne, of Poe's influence and of Rimbaud's fugue with Verlaine. A generation of truly modern writers emerges, all highly sophisticated, and all owing something to Flaubert and Baudelaire – James (b. 1843), Mallarmé (1842), Villiers de l'Isle-Adam (1838), Verlaine (1844), Huysmans (1848), and the mysterious Lautréamont (1846).

Villiers's talent petered out; he talked and drank it away, but his gifts were prodigious. 'Everything that's mine I owe to him' (Maeterlinck). Claudel, writing to Gide, recalls how in his young days he used to see Verlaine and Villiers 'with want in their eyes, wearing the remains of their talent like a moth-eaten old fur-piece round their necks'. Rimbaud aside, Mallarmé and Huysmans almost created the modern sensibility between them, while both Yeats and Valéry attended on the schoolmaster-poet who had discovered that the only universe he could bear to inhabit must proceed from his own head. Writing to Debussy about his setting of *L'Après-midi d'un Faune* Mallarmé said: 'Your illustration conforms exactly to my text except that it goes even further *dans la nostalgie et la lumière, avec finesse, avec malaise, avec richesse.*' Is not this what we mean by modern sensibility? It could never have been written before.

With the generation of Debussy (b. 1862), Yeats (1865), Gide (1869), Proust and Valéry (1871), Jarry (1873), we come within living memory and it is a short step to the generation of the 1880s, to Eliot, Pound, Lawrence and Joyce, to Virginia Woolf and Edith Sitwell and Marianne Moore, and from them to Hemingway, Cummings, Faulkner, Malraux, Huxley, Graves, and so to Auden and our own day. The French fathered the Modern Movement, which slowly moved beyond the Channel and then across the Irish Sea until the Americans finally took it over, bringing to it their own demonic energy, extremism and taste for the colossal.

As we look back across the drifting formlessness of contemporary literature, we see that the Movement had a shape – and that the peak period was from about 1910 to 1925, a period of creativity which included the Eliot of *Prufrock*, *The Waste Land* and *The Hollow Men*, the Pound of the lyrics and early cantos, the later Yeats, the heyday of Virginia Woolf and Lytton Strachey, the Joyce of *The Portrait*, *Ulysses* and the first *Anna Livia*, the poetry of Apollinaire and Valéry, the novel of Proust, the emergence of Hemingway, Cummings, Lewis, Wallace Stevens, W. C. Williams, Forster's *Passage to India*, Fitzgerald's *The Great Gatsby*, the preaching of Lawrence, the giggle of Firbank, the candour of Gide. It was also the great age of Cubism, and the beginnings of Surrealism, of Ravel and Stravinsky and Cocteau and the Russian Ballet. The Great War cut across the Movement, deflecting it but unable to stem its vitality. The late Twenties show a falling off but the angry Thirties introduce the political themes which sent many writers back to realism. At the end of the Thirties works like *Finnegans Wake* or Gide's *Journal* or *Between the Acts* resounds like farewells and epitaphs. Yeats (b. 1865), Joyce, Virginia Woolf (both b. 1882) are gone within six months of each other and everything the Movement stood for is dubbed 'degenerate art' – or converted to propaganda. The Titans depart, the theses begin.

As all objectives were gained and the complacent hypocrisy of the nineteenth century punctured, its materialism exposed, the Movement ground to a halt; technical innovations were by-passed, originality incorporated into the norm, until rebellion grew meaningless, though it may yet persist in authoritarian countries or where censorship and intolerance dominate as with unrevised attitudes to drug-addiction or homosexuality (Burroughs and the Beats) – and gone too the corresponding movements in the Arts – Post-Impressionism, Fauvism, Cubism, Surrealism, Abstract Expressionism – with their ramifications in many countries. It has nevertheless dominated the life-time of the over-forties, some of whom have never recovered from their youthful intoxication, and its survivors remain our grand old men.

~

In preparing this list I have tried to choose books with outstanding originality and richness of texture and with the spark of rebellion alight, books which aspire to be works of art. Realism is not enough. There is nothing specifically modern about realism and too often it goes with undigested documentary and unimaginative technique. Zola may be an exception but his full impact was made before the period. The other objections, however, apply to Dreiser, Wells, Bennett, Galsworthy, Lewis, Dos Passos, Farrell and many chain novels about a family. For similar reasons traditionalists are excluded and this means many Catholic writers. If we apply the awareness of Rimbaud, Baudelaire, Flaubert as a touchstone we must exclude as traditionalist not only Chesterton, Belloc, Kipling, Hardy (as a novelist) but Housman, De la Mare, even Robert Frost (Georgian-Wordsworthian-New England) and most of the poetry of Robert Graves. This is an important point since novelists, on the whole, are not avant-garde and depend solidly on tradition, even when their outlook is affected by the Modern Movement (David Garnett, Osbert Sitwell, Elizabeth Bowen, Anthony Powell, Carson McCullers). The new avant-garde novel or anti-novel (Beckett, Butor, Robbe-Grillet) falls just outside my date-line.

But awareness is not in itself sufficient. Arthur Symons, for example, was steeped in the Modern Movement, haunted by Baudelaire, the interpreter of symbolism for Yeats and Eliot and a prolific poet in his own right but he simply was not good enough. Genius was lacking, scholarship hazy, taste and talent spread too thin. Aldington was such another. Wilde imitated Flaubert in *Salomé* and Huysmans in *Dorian Gray* but his true gift (apart from conversation) lay in traditional Congrevian comedy. Synge, however, soaked like Wilde and Symons in the Symbolists, produced a revolutionary masterpiece. (This is nearly true of *The Ballad of Reading Gaol* which mounts a streamlined offensive on capital punishment and prison conditions but in the most hackneyed Ancient Mariner stanza, complete with archaisms.) It would be to fall into just the fault which we deplore in realism to include certain books because they are the first to defend abortion or explain relativity.

Furthermore, I have limited my list to French, English and American literature because, without knowing German or Russian, I cannot absolutely judge a book from a translation, however perfect, and because the dates at which translations appear confuse the time-scale. This means the exclusion of Tolstoy, Dostoievsky, Turgenev and Tchekov, of *Oblomov* and Bunin's *Gentleman from San Francisco*, of Rilke, Mann (alas for *Death in Venice*), of Kafka, Musil, Kavafy, Ungaretti and Sveyo, of Lorca and Pasternak; to include these writers would also enormously lengthen the list and I can only say that one hundred books is enough and that the three literatures I have chosen have always been in close communication.

I have also excluded translations except Waley's *Translations from the Chinese* which can surely be judged as an original contribution to our poetry, and Koestler's *Darkness at Noon* as it was first published in this country. I have assumed that we can all read French in the original but have also given the most recent translations of all French books mentioned.

Many good, even great books are not key books; they come too late in the day when the author is already well known and has made his mark on the Movement or they repeat an early success or explore a backwater. This problem is extremely difficult with Henry James or George Moore, for example, whose brightest novel, *Esther Waters*, is also one of his most derivative. Conrad poses a similar problem. And there are books which are marred by auto-intoxicated rhetoric like those of Thomas Wolfe (a plaster colossus) and the monologrolling of Henry Miller. Some 'key' writers do not, in my opinion, produce a key book. Verlaine is one of these unless we accept *Sagesse* (1881). Music is not enough either. This also applies to Laforgue whose poems, I feel, despite their influence on Eliot, are really very slender and whose *Moralités légendaires* are forced and whimsical. He died too young and so did Dowson whom I must fail to include for similar reasons.

The worst headache has been over writers whom I think ought to be in but whom I do not enjoy enough to feel prepared to take away with me into solitary confinement. Hypocrisy would certainly be found out so I hereby declare these blind spots: Claudel, Max Jacob, Saint-John Perse, Roussel (whose mechanistic anti-humanism is now coming into vogue), Faulkner (though I have chosen his easiest book), Éluard, whose poetry never seems to me to come to the boil (except in one or two war-time lyrics), Gertrude Stein, since I cannot stomach the torrent of her automatic writing nor the greedy show-biz of the autobiographies – and well-camouflaged anti-modernists like Max Beerbohm and the Baron Corvo.

The list is literary and one-culture, and must exclude scientific, historical and philosophical works because of difficulties of evaluation. The very thought of placing Bergson, G. E. Moore, Bradley, William James, Frazer, Freud, Spengler, Pareto, Bertrand Russell, Santayana, Wittgenstein and A. J. Ayer makes the anthologist shudder. Where is the frontier between science and literature? There is no space to indulge one's eccentricity. Works of reference are also excluded (Fowler), together with theories of literary criticism (Richards, Empson), books on art and by artists, anthologies and almost all criticism and biography. I have admitted three books of criticism: Wilson's *Axel's Castle*, Eliot's *Selected Essays*, and James's *Prefaces*. The only biography is *Eminent Victorians* – the only autobiographies are Gide's and Robert Graves's. (Henry Adams does not write well enough.) Most autobiographies fail as works of art through ancestor-worship or the inclusion of secondary material.

The last part of my list proved more treacherous than the beginning. While I feel 1880–1950 is right, the Forties are still painfully close. I made my selection here from some sixty books, trying to weigh *Between the Acts* beside *New Year Letter*, *Lord Weary's Castle* against *Under the Volcano*. When in doubt prefer genius, but how to be sure of it? '"*Mon Dieu! mon Dieu!*" *soupira des Esseintes* "*qu'il existe donc peu de livres qu'on puisse relire.*"' In a period where literary taste is changing so rapidly much may already appear incomprehensible. One seems to be sticking paper flags into a dissolving sand-castle, while in full erosion oneself. Try as we would to be objective, any such list (exhibition of compulsive pedantry or debt of gratitude?) is personal as a cardiogram. It may well prove the last unsponsored by a faculty.

~

A word on the numbering. Chain novels are treated as one (example: Proust). Very scarce but significant slim volumes are mentioned separately but numbered by the book of collected poems in which they first appeared. Thus Eliot's *Prufrock* and *The Waste Land* (30), count as one book, *Poems 1909–25*. These are the only liberties I have taken. For every book that I should like to put in, there is one that will have to come out. That, in a selection bridging seventy years, is where the squeeze is felt.

A List of One Hundred Key Books of The Modern Movement in England, France and America

THE HEROIC ERA 1880–1900

1 HENRY JAMES *Portrait of a Lady* (1881)

2 GUSTAVE FLAUBERT *Bouvard et Pécuchet* (1881, posthumous)

3 VILLIERS DE L'ISLE-ADAM *Contes Cruels* (1883)

4 JORIS KARL HUYSMANS *À Rebours* (1884)

5 CHARLES BAUDELAIRE *Oeuvres Posthumes* (1887)

6 ARTHUR RIMBAUD *Les Illuminations* (1886)

7 STÉPHANE MALLARMÉ *Poésies* (1887)

8 GUY DE MAUPASSANT *Bel-Ami* (1885)

9 EDMOND AND JULES DE GONCOURT *Journal* (published 1887–96)

10 JORIS KARL HUYSMANS *Là-Bas* (1891)

11 ALFRED JARRY *Ubu Roi* (1896)

12 HENRY JAMES *The Awkward Age* (1899)

THE PAX BRITANNICA

13 ANDRÉ GIDE *L'Immoraliste* (1902)

14 JOSEPH CONRAD *Youth* (1902)

15 JOSEPH CONRAD *The Secret Agent* (1907)

16 HENRY JAMES *The Ambassadors* (1903)

17 GEORGE MOORE *Memoirs of My Dead Life* (1906)

18 J. M. SYNGE *The Playboy of the Western World* (1907)

19 E. M. FORSTER *The Longest Journey* (1907)

20 NORMAN DOUGLAS *Siren Land* (1911)

21 D. H. LAWRENCE *Sons and Lovers* (1913)

22 GUILLAUME APOLLINAIRE *Alcools* (1913)

23 MARCEL PROUST *Du Côté de Chez Swann* (1913)

24 W. B. YEATS *Responsibilities* (1914)

1914–1918

25 THOMAS HARDY *Satires of Circumstance* (1914)

26 JAMES JOYCE *Portrait of the Artist as a Young Man* (1916)

27 FORD MADOX FORD *The Good Soldier* (1915)

28 NORMAN DOUGLAS *South Wind* (1917)

29 PERCY WYNDHAM LEWIS *Tarr* (1918)

30 T. S. ELIOT *Prufrock and Other Observations* (1917)
The Waste Land (1922)

31 PAUL VALÉRY *La Jeune Parque* (1917)
Charmes (1922)

32 GUILLAUME APPOLLINAIRE *Calligrammes* (1918)

33 GERARD MANLEY HOPKINS *Poems* (1918)

34 ARTHUR WALEY *One Hundred and Seventy Chinese Poems* (1918)

35 EZRA POUND *Lustra* (1916)
Hugh Selwyn Mauberley (1920)

36 WILFRED OWEN *Poems* (1920)

37 LYTTON STRACHEY *Eminent Victorians* (1918)

THE TWENTIES

38 D. H. LAWRENCE *Sea and Sardinia* (1921)

39 ALDOUS HUXLEY *Crome Yellow* (1921)

40 KATHERINE MANSFIELD *The Garden Party* (1922)

41 W. B. YEATS *Later Poems* (1922)

42 JAMES JOYCE *Ulysses* (1922)

43 RAYMOND RADIGUET *Le Diable au Corps* (1923)

44 RONALD FIRBANK *The Flower Beneath the Foot* (1923)

45 E. M. FORSTER *A Passage to India* (1924)

46 WALLACE STEVENS *Harmonium* (1923)

47 E. E. CUMMINGS *Tulips and Chimneys* (1923)
Is 5 (1926)

48 SCOTT FITZGERALD *The Great Gatsby* (1925)

49 ERNEST HEMINGWAY *In Our Time* (1924)

50 ERNEST HEMINGWAY *The Sun Also Rises* (1926)

51 ANDRÉ GIDE *Si le Grain ne Meurt* (1926)

52 WILLIAM PLOMER *Turbott Wolfe* (1926)

53 SOMERSET MAUGHAM *The Casuarina Tree* (1926)

54 VIRGINIA WOOLF *To the Lighthouse* (1927)

55 ANDRÉ BRETON *Nadja* (1928)

56 W. B. YEATS *The Tower* (1928)
The Winding Stair (1929)

57 D. H. LAWRENCE *Lady Chatterley's Lover* (1928)

58 EVELYN WAUGH *Decline and Fall* (1928)

59 HENRY GREEN *Living* (1929)

60 ERNEST HEMINGWAY *A Farewell to Arms* (1929)

61 ROBERT GRAVES *Goodbye to All That* (1929)

62 JEAN COCTEAU *Les Enfants Terribles* (1929)

63 IVY COMPTON-BURNETT *Brothers and Sisters* (1929)

64 HART CRANE *The Bridge* (1930)

65 T. S. ELIOT *Ash Wednesday* (1929)

66 EZRA POUND *Thirty Cantos* (1930)

67 EDITH SITWELL *Collected Poems* (1930)

THE THIRTIES

68 ANTOINE DE SAINT-EXUPÉRY *Vol de Nuit* (1931)

69 WILLIAM FAULKNER *Sanctuary* (1931)

70 VIRGINIA WOOLF *The Waves* (1931)

71 EDMUND WILSON *Axel's Castle* (1931)

72 T. S. ELIOT *Selected Essays* (1932)

73 W. H. AUDEN *The Orators* (1932)

74 LOUIS-FERDINAND CÉLINE *Voyage au Bout de la Nuit* (1932)

75 ALDOUS HUXLEY *Brave New World* (1932)

76 NATHANAEL WEST *Miss Lonelyhearts* (1933)

77 ANDRÉ MALRAUX *La Condition Humaine* (1933)

78 DYLAN THOMAS *Eighteen Poems* (1934)
Twenty-Five Poems (1936)

79 SCOTT FITZGERALD *Tender is the Night* (1934)

80 HENRY JAMES *The Art of the Novel* (1934)

81 MARIANNE MOORE *Selected Poems* (1935)

82 HENRI DE MONTHERLANT *Les Jeunes Filles* (1936–9)

83 HENRI MICHAUX *Voyage en Grande Garabagne* (1936)
Au Pays de la Magie (1941)

84 JEAN-PAUL SARTRE *La Nausée* (1938)

85 LOUIS MACNEICE *Autumn Journal* (1939)

86 CHRISTOPHER ISHERWOOD *Goodbye to Berlin* (1939)

87 JAMES JOYCE *Finnegans Wake* (1939)

88 GRAHAM GREENE *The Power and the Glory* (1940)

THE FORTIES

89 ARTHUR KOESTLER *Darkness at Noon* (1940)

90 W. H. AUDEN *Another Time* (1940)

91 STEPHEN SPENDER *Ruins and Visions* (1942)

92 T. S. ELIOT *Four Quartets* (1943–4)

93 GEORGE ORWELL *Animal Farm* (1945)

94 ALBERT CAMUS *L'Étranger* (1941)

95 ALBERT CAMUS *La Peste* (1947)

96 DYLAN THOMAS *Deaths and Entrances* (1946)

97 JOHN BETJEMAN *Selected Poems* (1948)

98 EZRA POUND *The Pisan Cantos* (1948)

99 GEORGE ORWELL *Nineteen Eighty-four* (1949)

100 WILLIAM CARLOS WILLIAMS *Paterson* (1946–51)

The Heroic Era 1880–1900

The period of French domination, when half a dozen masterpieces established a new sensibility (already apparent in some of Baudelaire's poems and many of his poems in prose). Some of these seminal works were first published in the Eighties and disseminated by Verlaine's *Les Poètes maudits* (1884) or Arthur Symon's *Symbolist Movement in Literature* (1899) or Moore's *Confessions of a Young Man* (1888): Swinburne, Meredith, Melville, Whitman are among Anglo-Saxon precursors. I consider the Nineties a dead end, essentially the English version of Symbolism, for, if we subtract the *fin de siècle* element, there is very little left. Mark Twain's *Huckleberry Finn* (1884) I think is over-praised, too involved and sentimental despite its prophetic use of American vernacular – a false dawn – and, therefore, although it has won the admiration of Eliot, Hemingway and Trilling, excluded.

~

The intellectual climate of the period can best be savoured in Huysmans's account of Des Esseintes's library in *À Rebours* (1884), particularly in its modern section which is uncannily prescient of our taste today. After citing Petronius, Apuleius, Villon, Pascal, he comes down heavily for Baudelaire. 'His admiration for that writer was boundless' and he gives a three-page analysis of the poet's '*insondable tristesse*', his disillusion and his style 'which above all others had the magical ability to pin down with a peculiar vitality of phrase the most fugitive and elusive psychological states, moments of morbid melancholy and exhaustion'; he particularly admired the *Mort des Amants* and the prose poem 'Anywhere out of this World', 'L'Ennemi' and his translation of Poe's 'Adventures of Arthur Gordon Pym'. He also admired Flaubert's *Tentation*, Barbey's *Diaboliques*, Goncourt's *Faustin*, Zola's *L'Assommoir*, and – among his contemporaries – Verlaine (particularly the poems 'Streets' or 'Dansons la Gigue' with its curious metre which was to be re-immortalized by Debussy), Tristan Corbière, eccentric author of *Les Amours jaunes* (1873), and above all Villiers and Mallarmé. He greatly appreciated the delicately supernatural tales of Villiers, the 'Intersigne' and 'Vera' which he thought a small masterpiece: '*Ici l'hallucination était empreinte d'une tendresse exquise*' (as in James's *Altar of the Dead*).

He praises four of the *Contes Cruels* for their ferocious wit and black humour, their savage denigration of the bourgeois epoch. He also enjoyed Charles Cros – but, beyond all, Mallarmé of whom, as with Baudelaire, he had had printed his own selection on special papers – *L'Azur*, *Hérodiade*, *Les Fenêtres*, *L'Après-midi d'un Faune*, each, of course, in highly significant bindings. No wonder his creator Huysmans was told in a review by Barbey that he must decide between the muzzle of a revolver and the foot of the cross! Ten years later, he had chosen – as several later revolutionaries in the Movement were to choose.

One can only wish that Des Esseintes had discovered Rimbaud and had also included an English section. He must, given the anglophilia which got him as far as the Taverne Anglaise in the Rue d'Amsterdam, have read Dickens as well as Poe – why not *Modern Love*, or Pater's *Renaissance*? One detects a reciprocal blankness between James and Huysmans. Yet the Eighties and Nineties are overshadowed by James whose work culminates at the end of the century in the brilliant series of novels and stories – the *Spoils of Poynton* and *What Maisie Knew*, *The Awkward Age* and *The Sacred Fount* and the series of tales dealing with the frustrations of the literary life, *Terminations, Embarrassments*, *The Two Magics*. To include more than one of these would capsize this little craft before it had left port. Where James, whose work moreover does not completely belong to the Movement, is concerned, I consider I have been able to make but a token selection.

The Pax Britannica

The years 1900–14 witnessed a ferment in the arts. Paris led, especially in painting (Cubism from about 1907), London, however, became the capital of prose and remained so till about 1920. French writers grew interested in fantasy, in cosmopolitan sophistication (Larbaud's *Barnabooth*, Gide's *Lafcadio*); their symbol was the amorous millionaire adventurer, cynical and melancholy in his wagon-lit. Gide founded the *Nouvelle Revue Française*, Rémy de Gourmont edited the *Mercure de France*. Proust retired from the world to prepare his great work. The Irish movement emerged (Moore, Synge), culminating in Yeats's 'Easter 1916'. The deaths (1909) of Meredith and Swinburne left James, Conrad and Hardy supreme by 1910, and the star of Bloomsbury rising. Official religion: sceptical realism (Shaw, Wells, Bennett); official opposition: romantic Catholicism (Chesterton, Belloc).

The trial of Oscar Wilde (1895) had left a blight on English literature from which Paris was still immune. The close connection, even the dependence of the men of the Nineties on Paris came to a stop. The Edwardian writers are not closely associated with French painters nor even with English ones. There was nothing to correspond with the Picasso/Apollinaire – Jarry/Bonnard Douanier Rousseau axis or with a literary-*cum*-artistic salon like Gertrude Stein's. It is arguable that writers have more to say if they do not derive too much satisfaction from music and painting but nevertheless on literary London – except for the Café Royal – a curtain of provincialism solemnly descends.

1914–18

The war dislocated the Modern Movement but did not destroy it. Some lost their faith in humanity, many were killed; nearly all had to cease writing. War poetry boomed while the spirit of revolt against the older generations grew more ominous (Sassoon, 1918, *Counter-Attack*). Of the three major war-poets Sassoon was the most conventional, depending on epigrams with a sting in the tail, Isaac Rosenberg (a private soldier from the East End) was the most original but the most unskilled in the handling of verse and only Wilfred Owen combined technical resource with profound feeling. Many war experiences were digested later while some of the best writing remained, in spirit anyhow, pre-war and was carried on in isolated back-waters (Joyce in Trieste and Zürich, Firbank in Oxford, Lawrence in Cornwall, Strachey and other pacifists on farms). The war, self-destruction of a golden civilization, was for most writers an intense and crippling disillusion, an interval for killing, dying, hating and lying. Many fell silent by the time they had apprehended the universal slaughter house to which they had been led.

The Twenties

The essential quality of the Twenties was release from strain, enthusiasm for experiment, hope for the future. It was the age of the Intellectual Mannerists: Douglas, Strachey, Pearsall Smith, Firbank, Van Vechten, Huxley, the Sitwells; of Cocteau, Morand, Fargue and Giraudoux; of brilliant women writers, Edith Sitwell, Virginia Woolf, Colette, Katherine Mansfield, Edith Wharton, Willa Cather and Gertrude Stein. Travel became a ruling passion. The first half of the decade was the more exuberant and 1922 has been described by R. P. Blackmur as an Annus Mirabilis. Demobilized American writers, fugitives from Prohibition and the Family Business, began to assert themselves as the centre shifted from London to Paris while Surrealism appeared with Breton's first *Manifesto* of 1924. The Café made way for the Night Club. In the last half of the decade the sense of liberation turned to increasing apprehension. The slump of 1929 was a time of suicides and conversions. War memoirs abounded, Wyndham Lewis wrote his early eulogy of Hitler (1930). The great frost of '29 drove the Expatriates home, shorn of their private incomes, restoring the Left Bank to Gide and Valéry.

It was a joy then to be alive. The Twenties had something of the Nineties about them in that there was still room for the *culte du moi*. Writers were not regimented, criticism was largely amateur, Eng. Lit. was something, in which Aldous Huxley had got a First, that went up as far as Chaucer. The afternoon train would land one in Paris on the spur of the moment and the cafés were crowded and living cheap. Each left-bank hotel harboured a memorable face – from Anderson to Wescott – and all were to be met with at Sylvia Beach's lending library. Germany was another adventure, and Italy or Spain. (One could live in Spain on ten shillings a day.) James was dead and Proust was dying but there were still great writers to be seen who were also fascinating – like Joyce and Lawrence – and young groups round the Sitwells or Gide or Breton or Strachey for whom everything seemed possible and all barriers down.

The Thirties

The disastrous decade. Infiltration of literature by destructive influences of Surrealism (sacrifice of critical standards to auto-intoxication) and politics (exhaustion of talent in lost causes like anti-Fascism, popular fronts, etc.). Increasing isolation and smugness of the non-political, increasing anger and controversy, frustration and anxiety culminating in war. Exceptions: some lonely figures liberated by the new fraternal feelings, some poets given new themes; expatriates, driven home by slump, develop social consciences. Nevertheless a good period to be young in, especially during the first years of hope with the world still keeping open for the traveller (Bali, Afghanistan, etc.). The modern impetus far from exhausted. One notices its nihilistic aspect flaring up in Céline, Henry Miller and in the spread of American gangster novels (Dashiell Hammett, Greene's *Brighton Rock*), and the revolutionary logic developing in Aragon, Éluard and early Spender, Day-Lewis and Auden: Cummings translates Aragon's banned political poem (*Front Rouge*). Spender collaborates with Éluard in poems of the Spanish war,

Malraux writes his novels of political action. Towards the end, Orwell and Koestler enter the scene. The aesthetic qualities and technical experiments typical of the Movement are confined to older writers, to Joyce and his contemporary Virginia Woolf (both 1881–1941) and to the group round *transition*. Auden is however by far the most naturally gifted poet since Eliot (who now concentrates on criticism and verse drama) and he writes with energetic facility in many forms. Dylan Thomas is the only successful Anglo-surrealist. Michaux and Queneau emerge in France as experimental writers and Sartre on the more conventional left wing. The decade, in America, of Frost and Faulkner, Stevens and Williams, with Cummings silting up. Pound is head-deep in polemics; Wyndham Lewis becomes a fascist; Joyce an icon; Yeats an angry old man. Gide and Valéry are no longer the gods they were in the Twenties. One might say that for the first time the new intake is not of the same quality as the generation of Lawrence (1885), and Eliot (1888), whom they will replace. There is a dearth of oxygen but far more constructive thinking came forth than in the Twenties, especially in New York and Paris, though fewer works of art. There is more here for the sociologist and the historian of the human spirit than for James's the 'lonely old artist man'.

The Forties

The Thirties ended in a blaze of nostalgia, with Joyce's *Finnegans Wake*, Gide's *Journal* covering fifty years, Breton's retrospective *Anthologie de l'Humour Noir*. Thus opened the frustrated Forties, five years of total war and five more of recrimination and exhaustion during which the Modern Movement unobtrusively expired. Surrealism gave way to Existentialism, the 'new criticism' flourished, Sartre edited Baudelaire's journals and Queneau recast *Bouvard et Pécuchet*. 'In my end is my beginning'; Queneau's *Exercices de Style* (1947) reduced the concept of literature to classified bathos. Breton, Bataille, Genet, Paulhan, Ponge and Michaux continued to experiment but Paris ceased to be the capital of the *avant garde*. The deaths of Yeats, Joyce, Virginia Woolf and Freud were followed by those of Valéry and Orwell, Dylan Thomas and Gide.

Why did the Movement peter out? Too many defectors in the Movement itself? Thus while Joyce, Gide, Valéry, Forster ('What I believe', 1939) and Cummings remained humanists of one kind or other to the end, too many seceded; some followed Huysmans into the religious fold (Eliot, Edith Sitwell, Waugh, Auden*), some became Fascists (Pound, Lewis), others Communists (Éluard, Aragon), others adopted an oriental religion (Huxley). Sartre went Marxist and quarrelled with Camus. Malraux became a politician – he who had introduced in *La Condition humaine* that literature of the condemned cell which was to produce such fine and characteristic work in the Forties – Hemingway's *For Whom the Bell Tolls*, Koestler's *Darkness at Noon*, Sartre's *Le Mur* and *Huis Clos*, Camus's *L'Étranger* and *La Peste* and Orwell's *Nineteen Eighty-four*. Perhaps the spirit of the Modern Movement persists today most strongly in the theatre (Artaud, Ionesco, Pinter), where there have been more conventions to overthrow. The recent publication of *Lolita*, *Lady Chatterley's Lover* and *Tropic of Cancer* has ended the battle with the censorship which began with the prosecutions of *Les Fleurs du Mal* and *Madame Bovary* more than a century ago. Genet's homosexual rhapsody, *Notre Dame des fleurs* (1948), carries the victory one stage further.

In 1961 I find the first epitaph – 'Robert Graves and the decay of Modernism' – as a title by D. J. Enright, while Spender has already been lecturing on them in the past tense (published as *The Struggle of the Moderns*, London, 1964) and the new poets from Larkin onwards are in arms against both the intellectualism of Eliot, and the emotionalism of Thomas. Professor Harry Levin, I am just informed, has delivered a Lecture on 'What *was* Modernism?'. Yet the twin features of the Movement, faith in the intellect as destroyer of pretences and illusions,

* 'We cannot in literature, any more than the rest of life, live in a perpetual state of revolution' – T. S. Eliot.

as man's true guide wherever it may lead, and the equally strong belief in the validity of the imagination, the enlargement of sensibility, the Côté Voltaire and the Côté Rousseau, or Stendhal and Chateaubriand, must surely continue to inspire a masterpiece, as in the days of Baudelaire, Rimbaud and Proust. For students who are growing up under new tyrannies and new orthodoxies such a list may prove more than a parlour game – a roll of honour; a prisoner's smuggled file; a home.

The Breakthrough in Modern Verse (1961)

When did modern poetry begin? And how? And what is it? These questions sound impossible to answer and so instead of replying to them, I should like to record some events which can be accurately dated and leave it to the reader to decide how far they are relevant.

One thing is certain, modern poetry exists; it has claimed new areas for its own, it has developed a new sensibility and enlarged our consciousness; there is something intelligent and energetic about it, an integrity, a depth of imagination which we recognise immediately and whose absence we are quick to detect.

~

The winter of 1907 was a cold one. One night the lecturer in French and Spanish at Wabash College, Crawfordsville, Indiana (he had taken a master's degree in Romance languages at the State University of Pennsylvania), went out late into a blizzard to post a letter. On the street he ran across a girl from a stranded burlesque show, penniless and hungry. He fed her and took her to his rooms, where she spent the night in his bed and he on the floor of his study. (We can believe this in 1907.)

When he left in the morning for his eight o'clock class, the two maiden landladies, the Misses Hall, went up to do the cleaning. They discovered his visitor and at once telephoned the President of the College and several trustees. The dismissed lecturer (he was then twenty-two) took a cattle-ship to Gibraltar and then walked through Spain and Southern France to Venice, where he published his first book of poems, *A Lume Spento*. Later in the same year he came to England, where he was to remain until 1921.

Ezra Pound had two very remarkable qualities: he was a poet and, despite his passion for the past, a deeply original one. He was also something rarer than a poet – a catalyst, an impresario, a person who both instinctively understood what the age was about to bring forth and who helped it to be born. We recognise this quality in Apollinaire, in Cocteau, in Diaghilev, in André Breton. Apollinaire also combined a backward-looking vein in his own poetry with a flair for discovering what was forward-looking in others; he was five years older than Pound and grew up at the centre of the modern movement instead of having to find his way there from the periphery.

Arrived in London in 1908, Pound produced two more books the next year, one of which was reviewed by Edward Thomas in *The English Review*, and he began to throw his weight about.* He formed a coterie of promising writers who lunched once a week to discuss poetry and very soon met Yeats, who was regarded as the outstanding poet of the 'nineties, a devotee of all that was aesthetic and occult: 'a great dim figure with its associations set in the past', Pound called him.

In these early books of Pound's the influences are from the 'nineties and the early Yeats, and Browning, especially the latter's method of introducing fully-drawn character studies by casual conversation ('That's my last Duchess') – and, of course, the formal rhyme-structures from the Provençal. Yeats was twenty years older than Pound and, for all his success, was becoming deeply dissatisfied with his work and his life, long sacrificed to an unhappy love-affair. There is no doubt that Pound's peculiar serum immediately began to take: 'This queer creature Ezra Pound, who has become really a great authority on the troubadours,' wrote Yeats to Sir William Rothenstein in December 1909. 'A headlong, rugged nature, and he is always hurting people's feelings, but he has, I think, some genius and goodwill.'

**Personae* (dedicated to 'Mary Moore of Trenton if she wants it') and *Exultations*. The *Review* was edited by Ford Madox Ford with assistance from Norman Douglas, Conrad and others.

~

1912 was an important year for Pound. He brought out his fifth book of poems, *Ripostes* (dedicated, incidentally, to William Carlos Williams), in which his authentic voice began to be heard. It is a tone of cool, relaxed dandyism, playing with the forms of the Greek and Latin epigram, yet capable of a deeper magic – as in 'Portrait d'une femme' ('Your mind and you are our Sargasso sea' or 'The Tomb at Akr Çaar', or his bleakly alliterative adaptation of the Anglo-Saxon 'The Seafarer'). At the end of the book Pound included the 'poetical works' of a new friend, the youthful T. E. Hulme.

> They are reprinted here for good fellowship; for good custom, a custom out of Tuscany and Provence; and thirdly, for convenience, seeing their smallness of bulk; and for good memory, seeing that they recall certain evenings and meetings of two years gone, dull enough at the time, but rather pleasant to look back upon.

This dates the poems between 1910 and 1912. Here is one of them [1908]:

> A touch of cold in the autumn night
> I walked abroad,
> And saw the ruddy moon lean over a hedge
> Like a red-faced farmer.
> I did not stop to speak, but nodded,
> And round about were the wistful stars
> with white faces like town children.

If that is not a modern poem – but we must hurry on. During the winter of 1912–13 Yeats was ill with a digestive disorder and sometimes unable to read. Pound came to read to him in the evenings, and even taught him to fence. (He also knew ju-jitsu and once threw Robert Frost over his back in a restaurant.) Wordsworth and Bridges were among the poets they read and discussed – at a later sojourn they read through the whole of Landor. Pound soon became indispensable and was taken on as Yeats's secretary. In the autumn of 1913 the pair settled down for the next three winters at Stone Cottage in Ashdown Forest. 'Ezra never shrinks from work, a learned companion and a pleasant one. . . . He is full of the Middle Ages and helps me to get back to the definite and concrete, away from modern abstractions; to talk over a poem with him is like getting you to put a sentence into dialect. All comes clear and "natural",' Yeats wrote to Lady Gregory.

It was then that they planned the selection of letters to Yeats from his father which Pound eventually edited (1917). Yeats passed on to Pound a prize for £50 which he received from *Poetry, Chicago* (editor, Harriet Monroe). I do not think it is far-fetched to see Pound's bias towards the 'definite and concrete' as influencing Yeats in the stupendous transformation, which bore fruit in his next book, *Responsibilities* (Cuala Press, 1914). It begins with the great prelude:

> . . . Pardon that for a barren passion's sake,
> Although I have come close on forty-nine
> I have no child. I have nothing but a book,
> Nothing but that to prove your blood and mine.

and ends with 'A coat' (first draft 1912):

> I made my song a coat
> Covered with embroideries
> Out of old mythologies
> From heel to throat;
> But the fools caught it,
> Wore it in the world's eyes
> As though they'd wrought it.
> So let them take it
> For there's more enterprise
> In walking naked.

'Yeats,' said Pound, 'is much finer *intime* than seen spasmodically in the midst of the whirl. We are both, I think, very contented in Sussex.' The main event was a visit to Wilfrid Blunt on his seventieth birthday, when Yeats made a speech and a group of poets, headed by Pound, presented the old poet-squire with a book each in a stone casket made by Gaudier-Brzeska. He regaled them with roast peacock 'in the pride of his eye'.* Pound's talent as an impresario led him naturally to editing and he was soon occupied with *Poetry, Chicago* (and Harriet Monroe), *The Egoist*, London (and Harriet Weaver), and Ford Madox Ford's *English Review*. He begins to mention the names of Lawrence, Lewis and Joyce, and by 1915 he is deeply involved in the successful transaction by which Yeats obtained for Joyce, then teaching in Trieste, a civil list grant of £75.

In 1914 he edited his first anthology, *Des Imagistes*, with poems by several well-to-be-known writers, Joyce, Aldington, H. D. He had also come to know Wyndham Lewis soon after his arrival and to be associated with him in *Blast* and also with Cubism and Gaudier-Brzeska about whom, in 1916, he wrote a book. *Blast* was a large, thick luscious magazine, the first number of which (1914) is rather disappointing. It held a dinner on the fifteenth of July. 'We were the first organised youth racket,' wrote Lewis afterwards.

In his *Gaudier*, Pound explains how his poems are written. He once saw several beautiful faces in the Paris Métro and, walking down the Rue Raynouard, 'found the equation, a pattern, little splotches of colour, like a non-representative painting'. He wrote a thirty-line poem and destroyed it as 'work of secondary intensity'. Six months later he made a poem half the length. A year later 'I made the following haiku-like sentence:

> The apparition of these faces in the crowd:
> Petals on a wet black bough.

I dare say it is meaningless.'

* January 18th, 1914. 'All the poets behaved well except poor X—.' The peacock was Yeats's suggestion and was followed by roast beef. A paper read by Yeats proclaimed, according to Pound, his new manner. The poets were Richard Aldington, F. S. Flint, F. Manning, John Masefield (absent), Sturge Moore, Victor Plarr and Yeats. Bridges, because of Blunt's political opinions, could not be invited, Belloc came down after lunch.

> 'We who are little given to respect,' declaimed Pound,
> 'Respect you, and having no better way to show it
> Bring you this stone to be some record of it.'

~

But his greatest discovery comes in a letter to Harriet Monroe of September 30th, 1914: 'I was jolly well right about Eliot. He has sent in the best poem I have yet had or seen from an American. PRAY GOD IT BE NOT A SINGLE AND UNIQUE SUCCESS. He is the only American I know of who has made what I call adequate preparation for writing. He has actually trained himself *and* modernized himself on his own.' The poem was 'The Love Song of J. Alfred Prufrock', which Harriet Monroe sat on warily till June 1915.

Pound's own programme was limited to three points which he had first published in 1913. He had dwelt on the necessity of distinct presentation of something concrete: on accuracy and economy of language – 'to use absolutely no word that does not contribute to the presentation' and, regarding rhythm, on the necessity of composing 'in the sequence of the musical phrase, not in the sequence of the metronome'. Eliot must have wholeheartedly accepted all three.

~

Thomas Stearns Eliot was born in Saint Louis in September 1888, and is three years younger than Pound. He comes of a distinguished New England family of Wessex origin and went up to Harvard in 1906. He spent a post-graduate year in Paris, 1910–11, and was in Germany with a travelling fellowship in the summer before the war. When the war broke out in 1914 he had moved to England, and was reading Greek philosophy at Merton College, Oxford, at the time he sent Pound his poems, for which Conrad Aiken had tried unsuccessfully to find a publisher.

As he dates them from 1909, these early poems of Eliot are really contemporaneous with the early Pound and with T. E. Hulme – but the year of his flowering is without question 1915, when 'The Love Song of J. Alfred Prufrock' at last appeared in *Poetry* (June). In July the second or war number of *Blast* contained the two 'Preludes' and 'Rhapsody on a

Windy Night', while 'Portrait of a Lady' was published in *Others* (U.S.A.) in September, and three more short poems in *Poetry* for October.

In November, Pound brought out his *Catholic Anthology* (catholic in taste, he meant), being 'determined to get Eliot between hard covers'. This is an astonishing book and certainly the first in the canon of modern poetry, containing, besides five poems by Eliot, a new poem by Yeats and poems by Carl Sandburg, William Carlos Williams, Maxwell Bodenheim and others. In 1914 Pound had married the daughter of Yeats's friend, Mrs. Shakespear. In 1915, Eliot too got married. This was also the year of Lawrence's *Rainbow* and Virginia Woolf's first novel, *The Voyage Out*.

In 1916 Eliot published four more poems in *Poetry* (including 'La Figlia che piange'), but his great year was 1917, when his first book, *Prufrock and Other Observations*, was published at a shilling by the Egoist Press, London, while his second, the anonymous *Ezra Pound, his Metric and Poetry*, came out in New York (November). 1915 had been the year of Pound's adaptations of Chinese poems, *Cathay*, and 1916 of his first volume of truly modern work – chiefly songs and epigrams – *Lustra*, a light-hearted narcissistic essay in linguistic deflation.

Dawn enters with little feet
Like a gilded Pavlova
And I am near my desire,
Nor has life in it aught better
Than this hour of clear coldness,
The hour of waking together.
[in a garret]

~

It will be seen that there is now an increasing acceleration, that the Pound-Eliot streams have become a river and that the whole movement, first of 'Imagists', then of 'Vorticists' (names chosen by Pound), like Cubism in France, was well under way by 1914, only to come up against the blind holocaust of the war. Hulme was killed, so was Gaudier-Brzeska; Lewis became a bombardier; Ford joined up; Joyce remained in Trieste and Zürich, although the 'Portrait of the Artist as a Young Man' continued to appear in *The Egoist*; Lawrence suffered persecution; neither Pound nor Yeats took any part in what the latter called the 'bloody frivolity' of the war. Eliot was trying to earn a living by journalism but eventually registered.

So this movement, in all its energy and subtlety, was maimed and permanently slowed down by the 'march of events'. These young men were denied the insouciant gaiety and freedom of experiment to which every new generation is entitled and also the opportunity of slow self-development through scholarly research. Yeats, however, found his voice in the Easter rebellion of 1916 and wrote his magnificent 'I have met them at close of day' in September of that year. His new-found realism dominated the next slim volumes, *The Wild Swans at Coole* and *Michael Robartes and the Dancer* (Cuala Press, 1917 and 1920). But Pound and Eliot by now were without a country, and it was to be ten years before these patriarchs of the Lost Generation finally adopted Erastian England and fascist Italy as their spiritual homes. Pound in England, with his shock of hair, red beard, ten-gallon hat and velvet jacket, striding about the streets with head thrown back and shouting out lines of his poetry, 'Damn it all! All this our South stinks peace' in Bellotti's, was, according to Lewis, always a fish out of water.

'Ezra started out in a time of peace and prosperity,' wrote Aldington, 'with everything in his favour, and muffed his chances of becoming literary dictator – to which he undoubtedly aspired – by his own conceit, folly and bad manners. Eliot started in the enormous confusion of war and post-war England, handicapped in every way. Yet by merit, tact, prudence and pertinacity, he succeeded in doing what no American has ever done – imposing his personality, taste and even many of his opinions on post-war England.'

~

These first books of our brief literary renaissance have a particular beauty. They come before the more self-conscious era of limited editions from costly private presses or the uniform assembly line of modern poets which we associate with Faber's. The *Catholic Anthology* (Elkin Mathews, 1915), with its Cubist cover, opens with Yeats's 'Scholars' ('Bald heads forgetful of their sins') and then goes straight into Prufrock:

> Let us go then, you and I
> When the evening is spread out against the sky
> Like a patient etherized upon a table;
> Let us go through certain half-deserted streets . . .

I can never read the opening of this marvellous poem without feeling that it is a piece of modern music, that I am sitting back in my seat at the first hearing of the Debussy Quartet – of which I am reminded by that sudden shatteringly discordant metaphor, 'like a patient etherized upon a table', in the third line. And as for the end –

> I have heard the mermaids singing, each to each,
> I do not think that they will sing to me.
> I have seen them riding seaward on the waves,
> Combing the white hair of the waves blown back
> When the wind blows the water white and black
> We have lingered in the chambers of the sea
> By seagirls wreathed with seaweed red and brown
> Till human voices wake us, and we drown.

– though we know it so well, the changes of mood – the flat beginning, the gathering crescendo with the harsh, astonishing vowel-sounds and rhymes, and the bold repetition of 'white', leading to the lovely dying cadence where 'red and brown' replaces the 'white and black' of the storm – never cease to intoxicate; like the three 'Preludes' and the 'Rhapsody', on the enormous thick blotting paper of *Blast*. How many realized that here was an urban lyricism, an absolutely original sensibility, something serenely new?

The winter evening settles down
with smell of steaks in passage ways
Six o'clock
The burnt out ends of smoky days . . .
The conscience of a blackened street
Impatient to assume the world.
I am moved by fancies that are curled
Around these images and cling:
The notion of some infinitely gentle,
Infinitely suffering thing . . .

~

To heighten the effect of these poems, or of a purely Cubist experiment like Pound's 'Dogmatic Statement on the Game and Play of Chess' (which is really a 'Vorticist' painting), or of the general Picasso-awareness of *Blast* under Lewis's dominating personality, one should contrast them with the ordinary poetry which was currently produced. 'The situation of poetry in 1909 or 1910 was stagnant to a degree difficult for any young poet of today to imagine' (T. S. Eliot). There was Bridges, to whom (in 1915) Yeats sent Pound's *Cathay*, and academics like Binyon and Sturge Moore, and there were the first two series of *Georgian Poetry* (1911–12 and 1913–15) edited by Edward Marsh. These were particularly disliked by Pound. The contributors to both series were Lascelles Abercrombie, Gordon Bottomley, Rupert Brooke, W. H. Davies, Walter de la Mare, John Drinkwater, James Elroy Flecker, Wilfrid Wilson Gibson, D. H. Lawrence, John Masefield, Harold Monro and James Stephens. Ralph Hodgson appeared in the second, G. K. Chesterton in the first.

I have read through both volumes but, *grisé par l'art moderne*, found them all lush or arid, whimsical or insipid. Pound thought Brooke the best of the bunch and his 'Fish' is, I think, an interesting poem, but to enjoy these warblers it is essential to forget Pound's three points and to like obsolete words with false sentiments and to listen to the metronome. There is no melodic line. There is one border-line case: Harold Monro, owner of the Poetry Bookshop and publisher of the *Chapbook* (not to be confused with Harriet Monroe, editress of *Poetry, Chicago*), who greatly encouraged the modern school and was gradually influenced by them. He alone appears in both *Georgian Poetry* and *Catholic Anthology*, and Pound and Eliot eventually wrote articles on him, treating him as a sincerely repentant late-comer. His poem 'Suburb' is already (1914) both pure Betjeman and a trailer for part of 'The Waste Land', or a story by Huxley.

> . . . In all the better gardens you may pass
> (Product of many careful Saturdays),
> Large geraniums and tall pampas grass
> Adorn the plots and mark the gravelled ways
>
> Sometimes in the background may be seen
> A private summer-house in white or green.
>
> Here on warm nights the daughter brings
> Her vacillating clerk
> To talk of small exciting things
> And touch his fingers through the dark.
>
> He, in the uncomfortable breach
> Between her trilling laughters,
> Promises, in halting speech,
> Hopeless immense Hereafters.
>
> She trembles like the pampas plumes,
> Her strained lips haggle. He assumes
> The serious quest . . .
>
> Now as the train is whistling past
> He takes her in his arms at last.
> It's done. She blushes at his side
> Across the lawn – a bride, a bride.

The stout contractor will design
The lazy labourers will prepare
Another villa on the line;
In the little garden-square
Pampas grass will rustle there.

~

It will be seen that I have not attempted to explain why or how Ezra Pound, born in Idaho (though really an Easterner), or T. S. Eliot (a New Englander from Saint Louis), were or became poets. It is our good fortune that some divine restlessness sent them forth on their travels and brought them to our shores, where Yeats and Ford Madox Ford and Harold Monro and Wyndham Lewis were waiting to receive them. Both Pound and Eliot had a very unusual combination of gifts – revolutionary élan, first-class minds, and a most fastidious and critical ear. One is always surprised by Pound's taste, he is indeed the Catullus (a *gamin* Catullus, wrote a reviewer) of Yeats's 'Scholar' poem which, I fully believe, was intended for him. De la Mare, too, had such an ear, but belonged, like Graves, to the traditional Georgian song-canon.

Perhaps the war, although it interfered with their natural pattern of growth, gave them both an additional stiffening. But whatever the cause, the two expatriates came of age. The Pound of *Lustra* is still a minor poet. With *Quia Pauper Amavi* he attains a stature which is worthy of the admiration since bestowed on him. The book was published by John Rodker at the Egoist Press in 1918 – since it was also the publisher of Lewis's *Tarr*, Eliot's *Prufrock*, Marianne Moore's *Poems* and Joyce's *Portrait of the Artist*, the Egoist Press has a claim to fame similar to Elkin Mathews before it, and the Hogarth Press immediately after. The book consists almost entirely of long poems and includes the first three Cantos and 'Homage to Sextus Propertius'. The Cantos have not yet begun to belch forth huge lumps of prose like a faulty incinerator and include the lovely Elpenor passage paraphrased from Homer, while 'Homage to Sextus Propertius', complete with howlers, grows better at each re-reading, a complete identification of one fame-struck, slightly wearying dandy with his dazzling archetype. The passage of time encrusts the howlers with a hoary rightness.

In 1917 Yeats got married and Ezra Pound was the best man, while in Chicago Margaret Anderson founded one of the brightest of all magazines, *The Little Review*, to which Pound was appointed foreign editor. He started her off with a splendid poem by Yeats, 'In memory of Major Robert Gregory', and Yeats announced his opinion in a generous letter: 'When I returned to London from Ireland, I had a young man go over all my work with me to eliminate the abstract. This was an American poet, Ezra Pound.' Pound also brought them stories by Lewis and the serialisation of Joyce's *Ulysses*, which began in 1918: both these ended in disaster, for several numbers of the magazine were banned on account of them although Miss Anderson was defended by the Maecenas of the whole group, the Irish-American collector John Quinn.

The Irish rebellion, closely involving two of the women he loved (Maud Gonne's husband, John MacBride, was shot), was an extraordinary inspiration to Yeats and events in Ireland continued to arouse him till his visit to Oxford –

> When long ago I saw her ride
> Under Ben Bulben to the meet
> The beauty of her country side
> With all youth's lonely wildness stirred,
> She seemed to have grown clean and sweet
> Like any rock-bred, sea-borne bird;
>
> Sea-borne or balanced on the air
> When first it sprang out of the nest
> Upon some lofty rock to stare
> Upon the cloudy canopy
> While under its storm-beaten breast
> Cried out the hollows of the sea.

1922 was the year of triumph for Yeats. His *Later Poems* came out, illustrating his whole development from *The Wind among the Reeds* to

The Second Coming, from 1899 to 1921. He also brought out his autobiography, *The Trembling of the Veil*, and a volume of his plays and eight more poems, including 'All Souls' Night' (the beginning of his intellectual manner), at the Cuala Press. Although Middleton Murry thought the *Wild Swans at Coole* (1919) 'eloquent of final defeat' and Pound pronounced him 'faded' in 1920, the greatest triumphs of his poetic life were all before him.

Eliot however seemed to be making heavy weather by 1917 and after failing to earn his living from journalism took up working in a bank. His poetic output fell off slightly. There were four poems (three in French) for *The Little Review* in July 1917, four more in September 1918, three in 1919, the superb *Gerontion* in 1920, and then nothing till 1922. These were the years when Eliot was making a reputation as a critic, the years of his first collection of essays in *The Sacred Wood* (1920), and during which the Prufrock volume, enlarged by the new poems which appeared as the Hogarth Press *Poems* (1919), became *Ara Vos Prec* in 1920 (with *Gerontion*) and *Poems* 1920 in America.

In 1918 Sweeney comes on the scene, sensual among the nightingales, and a major difference between Eliot and Pound grows more apparent: Eliot understands suffering, 'the last twist of the knife' and becomes a deeper, ultimately Christian writer. Pound remains light-heartedly pagan, open to wonder and moments of lyrical sadness, but never portraying a stronger emotion than indignation, and that very rarely. His Hell, as Eliot was to point out, is for Englishmen he didn't like, not for himself. In *Lustra* Pound claimed that this cool, formal, elegiac dandyism was the best way to puncture the Georgians, the lush Swinburnian and Tennysonian cadences, the romantic inflation. He called it a 'work of purgation of minds'. Lacking the tragic sense of life which leads to the understanding of other people, his portraits as a result grow increasingly artificial, 'an art in profile'. Propertius is there without his anguish; and Pound's other major poem describes Hugh Selwyn Mauberley, an anglicised Prufrock who has walked out of Henry James to be intaglio'd by Gautier and who is too much a cardboard man even to be hollow. But *Mauberley* (Ovid Press, 1920), in which Pound bids his lethargic English audience a disdainful farewell, is a chain of lyrics flung out like a pattern of islands – 'scattered Moluccas' which are a perpetual delight.

As whole books have been written about these exquisite poems and a Warden of All Souls has devoted much space to annihilating their defunctive music, I will only say that every other one seems perfect. [They include the most bitter anti-war poem ever written.] 'His true Penelope was Flaubert': that is what distinguishes Pound from all other revolutionaries; he flies his jolly roger from the ivory tower. Both *Quia Pauper Amavi* and *Mauberley* went unsold and uncelebrated and his increasing dislike of post-war England – where the Sitwells had replaced his own shock-troops, and where the gay demobilised second wave with Huxley, Graves, Robert Nichols and Sassoon gathered at the Café Royal and Tour Eiffel instead of Bellotti's and the Vienna Café – as well as his native restlessness drove him in 1921 on to Paris where he could continue to be foreign editor of *The Little Review* and discover the novelist Hemingway, the poet Cummings and the composer Antheil all within a year of his arrival. Here Joyce, financed by Miss Weaver at Pound's suggestion, had preceded him. He there ceases to be the clear-sighted troubadour and becomes the full-blown international exhibitionist, Gertrude Stein's 'Village Explainer', Lewis's 'Revolutionary Simpleton'. He had, however, one more midwifery duty to perform.

December 24th, 1921: Letter to T. S. Eliot

. . . The thing now runs from 'April' to 'Shantihk' without a break. That is nineteen pages and let us say the longest poem in the English langwidge. Don't try to bust all records by prolonging it three pages further. . . . Compliments, you bitch. I am wracked by the seven jealousies. . . .

March 18th, 1922: Letter to William Carlos Williams

Eliot, in bank, makes £500. Too tired to write, broke down; during convalescence in Switzerland did 'Waste Land', a masterpiece, one of most important nineteen pages in English. Returned to bank and is again gone to pieces physically. . . .

Of course I'm no more Mauberley than Eliot is Prufrock. Mais

> passons. Mauberley is a mere surface. Again a study in form, an attempt to condense the James novel. Meliora speramus. . . .
>
> Eliot's 'Waste Land' is I think the justification of the movement, of our modern experiment, since 1900. It should be published this year.

It was. One should read it every April. In America it won the Dial prize and came out both in the magazine and as a book; in England it appeared in the first number of the *Criterion*, which Eliot was to edit and which also contained a review of *Ulysses*. The *annus mirabilis* of the modern movement was drawing to a close. Yeats's *Later Poems* and *The Waste Land*, *Ulysses* and *Women in Love*, *Jacob's Room* and Valéry's *Charmes*, with *Le Serpent* and the *Cimetière Marin* – the breakthrough is complete. I have left out two important minor poets, Marianne Moore (also from Saint Louis), who was first published in 1921, and the war-poet Wilfrid Owen (1920), and one major one – Edith Sitwell, because she deserves a study in herself and grew up in total isolation from any of these influences – a Christina Rosetti crossed with Pope – maturing considerably later. Her early works, especially *Façade* and *Bucolic Comedies*, and the poems in *Wheels*, do belong to this period, but it would not be easy to relate them, because they still tend to be formal exercises in technique until the *Sleeping Beauty* (1923).

In fact the Sitwells' part in the breakthrough, with their magazines *Wheels* and *Art and Letters*, is a separate, almost a self-contained subject. When Wyndham Lewis started to attack her, Yeats wrote to him (1930):

> Somebody tells me that you have satirized Edith Sitwell. If that is so, visionary excitement has in part benumbed your senses. When I read her 'Gold Coast Customs' a year ago, I felt, as on first reading 'The Apes of God', that something absent from all literature for a generation was back again, and in a form rare in the literature of all generations, passion ennobled by intensity, by endurance, by wisdom. We had it in one man once. He lies in St. Patrick's now, under the greatest epitaph in history. Yours very sincerely, W. B. YEATS.

In the *Pisan Cantos* (1949) Pound, who has at last become acquainted with grief in his solitary cage at an American prison camp, recalls these formative years and 'lordly men to earth o'ergiven' – Hulme and Ford and Blunt opening the door 'from a fine old eye the unconquered flame' and his three winters with Yeats

'At Stone Cottage in Sussex by the waste moor'.

The Position of Joyce (1929)

James Joyce has brought out a new book. It is a fragment of a longer one, and is called *Anna Livia Plurabelle*. We are used to the reputations of authors fluctuating from year to year, but Mr. Joyce's also fluctuates from place to place. He is resented in Ireland, neglected in England, admired by a set in America, and idolized by another in France. In every nation there is a general public and a literary public. In Ireland the general public is provincial and priest-ridden. It cannot forgive Joyce his blasphemy nor his contemptuous parodies of Irish jingoism. The other, the smaller public, has chosen escape in a romantic return to the past, characterized by a special lyric note of easy and indefinable melancholy born of self-pity. Joyce is a realist, and out of touch intellectually with that generation. 'Michael Roberts remembers forgotten beauty. He presses in his arms the loveliness which has long faded from the world. I desire to press in my arms the loveliness which has not yet come into the world.' Thus Joyce's only disciples in Ireland are the young realists of the post-rebellion period. In England the literary public is governed by good taste. Cautious as the cenotaph, the critics decide the value of a book in terms of 'delicious' and 'charming'. The general public is equally conservative, and the fate of a book like *Ulysses* (so hopelessly unpresentable when submitted to the Chelsea canon) is decided in advance. It is in America, where there is a large and less sophisticated general public, and in Paris, where there are a great many young writers anxious to experiment in literary form, that the 'Ulysses generation' has grown up.

Mr. Forster, in his lectures on the novel, states perfectly the English attitude to Joyce, the bad bogy-man of letters. '*Ulysses*,' he writes, 'is a dogged attempt to cover the universe with mud, an inverted Victorianism, an attempt to make coarseness and dirt succeed where sweetness and light failed, a simplification of the human character in the interests of Hell.' It is also an 'epic of grubbiness and disillusion . . . a superfetation of fantasies, a monstrous coupling of reminiscences . . . in which smaller mythologies swarm and pullulate, like vermin between the scales of a poisonous snake.' 'Indignation in literature,' adds Mr. Forster, 'never quite comes off,' and the passage I have quoted does little except to express the general attitude of English culture towards novelty, and to prove that the vocabulary of scandalized vituperation is drawn from the reptile-house in every age.

'Indignation' is not a quality of Joyce's work, but 'the raging of Joyce seems essentially fantastic, and lacks the note for which we shall be listening soon,' continues Mr. Forster, who proceeds to classify *Ulysses* as belonging to the period of *Zuleika Dobson*. Let us get a clear idea of *Ulysses* before we try to estimate the later work of its author. James Joyce is, by temperament, a medievalist. He has always been in revolt against his two greatest limitations, his Jesuit education and his Celtic romanticism. Each of his books reveals a growing fear of beauty; not because life is not beautiful, but because there is something essentially false and luxurious in the 'Celtic Twilight' approach to it. This tinsel element is very strong in Joyce's early poems, and is contrasted with an equally pronounced repulsion from it in *The Portrait of the Artist.** In *Ulysses* he has got it in hand, and is experimenting in other approaches to beauty; the pagan simplicity of Mrs. Bloom's reverie, the mathematical austerity of the catechism which precedes it. Only Stephen Dedalus, the Hamlet young man, thinks automatically in the diction of the Celtic Twilight; but in him the remorse, the guilty sense of loneliness which attacks brave but weak men who destroy the religious framework of their youth, has fused with his minor poet melancholy, and gives to his reverie the quality of a Greek chorus. Stephen Dedalus, in fact, equips the *Ulysses* generation with a fatalism, a dramatization of

*Editor's note: the correct title of James Joyce's first novel is *A Portrait of the Artist as a Young Man.*

their own forebodings, and with the medieval quality so rare in America, so reduced in England, so rife in Europe – the Tragic Sense of Life. This is the great link between Joyce and Proust, otherwise so misleadingly compared. Both the Irishman and the Jew possess the tragic intelligence; the idea that life can only be appreciated, can only be lived even, if the intelligence is used to register all the beauty and all the intimacy which exist in ironic contrast to the unrelieved gloom of squalor and emptiness, mediocrity, disease, and death.

> For all our wit and reading do but bring us
> To a truer sense of sorrow.

The whole climax of *Ulysses* is a single moment of intimacy, when Bloom, the comic character, rescues Stephen in a drunken brawl. Bloom had a son who died, Stephen a father who is alive; but for this instant of spiritual paternity all the swelter of that urban summer, all the mesembrian pub-crawls of Bloom and Stephen, the 'vermin' and the 'scales' and the 'serpents', move into place. The central emotion of *Ulysses* is not indignation, but remorse; and remorse, though perhaps second-rate in life, is an emotion which usually succeeds in literature. Expiation and the sense of doom, which form the essence of Greek tragedy, are only a variation of this feeling; and though in real people remorse seems so feebly static, its very tranquillity and remoteness from action lend it a glassy literary beauty. In *Ulysses* Stephen dwells in the consciousness of having hastened his mother's death by his atheism, Bloom feels obscurely his father's suicide and the troubled history of his people, while all Ireland seems listlessly aware of its destiny. Perhaps the most typical scene in *Ulysses* is that in which Stephen, who has run away from the squalor of his father's house, comes across his young sister also trying to escape her environment without the help he might have given:

> He turned and halted by the slanted book cart. Twopence each, the huckster said, four for sixpence. Tattered pages. *The Irish Beekeeper. Life and miracles of the Curé of Ars. Pocket Guide to Killarney.*
>
> 'I might find there one of my pawned school prizes.'

'What are you doing here, Stephen?'

Dilly's high shoulders and shabby dress.

Shut the book quick. Don't let see.

'What are you doing?' Stephen said.

A Stuart face of nonsuch Charles, lank locks falling at its sides. It glowed as she crouched feeding the fire with broken boots. I told her of Paris. Late lieabed under a quilt of old overcoats, fingering a pinchbeck bracelet; Dan Kelly's token.

'What have you there?' Stephen asked.

'I bought it from the other cart for a penny,' Dilly said, laughing nervously. 'Is it any good?'

My eyes they say she has. Do others see me so? Quick, far and daring, shadows of my mind.

He took the coverless book from her hand. Chardenal's *French Primer*.

'What did you buy that for?' he asked. 'To learn French?'

She nodded, reddening and closing tight her lips.

Show no surprise, quite natural.

'Here,' Stephen said, 'it's all right. Mind Maggie doesn't pawn it on you. I suppose all my books are gone.'

'Some,' said Dilly, 'we had to.'

She is drowning. Agenbite. Save her, Agenbite. All against us. She will drown me with her, eyes and hair. Lank coils of seaweed hair around me, my heart, my soul. Salt green death.

We.

Agenbite of Inwit. Inwit's Agenbite.

Misery.

This quotation reveals many other aspects of the book; the old word for remorse, for instance, becomes one of those snowball phrases with which *Ulysses* is packed. Appearing continually in the characters' day-dreams, they gather momentum from each association, echoing through the chapters till by the end they are charged with as much personality as the thinkers themselves. Then the drabness of the scene, the halting, trite dialogue, illustrate the other side of *Ulysses*: the attempt to create beauty out of city life, and style out of the demotic English which is spoken in therein. Every year more people's lives are passed in towns than in the country; but while there is a whole vocabulary of rural beauty, there is so far only the slenderest aesthetic of cities, the roughest technique in appreciating them. What Baudelaire and Laforgue did for Paris, or Mr. T. S. Eliot for modern London, Joyce has done for Dublin: and at a time when Yeats and Synge had monopolized the Gaelic side of the Irish, he was able to create a language out of the demotic commercial speech of the anglicized burghers of Dublin itself. Literary English has become very hackneyed, as a glance at any book of essays or a preface to an anthology at once will show, and Joyce in *Ulysses* set out to revive it by introducing the popular colloquial idiom of his own city, by forming new words in the Greek fashion of compound epithets, by telescoping grammar, by using the fresh vocabulary of science manuals, public-houses, or Elizabethan slang. Here, for instance, are two quotations, one to illustrate the city aesthetic, the note of Celtic melancholy introduced into the descriptions of an urban summer sunset by the Hill of Howth, where Bloom had once made love; the other, an example of Joyce's highly latinized English, which produces an effect of austere rhetoric and elaborate original rhythm.

> A long-lost candle wandered up the sky from Myrus' bazaar in search of funds for Mercer's hospital and broke, drooping, and shed a cluster of violet but one white stars. They floated, fell: they faded. The shepherd's hour: the hour of holding: hour of tryst. From house to house, giving his everwelcome double knock, went the nine o'clock postman, the glow-worm's lamp at his belt gleaming here and there through the laurel hedges. And among the fine young trees a hoisted linstock lit the lamp at Leahy's Terrace. By screens of lighted windows, by equal gardens, a shrill voice went crying, wailing, '*Evening Telegraph* – stop press edition! Result of the Gold Cup races!' And from the door of Dignam's house a boy ran out and called. Twittering the bat flew here, flew there. Far out over the sands the coming surf crept, gray. Howth settled for slumber, tired of long days, of yumyum

rhododendrons (he was old) and felt gladly the night breeze lift, ruffle his fell of ferns. He lay but opened a red eye unsleeping, deep and slowly breathing, slumberous but awake. And far on Kish bank the anchored lightship twinkled, winked, at Mr. Bloom.

What play of forces, inducing inertia, rendered departure undesirable?

The lateness of the hour, rendering procrastinatory: the obscurity of the night, rendering invisible: the uncertainty of Thoroughfares, rendering perilous: the necessity for repose, obviating movement: the proximity of an occupied bed, obviating research: the anticipation of warmth [human] tempered with coolness [linen], obviating desire and rendering desirable: the statue of Narcissus, sound without echo, desired desire.

Besides this he directed a campaign of parody against the whimsy and archaism latent in English prose style. It is indeed as an enemy of 'literature' that Joyce really might appear to Mr. Forster as working 'in the interests of Hell'. Though he did not originate the 'stream of consciousness' as a form of writing, he saw that by recording the thoughts of each character he could take shorthand liberties with their syntax as well as get nearer to their selves. He too, among those who have used this method, is the only one to have grasped that people, besides thinking differently, think at a different pace. Mrs. Woolf, whose *Mrs. Dalloway* is in many ways a feminine adaptation of one idea of *Ulysses* to English good taste, tends to make all her characters think in the same tempo. She gives us anatomical slices; not human beings, but sections of them, which portray the doubts, the tendernesses, the half-hopes and half-fears of the human mind all conceived in the same mood of genteel despair. Bloom, Mrs. Bloom, Stephen, however, and the nameless Cyclops narrator possess mental processes which are quite incomparable with each other. Bloom's mean, good-tempered, second-rate, scientific curiosity colours all his commonplace meditations. Stephen's bitterness, imagination, and petulant intellect quicken feverishly the pulse of his thought. The racy, cynical and shamelessly prejudiced gusto of the Nameless One transforms his narrative into the whirl of the winds of

Aeolus that it is meant to symbolize, while elaborate journalese retards the speed of the book for those chapters when the action is at a standstill. Lastly, the even breathing of Mrs. Bloom times with her steady physical reverie, her pagan meditation so free from Stephen's medieval anguish, Bloom's scepticism, or the problems which faced the morning of the one, the evening of the other, and their common night.

The link between the new work of Joyce and *Ulysses* is chiefly one of language; though both are united by the same preoccupation with the aesthetic of cities, with the absurdity of our Jewish-American democracy, and with the capacity for being beautiful which this democracy yet retains.

Here are two quotations, one showing the Hill of Howth again treated in a symbolic manner, the other the praise of Dublin, rhetorical as cities are – Earwicker (the Danish castle) is bragging to his wife, the Liffey, of all he has done for her. I have annotated the text so that the complexity of the portmanteau language may be gauged.

> '"Old Whitehowth is speaking again. Pity poor Whiteoath! Deargone mummeries, goby. Tell the woyld I have lived true thousand hells. Pity please, lady, for poor O.W. in this profoundest snobbing I have caught. Nine dirty years mine age, hairs white, mummery failing, deaf as Adder. I askt you, dear lady, to judge on my tree by our fruits. I gave you of the tree. I gave two smells, two eats: my happy blossoms, my all falling fruits of my boom. Pity poor Haveth Children Everywhere with Mudder. That was Communicator a former Colonel."'

> '". . . And I built in Urbs in Rure for mine elskede, my shiny brows, an earth closet wherewithin to be quit in most convenience from her sabbath needs: did not I festfix my unniverseries, wholly rational and got alike [three Dublin universities national and godlike with Trinity to suggest the holy]; was not I rosetted on two stelas of little Egypt, had not rockcut readers, hieros, gregos, and democriticos [the Rosetta stone]; and by my syvendialed changing charties Hibernska ulitzas made not I [allusion to superimposing a street map on an older one and rotating it to find what streets lie along a Roman road. Ulitza is the Slav

for a street, but in this case is also a prophecy of Ulysses and his labours] to pass through 12 Threadneedles and Newgade and Vicus Veneris to cooinsight. [Allusions to Ulysses, to Newgate prison on the Roman Road.] Oi polled ye many, but my fews were chosen: and I set up twin-minsters, the pro and the con [Christchurch and the pro-Cathedral] woven of peeled wands and attachattouchy floodmud [Italian root, 'sticky'] arched for the convenanters and shinner's rifuge; all truant trulls made I comepull, all rubbeling gnomes I pushed, go go; and thirdly for ewigs I did reform and restore for my smuggy piggiesknees her paddy palace on the cross-knoll [St. Patrick's restored] and added there unto a shallow laver to put out her hell fire and posied windows for her oriel house and she sass her nach, chilly-bombom and 40 bonnets, upon the altarstane, may all have mossyhonours!

'I hung up at the Yule my pigmy suns helphelped of Kettil Flashnose [electric lights introduced in Dublin under Kettle, the chief of the electricians and descendant of Kettle Flatnose, an original Dane settler] for the supper hour of my frigid one, coulomba mea, frimosa mia, through all Livania's volted ampire from anods to cathods, and from the topazolites of Mourne by Arcglow's sapphire seamanslure and Waterford's hook and crook lights to the polders of Hy Kinsella [old Danish beacons].'

The ordinary man of letters, when faced with modern civilization, plays the ostrich with its head in the sand. A very whimsical, arch, mock-apologetic, and well-subsidized ostrich too. In fact, they are the paid entertainers of democracy, the jesters who are allowed the licence of bewailing the rattle of hansom cabs, of beginning every sentence with 'I must needs avow that I have never seen eye to eye with those who,' and ending 'nevertheless, to my thinking, when all is said and done. . . .' Of course, there is no law compelling anyone to belong to his period; but not to belong to it, is to take sanctuary, to eke out a whimsical existence and an archaic style in a half-timbered Utopia, visited, like an Elizabethan teashop, by the most insipid of the public one would wish to avoid. If *Ulysses* is largely a parody of literary manners, a dissatisfaction with style, the new work of Joyce is a parody of language, an attempt to create a new vocabulary for literature itself. And both, which readers are unwilling to see, are meant to be funny. After all, the ballad of the Jabberwock has passed into the accepted treasury of English humour; yet when the method Carroll used to reinforce words with double meanings is applied to contemporary prose, which surely needs it, the result is that we label the originator mad.

Literary language in England has become very far removed from conversation, nor is it able to profit, like American, from a rich background of polyglot slang. All literary words in addition tend to be used, especially by Georgian poets, without a due conviction of their meaning, and this depreciates the currency so that most epithets become like the dead notes on an old piano, which go down when they are sounded, but do not come up. The best instance of this is the penultimate passage of *The Oxford Book of English Prose*. The new language of Joyce is only a kind of piano-tuning, whereby he tightens up certain words by grafting fresher foreign equivalents on to them, approximates them to other words to strengthen their own vigour, above all puns with them freely, and gives words a synthetic meaning, with which either to express life, or simply to make a series of academic jokes. The experiment may be a failure, just as Esperanto or phonetic spelling may be a failure, but there is nothing that is contrary to reason in the idea itself. The chief defect of Mr. Joyce's new language is that, so far, it has swamped the lyrical quality of his other prose writings; he has not attempted purple patches in it so much as rhetorical imitations of them. Here is the close of a fable called 'The Mookse and the Gripes', which can be compared with Bloom's city sunset, quoted above:

> The shades began to glidder along the banks, dust unto dusk, and it was as glooming as gloaming could be in the waste of all peaceable wolds. The mookse had a sound eyes right but he could not all hear. The Gripes had light ears left yet he could but ill see. He ceased. And he ceased and it was so dusk of both of them. But still one thought of the deeps he would profound on the morrow and still the other thought of the scrapes he would escape if he had luck enough.

The new book is full of fables, because the whole of the first part is really a *surréaliste* approach to the prehistory of Dublin, the myths and legends of its origin, Duke Humphrey and Anna Livia, the mountain and the river, from a black reach of which the city took its name. The first words 'riverrun brings us back to Howth Castle and Environs' suggest the melodies to follow. All the urban culture of Ireland is by origin Scandinavian; and, to emphasize this, Joyce has introduced the greatest possible amount of Norse words into his description of it. There are four parts to the new work of Joyce: the first is a kind of air photograph of Irish history, a celebration of the dim past of Dublin, as was *Ulysses* of its grimy present; the second is an interlude in a barn near Chapelizod; some children are playing, and react unconsciously the old stories of the first (Iseult of Ireland linking in the suburb's name); and the third part, jumping from the 'past events leave their shadows behind' of the first, to 'coming events cast their shadows before,' deals in four sections with the four watches of one night. As this is literary criticism, I cannot go into the metaphysics of Joyce's new book, which are based on the history of Vico and on a new philosophy of Time and Space; but two other things emerge, the same pre-occupation of the author with his native town, his desire to see all the universe through that small lens, and his poetic feeling for the phases of the dusk, for that twilight which originally gave the Celtic revival its name. The book opens in a museum with a mummified description of the battle of Waterloo:

> 'This is the way to the museyroom. Mind your hats goan in! Now yiz are in the Willingdone museyroom. This is a Prooshious gun. This is a ffrinch. Tip. This is the flag of the Prooshious, the Cap and Soracer. This is the bullet that byng the flag of the Prooshious. This is the ffrinch that fire on the Bull that bang the flag of the Prooshious. Saloos the crossgun! up with your pike and fork! Tip. (Bullsfoot! Fine!) This is the triple-won hat of Lipoleum. Tip. Lipoleumhat. This is the Willingdone on his same white harse, the Cokenhape.'

Monotonous as the tap of a lecturer's pole, rusty, archaic, the old contraptions of history reveal themselves, the past lumbers slowly into being under the touch of the chirpy guide. The museyroom, the sight-seers, moving dustily among the dregs of the forgotten battle, clank into place in the uncouth language; we are looking at the earth from a long way away, perhaps as one might look at it by overtaking the light rays – by turning a telescope on the Dark Ages, from some planet so far that it still could watch them going on. 'Only a fadograph of a yestern scene.'

> So, now idler's winds turning pages on pages, annals of themselves timing, the cycles bring fassilwise to pass how. 1132 A.D. Men like to ants or emmets wondern upon a groot hwide Whallfisk which lay in a Runnel. Blubby wares up at Ublanium.

Figures emerge from the chronicle: in this early Dublin, Irishman meets Norseman, typical of all misunderstanding since the days of Babel. The Irishman begins:

> 'Hop! In the name of Anem this carl on the kopje a parth alone who the Joebiggar be he? Forshapen his pigmaid hoagshead, shroonk his plods-foot, me seemeth a dragon man.... He is almonthst on the kiep fieg by here, is Come-stipple Sacksounn, be it junipery or febrewery, marracks or alebill, or the ramping riots of prouriose and froriose. What a quhare soort of a mahan. It is evident the minchindaddy. He can prap-sposterous the pillowy way to Hirculos pillar. Scuse us, chorley guy! You tollerday donsk? N. You tolkatiff scowegian? Nn. You spigotty anglese? Nnn? You phonio Saxo? Nnnn. Clear all so! Tis a Jute. Let us swop hats and excheck a few strong verbs weak oach eather yap-yazzard abast the blooty creeks.'
>
> Jute: Yutah!
> Mutt: Mukk's pleasurad.
> Jute: Are you jeff?
> Mutt: Somehards.
> Jute: But you are not jeffmute?
> Mutt: Noho. Only an utterer.
> Jute: Whoa! Whoat is the matter with you?
> Mutt: I became a stun a stunner.

By and by other heroes appear, Shaun the Rabelaisian postman, sly Shem, his writer brother, H. C. Earwicker (here comes everybody) (alias the Hill of Howth), the typical great man of the new democracy, and his bride, the lovely Anna Livia.

~

Writers are on safest ground when they confine themselves to what interests them, and the key to this obscure and difficult book is the author's *pietas* for his native city. Joyce's life has been nearer to the classical tradition of great writers than to the Victorian comfort of the men of letters of today. His existence resembles that of the old Greek poets, a youth spent in city politics and local revels, then banishment to foreign places, the publication of a masterpiece after ten years, as Dedalus promised, with his weapons 'silence, exile and cunning'. Now his whole art is applied to celebrating his native town, though his feelings for Dublin, its squares and stews and beery streets, its hills and foreshore, seagoing Liffey and greenbanked Dodder, is very different from the provincial quality of Irish patriotism and is more akin to the pagan sentiment of birthplace. There is nothing flamboyant in his tender attitude to the 'poor little brittle magic nation, dim of mind'.

Anna Livia is an episode from this book describing the legend of the Liffey. Two old washerwomen stand on each side of the stripling river and gossip away as they pound the clothes. ('O tell me all about Anna Livia.') They talk of Earwicker's affair with her under his other identity, of Duke Humphrey, and gradually their language breaks into a melody of water music, a kind of paean, like the praise of the brook Kishon, into which the names of every conceivable river are brought in as onomatopoeic train-bearers.

> . . . She sideslipped out by a gap in the devil's glen while Sally her nurse was sound asleep in a shoot, and fell over a spillway before she found her stride and lay and wriggled in all the stagnant black pools of rain under a fallow coo and she laughed with her limbs all aloft and a whole

grove of maiden hawthorns blushing and looking askance upon her.... And after that she wore a garland for her hair. She pleated it. She plaited it. Of meadow grass and river-flags, the bulrush and the water weed, and of fallen griefs of weeping-willow.

Occasionally the charwomen break in with their own troubles:

'O my bach! my back! my back! I'd want to go to Aches-les-Pains ... spread on your bank and I'll spread on mine. It's wat I'm doing. Spread! It's turning chill. Der went is rising.'

Gradually the widening stream carries them apart as the night falls, for they are standing on the two banks of the infant river as on a moving stairway, and the gap between them has widened as the Liffey leaps, in the words of her song, 'to the slobs of the Tolka and the shores of Clontarf to hear the gay aire of my salt troublin' bay and the race of the saywint up my ambushure.' When night falls, the old women shouting across the dark cannot understand each other; still gossiping, they are transformed into an elm and a stone, the strange obscurity of the old myths from which they have emerged gathers about them, and the *motif* of the past of Ireland is re-echoed in their dumb block-like language; for the Mookse and the Gripes had suffered the same fate, mortal beside the immortal river:

'... and it was never so thoughtful of either of them. And there were left now only an elm tree and but a stone. O! Yes! and Nuvoletta, a lass.'

The end of the *Anna Livia* marks another of Joyce's extraordinary descriptions of dusk:

'Whawk? Can't hear with the waters of. The chittering waters of. Flittering bats, fieldmice bawk talk. Ho! Are you not gone ahome? What Tom Malone? Can't hear with the bawk of bats, all the liffeying waters of. Ho, talk save us! My foos wont moos. I feel as old as yonder elm. A tale told of Shaun or Shem? All Livia's daughtersons. Dark hawks hear us. Night! Night! My no head halls. I feel as heavy as yonder stone. Tell me of John or Shem? Who were Shem and Shaun the living sons and daughters of? Night now! Tell me, tell me, tell me, elm! Night night! Tell me tale of stem or stone. Beside the rivering waters of, hitherandthithering waters of. Night!'

The best way to read Joyce's new book, apart from this rare reprint of *Anna Livia*, is in a quarterly called *Transition*, edited by Americans living in Paris. The contents are often as grotesque as the idea is enterprising. But we have no paper for literary experiment in England, and literature is, after all, as technical a business as medicine or engineering. *Transition* is sometimes a silly magazine, and sometimes intensely amusing, for, like most rebel journals, its satire is on safer ground than its originality; but it is the only one which publishes the honest, sometimes fascinating, often incoherent research of those who take new literature seriously in every country. Of course, it is not possible to pronounce a verdict on Joyce's work while it is still fragmentary. The best that this article can hope to prove is that the new work of Joyce is respect-worthy and readable. There is nothing insane in its conception nor bogus in its execution. Though to many a spinster fancy it probably will continue to lack the 'note for which we will be listening soon', to others it promises amusement and a most interesting and strange approach to life and beauty. In short, it is an experiment. We are content to accord the wildest tolerance to the latest unintelligible – even uncommercial – pamphlet of Einstein – can we not admit a little of the same tolerance to something in writing which we do not understand? It must be remembered that Joyce, besides being a lover of words, is an Irishman under no obligation whatever to rest content with the English language, and also that, while our Literature, unaware of a decline of the West or a defence of it, grows daily more bucolic and conservative, Continental Letters are nourished on an exhilarating sense of an uncertain future which makes the liberties of their volcano dwellers permissible – and which we are entirely without. Literature is in essence a series of new universes enforced on a tardy public by their creators. This one may be a fake, but it is not from a writer who has previously given us fakes; it may be a failure, but it is surely an absorbing one, and more important than any contemporary success. I, personally, am biased as a critic by nationality, and by the same feeling for geography and Dublin, but still more by the enthusiasm which comes to everyone when they discover themselves through a book – a service which Joyce, Proust, and Gide have rendered generally to almost all our thinking generation; for me any criticism of *Ulysses* will be affected by a wet morning in Florence, when in the empty library of a villa with the smell of wood-smoke, the faint eaves-drip, I held the uncouth volume dazedly open in the big armchair – Narcissus with his pool before him.

James Joyce
(1941)

This is no time to attempt a critical estimate of Joyce. Wilson's forty pages in *Axel's Castle* (Scribners) have done that best. He has died this week, but it will be a year or two before anything can be said about him which is worth saying. In the next period of expansive leisure, when we can read again and reassess the past, he may well take the place which Henry James has lately occupied, that of the Forerunner in vogue, the fine product of a vanished and alien civilisation which by its completeness and remoteness stirs the imagination and so enters into communication with its successor. Joyce was the last of the Mammoths, not perhaps quite the last, for there is still Gide, Claudel, Vuillard, Bonnard, in France, but I know of none in America and England, and by Mammoths I mean those giant inhabitants of the middle class who believed in life for art's sake, and were prepared to devote sixty or seventy years of unremitting energy and patience, all their time, all their money, all their mind to it. We see them browsing in small herds through the 'sixties and 'seventies and 'eighties, Impressionists, Post-Impressionists, Ivory Tower dwellers, Realists, Parnassians, their food the experience of a lifetime obtained through a giant curiosity, a private income and a deep sense of security, for their protective bourgeois colouring, their rich dark suits and stiff collars, their comfortable homes and devoted women disguise them completely and merge perfectly into the contemporary bourgeois landscape. With the turn of the century the herds thinned out, the feeding grounds deteriorated, the last war had somewhat the effect of an ice age yet the pastures which had supported Cézanne and Flaubert, Degas and Henry James continued to nourish Moore and Yeats and Proust, Joyce, Gide, and Valéry. Now most of them are gone and the ice cap is returning with velocity.

Joyce was not a revolutionary. His life contained only one revolutionary gesture, his departure from Ireland after the final suppression of *Dubliners* (1912) which was to have been brought out in 1904. He produced a fierce poem, *Gas from a Burner* (1912), which contains some excellent hate of Ireland, and left his country never to return. He then taught English in the Berlitz schools, where he was working at Trieste when the last war broke out, after which he moved to Zurich. It is odd to think that there must exist many Italians who learnt their English from this lord of language, who was quietly acquiring every known tongue in his spare time. *Dubliners*, an admirable collection of short stories, was finally published in 1914. It shows Joyce torn between the realism of the 'modern movement' and a decadent Celtic romanticism. In 1916/7 he published *A Portrait of the Artist* through the Egoist Press. It is a quite remarkable book, adult, sensitive, unreassuring, in which the two veins of Dublin realism and Celtic romanticism are woven into an elaborate fugue. After the publication of *Ulysses*, which was due to the courage and devotion of Sylvia Beach, he became, through a private benefaction, financially secure, and was able to live the kind of life he wanted, which was that of a well-to-do high priest of art, remote from equals and competitors and not too accessible to admirers, in a luxurious apartment in the Rue de Grenelle. It was there that I used to go to see him, or else in his room at the American hospital in Neuilly, when I was writing an article on *Ulysses* and *Work in Progress*. I had read *Ulysses* with passion; it is very much a young man's book, packed with the defeatism and the guilt of youth, its loneliness, cynicism, pedantry and outbursts of bawdy anarchist activity. Guilt about a dying mother, boredom with an actual father, search for a spiritual father, reliance on robuster friends, watery and lecherous cravings for girls, horror and delight in failure, horror and fascination for the gross calm, bitchy, invincible feminine principles as exemplified in Molly Bloom, 'Queen of Calpe's rocky mount, the raven-haired daughter of Tweedie'; it was like, and always will be, nothing one has read before.

At that time there was a complete cult of *Ulysses*. Books were written about it. Stuart Gilbert provided a fascinating crib; there was a map of Dublin with the journeyings of Bloom and Stephen in different coloured inks, and on 'Bloom's Day' (June 16th) there was a celebration, Joyce going to the country with a few friends and admirers for a picnic, one of which was ruined by a clap of thunder for which Joyce had a genuine terror. I could not write about *Work in Progress* without having it explained to me and so my talks with Joyce ended up in my being put on to construe. 'Now, Mr. Connolly, just read this passage aloud and tell me what you think it means.' 'It's about the Danish walls of the original Danish encampment – er – I mean Dub-b-lin – the black ford? Ford of the oxen? Hill on a fort?' 'No, no, no – I refer to the three cathedrals of Dublin, Mr. Connolly, the only city, you know, to have three cathedrals.' It was not quite like being at school, it was like going to breakfast, after one had left school, with one's schoolmaster. In theory you were grown up, in practice you weren't. After one difficult passage about Roman Dublin intoned by Joyce in his magnificent voice, he paused. 'You know, of course, to what I refer, Mr. Connolly?' 'No, not exactly.' 'I refer' – there was a moment of acute embarrassment – 'I refer to a Lupanar.' After the tutorials he would go to the piano and sing Dublin street ballads with a charming, drawling, nasal parody of the old itinerant singers. He talked endlessly about Ireland. 'I am afraid I am more interested, Mr. Connolly, in the Dublin street names than in the riddle of the Universe.' He was even interested in Irish cricket, and always, when I knew him, wore the white blazer of an obscure Dublin club. He was very proud of his family, and like all the Anglo-Irish, a snob. In Paris he liked good food, especially a Montparnasse restaurant called Les Trianons, and going to the opera and order and wealth. Sometimes, however, he went out with Hemingway or Lewis and got drunk. He always seemed to be two men, the legendary Joyce, blind but patient, pompous, cold, easily offended, unapproachable, waiting to be spoken to, with a strange priestly blend of offended dignity, weakness and intellectual power and underneath the warm, sympathetic bawdy Dublin character. In the years to come something really important could be written about him. Revolutionary in technique, yet conservative in everything else, so deadly respectable in his life, so fearlessly sensual in his writings, so tortured with the lapsed Catholic's guilt – the '*Agenbite of Inwit*', so obsessed with his own youth that his clock seemed literally to have stopped on June 16th, 1904, and yet so determined to create a mythical universe of his own. We will never have the time, the security or the patience in our lifetime to write like him, his weapons 'silence, exile and cunning' are not ours. I hope but only for the time to read through him and one day make a study of this literary anti-Pope, this last great mammoth out of whose tusks so many smaller egoists have carved their self-important ivory towers.

Ezra Pound
(1969)

It was after some letters about the *Pisan Cantos* and a suggestion from Olga Rudge, that I found myself on my way to Venice to attend Pound's eighty-fourth birthday (October 30, Scorpio). I knew Venice only in spring and summer and was unprepared for the overwhelming beauty of the city at this last moment of sunshine with all tourists gone. Pound's references are surprisingly few. He published his first book there (rarest of all the moderns), at his own expense when he came to Europe in 1908. *A Lume Spento* (*With Tapers Quenched*) has since been reprinted, with additions, in both Italy and America. According to his daughter, Mary de Rachewiltz, Pound lived at that time at Calle dei Frati, 942, in the San Trovaso quarter near the Accademia.

> I sat on the Dogana steps
> For the gondolas cost too much that year,

he wrote in Canto 3, but his best evocation of Venice is in the *Pisan Cantos* (No. 76). I might say in passing that I think the *Pisan Cantos* are among the greatest poems of the last war, indeed of our time, a *canción del prisoniero* in which the war is seen like the reflection of distant cloud-shadows, in which the detail of daily life gives way to the blaze of memory, memory operating without books, friends, letters or any outside assistance. I prefer them to 'Four Quartets' and cannot praise them higher than that.

> Under the two-winged cloud
> as of less and more than a day
> by the soap-smooth stone posts where San Vio

meets with il Canal Grande
between Salviati and the house that
was of Don Carlos
shd/I chuck the lot in the tide-water?
Le bozze 'A Lume Spento'
And by the column of Todero
shd/I shift to the other side?

Trovaso, Gregorio, Vio . . .

The blue soap-stone posts are still there on the corners of the Canal San Vio and the Palazzo Loredan, where we were lunching. Everything in Venice is still there: if one was set down there five hundred years ago, we would still find our way. 'The House that was of Don Carlos' is now Count Cini's Loredan.

Our host, Count Cini, was an old friend of Pound's, an outstanding octogenarian whose fortune is devoted to his foundation on the island of San Giorgio. I had not seen Pound for two years. He seemed if anything younger. He was not so thin, he was not so depressed, he did not pick at his hands; he wore a well-cut light blue suit, a felt hat and carried a malacca cane. He was silent as ever, silent as the lanes of Venice after London traffic, but the silence held no more terrors; it was of two kinds, benevolent or else simply abstracted, like a light switched on or off. It did not prevent him from jumping in and out of launches and vaporettos or striding about Torcello. I bought him a pocket Virgil as a birthday gift and suggested he open it at random and take a 'Sors Virgiliana'. 'Bello,' he said and showed me with his finger:

. . . Caesar dum magnus ad altum
Fulminat Euphraten bello . . .
Illo Virgilium me tempore dulcis alebat
Parthenope, studiis florentem ignobilis oti.

'While great Caesar was smiting the wide Euphrates with war,' I translated, 'Soft Naples was nourishing me, Virgil' – and then suddenly I stuck, unable to parse the rest. Pound waited, with mild blue eyes fixed on his Boswell. I skipped hastily and went on to the last line, '*te patulae cecini sub tegmine fagi.*' 'Singing of you, Tityrus, under the shade of a spreading beech.' (What in hell was '*patulae*'?) – Pound waited. Was he going to correct me? Why was I translating for him at all? It was a bad moment.

Luckily it was time to go. The Count was a gourmet. The meal was a celebration. We had place-cards and menus and rows of gold-engraved glass goblets. I shall never forget the white truffles in cheese sauce and it took them a long time to forget me. We ate persimmons and local muscats and white figs while the Count's beautiful Roman wife cut up an apple for Mr Pound. After luncheon the guests gathered round and the Count toasted the Maestro in Marc de Bourgogne and he drank back. The sun streamed through the huge windows of the piano nobile; children appeared, poets, beautiful women, coffee, chocolates – footmen looked genially on. Boswell blundered around getting in the way.

I went to Pound's home for his own birthday party, a mixture of Americans and Italians, painters, sculptors, writers. Peter Russell, once editor of *Nine* and a devoted Ezraphile now living in Venice, read a poem in his honour; we drank champagne, and a cake arrived with eighty-four small candles. I realised he was the same age as the ageless Duncan Grant. The patriarch gave two great puffs like the Cyclops' bellows and blew them all out.

I soon found myself back on the old problem. Where would one live in Venice, or even in which hotel? Was it not Leslie Hartley who had plumped for the sunny Zattere? The churches of this magic area of Dorsoduro began to fall into place. San Trovaso with its slightly down-at-heel canals and mystery, the Gesuati, the gayer residential quarter of San Gregorio and finally the never-failing miracle of the Salute, with the Dogana Steps at the point. Across are the bristling dollar strongholds, from the Gritti, urbane as ever, to the windows of Harry's Bar.

It was here we met the next morning to take the launch for Cipriani's at Torcello. The sun raised a tan on the cheek, danced over the immeasurable peace of the lagoon, islands covered with reed-beds, before the launch drew up at the restaurant steps. Fish soup, grilled scampi, more muscats. In the garden the pomegranates were ripe, a scarlet flush on each little tree, it was hot enough to lunch out; the campanile and ochre bricks of the church (the oldest in Venice) glowed against the blue sky. We talked of the book of essays, *New Approaches to Ezra Pound* (they liked Christine Brooke-Rose's contribution), and the new edition of Charles Norman's biography. I mentioned that Norman thought Frederick Manning had attended the poet's luncheon at Wilfrid Blunt's and Pound shook his head indignantly. We talked about the six poets; of Aldington's verse he said 'I don't remember much of it'; of Henry James, and Eliot's letters, of the forthcoming edition of *The Waste Land* with Pound's emendations from the mss. He ate very little and was afraid that Miss Rudge, most abstemious of Bostonians, would drink to excess.

One had the feeling that everywhere he went Pound was a revered and popular figure. To the Italians he is not a traitor but a martyr or rather a loyal friend who had stood by them in bad days. His enemies would one day be as forgotten as Dante's. I say 'we talked about', 'we discussed', but in fact Miss Rudge, his daughter and I talked while Pound either bestowed on us the elixir of his silence or absented his being altogether.

After a walk in the Basilica where the German television had recently made a film of Pound we sped back over the green water. More hotels . . . Miss Rudge recommended the Riva del Schiavoni in winter. In summer the noise and trippers were terrible. The pigeons had turned the piazza into a chicken run, tourists lay swigging on the ground. They should all pay an entrance fee. I went back before dinner. Pound was playing records of early music. He has a studio at the top of the house, a bedroom below, a salon on the ground floor. We returned to my favourite topic, who's who in the *Pisan Cantos*. Restaurants in the *Pisan Cantos*: Dieudonné, London; Mouquin, New York; Voisin, Paris; the Greif, Bolzano; Schöners, Vienna; Robert's, New York; La Rupe, Rome. 'No longer, *finito*.' 'But the Taverna – is it the Taverna here?' 'No,' barks Pound. 'Where then?' 'I can't remember.'

Next morning I went round to say good-bye; Pound was sitting up in bed; the ladies produce biscuits and a *canarino* (a decoction of lemon rind) for me. Ideal beverage! I bring tuberoses, the last of the season, and some of the little black grapes which taste of strawberries. We talk of Beckett (Pound is very happy about his Nobel Prize) and about his 'Jewel Box', Santa Maria dei Miracoli, which on their recommendation I had just seen for the first time. The carved 'sirens' of Tullio Lombardo are in the Cantos, too. I bid farewell to the poet-friend, this wisp of history, to the solace and the sunshine. The bells ring out

'Trovasco, Gregorio, Vio . . .'

Miss Rudge comes with me to the airport launch. She tells me Pound's latest dream. 'He lost all his money so he got a job as a builder's labourer carrying two long planks over his shoulders. He was much younger then.'

T. S. Eliot
(1965)

'Whatever happens read "The Waste Land" by T. S. Eliot – only read it twice. It is quite short and has the most marvellous things in it – though the "message" is almost unintelligible and it is a very Alexandrian poem – sterility disguised by superb use of quotation and obscure symbolism – thoroughly decadent. It will ruin your style . . .' So I wrote as an undergraduate at Oxford to another at Cambridge in the winter of 1923–24, shortly after the appearance of the Hogarth Press edition.

For what can convey the veritable brain-washing, the total pre-occupation, the drugged and haunted condition which this new poet induced in some of us? We were like new-born goslings for ever imprinted with the image of an alien and indifferent foster-parent, infatuated with his erudition, his sophistication, yet sapped and ruined by the contagion of his despair. Housman, Flecker and the Georgians all melted away overnight. At that time his earlier poems were hard to come by and I still have the transcript I made of 'La figlia che piange' from Sir Maurice Bowra's copy of 'Ara Vos Prec'.

By early 1925 the first version of 'The Hollow Men' had appeared in *The Criterion* and later in that year came the *Poems 1909–25* which marked the culmination of early Eliot, the handsome pagan from Harvard with his Harlequin good looks, his luminous Luciferian expression, of whom one could find out nothing but that he was poor and unhappy and had worked in a bank and sometimes stayed at nearby Garsington. His favourite poets were clearly Dante, who supplied so many of his epigraphs, and the minor Elizabethans. It was not known then how much he owed to Laforgue (he was so much better than Laforgue).

Then in 1926 and early '27 the two dramatic 'Sweeney' fragments appeared in his *Criterion*, followed in August 1927 by his first religious poem, 'The Journey of the Magi', and – in 1928 – by two sections of 'Ash Wednesday'. During 1927 he became a British subject and proclaimed his conversion to the Church of England ('A Song for Simeon' and 'For Lancelot Andrewes', 1928).

Eliot's literary span has lasted fifty years, from 1915 when 'The Love Song of J. Alfred Prufrock', 'Portrait of a Lady' and the Preludes and 'Rhapsody' were published in little magazines ('Prufrock' in Pound's *Catholic Anthology*) up to his death.

He was born in St Louis, Missouri, on September 26, 1888, the seventh and youngest child of Henry Ware Eliot, president of the Hydraulic Press Brick Co. of St Louis, and Charlotte Chauncy Stearns of Boston, author of a dramatic poem on the life of Savonarola. The Eliots came over *circa* 1650 from East Coker, Somerset, and were mainly merchants of Boston: but the poet's grandfather, the Reverend William Greenleaf Eliot, had gone west to St Louis and established the first Unitarian church in that city.

Two of his four sons entered the ministry. Eliot went to Harvard where he was Bertrand Russell's most brilliant pupil; he continued a post-graduate course in philosophy which took him to Paris and in 1914 to Germany on a travelling fellowship until the war. By the winter of 1914 he had got to Merton College, Oxford, through his thesis on Bradley – but Merton and its married dons made him long for London. 'Come, let us desert our wives and fly to a land where there are no Medici prints, nothing but concubinage and conversation. Oxford is very pretty, but I don't like to be dead.' And so, for the rest of his life, London it was.

I suppose no great poet since Johnson has been so much a Londoner or written so elegantly about it; one could never imagine him with a week-end cottage. It has often given me satisfaction just to think that he was somewhere around, as loyal subjects feel when they see the Royal Standard floating from the Palace. In Russell Square one might run across 'his set imperial face' or near his club in Pall Mall or in Gloucester Road or Chelsea. I believe that his devotion to London shortened his life, for two winters ago he put off going abroad for so long that he went down with acute bronchitis in the first bad fog.

'Pound is rather intelligent as a talker; his verse is touchingly incompetent,' he wrote to Conrad Aiken before falling under the spell of 'il miglior fabbro' (it was Pound who took over from Aiken the task of getting Eliot published successfully). Critics have been so occupied in recognising Eliot's debt to Pound that they have ignored Pound's debt to Eliot. Surely the change from the epigrams of 'Lustra' to 'Homage to Sextus Propertius' owed something to the academic seriousness of the younger mind and Pound's 'Mauberley' to the dazzling rhymed quatrains of the Sweeney poems of 1919?

I find I keep returning to the early Eliot and his poetry; it was after all the moment when the key fitted the lock, when the time was ripe for a poetical revolution incorporating urban life and its new vernacular; and he and Pound made it, only to look back, over the corpses of the slaughtered Georgians, to their own vision of the traditional past – Dante and Cavalcanti, or the French nineteenth century – and fall backwards to embrace it.

In addition there is something deeply enigmatic about the youthful Eliot with his intellectual gifts; it is seldom that a mind with so elastic a grasp of mental concepts can turn out such haunting poetry, or that such a mind should inhabit that formal and elusive body, which took boxing lessons and affected a discreet dandyism.

Professor Kenner called his book on Eliot *The Invisible Poet*, partly in allusion to the way in which all his tracks had been covered. I know of no lyric poet who has so completely disguised the clues, leaving only the harrowing sense of personal grief and loss lurking in the poems – 'the last twist of the knife'. This withdrawal of any affirmative personality, according to Hugh Kenner, 'has allowed his work to be discussed as though it were the legacy of a deceased poet and, like such a legacy, it invades the reader's mind and there undergoes an assimilation which soon persuades us that we have always possessed it.' It is this assimilation of such a completed life-work of poetry and criticism that makes his death less difficult to bear.

In 1915 Eliot married Vivien Haigh-Wood and moved to London. It was a most unhappy marriage and is likely to figure largely in many future accounts as an explanation of so much of his reticence. *The Waste Land* was written in Switzerland recuperating from some kind of break-down ('the nightingale sings of adulterous wrong'), and the marvellous penitential sequence of 'Ash Wednesday' was dedicated to her. She became mentally deranged and remained ill for many years, dying in 1947.

> The golden foot I may not kiss or touch
> Glowed in the shadow of the bed
> Perhaps it does not come to very much
> This thought this ghost this pendulum in the head
> Swinging from life to death
> Bleeding between two lives
> Waiting that touch . . .
>
> —From a poem in *The Tyro*, 1921

Eliot's middle period covers his dominating years as a critic and editor, his lectures, his best essays, his first verse plays: *The Rock*, *Murder in the Cathedral*, and *The Family Reunion* (1939) (to my mind the loveliest and the most original, though not the most actable), some of his own favourite short poems like 'Virginia' and 'Cape Ann', and his two masterpieces, 'Ash Wednesday' and *Four Quartets*. One might include his two prose masterpieces *Selected Essays* (1930) and *The Use of Poetry and the Use of Criticism*.

'He introduced a severity and astringency into criticism which were long resented, but which eventually compelled respect when backed by the prestige gained by his work in poetry' (Robson). He planted many a stiletto, painlessly, in a fatal spot – and some of his early definitions, from *The Sacred Wood* onwards, have the perfection of his best lines of verse. As, of the poet, 'What happens is a continual surrender of himself as he is at the moment to something which is more valuable. The progress of an artist is a continual self-sacrifice, a continual extinction of the personality.'

As the years went by, the astringent, sparkling quality deserted Eliot's prose, which was apt to become arid and sometimes pontifical, bowed down by the honours and ex-cathedra authority which society had bestowed on him. During the war he suddenly found himself accepted as something we were fighting for, like the Four Freedoms or Big Ben. In the Thirties the image had been formed of the cat-addict and cheese-taster, the writer of pawky blurbs, the church-warden, the polite deflater.

But all this time 'Four Quartets' were in gestation, the greatest single poem of the first half of the twentieth century. The Quartets are still baffling and few possess the philosophical training as well as the critical equipment to unravel them, but one can read them again and again discovering new consonances, familiar truths and fresh meanings. No one has written, throughout a long life, so movingly about death, ever present from Phlebas to the serene passing of the Elder Statesman, and no poet has so elegantly mocked human pretensions and the trappings of fame, orders and decorations, honours and emoluments.

Yet he has been carried through time and death to a state of mystical rapture where 'fire and the rose are one'. The rose-garden has always been his symbol of happiness.

In 1957 Eliot married his 'confidential clerk', Miss Valerie Fletcher, and gained the human happiness which by a tragic mistake he had for so many years been denied. In what I believe to be the last poem he wrote, the dedication to his last *Collected Poems*, he comes back to the rose-garden:

> No peevish winter wind shall chill
> No sullen tropic sun shall wither
> The roses in the rose-garden
> which is ours and ours only.

I would like to quote from a letter of last autumn so typical of his humility and candour:

> I was particularly touched by the way in which you referred, in reviewing my *Collected Poems*, to my last dedicatory poem to my wife.

> You were the first sympathetic reader and critic to call attention to the unusual fact that I had at last written a poem of love and of happiness. It would almost seem that some readers were shocked that I should be happy.

Like many admirers of Eliot I could never see enough of him. One longs for his Letters to get to know him better. I suppose my crowning moment was at a party I gave when he had won the Nobel Prize and where the poet, John Hayward, and myself read 'Sweeney Agonistes' at a late hour, Eliot singing 'Under the Bamboo Tree' for us. Although by his reserve he carried the prestige of literature far into enemy country he relaxed into gaiety when he could. His three last plays brought him an enormous audience and lost him some of his earlier admirers – unjustly, for in its way *The Cocktail Party* is just as original as *The Waste Land*. I am reminded of what Valéry, Eliot's closest French counterpart, once wrote about Mallarmé.

> Our beloved Mallarmé, the great event of our youth, always present and always perceptible and recognisable in the minds and judgements of everyone who approached him and revered him, and who accepted him as different from anyone else whom they would ever meet, martyr and confessor of the will to perfection.

e. e. Cummings
(1962)

I have lately felt aware of a worry at the back of my mind about the death of the American poet E. E. Cummings who liked to be known as e. e. cummings. It is an added misfortune to die at the end of August or beginning of September when all one's friends are away in the hills or on the beaches; the event appears slightly unreal for there are no critical estimates or personal tributes. That was what was at the back of my mind, the feeling that I had missed something, that at any moment I would open a paper and find the tribute and the estimate I expected. But months have passed and once again the thought arises which all must feel as they grow old, that it is they who are the custodians of the dead, and that if they wish to read something about one of them they will have to write it themselves.

Here is what I expected:

Edward Estlin Cummings was born in October, 1896, in Cambridge, Massachusetts where his father was a Unitarian minister. He was educated at Harvard like his father, went to France in the first world war, wrote an extraordinary war book, *The Enormous Room* (1922), fell in love with Paris for two years, then returned to America and devoted his whole life to painting and poetry.

He was a natural anarchist who made no concessions to authority and remained all his life a poor man, one of the very few poets to have no other jobs. He insisted on making typography part of the structure of his poems; this intrigued some and alienated many. It was not an affectation but part of his preoccupation with language, the heresy, one might call it, of Mallarmé's *Coup de dès*.

He lived most of his life in Patchin Place, New York, which somehow reminded me of Margaretta Terrace, Chelsea. He was a man of very great charm, with a lovely wife, absolutely authentic in all his personal relations because he would not recognise any others. He set a high standard of friendship and perhaps was too easily disappointed. He enjoyed his painting as much as, probably more than, writing poetry. He was built like a rather rangy pelota player with a long Etruscan face which looked very well in a beret. He could metamorphose at will from the Harvard man of letters to the East Side tough, talking venomously out of the side of his mouth. He was one of the people in America I most wanted to get to know and it was worth it; we had some French meals at the Lafayette and I introduced him to Auden whom he had never met, and I published a book of his, *One Times One*, when I got back. It proved quite unsaleable. He was a very isolated figure, but far too happy to be lonely. He began to obtain a lot of recognition in the 'fifties, but I don't think he cared much about it; he was used to feeling indignation and to taking the offensive against all life-haters, from intellectual Marxists to venal critics and the complacent American bourgeoisie.

When a young man, in his Paris days, he seems to have undergone a manic visitation from the Muse; his long prose work and five volumes of poetry all came pouring out in two or three years (1922–25) and he could also hold forth all night without pausing, looking like a sophisticated Apache. These poems, I think, are his best work, and at this time he had the entrée to *The Dial* through Gilbert Seldes and Scofield Thayer and also won the admiration of Ezra Pound.

He must have been a little like a rougher, uncorrupted Scott Fitzgerald, an American romantic turning realist. His favourite form was the Shakespearean sonnet which he broke up into a violent, almost colloquial medium. His best poems remind me of Catullus; there is a controlled fury about them, an erotic exhilaration. I don't know of anyone who has so caught the excitement and despair of brothels and speakeasies in the Prohibition days, in that New York from which the other expatriates kept away.

The 'thirties was a bad time for him as for so many writers of his generation. Unlike Fitzgerald, he was not almost forgotten, but went off into polemic and had great difficulty in finding a publisher, though he must have been the only poet to have discovered as a patron a tame printer, Mr S. A. Jacobs, who welcomed his typographical challenge. During the war his poetry picked up again and since then he has been in all the anthologies. I do not feel, however, that his later poetry was his best. He was a lyric poet who continued to celebrate love and spring and young lovers with all his warmth and to hate death and conformity, cowardice and apathy – but who to some extent lacked an intellectual growth within so that his hymns to love and life could appear sentimental and his satirical typographical cryptograms grow wearisome.

Anarchist attitudes age badly, and I think to get the feel of authentic Cummings one must turn back to the earlier poems of *Is 5* (his fifth book, 1925) or the larger revision of his first poems, *Tulips and Chimneys*. There we will find sudden illumination, as if we are watching the lights go on along the Boulevard from the window of some dingy hotel bedroom or waiting for a girl in a New York speakeasy on a winter afternoon.

Dick Mid's large bluish face without eyebrows
sits in the kitchen nights and chews a two-bit cigar,
waiting for the bulls to pull his joint. . . .

The total silence surrounding Cummings's death made me wonder if it were not part of a larger ignorance, if today the two alienated cultures are not art and science but British and American. I began to consider how many people in this country have read, as well as Cummings, Wallace Stevens, William Carlos Williams or Hart Crane.

Hart Crane was a frenzied middle-western alcoholic homosexual whose passion was to write like Rimbaud and who succeeded. He is nearly as important as Dylan Thomas, who greatly admired him, and when he was drowned in his early thirties (1932) was at work on a fascinating group of tropical poems, *Key West*, an adult change from his overloaded but magnificent sequence about Brooklyn Bridge.

He wrote best when drunk, with the gramophone playing the same piece of jazz all night, awaiting some magical *donnée* in the manner of Francis Bacon. And if that seems surprising, how much more surprising is the case of Wallace Stevens, a poet of great intelligence and exquisite fancy who clung all his life to the insurance business and became managing director of a large company from which he refused to retire at seventy-five. And of Dr Williams, who has been in every *avant-garde* magazine since 1920 and remained a suburban G.P. His last book, *Paterson V*, has some of the best lines on old age since Yeats.

And while we are about it, how many Americans know what a wonderful poet we have in Mr Arthur Waley, whose translations from the Chinese from 1916 onwards were really the profound answer to both the academic and the Georgian styles and which performed – or could have performed – the same liberating function that Dr Williams did, with his 'Nantucket' or 'By the Road to the Contagious Hospital'.

And how many English know it either?

Ernest Hemingway (1961)

By the death of Ernest Hemingway we have lost a Titan: whatever judgment we make upon his books the man was of the stature of a great novelist. He had the energy, the endurance, the personal grandeur of the Balzac, Stendhal, Flaubert, Tolstoy category. I do not think he was a great novelist but he was of the material of which great novelists are made, a Titan who still had it in him to become a god.

That we cannot put him on the highest level is not to his discredit. It is because he chose so completely to represent his era that he could never escape from its limitations; he was at heart a romantic poet who used fiction, even journalism, as his medium. It was writers as artists whom he admired – not novelists whose craft he studied. One cannot imagine him writing a book on the novel.

His first book was called *Three Stories and Ten Poems*, his first two novels were long short stories. His real novels are only three: *A Farewell to Arms*, *For Whom the Bell Tolls*, and *Across the River and Into the Trees*. He is not a novelist in the sense in which Henry James was, or Joyce or Arnold Bennett or Dreiser – or even Virginia Woolf, another poet. What concerned him was getting down the poetic nature of his own experience, not the construction of a novel as a work of art which would enforce on him its own laws.

The experience he wished to communicate could go into several moulds: the prose poem (like the first version of *In Our Time*), the didactic essay (*Death in the Afternoon*), the travel book (*Green Hills of Africa*), journalism (the articles on deep-sea fishing in *Esquire*, on the *Dangerous Summer* in *Life*), or a film like *Spanish Earth* which is pure Hemingway and a great film which should be shown again. But above all his medium was the short story: *The Sun Also Rises* and *A Farewell to Arms* were begun as short stories and *To Have and Have Not* included one, while some of his short stories have the depth and completeness of novels. Of these the greatest in my opinion is *The Snows of Kilimanjaro* which has all the elements of an autobiographical novel and, in the present circumstances, a prophetic, almost unbearable sadness.

Wonderful as so many of these stories are, and diverse in content, they never take one away from the central point of Hemingway's genius; his stance of a romantic poet in the twentieth century. All are based, almost without exception, on the relationship between man and death, on the confrontation of man's nobility and courage with his ineluctable adversary.

> When you were young you gave death much importance. Now you give it none, you only hate it for the people that it takes away.

So he wrote in 1938, but it was not true: the world was already taking on a new lease of death and very soon Hemingway was giving it his full attention from the death of Robert Jordan in *For Whom the Bell Tolls* to that of Colonel Cantwell in *Across the River and Into the Trees*. In fact everything he has written springs from the romantic protest.

> *'Tis a fine thing to dance and sing*
> *While the bells of death do ring—*

They dance and sing in *The Sun Also Rises*; in other books they talk and drink – but always against the same background. War provides the obvious arena for brave men to face death but Hemingway, in time of peace, also made his study of bullfighting because it is a sport in which the competitors risk their lives against death personified: boxing was a pale echo of this and gang-warfare provided another peacetime field of study. Big-game hunting and fishing also had their place, even skiing. But tennis, for example, of which Hemingway was fond, had no mention in his stories because it held no danger.

I suppose no writer has ever written so consistently of the 'moments of truth' when death stalks the adventurer (and less about lingering diseases, financial suicides, or bed-side quittances where the drama is lacking) and I cannot accept Hemingway's own explanation:

> The only place where you could see life and death, i.e. violent death now that the wars were over, was in the bull-ring and I wanted very much to go to Spain where I could study it. I was trying to learn to write, commencing with the simplest things, and one of the simplest things of all, and the most fundamental, is violent death.
>
> (*Death in the Afternoon*)

Hemingway was already writing about dying bull-fighters in 1923, and he had been reporting the atrocities of the Turko-Greek war before that, besides being badly wounded in 1918.

One of his *Ten Poems* described a suicide in Montparnasse and his father committed suicide in 1928; and although Hemingway made Colonel Cantwell in *Across the River and Into the Trees* say 'no horse called Morbid ever won a race' I would assert that he must have had from boyhood a preoccupation with death and violence, an imagination drawn irresistibly towards the macabre – a common attribute of genius. His earliest stories, written when he was seventeen, already dealt with crimes of violence and crooked boxers.

Ernest Hemingway was born July 21st, 1899, in Oak Park, a suburb of Chicago. His father was a doctor, his mother was artistic and went in for music and painting. Their summers were spent in the wild lake district of Northern Michigan with its woods and Indians. Here his father taught him to shoot and fish:

> They were seated in the boat, Nick in the stern, his father rowing. The sun was coming up over the hills. A bass jumped, making a circle in the water. Nick trailed his hand in the water. It felt warm in the sharp chill in the morning.
>
> In the early morning on the lake sitting in the stern of the boat with his father rowing, he felt quite sure that he would never die.

At school he became both an athlete and an omnivorous reader and very soon a writer who went to work on the *Kansas City Star* rather than go to a university, before joining the American Red Cross. (His sight was too bad for the Army.) His Italian war-time experiences are described in *A Farewell to Arms*, his childhood and adolescence in *In Our Time*, that subtle counterpoint of stories and anecdotes which contrasts the war-time chaos and violence of Europe with the happiness of growing-up in Michigan.

Then came the formative years in Paris (so handy for Spain) which gave us the Hemingway we know. Only a year separates the publication of the complete *In Our Time* (1925) from the nineteen-twentyish best-seller *The Sun Also Rises* (1926), from which moment Hemingway was famous and evermore remained so, in the big lights and the big money, unable ever to hide from them.

He was an extremely handsome young man of superb physique, dazzling teeth, a British officer moustache, great courage; no one so physical and athletic had ever found his way before to sit at the feet of Flaubert, Joyce, Pound or Gertrude Stein. To his study of violent death he brought his exúberant gaiety, immense vitality, a wicked satirical gift and a lyrical sense of words, of their placing and timing.

Gertrude Stein made a writer of him out of a reporter; but his dialogue, which is flowing, natural and inevitable, was his own contribution. He had one grave fault which sprang I think from something warped in his character, a sadistic facetiousness which went with a tendency to sentimentality.

It took several forms; sneering at intellectuals, making smarty wise-cracks in what should have been naturalistic dialogue, needling homosexuals, exulting in unpleasant details in the hope of giving offence, revelling in phony characters like the bloodthirsty little old lady in *Death in the Afternoon* or the suffering of hyenas in *Green Hills of Africa* or the thought-train of that Soames Forsyte in battledress, Colonel Cantwell in *Across the River and Into the Trees*.

The excessively male audience for which most of his journalism and some of his stories were written tended to bring this out and it accounts for the considerable critical coldness on the part of those who shrank from this uneasy vulgarity.

Hemingway, as a writer, was very conscious of his own failings. After the enormous success of *A Farewell to Arms* (1929) he encountered unpopularity with his two guide books to bull-fighting and kudu-slaying, and his socially-conscious novel *To Have and Have Not* was not a success although it is quite one of his best books, beautifully constructed and marvellously written.

He was saved from the bloated lethargy of success by the Spanish war which brought the romantic love of his life, the Iberian peninsula and its people, into historical greatness. He gave most of his fortune, forty thousand dollars, to the Spanish Medical Aid and this gesture alone set him absolutely apart from all other writers: it was worthy of a Titan, like his film, his despatches from Madrid and the encouragement afforded by his great prestige and loyal personality. 'Writers are forged in injustice as a sword is forged. . . .'

In Spain, as for so many others, his youth ended and after the war he went back to Cuba, where the shaggy grey-bearded bespectacled 'Poppa' was born. His moment of glory as a man, if not as a writer, was in Normandy and Paris at the Liberation. Although a war correspondent he had somehow become a tank commander and led his regiment to the relief of the Ritz, the Travellers Club, and Sylvia Beach's bookshop, where, twenty years before, he had begun.

The proof of this last ten years will be his great war novel with its vast size and many deletions. Will it justify the artist who continued to work away inside the over-garlanded, over-celebrated, touchy, arrogant and run-to-seed 'great man' as he appears in the famous *New Yorker* interview? His last two years were built round his visits to Spain and his identification of all his youthful '*aficion*' with the career of the young bull-fighter Antonio Ordoñez whose father he had known and whose father he was becoming.

I would like to give a brief anthology but there is no room. I would include the last page of *A Farewell to Arms* because he rewrote it so many times; the whole of the twentieth chapter of *Death in the Afternoon*, the inventory of his beloved Spain; the whole of *In Our Time* because it is such a good first book; the two suppressed opening chapters of *The Sun Also Rises* (so that we can read them); the last chapters of *To Have and Have Not* and the first sentence; many, many stories, even extracts from his *Death in Venice* (*Across the River and Into the Trees*); the wonderful digressions on Paris and the Gulf Stream in *Green Hills of Africa* and the whole of his remarkable interview in *Paris Review*. No one has written more knowledgeably about sudden death or with more poetry about physical pleasures and the joy of living, no one has worked harder to give his prose a new dimension, a prose which he thought could never be written, 'without tricks and without cheating. With nothing that will go bad afterwards'.

Evelyn Waugh: Was this Journey Really Necessary? (1960)

When we are young we travel to see the world, afterwards to make sure it is still there. In *A Tourist in Africa* Mr Waugh makes a routine check-up on various places which had delighted him as a youth. Aden? 'Here, Sir.' Zanzibar? 'Here, Sir.' Mombasa? 'Here, Sir.' Dar-es-Salaam? 'Here, Sir.' Happy Valley? Silence – and the blue pencil strikes it off the roll. I know the obsession by which re-visiting places where one has once felt becomes a substitute for feeling, but it does not make for the best kind of travel book. In fact *A Tourist in Africa* is quite the thinnest piece of book-making which Mr Waugh has undertaken and must be viewed in relation to the labours on Father Ronald Knox which preceded it.

It is not that Mr Waugh has seen so much already, although many of these places he seems to have visited only the year before, but that the particular pose he affects – of an elderly, infirm and irritable old buffer, quite out of touch with the times – is hardly suited to enthusiasm, a prerequisite of travel-writing. His book is full of little bread-and-butter letters, but, on the whole, his motto seems to be like Yeats's lines:

On life, on death
Cast a cold eye.

The fact must be faced, however, that there are people who are interested in every single word Mr Waugh writes, and I am one of them. While deploring the perfunctory and blasé handling of his material, the rows of short sentences, the occasional carelessness, such as misquoting Tennyson, using words like 'insomnious', together with his indifference to scenery, and all forms of wildlife (so unlike the descriptions of Kenya in *Remote People*), I can still assert that the magnetism of his extraordinary personality breaks through and that one is loth to part from it, even when he is on the level of:

> Mrs. Newman forbade one to go to this hotel and very kindly put me up for the night in her own cheerful villa. That evening she collected some of her neighbours for cocktails . . . All were most welcoming to a rather travel-worn stranger.

He is really at his best in Europe, in his description of Genoa, and I wish he could have included his articles for the *Daily Mail* on European cities, for he has reached the age when one writes much better if one is comfortable and not too hot or too cold. There is one exception; when kindled by his faith, his pen surmounts other obstacles, and he describes Father Groeber's school of native wood-carvers at the Serima mission in Southern Rhodesia with vivacity. Emin Pasha also kindles his interest.

What would we learn of (1) Africa (2) Mr Waugh – if we had only this book to go by? That we must travel by sea, not air, that the coast towns are too hot, that Mombasa is the best of them, that we must avoid British-owned hotels, that the hospitality of the landed gentry of the White Highlands has been replaced by that of government officials, that there is some jealousy among them, that the Eastern Highlands of Southern Rhodesia round Umtali are an unspoilt paradise ('Perhaps the development of this district may provide the elderly and well-to-do with a more dignified resort than the beaches where they now exhibit themselves. The craze for sunburn has lasted long enough').

On racialism, nationalism, the colour bar, even the ground-nuts scheme, Mr Waugh is without prejudice. He disapproves, but will not let them spoil his holiday. He defends the Aden smells:

> It is always a wonder to me that the English – who cheerfully endure the reek of cabbages, diesel fumes, deodorisers, fish and chips, gaspers, ice-cream – fight shy of 'native streets'.

'Paris at the cocktail hour. How gaily I used to jump into a taxi and visit the bars while the train crawled round the ceinture. Nowadays, hard of hearing and stiff in the limb, I sit glumly in my compartment.' That really is a bad sign, especially with a good restaurant in the Place d'Aligre close to the Gare de Lyon. About planes and boats he is rather unfair. The menus on boats are good, but the food is often deadly dull, and nothing on a plane is as bad as having to share a cabin or even a table in the restaurant with the same people for a week.

To travel first class, on the other hand, on a Comet or a Caravelle from London to Rome, Madrid, Athens or Tripoli compared to any other means of getting to such places is absolute bliss. But I have made a mental reservation on the *Pendennis Castle*, noted the excellent library on the *Rhodesia Castle* (for the East Coast Route) and not forgotten the German hotel at Kibo. 'A very pleasant bedside book,' the blurb says of *A Tourist in Africa*, and so it is. But what a drubbing I should get if I had written it.

Apotheosis in Austin
(1971)

'First they'll crab you – then they'll crib you,' Desmond MacCarthy used to say, and that seemed to be the fate of my *The Modern Movement: a Hundred Key Books* (Deutsch 75p), marred by misprints, savaged by critics and immediately followed up by a polymath compendium which included scientists and film stars as if to prove how mine should have been done.

Only in booksellers' catalogues did my own selection and phrasing – fruit of years of love and worry – begin to make headway.

Meanwhile, the book became rare, then out of print with no signs of anybody wanting it. But in that great good place, Austin, headquarters of the University of Texas, the librarian, Mary Hirth, in charge of the vast collection of contemporary British texts and of many others, realised that my list corresponded closely with their holdings and could be used as a frame:

> The proverbial bell rang [she wrote later]. As I read the list of titles it rang louder and louder, and the first problem of preparing an exhibit was solved – the choice of a theme.

I had included British, French and American authors only, from 1880–1950, writers whom I could read in the original.

Only two translations had been included. Waley's *170 Chinese Poems*, and Koestler's *Darkness at Noon* (the one book of which Texas does not possess a first edition).

Texas' agents soon acquired some magnificent French examples to fill gaps, including a presentation copy from Verlaine of Rimbaud's 'Illuminations' and from Proust – of Swann – to 'Celeste Gineste loving wife of Odilon Albaret in memory and recognition of my deep affection for them both' together with an unpublished poem to her.

The Exhibition was postponed for more than a year for various reasons. When at last it was about to open I set off, in the first week in May.

The immense boredom of crossing the Atlantic, the sadness of the ice-packs off Labrador, the charm of immigration officials, the limbo of airports. Twenty hours in planes and airports since I heard the cuckoo at home at 5 a.m. Now it is night in Texas with heat and humidity in the eighties and I unpack in an enormous double room in a hotel which is called a club to be able to serve liquor and which provides appetising Southern food and iced tea.

Next morning I met John Lehmann, Virgil for once to my Dante, and the organisers of the Exhibition, Warren Roberts (bibliographer of Lawrence), Mary Hirth, and later William Ransome who master-minded the huge operation which put the Texas collections above all others. They are a very small, expert, modest, dedicated group, those of 'The Humanities Research Center' who provide the great archives on which future students will draw on for their researches. The number of requests to consult the archives remains at between 200 and 300 a year, half of which come from American universities outside Texas and another quarter from abroad.

Favourite subjects are D. H. Lawrence (an easy winner) with thirteen dissertations, then Joyce with seven, Pound and Tennessee Williams with five, Eliot, Shaw, Orwell, Dylan Thomas with four, Tennyson, T. F. Powys, Faulkner and Céline with three.

Austin is a pleasant city with a capitol in pale cold granite whose dome is illuminated at night. The plains of the gulf stretch to one side; low hills covered with Mediterranean scrub to the other announce the beginnings of the West. The poor whites are Mexicans, there is no sign of racial tension and only a few skyscrapers from one of which a psychopathic student, Charles Whitman, after murdering his parents, gunned down fourteen victims in 1966.

The university is pleasantly shaded by many evergreen trees, oleanders and jacarandas bloom, mocking birds abound and large black grackles, the academic buildings are sensible and well-ordered, the campus is soothing. A new 'Humanities Center' is rapidly nearing completion, big enough to house all the various branches and archives.

On the ground floor at the Center are two cases of my MSS, association copies – of which, more, as they say, anon. On the fourth floor is the exhibition proper, each case festooned with corrected galleys of my book, like strands of seaweed, and photographs or self-portraits of writers until they seem to come alive before one. Treasures include the MSS of Forster's *Passage to India*, Greene's *The Power and the Glory*, Huxley's *Brave New World*, much Dylan Thomas and 150 pages of Flaubert's notes for *Bouvard*. To be associated with these riches is to be given a sense of belonging to the tradition, a boost to the ego for one's diffident London self.

A long corridor runs outside which forms a 'gallery of British worthies'. Here are portraits of Eliot by Gerald Kelly, Auden by Coldstream, Yeats, Joyce, drawings by Lewis, an excellent Betjeman by Buhler, busts of Conrad and Eliot by Epstein; so many writers one has known and some one has loved. I am seized by an overwhelming emotion like Encolpius in the Picture Gallery. The Portraits of the Artists – so intelligent, so immaterial, so aloof and reposeful – form an overwhelming tribute to the dignity of our occupation. The gallery is like the aisle of a cathedral whose side-chapels are the cases full of reliquaries and ex-votos.

On another floor is the archive – the columbarium, the Père Lachaise – the filing rooms where one walks down narrow corridors with urn-like boxes of material on each side – Edith Sitwell with the largest deposit. Here all the hopes and worries and tax troubles and fan-mail, the contracts and the loveletters, the rows and reconciliations come to rest.

Who knows what secrets lie incarcerated, awaiting the ultimate deadline when the dissertations will uncover the true facts. I felt like Gray in his country churchyard or Evelyn Waugh, discovering Forest Lawn.

Evelyn Waugh . . . now I remembered that I had glimpsed his handwriting in my show-case, in a handsomely bound copy of *The Unquiet Grave*. I went back to have a look. The book had vanished. I found it had been closed and put aside but by pleading obtained permission to have it back and hold it in my hands. (Texas have bought the complete contents of Evelyn's library including his book-shelves, desk and armchairs.) Was I not the hero of the hour? Could any of my wishes be denied?

The afternoon was young – I had lunched well on Mexican food and the pink Texan grapefruit, best of its kind. My body relaxed in the sun, my heart was back in London, the London of grime and buzz-bombs, of uniforms, of sand-bags and rationing, of *Horizon* and Palinurus. This is what I read:

> Why should I be interested in this book? Because I have known Cyril more than twenty years and enjoy dining with him? Because, alone in Dubrovnik, I have not much else to occupy me? Rather because Cyril is the most typical man of my generation. There but for the Grace of God, literally. . . . He has the authentic lack of scholarship of many of my generation. He read Freud while getting only a third in Greats, the authentic love of leisure and liberty and good living, the authentic romantic snobbery, the authentic waste-land despair, the authentic high gift of expression. Here he is in war-time, in Bloomsbury, strait-jacketed by sloth. . . . Quite clear in his heart that the ills he suffers from are theological, with the vocabulary of the nonsense-philosophy he learned, holding him back. The Irish boy, the immigrant, homesick, down at heel and ashamed, full of fun in the public house, a ready quotation on his lips, afraid of witches, afraid of the bog priest, proud of his capers: the Irishman's deep-rooted belief that there are only two final realities – Hell and the USA.

Worse was to follow: on page after page Evelyn recorded his disapproval, his hate (and, dare I say, envy), referring to me as 'Paddy' or as 'a lady novelist' or a shabby journalist frequenting Lady Cunard's salon at the Dorchester. When, towards the end, he began to interpolate a few words of praise, one felt like the victim of torture who gets an occasional cup of water dashed in his face.

I suppose what I minded most was the contempt which emerged from a writer for whom for twenty years (1923–43) I had looked upon as a friend. His comments, greatly toned down, were used in his review in the *Tablet*. I suppose Hugh Walpole went through this over *Cakes and Ale*, but Maugham at least could plead that he meant someone else. The dead make no such excuses.

Well, here was the wicked godmother at my exhibition's christening. How many other mines and booby-traps lurked in the archives? I began to smart most at the assumption that I was a bog-trotting, lapsed Catholic immigrant in fear of Hell Fire. My Anglo-Irish grandfather, High Sheriff of Dublin, a land-owning pillar of the Kildare Street and Carlton Clubs, used bogs only for snipe-shooting: my father's grandfather was an impeccably Protestant Rector of Bath; I had worked hard at Oxford but on extra-curricular subjects and had collected a Laming Fellowship at Queen's provided I had got a second in History and not a third.

For the rest of my stay in Texas I remained obsessed with Evelyn, and on my return flight I attributed every sudden turbulence to him. I beheld the bloated, puffed-up face of my old club-mate with the beady eyes red with wine and anger, his cigar jabbing as he went into the attack. A certain coarseness of heart, I thought, marred his work.

And yet – if he hated me so, why did he present *Horizon* with 'The Loved One' free of charge and bear with all my suggestions about it, why did he ask me to stay or want to take me to the South of France? Did Taffy have some secret affection for Paddy to which he could never admit? I shall never know until Texas gives up all its secrets. Among them is an admirable piece of writing, a diary Evelyn kept after his return from Crete. It has been much drawn upon for his war novels but remains a basic statement of what happened to him and how he felt in those days in Cairo, Whites Club, and the Commando camp in Scotland. I see how one couldn't expect much sympathy for *The Unquiet Grave* from this crusader in battledress. I managed to extract the last sentence, so completely typical of Evelyn in his prime as a man and a writer:

> 28 October 1942
>
> My 39th birthday. A good year. I have begotten a fine daughter, published a successful book, drunk about 300 bottles of wine and smoked 300 or more Havana cigars. I have £900 in hand and no grave debts, health excellent except when impaired by wine, a wife I love, agreeable work in surroundings of great beauty. Well, that's as much as we can hope for.

George Orwell
(1968)

This splendid monument* is erected by Sonia Orwell and Ian Angus, who is in charge of the Orwell archive at London University. Orwell made a request that no biography should be written; this constitutes the nearest equivalent, since so many of his letters are included. Thus, of nine letters to me which appeared in the hundredth number of *Encounter*, seven are reproduced here and two 'non-vintage' ones are left out, while two paragraphs omitted from the *Encounter* versions are restored, and rightly. I mention this to illustrate the quality of the editing.

There is not much wholly new material in this book, yet sixty per cent of it is unfamiliar – articles and reviews retrieved from forgotten publications. The Wigan Pier diary, the complete war diary, the notes on the Spanish militia and the Orwell revealed by the hundreds of letters may be considered as new material, which alone justify the outlay on these four volumes. Volume IV includes *Such, Such Were the Joys*, hitherto available only in America. It is, to my mind, his most important autobiographical fragment and perhaps his best essay, running to forty pages, written in 1947:

> I am sending you separately a long autobiographical sketch which I originally undertook as a sort of pendant to Cyril Connolly's *Enemies of Promise*, he having asked me to write a reminiscence of the preparatory school we were at together . . . It is really too libellous to print but I think it should be printed sooner or later. (To F. J. Warburg)

* *George Orwell: The Collected Essays, Journalism and Letters*, edited by Sonia Orwell and Ian Angus. 4 vols. (New York, 1968).

What is important about this essay is the picture it gives of Blair (his real name) as a boy; his account of the school can be verified, the remainder not. The effect is magical: one enters the antechamber, shrinks, slips through the 'windowpane' of his prose and there one is, back again, among the cramming and the hunger and the smells, a little boy in corduroy knickers and a green jersey.

> That was the pattern of school life – a continuous triumph of the strong over the weak . . . Life was hierarchical and whatever happened was right. There were the strong, who deserved to win and always did win, and there were the weak who deserved to lose and always did lose, everlastingly . . . I had no money, I was weak, I was ugly, I was unpopular, I had a chronic cough, I was cowardly, I smelt, I was an unattractive boy . . . But this sense of guilt and inevitable failure was balanced by something else: that is, the instinct to survive.

I have reported, in reviewing George Woodcock's *The Crystal Spirit*, a certain softening in my own attitude to St Cyprians. This was due to getting possession of my school reports and the headmaster's letters to my father, and some of my own letters home. They revealed a considerable distortion between my picture of the proprietors and their own unremitting care to bring me on. At this point I hear Orwell's wheezy chuckle. 'Of course, they knew they were on to a good thing. What do you think was our propaganda value to them as winners of Eton scholarships – almost as good as being an "Hon."'

Orwell claims to have been taunted by the headmaster for paying reduced fees – but we had no inkling of this. History, if it can be bothered, will probably show Mr Wilkes to have been an extremely conscientious, though unimaginative and perhaps unlovable man; and Mrs Wilkes to have used too much physical violence and emotional blackmail, and to have vented some personal bitterness on the boys. Yet she was warm-hearted and an inspired teacher. The worldliness and snobbery of the Wilkeses which Orwell so much condemns was characteristic of the competitive middle class of the period, not a singular aberration. 'A couple of silly, shallow ineffectual people, eagerly clambering up a social ladder which any thinking person could see to be on the point of collapse.'

Half a century ago it had not collapsed, nor does it show all those signs of collapsing even now. A knighted grocer still cuts more ice than a writer on most social occasions; the Cavendishes, Capels, and Mildmays, or the Scotch lairds at whom the Wilkeses set their caps so successfully, are still a draw in the world of scholastic private enterprise. So many children enjoy pageantry that the supply of snobs is constantly renewed. It has been suggested by Mr Gow that Orwell and I were rebels who would be bound to criticise any educational institutions; but this is to underrate the voodoo-like quality of St Cyprians. Gavin Maxwell found it unchanged ten years later and I have heard of old boys who taught their children to shake their fists at the now deserted playing-fields, as they drove past.

> England is the most class-ridden country under the sun. It is a land of snobbery and privilege ruled largely by the old and silly. (1940)

Orwell was a political animal. He reduced everything to politics; he was also unalterably of the Left. His line may have been unpopular or unfashionable, but he followed it unhesitatingly; in fact it was an obsession. He could not blow his nose without moralising on conditions in the handkerchief industry. This habit of mind informed everything he wrote. *Animal Farm* and *1984* are political novels, *Homage to Catalonia*, *The Road to Wigan Pier* and all his essays ask a *cui bono* and try to unseat the profit-makers, whoever they be. This ruling purpose is the secret of his best writing but far too evident in his worst. If we look dispassionately at his achievement, we notice the enormous preponderance of journalism in these four volumes.

Orwell slipped into the last war as into an old tweed jacket. He settled down in 1939, to the BBC or the Literary Editorial chair of *Tribune*, or as London correspondent to *Partisan Review* (New York) to watch his dream come true – a People's War. He had seen it nearly happen in Spain, now it seemed inevitable. This time the gamble must come off, *Revolution or Disaster*. A series of defeats would topple the

British ruling class; in the nick of time the People would kick them out and take control, snatching victory at the last moment, as happened in revolutionary France. Churchill must go, even Cripps must go. Red Guards in the Ritz! Long live the People's Army and the Socialist Home Guard.

This point of view, apart from not being borne out by the facts, limited Orwell. He was anti-Churchill, anti-Stalin, anti-Beaverbrook, anti-American, except for the Trotskyites of *Partisan Review*. He felt enormously at home in the Blitz, among the bombs, the bravery, the rubble, the shortages, the homeless, the signs of rising revolutionary temper.

But the political crisis he 'expected for the better part of two years' never materialised. Churchill remained, so did top-hats, titles, officers, the Ritz, Margesson, money, all the bad old things. By 1945 it was too late. Socialism had become respectable. Orwell admitted this, but it is doubtful if he ever admitted what a vast quantity of words he had wasted.

My idea of Hell is a place where one is made to listen to everything one has ever said. But if this punishment be more than one could bear, then to listen to everything one said during the war would be hell enough. The war confined many ambitious, articulate and frustrated publicists to a small space with no outlet but discussion. As Orwell's editor puts it, 'he must have written hundreds of thousands of words during those years.' Being Orwell, nothing he wrote is quite without value and unexpected gems keep popping up. But O the boredom of argument without action, politics without power.

What is the importance of these four volumes? First, the letters. We are never likely to get such an opportunity again, for though not one of the best letter-writers Orwell was certainly candid. In his letters to women friends, like Brenda Salkeld or Eleanor Jaques, we hear him speaking, as in his letters to friends like Geoffrey Gorer, Julian Symons or Jack Common, who appears out of the blue, or rather the pink, with an enormous bundle. As I wrote about his letters to me, 'He was a man, like Lawrence, whose personality shines out in everything he said or wrote.'

Next, the non-political essays and reportage – or rather those in which his literary gifts outweigh his political message. Some of these are well known, but it is no bad thing to have them all together. Such are *Why I Write*, the letter about *Ulysses*, the review of *Tropic of Cancer*, *Shooting an Elephant* and *A Hanging* in Volume I or *Boys' Weeklies* which I published, with Frank Richards's unexpected and admirably written reply. Volume II gives us his memories of the Spanish War, and his fascinating war diary, so much better than the journalism he spun from it. Volume III has the Wodehouse article, the Dali assault.

Volume IV contains his famous rules for writing ('if it is possible to cut a word out cut it out,' etc.); his autobiographical letter to his old tutor, Professor Gow; his gloomy but delightful article on book reviewing; and also *Books and Politics*, *How the Poor Die*, *The Falling Off of Writers*. ('Many writers, perhaps most, ought simply to stop writing when they reach middle age') – and of course, *Such, Such Were the Joys*. His illness clouds his later letters with his account of hospitalisation and his removal to a sanatorium; and we catch only an echo of his contemplated article on Evelyn Waugh. Of Graham Greene, Orwell wrote: 'I have even thought that he might become our first Catholic fellow-traveller.'

Waugh was a different matter. I arranged for Evelyn to visit him at Cranham, near his Cotswold home, and he reported that Orwell 'was very near to God.' Orwell's conclusion: 'Waugh is about as good a novelist as one can be while holding untenable opinions.'

His last diary concludes with a devastating analysis of upper-class English voices which must have haunted him from St Cyprians School Sports. 'No wonder everyone hated us so.' How typical to shoulder the blame for them!

Samuel Beckett: *Watt, Malone Dies, Molloy* (1958)

These three volumes might be described as prolegomena to *Waiting for Godot*, and bear the same relationship to it as *Three Lives* and *The Making of Americans* to the *Autobiography of Alice B. Toklas*.

In my opinion *Waiting for Godot* is an original masterpiece of the theatre, and therefore anything which has contributed to it is of interest. I am not so happy about its successor *Fin de Partie*. *Godot* is a fresh assault on a universal problem. *Fin de Partie* is the statement of a private one, in which a dying Prospero and Caliban assert the validity of the human order (master and servant, will and action) against a collapsing universe.

The meaning of authority is also a preoccupation in these three books. Watt is a servant employed by Knott and this early novel is close to *Fin de Partie*, while there is also a resemblance between Watt and Lucky, 'stopping, and laying down his bags, and picking up his hat, and setting it on his head, and picking up his bags, and setting himself, after one or two false starts, again in motion. . . .'

The success of *Waiting for Godot* depends on three circumstances, that the audience be attuned to the atmosphere of hope and bewilderment in which some supernatural event is expected, that the extraordinary creatures with whom Beckett's world is peopled can be mimed in terms of human clowning, and that the particular melody of reiteration and silence, the notation of Beckett's word-music, gets across. To this extent Beckett is deliberately writing for the theatre.

In these novels, however, there is little or no dialogue. *Malone Dies* is a sombre soliloquy in which one or two shadowy characters appear;

and in the other two the page is unbroken except for an occasional questionnaire. I must now come forward and say that I do not see how these books can be read for pleasure, and that I consider that I have read them in order to protect the public from some of the hazards of a hebdomadist's occupation.

They are literary exercises, metaphysical limberings up before the author's first platform appearance. Shandean divagations in the elaborate *avant-garde* manner of the day before yesterday.

What is Mr Beckett's world? Expatriated Dubliner, lapsed Christian, ex-secretary of Joyce, he brings to it the atmosphere of the later chapters of *Ulysses*. His characters are all solitaries; lonely men whom God has let down and from whom man has turned away in disgust. They are semi-invalids, hunchbacks, spastics, epileptics who have replaced love and sex ('a mug's game, and tiring on top of that') with masturbation and nose-picking. Urinating and defecating play an enormous role, partly to emphasise man's fallen nature, partly because to the solitary invalid such pleasures are uncertain and important, hazardous and unpredictable, synonymous with the human gaucherie.

Place and time are of no importance; there is usually some town with a name like 'Bally' or 'Hole'; scenery is a matter of clouds seen from a window: the past is murkily remembered, the present non-existent, family ties are few and far between: ' "She died in giving me birth," said Mr. MacStern. "I can well believe that," said Mr. de Baker.' All Mr Beckett's characters are deformed or hideous and move in a terrifying atmosphere of rejection, abandonment and guilt.

An appalling perception of the degrees and fine shades of human misery seem to fill Mr Beckett with horror and compassion; he knows that old age, as a French writer put it, is a process of being flayed alive and he is determined to make his report on it. On the other hand his Irish wit and realism tell him that there is nothing people cannot eventually get used to. An impotent Prometheus shakes his fist at the heavens while adding another straw to the human camel beside him.

Watt is an early novel written in English and with considerable playfulness. The theme is servant and master, with an elongated tubular schizophrenic Caliban and an elusive Prospero. It is based on a kind of linguistic compulsion neurosis, as if the formula *abc, acb, bca, bac, cba, cab*, or one of four or five letters had been employed throughout.

> He read the book of the play, and the play of the book, and the book of the play of the book and the play of the book of the play and the book of the book of the play and the play of the book of the book and the book of the play of the play and the play of the play of the book and the book of the book of the book and the play of the play of the play. He must make time for reading.

This is an imaginary example of the form of logical stammer with which Mr Beckett is able to fill many pages, building up to a laugh which is in reality a pure release from tension at the end. I suppose Watt could be called a comic character, as he eventually takes to inventing the order and spelling of all his sentences – another schoolboy game. But Malone is more formidable, passing slowly into delirium or uraemia in a passion of isolation, like a sitter to Francis Bacon. The going is heaviest here. *Molloy* is perhaps better in the French, though I was never able to read it.

One is left with the feeling that this last eccentric of Irish prose is lacking in some gift – perhaps genius, *suineg spahrep* – whose presence shone out in Joyce and illuminated our way through the labyrinth.

> To be buried in lava and not turn a hair, it is then a man shows what stuff he is made of. To know you can do better next time, unrecognisably better, and that there is no next time and that it is a blessing there is not, there is a thought to be going on with.

Such stoicism is the nearest he comes to a positive message. I am afraid that after reading these three books, which I am delighted to see are now available in England, one realises that to write a really good play is not just a matter of long practice and the crystallisation of obsessions but of superlative luck.

W. H. Auden: Some Memories
(1974)

> Personal song and language . . .
> Thanks to which it's possible for the breathing
> Still to break bread with the dead. . . .

A few years ago it would have been easier: memories would have come crowding in, it remained only to sift them and bring them up to date with our last meeting, for I still saw him regularly when he came to England. But since he had made his home in Oxford we hardly met, except through Stephen Spender. Age still finds me devoted to my old friends but increasingly reminded that it is a one-way traffic so that I anticipate their rebuffs from an instinct of self-protection. I used to imagine the old as yarning away together or locked in pregnant silence like Tennyson and Carlyle. But age is not like that: the old are diminishing universes racing further and further apart, piling up space between them, unable to cope with the simplest mechanics of meeting. Artists can be touchy, frivolous and unforgiving, and often the only way to catch a glimpse of our old friends is at a memorial service or a literary award. 'O yonge freshe folke' be warned; friendship is for those who strenuously pursue the same goal; cultivate it now and do not put it off 'for when there will be more time' – time there may be but also death, weariness and estrangement.

I endangered our relationship at a recent meeting by telling Wystan that I could not agree to destroy his letters, that I did not think it scandalous that Keats' love-letters should have been published or the sonnets of Shakespeare, nor rejoice in the burning of Byron's journal. I could not wholly deplore the public's curiosity about artists' lives (better than none at all). But Wystan saw himself by now as a great gentleman, 'I am afraid I have become very square in my old age,' he answered:

> The class whose vices
> he pilloried was his own,
> now extinct, except
> for lone survivors like him
> who remember its virtues.

I have disobeyed his wishes by keeping his letters; worse still, I shall want to quote from them.

I have to hew my way back through the wilderness of time to rediscover the dazzling adornment of my youth, the one indisputable genius – 'water-fluent tea-drinking' – whose friendship I could once enjoy on an equal footing. I should perhaps mention in passing that when I am moved by the work of a contemporary my instinct is to wish to get to know him, and that once we have become acquainted, he can do no wrong. Some, like George Orwell and Evelyn Waugh, were already my friends before they revealed their talent, others like Dylan Thomas proved too alien to assimilate, or, like Hemingway, were always somewhere else.

At that time (the early thirties), poetry seemed to have exhausted itself; Eliot had gone religious, the Georgians moribund; Edith Sitwell appeared to be resting after giving us her *Collected Poems* of 1930 and Geoffrey Grigson had not quite started *New Verse*. *New Signatures*, *New Writing* – everything *new* but the *New Statesman* was still in the womb.

I first heard of Wystan through Tom Driberg's column in the *Daily Express* when he required of his large public 'Awareness of Auden', referring, I think, to the *Poems* of 1930, but it was the *Orators* (1932) which deeply moved me, while I found the chilly Marxism of *The Dance of Death* rather intimidating. But it was not Auden but Spender whom I was to meet after he wrote me a long letter from the island of Mlini about *The Destructive Element*, which I reviewed in the *New*

Statesman. We became firm friends and still are. Isherwood also I was to get to know well and it was he who told me to look up Auden at his hotel in Valencia where I was to return in my reporting on the Spanish war; I went there with my wife and Ran Antrim, who at that time described himself as 'me good pink peer', and we were rather cosseted except for a strict examination by the Comintern agent for whom I produced a letter from Harry Pollitt, the Secretary of the Communist Party. Auden, who was working for the government radio, seemed overjoyed to meet us and ordered a bottle of Spanish champagne, a detail which delighted Isherwood, who said it would have convinced him that it was the real Auden and not some impostor. I was at once obsessed with his appearance which penetrated deep into my subconscious so that I often dreamt about him. (The last time was January 1973.) Fortunately there are many photographs of the youthful Auden, as he remained till the end of the last war; the solid cragginess came later. He was tall and slim, with a mole on his upper lip, rather untidy tow-coloured hair in a loop over his forehead with extraordinary greenish eyes suggesting that iceberg glare he liked to claim from his Norse ancestors. His voice was unforgettable, with no trace then of an American accent, he was charming but ruthless, and certainly, like Isherwood, a Marxist of sorts, but less close to Communist orthodoxy than Day Lewis or Spender. My feelings towards him were entirely platonic: I was passionately fond of his poetry and desired his friendship but my subconscious demanded more and I was put out by a dream (based on his ballad) in which, stripped to the waist beside a basin ('O plunge your hands in water') he indicated to me two small firm breasts; 'Well, Cyril, how do you like my lemons?' Though not homosexual, I was, I hope, without any prejudices, and so was my wife Jean who became one of Wystan's closest women friends, the first, I believe, to call him Uncle Wiz and whom he described in her copy of his *Epithalamium* as the only woman who could keep him up all night.

After Valencia (May 1937), we soon met again in Barcelona where he took a photograph of Antrim playing chess and where, after a good lunch with much Perelada Tinto, we went for a walk in the gardens of

Monjuich. By the remains of the old International Exhibition Auden retired to pee behind a bush and was immediately seized by two militia men – or were they military police? They were very indignant at this abuse of public property and it took several wavings of Harry Pollitt's letter to set him free. I think the incident was important for it revealed the misunderstanding between the revolutionary poet who felt disinhibited by the workers' victory and the new bureaucracy to whom the people's gardens deserved more respect than ever before. I suppose we were in as much danger then as we had been during the shelling of Valencia. By the time we left a few days later it was clear to all of us that the government could not win. I see, by the way, that I reviewed *The Dog Beneath the Skin* for the *New Statesman* on 12 February 1936, and 'Spain' on 5 June 1937 whose ending:

> History to the defeated
> may say 'alas' but cannot help nor pardon

he has crossed out in my copy and written 'This is a lie.' The first contemporary inscription I possess is in *Look Stranger* with an unpublished quatrain sometime in 1937. I did not much like *The Dog Beneath the Skin* perhaps because I had found the hero, Francis Turville Petre, a little too much.

> I raise myself upon an awkward elbow
> and mourn beside the open window
> those two who fell at Pressan Ambo

The Ascent of F6 seemed to me a far better play.

One of the drawbacks of being a professional critic is that one sometimes cannot get out of reviewing a friend's books although one is disappointed. I once apologized to Wystan for one of these infrequent disparagements, 'O that's all right,' he answered, 'I didn't mind. I thought "It's just Cyril".' 'And is that what you would have said if I had praised it?'

I have said that he was ruthless and I do not mean only that he was intellectually tougher; he was uncompromising in his feelings, in his coherence of idea with action. He was hard-edged and unmellowed, wanting the benevolence of his later years. I remember once discussing my father and my difficult relationship with him. Wystan was adamant. 'Those people just batten on one, real emotional harpies, they've got to be taught a lesson. Stand up to him, make him see you don't need him any more.' ('From the immense bat-shadow of home deliver us.') Shortly afterwards my father lunched with me in Soho, a treat he always enjoyed, and on the way back I stopped the taxi outside my door in Chelsea (he lived in South Kensington). He clearly expected to be invited in for a talk and a brandy but I bade him an abrupt farewell and gave the driver his address. Clutching his two thick cherrywood sticks with the rubber ferrules, his legs crossed, his feet in pumps, for owing to arthritis he could not stoop to do up laces, he fingered his grey moustache while a tear trickled down his cheek. I don't know which of us felt more unhappy.

Freud's way-out colleague Dr Groddeck was to blame here, for Auden took him more seriously than Marx; he was more at home then among biologists and doctors than humanists; he knew German but little French and he was insularly devoted to northern England.

How much more difficult it is to write about a poet than his work. I keep trying to describe Wystan yet I feel I am but making a grotesque waxwork because I cannot communicate the mysterious certainty of inspiration that covered old envelopes with his tiny crabbed writing. He never seemed to erase and never to be at a loss – 'nothing superfluous and nothing wanting'.

To experience the impact of his early poetry one should re-read it in the magazines in which it first came out. *Oxford Poetry*, *New Country*, *New Signatures*, *New Writing* ('Lay your sleeping head my love') above all, *New Verse*. Grigson's little sixpenny, so well-printed and composed, was a joy right up to its special Auden number but editorial enthusiasm was counteracted by the spleen of his *alter ego*, who saw himself as a *chef d'école* like Breton. But he admired and loved Auden who got no worse chastisement than a comment that 'there was a smell of light verse in the air' (1938).

I always felt that the influence of Shakespeare's sonnets (later to be dismissed by the old Anglican arbiter as the height of bad taste) was extremely stimulating to the younger poet seeking to revive a convention in which it was possible to celebrate homosexual love. Hence those five sonnets, which he never reprinted, among the loveliest he has written I have always thought (*New Verse* No. 5, October 1933):

I see it often since you've been away:
The island, the veranda and the fruit;
The tiny steamer breaking from the bay;
The literary mornings with its hoot;
Our ugly comic servant and then you,
Lovely and willing every afternoon.
But find myself with my routine to do,
And knowing that I shall forget you soon.
There is a wound and who shall stanch it up?
Deepening daily, discharging all the time
power from love. . . .

These magical first lines of his!

The latest ferrule now has tapped the curb

or

August for the people and their favourite islands

or

Out on the lawn I lie in bed
Vega conspicuous overhead

or

A shilling life will give you all the facts

In a brief list of my friends in 1937 (I am a compulsive list-maker) I end with '?Wiz' – and one of my pleasantest moments was when I lent him my tails to go to the Palace to receive his gold medal from the King and he came straight back to tell us about it. I shared with Brian Howard the position of his social adviser but Brian, more assiduous, soon cut me out. The next year witnessed his departure with Isherwood for China and in October the publication of my *Enemies of Promise* so eulogistic of his prose and verse. *4 February:* 'The Indian Ocean is crashingly dull. We take the best part of a week to cross it. You're to get that book finished before we return or there'll be big trouble . . .'.

Hong Kong: 'We are living in a baking hut, but move to the Vice-Chancellor's house today. The ambassador saw us while he was dressing, and tomorrow we call on the bishop. Love Wystan.' 'It's Uncle Wiz's birthday. This evening we're giving a big Chinese supper-party. We're off to Canton next week. Love C.'

> *15 November 1938* [*Birmingham*]: I have just finished reading *Enemies of Promise*. . . . As both Eliot and Edmund Wilson are Americans. . . . I think *E. of P.* is the best English book of criticism since the war, and more than Eliot or Wilson you really write about writing in the only way which is interesting to anyone except academics, as a real occupation like banking or fucking with all its attendant egotism, boredom, excitement and terror. I do congratulate you on a brilliant but also solid and moving book.

On their way home from China they had passed through America and had both made friends whom they found they had missed more than they had expected. Abruptly they struck camp and migrated to the USA sufficiently near the outbreak of war to incur some hostile criticism. Soon afterwards the intellectual ties reasserted themselves and Auden began to send his American-based poetry to *Horizon* and *New Writing*. (I published his elegy on Freud in March, 1940.) It soon became clear from his important transitional poem, *New Year Letter* (first published in the USA as *The Double Man*) that Auden had undergone a change of heart as well as of scene. *On this Island* (*Look Stranger*) is British, *Another Time*, transitional, *New Year Letter*, American, prelude to *The Age of Anxiety* and the Christian poetry of *For the Time Being*. We had met again, briefly, in 1945 when he passed through London in his pale American officer's uniform and his flat 'a's' ('gas' rhymed with 'mask').

> *28 November 1946, New York:* Wystan charming, though very battered-looking. More American than ever and much less self-conscious than in London. . . . On to chez Chester. At last the luxury of poverty, stairs (no lift), leaking armchair and an exquisite dinner – with really good European conversation; arguments about poetry and Lorca. Mysticism and fucking, according to Wystan, are the two extremes where man forgets himself and art consequently can't be made. Much conversation about the USA and Wystan continues to propound his point of view (see his Introduction to Henry James' *American Scene*), he is quite pro-British and defends this also. He always reverts to the same argument which I think is true for him – in the USA he receives anonymity, more money (he made ten thousand dollars this year and bought a mortgage) and his desire is gratified for a large, open, impersonal new country.
>
> Away from the 'bat-shadow', Auden warns us of the perils of the big city, hold-ups, the proper use of the subway system, and jumping to it at the traffic lights, his welcome is like that of the town mouse to the country one.

> Dearest Cyril,
> Chester and I sail from here on 7 April [1948]. I hope very much you will be in London then to look after us. It would be lovely if you could meet us at Victoria (you can be the town mouse this time). By the way have you ever read *Tender is the Night*? I did for the first time this summer and found it magnificent – probably the best American novel since H.J. It made me bawl like a baby.

This return visit was after the appearance of the American number of *Horizon* which contained *The Fall of Rome* which he dedicated to me. I believe or rather I hope that it is true that I had asked him to write me something that would make me cry. It is a beautiful poem and like all the true expressions of his genius there is something totally unpredictable about it (those reindeer) yet even so one finds, as once his scientist was Groddeck, that now Sheldon had taken over – 'Cerebrotonic

Cato . . .'. I also published *In Praise of Limestone*.

I think this is the moment to stop, just before Auden's private face grew, through no choice of his own, irrevocably public, finally to settle into that striated Roman mask of luminous authority which it became harder and harder to penetrate. In 1972 I was invited by Alasdair Clayre to the All Souls *Encaenia* where, resplendent in cap and gown, Wystan was made a Doctor of Letters. 'Why, Cyril, what on earth are you doing here?' 'I came to find *you*,' I answered. It was the only time I had ever seen him at a loss.

Albert Camus: Introduction to *The Outsider* (1946)

The Outsider is the first book of a writer, now in his middle thirties, who played a notable part in the French Resistance Movement, who edited the daily paper, *Combat*, and whose name has been closely linked with Jean-Paul Sartre in the forefront of the new philosophical and realistic school of French literature. As well as this novel, Albert Camus has produced between 1942 and 1944 two plays, *Caligula* and *Le Malentendu*, and a book of essays, *Le Mythe de Sisyphe*. But he has an even more distinctive quality which colours all his work. He is an Algerian.

What is an Algerian? He is not a French colonial, but a citizen of France domiciled in North Africa, a man of the Mediterranean, an *homme du midi* yet one who hardly partakes of the traditional Mediterranean culture, unlike Valéry whose roots spread from Sète by way of Montpellier to Genoa; for him there is no eighteenth century, no baroque, no renaissance, no crusades or troubadours in the past of the Barbary Coast; nothing but the Roman Empire, decaying dynasties of Turk and Moor, the French Conquest and the imposition of the laws and commerce of the Third Republic on the ruins of Islam. It is from a sultry and African corner of Latin civilization that *The Outsider* emerges, the flower of a pagan and barrenly philistine culture. This *milieu* has a certain affinity with the Key West of Hemingway, or Deep South of Faulkner and Caldwell, with those torrid American cities where 'poor whites' exist uneasily beside poor blacks; in fact the neo-paganism which is common to both civilizations, together with Camus's rapid and somewhat colloquial style, have caused some critics to consider *The Outsider* merely as a French exercise in the American 'tough guy' manner. But the atmosphere is not really similar. *The Outsider* is not at all a morbid book, it is a violent affirmation of health and sanity, there are no monsters, no rapes, no incest, no lynchings in it; it is the reflection, on the whole, of a happier society. Monsieur Sartre asked, in a recent interview, if his friend Camus is also an 'existentialist', replied 'No. That's a grave misconception. Although he owes something to Kierkegaard, Jaspers, and Heidegger, his true masters are the French moralists of the seventeenth century. He is a classical Mediterranean. I would call his pessimism "solar" if you remember how much black there is in the sun. The philosophy of Camus is a philosophy of the absurd, and for him the absurd springs from the relation of man to the world, of his legitimate aspirations to the vanity and futility of human wishes. The conclusions which he draws from it are those of classical pessimism.'

We possess a valuable piece of evidence which bears out this theory. In 1936 and 1937 Camus wrote two or three essays which have since been reprinted as *Les Noces*. No writer can avoid in his first essays the mention of the themes which are crystallizing for his later work. Two melodies emerge in these papers, a passionate love for Algiers and for the harsh meridional ecstasy which youth enjoys there, and also an anger and defiance of death and of our northern emphasis upon it. These are the two keys to *The Outsider*.

> 'Le bourreau étrangla le Cardinal Carrafa avec un cordon de soie qui se rompit – il fallut y revenir deux fois. Le Cardinal regarda le bourreau sans daigner prononcer un mot.'
>
> STENDHAL: *La Duchesse de Palliano*.

This quotation at the head of *Les Noces* might stand as a motto for the novel.

In his essay in *Summer in Algiers* Camus introduces us to the kind of *milieu* we will meet in the later book.

'Men find here throughout all their youth a way of living commensurate with their beauty. After that, decay and oblivion. They've staked all on the body and they know that they must lose. In Algiers, for those who are young and alive, everything is their haven and an occasion for excelling – the bay, the sun, the red and white checkerboard of terraces going down to the sea, the flowers and stadiums, the fresh brown bodies . . . But for those whose youth is past no place exists, no sanctuary to absorb their melancholy.'

Farther on he gives a brief account of the ethics of these athletes. 'The notion of hell, for instance, is here no more than a silly joke. Such imaginings are only for the very virtuous. And I am convinced that the word virtue is entirely meaningless throughout Algeria. Not that its men are without principles. They have their moral code. 'We don't "chuck" our mothers, we make our wife respected in the street, we are considerate to the pregnant, we don't attack an enemy two against one, because it's "cheap". Whoever doesn't keep these elementary commandments "is not a man" and the business is settled.'

'There are words whose meaning I have never clearly understood,' he continues, 'such as the word sin. I know enough, however, to see that these men have never sinned against life, for if there is a sin against life, it is not perhaps so much to despair of life, as to hope for another life and to lose sight of the implacable grandeur of this one. These men have not cheated; lords of the Summer at twenty through their joy of living, though deprived of all hope they are gods still. I have seen two die, horrified but silent. It is better so. That is the rude lesson of the Algerian dog-days.'

So much for the ambience of *The Outsider*. When we study its philosophy, the limpid style disguises a certain confusion. According to one critic, the Outsider himself represents the drying up of all bourgeois sources of sensation, and the complete decadence of renaissance man; he is a 'poor white'. According to another, Maurice Blanchot, he grows out of character in the last pages, when he becomes too articulate, and thus destroys the unity of the book. I don't agree with either. Meursault represents the neo-pagan, a reversion to Mediterranean man as once he was in Corinth or Carthage or Alexandria or Tarshish, as he is to-day in Casablanca or Southern California. He is sensual and well-meaning, profoundly in love with life, whose least pleasures, from a bathe to a yawn, afford him complete and silent gratification. He lives without anxiety in a continuous present and has no need to think or to express himself; there is no Nordic why-clause in his pact with nature. The misfortunes into which he is led by his lazy desire to please and by his stubborn truthfulness gradually force the felt but unspoken philosophy of his existence to emerge into the open, and finally to express itself in words. To understand this last outburst we must study Camus's attitude to death. In his essay on the Roman ruins of Djemila he makes clear how much he admires the fortitude of the pagan ending, even as he shares the sure-set pagan passion for life. 'What does eternity matter to me? To lose the touch of flowers and women's hands is the supreme separation.' In his long essay on suicide in *The Myth of Sisyphus* he introduces his conceptions of the Absurd. 'Everything which exalts life adds at the same time to its absurdity,' he says in *Summer in Algiers*, and comes to the conclusion in the *Myth* that 'the Man under Sentence of Death is freer than the suicide – than the man who takes his own life'. The Suicide is a coward, he is one who abandons the struggle with fate, the Condemned Man, however, has the chance to rise above the society which has condemned him and by his courage and intellectual liberation to nullify it. The egotism of suicides with their farewells and resentments is sometimes grotesque, the dignity of a brave man on the Scaffold never. In his own words, 'The precise opposite of the suicide is the man who is condemned to death . . . The God-like disponibility of the condemned man before whom the prison gates open one day just before dawn, his incredible disinterestedness about everything except the pure flame of life within him, here I am quite sure that Death and Absurdity are the principles which generate the only rational Liberty – that which a human being can experience with body and soul.'

Having said all this, I will leave the reader to form his judgment. The Bourgeois Machinery with its decaying Christian morality, and bureaucratic self-righteousness which condemns the Outsider just because he is so foreign to it, is typical of a European code of Justice applied to a non-European people. A few hundred miles farther south and 'a touch of the Sun' would have been readily recognized, no doubt, as a cause for acquittal, in case of a white man accused of murdering a native, but part of the rigidity of the moribund French court is the pompous assumption that Algiers is France. On the other hand it is a failure of sensibility on the part of Camus that the other sufferer in his story, the Moorish girl whose lover beats her up and whose brother is killed when trying to avenge her, is totally forgotten. She too may have been 'privileged' to love life just as much, so may her murdered brother, for they too were 'foreigners' to the Colonial System, and a great deal besides. But the new paganism, I am afraid, is no kinder to women than the old.

Nevertheless something will have to happen soon and a new creed of happiness, charity and justice be brought to men. *The Outsider* is only a stage. He is a negative destructive force who shows up the unreality of bourgeois ethics. It is not enough to love life, we must teach everyone else to love it, we must appreciate that that happiness is consciousness, and consciousness is one, that all its manifestations are sacred, and it is from these newer schools of novelists and poets in all countries that one day we will learn it.

Albert Camus: Symbol of an Epoch (1961)

The death of Albert Camus in a motor accident on the Lyons–Paris road just over a year ago marked the end of an epoch, the period of anti-fascist writing and '*la littérature engagée*' of which he was a symbol, being to the Resistance what Malraux had been to the militant Thirties. His Nobel Prize in 1957 was an award like a medal won on the battlefield 'for his important literary production which, with clear-sighted earnestness, illuminates the problems of the human conscience of our times.'

He hated both injustice and violence and believed in liberty and goodwill, and so came to adopt a political position nearer to certain pre-war anarchists than to the closely reasoned Marxist Socialism of Sartre. Hence their quarrel, for Sartre is apt to make one feel that he is the only person who can criticise Russia without being a reactionary, and his qualifications as a philosopher were also sufficient to pulverise Camus's pretensions in that direction. But he could not destroy Camus's style, which is both lucid and precise as well as imaginative and poetic – as one would expect from a philosophic footballer with a passion for Mozart.

It is difficult to predict what kind of writer he would have become had he survived, but one can be sure that his death has placed him as the cult-figure of the French Resistance, a symbol of the youth of the generation which governs France today. He had a most charming personality, a brittle ironical manner, something about him of a capuchin or Humboldt's woolly monkey, an extremely intelligent, slightly melancholy gentleness, with strong convictions underneath.

Like Orwell he had won a position of his own, right of left and left of right, through the probity of his character and the independence of his thought.

And so, as the legend begins to crystallise, this is a good moment for Messrs Hamish Hamilton to bring out these two books:* and I think it is a good thing to reprint his novels and not his plays, none of which seems to me to be of permanent interest, though *Caligula* has a bloodthirsty craziness appropriate to the moment it was written.

Of the three novels, *La Peste* I think falls short of greatness and, since it aimed at greatness, must be regarded as a failure because Camus was unable to create character. In his two long short stories he can portray an individual but is not forced to attempt the three-dimensional. Both these, *The Outsider* and *The Fall*, are near-masterpieces: *The Outsider* is the name I chose for *L'Etranger* – the man who does not belong anywhere, who lives by a blind, profound instinct for his physical happiness which renders him immune to all conventional feelings. His apparent lack of response shows up the artificial standards by which the rest live.

The Fall is another study in an extreme individual, one whose whole life is ordered by a guilty conscience even as the Outsider's is arranged by a total lack of conscience. It is a very mannered little book but has given me a lot of pleasure on a second reading, as have the three or four short stories which wind up the volume.

I am sorry the selection of essays does not include Camus's first piece, 'Summer in Algiers', which dates from 1937. The selection, however, was made by Camus himself and stresses most of the main qualities to which he laid claim: his concern and 'engagement' with political events, and his basic optimism, and his belief in 'fecundity'.

I was delighted to re-read his magnificent essay on capital punishment, which brings him into line with Koestler, Charles Duff and other pamphleteers on this subject. The guillotine was invented as a humane

* *The Collected Fiction of Albert Camus* and *Resistance, Rebellion and Death*.

method of killing, but, of course, owed its success to its qualities as an instrument of mass-production, an assembly line for human heads. Camus produces some evidence to suggest it is very cruel indeed, apart from the inhumanity of the executioners, who refer to their victim as '*le client*' or '*le colis*' (the parcel).

On Algerian affairs Camus as a rule kept silence, but when he did speak out it was to plead for the civilians of both races and to attack the extremists. He believed in a federal solution along Swiss lines (the Lauriol plan). One does not find the denunciation of military torture that one would expect. As an Algerian himself, however, Camus was convinced of the basic unity of all the inhabitants of the country, though against the colonist's pretensions. Without federation:

> Algeria will be lost and the consequences will be dreadful for the Arabs and the French. This is the last warning that a writer who for twenty years has been devoted to the service of Algeria feels he can voice before resuming his silence (1958) . . . Although I have known and shared every form of poverty in which this country abounds, it is for me the land of happiness, energy, and of creation.

The most interesting essays are those in which Camus tried to state his position as an artist. He remained acutely concerned with the problem of a writer's relationship to the events of his time, he saw the dangers of being swamped by politics, of becoming a Marxist rubber-stamp, and he was also convinced that art-for-art's sake was dead, that the writer could no longer be an anti-bourgeois rebel, since the changes in class structure made such rebels ridiculous. He thought both social-realism and abstract art the two conventional uniforms:

> For about a century we have been living in a society that is not even the society of money (gold can arouse carnal passions), but that of the abstract symbols of money. The lie of art-for-art's sake pretended to know nothing of evil . . . but the realistic style, even though managing to admit mankind's present unhappiness, betrays that unhappiness by making use of it.

It seems to me that all this talk about the position of the artist is a waste of time, a 'making with the blocks', a symptom of flat, stale, though profitable, self-consciousness. Camus, who 'learnt his ethics from sport', learnt his aesthetics from the Resistance movement: it left him conscious of a following, of a duty to lead, and therefore to clash with other leaders. Perhaps, like Henri Michaux, he should just have written.

Dylan Thomas
(1960)

[E. W. Tedlock, *Dylan Thomas: The Legend and the Poet* (Heinemann)]

'Pushing up theses,' that is the euphemism which men of letters use for being dead; a long littleness of dons lies ahead of us, unless we have been afflicted with the curse of lucidity: now comes a symposium of thirty-eight writers to describe Dylan Thomas as they knew him, or to discuss his work.

Professor Tedlock has reprinted many scattered pieces about Dylan Thomas, not usually giving their dates, so that some of them conclude with the hope that, in the future, he will change his tactics; some even are unaware of the impending war which was to produce his greatest poems.

I myself came across the other day my review of *The Map of Love* for the *New Statesman* in 1939, and was surprised by the patronising tone which I adopted. Three things were to happen to Dylan Thomas after 1939; the poems in *Deaths and Entrances*, the emergence of the actor and reciter and broadcaster, and his early death; and none of this is adumbrated in some of these articles about him.

The biographical glimpses, however, take us right up to the final 'insult to the brain' which is now as familiar to us as the horn-wound which killed Manolete or the rose-bush which pricked Rilke. This publicity aspect of Thomas which links his death to Rupert Brooke and Rudolf Valentino in an apotheosis of the absurd, surely needs a few years to settle, and I am inclined to recommend *The Legend and the Poet* only to those who wish to read everything written about him, not to those who are still ignorant of his 'craft and sullen art'.

Since the book is in two halves we must judge them both separately. The first, the reminiscences, contains some fascinating material, by Messrs. Durrell, Davenport and others, including the verbatim report of one of Thomas's lectures on the poetry circuit. One must imagine the exhausted performer facing the usual circle of enlightened students, all of course thesis-minded, and the inevitable 'creative-writing' teacher whose ambivalent attitude to visiting authors has often been analysed. This one took place at the university of Utah:

'Is it ever fair deliberately to confuse the reader?'

Thomas: 'I thought someone would take me up on that. No, it is a deliberate avowal of your own inefficiency. It is impossible to be too clear . . . I am trying for more clarity now. At first, I thought it enough to leave an impression of sound and feeling, and let the meaning seep in later, but since I've been giving these broadcasts, and reading other men's poetry as well as my own, I find it better to have more meaning at first reading.'

'But on the other hand, isn't it possible to narrow and fix a meaning to the exclusion of richer levels of meaning?'

Thomas: 'O God, isn't education wonderful! . . .'

He dealt an even deadlier thrust at the thesis-industry when a student asked, 'How do you tell if a poem is good or not?'

'If I like it.'

'But what do you go by?'

'I like one because it is better than the others.' (Silence.)

The professor had to suppress this heresy. 'Perhaps we should do as you suggest and like a poem because we think it better than others, but students have to pull it apart and analyse why they like it and write it all down for the professor.' (Very long pause.)

And professors have to pull it apart too, in order to contradict other professors, which they do in the second half of this book, where the same lines appear and re-appear to be given quite different interpretations. On the whole, the unfriendly reviews linger longer in the memory because Mr Grigson and one or two others do show up the truth of the admission that Thomas made in jest, that sound and feeling preceded meaning, and that the famous letter to Henry Treece, on his method of composition, should be taken with a grain of salt. Thomas loved to parody himself and everyone else; his mixture of genius and humility allowed him to by-pass all the usual paraphernalia of poets; about his meaning or method of work he would say whatever he felt you would like to hear. Although he was a most conscientious craftsman and took infinite pains in the writing of his poems, he liked to sell them to editors for cash down and then it was extremely difficult to get him to correct a proof, 'because poets did not go to offices like businessmen'.

An error I should like to correct is that the visits to America (to make money for his English income tax) were the cause of the alcoholism which led to his death. The closeness of death is present in all his poetry and when I first knew him, soon after he had come to London, he was determined to drink as much as possible and to imagine that he had T.B.

He was already obsessed with the idea that a poet should die young and live in such a way as to risk his own destruction. At an age when many an undergraduate is doing the same thing, it did not seem pernicious that he should aim at the intoxication of a Marlowe, a Baudelaire, a Rimbaud, or a Dowson, because he seemed able to do without drink for his creative country-periods, and because he was still a young poet, not the heavy-drinking Fleet Street character which he afterwards became.

Of course, his detractors are right in that some of his poetry is merely surrealist and consists of heavily-flogged imagery which belies all meaning – but despite this he was a genius and when he could weld his own backward-looking religious and romantic sensibility into the new forms he desired, he created a new poetry: as Hugo said of Baudelaire, a '*frisson nouveau*'. That his imitators are so artificial and empty does not prove that his poetry is bad, only that it is inimitable.

So one comes back to Dame Edith Sitwell and the other appraisers of his work in this volume for, despite the limitations of his genius, which could operate only in a narrow range of central ideas – childhood – birth – sex – crucifixion – death, it can carry us into the world of great art, while the critical examinations here gathered together in the end generate only weariness. The author of one of them complains that Thomas could have just as well written 'the synagogue of the water-bead, and the round Zion of the ear of corn', as the reverse. But he didn't (ears of corn are not round), and what he did write was better, and no one else could have thought of it.

The death of a young poet, as Mr Karl Shapiro writes in the concluding essay, inflicts a psychic wound upon the world and is the cause, among poets themselves, of frightening babbling and soothsaying.

The Beats
(1960)

'Along with others I hung around with in the 'twenties, I had indulged in marijuana.' When square egghead Cyril Connolly came to this sentence* he nearly flipped his wig. Like this cat Lipton could be as old as him – and if he could make the scene among the beatsters why not me? And soon Connolly had gotten himself a pad in Venice West, the new *Thebaid* of Los Angeles where all the mad things were happening which made San Francisco's North Shore look like Greenwich Village.

'First thing you got to change,' said the gentle oldster, 'is your name.' We were squatting on a mattress in Itchy Gelden's pad with Mr Lipton's tape-recorder purring away. 'Like why should the poor square need a name? He's among friends!' Itchy's tolerance was proverbial. Then Angel Dan Davies spoke up with a rattle of his Bongo drums. 'There's only one name a man needs, man, and that name, man, is – man.' 'Like Mortal Man,' said Chuck Bennison, and from that moment Cyril Connolly was dead and Mort Conamore was born, with nothing more to do but play it cool and bring up his wind.

At first it looked like Mort would never 'relate'. He had to forget more than all the rest had ever learnt and that wasn't saying much. He cut down to two shirts and one pair of jeans and let his beard grow. 'The beard,' he will tell you, 'just grew naturally out of not shaving for a few weeks. It's my letter of resignation from the rat-race.' Angel considered the greying mould. 'Like Mort, that letter took a long time.'

> Dostoievski is an all-pervading influence that, for this very reason, no-one thinks of mentioning. Tolstoy, Andreiev, Turgenev and Lermontov

* In *The Holy Barbarians*, by Lawrence Lipton (W. H. Allen).

are known only by name. Thomas Mann and Marcel Proust are honoured and unread classics. William Saroyan's early short stories are sought out in yellowing paperbacks, and in some quarters he is listed as an 'influence' among beat writers. Henry James is tough going for them.

Mort was quick to throw the whole lot overboard and because he had met Henry Miller, Dylan Thomas and Gregory Corso (in Venice Europe) some of the cats took kindly to him. When offered marijuana, he had a good alibi, 'Like, man, I don't smoke.'

For spiritual satisfaction was what Mort was seeking and he turned to the 'Holy Barbarians' who in his youth would have been called 'anarcho-pacifists' to see if they could provide it. These lemmings, in full flight from the American industrial system, 'a total rejection of the whole society', had stopped on the verge of the Pacific without the know-how to throw themselves in.

'Art is love' says artist Wally Berman, and his words are scrawled on the walls of the Venice West Espresso Café. 'Art is love is jazz is work (sex) is pot (marijuana) = Zen' hazarded Mort one evening and was rewarded with a burst of crazy silence. He was trying hard with his vocabulary by now and forgetting a thousand facts a day. One morning all the Sèvres date letters went, another day it was the Roman Emperors, the Popes and the Kings of England. 'There are no trees in Venice West,' Angel told him – 'You can forget your botany and your first editions, man, we don't look for hallmarks on a can of beer.' Alcohol, however, was permitted. 'William Carlos Williams evidently puts no stock in trance or drug-induced hallucination, nor does Kenneth Patchen, although both, and Rexroth as well, have praised wine as a disinhabitant' (p. 254).

Unfortunately Mort found that Mr Lipton's glossary of beat terms was quite different from Caroline Freud's (in *Encounter*). 'Lay some bread on me' means 'Lend or give me some money' and, when he tried it, Mort agreed with Mr Lipton that 'the alienation of the hipsters from the squares is now complete.'

'It was the mad season in Venice West. Things were happening and if you were really *with it* you couldn't show it any better than by flipping your wig.'

Things were happening everywhere now; in San Francisco, in New York, in Chicago, New Orleans, Seattle. And people were converging on Venice West from everywhere to tell about them. 'Like more and more people everywhere are just giving up,' was Mort's comment. 'The squares are breaking.' But he still couldn't quite make it. Like Gide, his drug was lucidity. He couldn't blame reason for all that was wrong in the world.

It seemed to Mort that jazz, sex and marijuana could only afford physical sensations which, however disturbing, would never alleviate his craving for a lightening of his own opacity. He was never 'way out', only just round the corner. The intoxication which this new trinity offered was purely sensual and therefore subject to the law of diminishing returns. There was not enough inspiration to go round.

The art of the beat generation which rejects all technique and criticism and relies on the purely personal statement ('Like Art, Man' was the title of one exhibition) in any handy material is like the private devotions of a mystical sect – incommunicable. Mr Lipton gives a tape-recorded conversation about a funeral, which no one attended. Angel: 'If a culture has a ritual, a real living ritual, it doesn't matter what you do with the body. The only thing that matters is what the living make out of it – out of the fact of death – and that means the fact of *life*, the meaning of life. Marriage is *one* thing. Mating. Love. I can do something with that. I can understand it. But dying – wow – death. I don't know *what* I'd do with it. Like I don't even know what it is.'

Something stirred among Mort's obliterated memories. 'Dying – wow!' Where had he read that? '*Wa! Wa!* Who is this heavenly ruler who can lay low the great ones of the earth?' The last words of King Wamba. Was this all they could tell him? He looked up one more phrase in Mr Lipton's glossary: 'Cop out – to settle down – go conventional. In some circles you may be charged with copping out if you shave off your beard.' Next day the British Consul laid some bread on him and he was disinhabited.

Poetry Today
(1970)

We are all living through a technological revolution far more significant than the political one. We see it all around us but we are not conscious of its effect on our minds and our habits of thinking and feeling. Someone like Marshall McLuhan may give us a bit of a jolt. In my case, I was shaken by Mr Gore Vidal's suggestions that the literature of the future will consist of the collected telephone conversations of Truman Capote – recorded on a disc the size of a postage stamp for the international word-bank.

Poetry is the earliest form of literature, and in the form that we know it is about 3,000 years old. Poets are known by name and fame from Homer onwards; their manuscripts have been copied and edited and collected since the Alexandrians. The Romans copied these books and their own poetry circulated by wax tablets and papyri and, later, parchment. The monks copied them in the Dark Ages, the Renaissance princes competed for them. Petrarch was antiquarian as much as poet. Virgil, Horace, Ovid ruled from their tombs. This preeminence of poetry, of the poet as 'unacknowledged legislator' has lasted into our own day together with his instrument, the 'slim volume'. To mention a few of these: Shakespeare's sonnets and his *Venus and Adonis*, Milton's early poems, Pope's *The Rape of the Lock*, Gray's *Elegy*, Wordsworth and Coleridge's *Lyrical Ballads*. The *Lyrical Ballads* were an experiment about to be tried by Coleridge and Wordsworth, to see how far the public taste would endure poetry written in a more natural and simple style than had hitherto been attempted, discarding the artifices of poetical diction, as Coleridge told the adoring Hazlitt . . . To come to our own time, Eliot's *Prufrock* and *The Waste Land*, Pound's *Lustra*,

Frost's *North of Boston*, Dylan Thomas's *18 Poems*, Auden's early poems, Yeats' later ones have all seeped into our heart and sensibility. The impact is of the poet through his slim volume reaching a small group of devoted readers, mostly young, whence his ideas and inventions proceed to germinate. When one of the readers is himself a poet a chain reaction is set up. The lonely, gauche, dedicated figures communicate with each other: Keats looks into Chapman's *Homer*, Swinburne meets Landor; Valéry, Mallarmé; Beckett and Bunting meet Joyce and Pound; Auden and Spender were published by Eliot and became his friends. Edith Sitwell never ceased to champion Dylan Thomas. When Flecker wrote a poem 'to a young poet a thousand years hence' he imagined the same kind of shared emotions and experience that he might himself have derived, for example, from Catullus. Pound's *Homage to Sextus Propertius* is another identification with the past. All the poets in fact behave as if they were members of the same club, from the Mermaid Tavern to the Rhymers at the Cheshire Cheese, where Yeats met Dowson and Lionel Johnson. These poets were already having great difficulty in supporting themselves and they were victims of the central problem, the occupational disease and contradiction of the poet, the constant preoccupation and obsession with a way of life whose demands are unrecognized by society. Poets are under compulsion to write poetry, but nobody is compelled to read it. A conspiracy binds the author of the slim volume to his reader: that both can afford it. As Mr Nixon, based on Arnold Bennett, says to Ezra Pound, who appears in his own poem as Mauberley:

. . . as for literature
It gives no man a sinecure,
And no one knows, at sight, a masterpiece.
And give up verse, my boy.
There's nothing in it. . . .
. . . the 'Nineties' tried your game
And died, there's nothing in it.

The legend of the penniless poet, immoral, arrogant, probably alcoholic, persists through Dowson, Lionel Johnson, Verlaine, Hart Crane, Dylan Thomas, but there have also been poets of the first rank who are immensely successful: Yeats, Eliot, Auden, Frost, Wallace Stevens, Valéry, Neruda, Dame Edith Sitwell, Sir John Betjeman. Others like Pound, Robert Graves or Robert Lowell take violent evasive action to elude their fame. One poet, Senghor, is a head of state (Senegal); another, Chairman Mao, of a vast empire, but on the whole successful poets have either taught or lectured or become publishers or critics. Yeats was the exception. Thus Eliot was publisher, lecturer and critic, Auden, teacher, lecturer and critic, Frost, teacher and poet-in-residence; Stevens was vice-president of the Hartford Accident Company.

Nobody can write poetry all the time: the problem is to earn a living in a way conducive to being able to continue to write poetry when the torrents of inspiration arrive. The poet-in-residence at American universities is a happy solution. Teaching jobs are mentally exhausting but provide long holidays with pay. Criticism uses faculties which are usually highly developed in poets, though they may tend to get swamped by other people's work. True patronage, where a rich woman supports a poet by giving him an allowance or marrying him, is apt to turn sour. The poets who will brook no discipline often succumb to drink or write worse than if they had a job in a bank. In youth poetry will force its way out anyhow, in middle age the wisest cosseting may fail. 'My capacity for even the simplest business undertaking is negligible; it sounds as if I'm trying to plead for notorious vagueness of the Dreamy Poet but really I'm a complete nitwit when it comes to replying to people, organizing anything, making any sort of deal, keeping very tiny affairs in order.' (Dylan Thomas to his agent in 1937.)

It was Berenson, one of the last of the aesthetes, who said he would only read poetry that was beautifully printed on good paper with wide margins. The first half of this century, from 1890–1945, was in fact the age of the private press. These presses did nothing to discover poets (exception: the Hogarth Press and *The Waste Land*, *The Black Sun* and *The Bridge*, and one or two others) but everything to preserve them. The work of Yeats' lyric poetry appeared in the slim volumes of the

Cuala Press, and there were many others. They did not bring the poet much money but his profits were regular and safe. In the last fifty years the sale of new volumes of verse has remained exactly the same. Five hundred to 1,000 copies of each book sell, unless the poet is exceptionally well-known. Many poets falter between 300 and 500 copies; only rarely will a new poet like Brian Jones reach about 3,000 with his first book.

The very few established poets like Eliot, Frost, Auden, Betjeman, do much better. Robert Lowell expects to sell about 10,000 copies in two years, followed by 25,000 in paperback for which he would earn less money. Fees from anthologies mount up as well. The cost of living has increased more than the prices of books but the poet can at least get a good price for his manuscripts, which went for next to nothing till after the last war. But what can he earn compared to a painter?

The poet is therefore compelled to tackle the new mass media and sell his voice and his face as well as his poetry: he can give lectures and readings, as of old, and also make tapes and recordings and attend festivals and congresses; he is heard and seen, then, so what matter if he be read?

But the worst effects of the technological revolution are on the sensibility of the reading public. Children grow up to view, not to read; the book loses its mystique; not for them the impact of *À Rebours* on Dorian Gray, and the population explosion dims the Romantic frisson, the moon, the stars, the nightingale ('The music of the moon sleeps in the brown eggs of the nightingale'). The countryside with its every detail, as noted by Tennyson or Hardy, even the sea and the shore, the woods and the mountains, half the subject matter of poetry, lose their magic for the new race of apartment dwellers. The appreciation of poetry tends to be confined more and more to the poets themselves, its place being taken by pop music. Dylan slew his thousands/Bob Dylan his tens of thousands. The Beatle lyrics are as widely known as any poetry has ever been, but they do not stand up without the music, any more than a blues or a Spanish *copla*. Some poets like Christopher Logue or Allan Ginsberg strive to be popular, but even they must return to the academic and end up in the text book. How much of Auden's popularity, for example, comes from the academic world in which he teaches and is taught? How much do the young who find modern poetry on their syllabus really enjoy it? And yet, though there are few great poets alive and these have made their reputations with an ageing public, poetry itself is more interesting and experimental than it has ever been because it has opened the doors of sensibility to admit surrealist poetry, abstract poetry, concrete poetry, and tries to express itself as experimentally as modern painting. 'Concrete' poetry has enormous possibilities for group manifestations. Poems can thereby become visible structures like the human chess that used to be played in the square at Cracow. In its two branches, the festival and the campus, spoken poetry gains in authority, the Poet-in-Residence need do no more than say 'Try the Pork,' like Frost in Nabokov's *Pale Fire*.

Who are these younger poets? Any English group would include Ted Hughes (the work of whose late wife, Sylvia Plath, is now coming into its own), Thom Gunn who lives in California, Philip Larkin, our most significant poet since Dylan Thomas. His poem *1914* manages to compress all the futility and tragedy and unthinking heroism of World War I into a few stanzas. Written before *O What a Lovely War*, it performs the same catharsis, a poem I would choose, if asked to illustrate what poetry can do. Charles Tomlinson, Peter Porter, Charles Causley, Peter Redgrave, D. J. Enright, George Macbeth, Brian Jones are all interesting. These poets, and particularly Gunn, Hughes, Larkin and Enright, aim at a certain reticence, a dryness, a manipulation of language which leaves nothing exaggerated or unclear; they have plenty to say but they are extremely economical in the way they say it. One hesitates to use the expression 'silver age', perhaps 'platinum' is more suggestive, a precious metal which has no romantic echoes or overtones.

America boasts two major poets, Auden and Lowell. The first has produced some of his most moving poetry recently in *About the House*, the other, one of the largest collections of lyrics (*The Notebooks*) to be written. It is also the home of Marianne Moore. In Spain we have

Robert Graves, in Italy Ezra Pound, in France Jouve and Aragon. The Black Mountain Poets leave me cold; I have a blind spot for Olson, Duncan, Creeley, and I'm only just beginning to enjoy Allen Tate and John Crowe Ransom, while Cummings, Crane and Lowell have always been an inspiration.

I have loved poetry all my life, I remain the ideal *lecteur* for the poets whom I understand, for I am a sound box, a record player, an aeolian harp who gathers up and stores innumerable fragments, and for me, to love the poem is to love the poet who wrote it and become his man.

Determined on Time's honest shield,
The lamb must face the tigress.

Why do these two lines from Auden's *As He Is* haunt me perpetually these days? I mentioned them to a political friend who seized on them to address a meeting of Israeli bankers – for poetry, when not too concrete, has the power to generate action:

The world hath conquered, the wind hath scattered like dust
Alexander, Caesar, and all that shared their sway.
Tara is grass, and behold how Troy lieth low—
And even the English, perchance their hour will come!

The four lines from the Irish are better translated by Frank O'Connor with the last line:

Maybe the English too will have their day.

But the first version of this eighteenth-century poem is by P. H. Pearse, the leader of the Irish rebellion of 1916. 'We find Irish hate of the English expressing itself suddenly and splendidly in many a stray stanza,' he noted. Who knows but this stanza may well have set him on his fatal path to the firing squad?

The Novel-Addict's Cupboard
(1936)

'Other people's hobbies,' as one book-collector has remarked, 'are always ridiculous,' so I will do no more than say that about two years ago the printed words 'Second edition, second issue, seventh thousand, first published in . . . reprinted in . . .' suddenly became to me the most horrible stains and blots on a book imaginable. And cheap editions, travellers' libraries, anti-travellers' libraries; ghastly! There is some point in collecting ancient first editions, for in the seventeenth and eighteenth centuries they differed often very considerably from succeeding texts, and were, also, lovely objects. But I collect modern ones, the seven-and-sixpenny poisons. They are cheaper and one has the pleasure of backing one's judgment, generally wrongly, against the whole weight of middlebrow, sentimental, childhood-loving, and pedantic opinion represented by booksellers' catalogues. I still do not collect books unless I think I shall enjoy reading them, but I do not expect that phase to last. Reading, in book-collectors, is replaced by a kind of fidgeting motion, balancing the book in the left hand, opening it and shutting it with the right, and exclaiming 'But that's not really his first book at all, you know,' or some other holy rubric. But as a good many of my books are novels, it may be of interest to recall a few in the hope of suggesting some new titles for the novel-addict or reminding him of some old ones. Incidentally, it will be proof that there was once a time when I enjoyed fiction. Where the authors are American, I try to get the American editions, as the English are so often altered, but there is no book I am going to mention that is not in some form cheaply and easily procurable. I can't afford *South Wind*, *The Way of All Flesh*, *Human Bondage*, or the *Old Wives' Tale*, so you must imagine them filling shadowy blanks to begin with, and there are some publishers whom I refuse to collect, because all their novels look exactly alike, and destroy my conception of a book-shelf, which should be a mass of gaudy variety.

E. M. Forster, *Howards End*, *Room with a View* (Arnold). *Howards End*, written in 1910, introduces the first post-war young highbrow, with a post-war name (Sebastian), and a simplified form of writing in full revolt against Henry James. But an artist's revolt – not a philistine's, like Wells'. The themes of Forster's novels are always the breaking down of bridges and barriers – between English and Indian, between the intelligentsia and the bourgeoisie (*Howards End*), between soldier and scholar (*Longest Journey*) – he is really anti-highbrow, in the sense that he dislikes nothing more than intellectual presumption and spiritual pride. He is consequently a revolutionary writer, one of the first to attack the individualism of the 'nineties, to find the crack in the ivory tower; his heroes are plain men and plainer women, his motto 'only connect' – yet as a writer he is an artist always. I think *Howards End* is his best book, the *Longest Journey* (which started the Wiltshire trek) second. He has written only one book since 1910, and is still waiting for English fiction to catch up.

Henry James, semi-complete. I get an inconceivable pleasure from a Henry James book when I am able to finish it, but too often I can only flounder out a few yards and then have to retreat. For others in this plight I recommend his long short stories, particularly *The Lesson of the Master*, *The Aspern Papers*, and *The Death of the Lion*. They enshrine the subtlest vanities and disappointments of the pursuit of letters for all time. Another remedy is to read anecdotes of Henry James. He is the last of the great writers to be a great man, and even the dirtiest pens take on a new quality when they write about him – enough to send one back to his books again. Or read his letters – that one in which he so pathetically reminds Gosse that he is 'insurmountably unsaleable' and says of his collected edition, like Ozymandias, 'look on my works, ye mortals, and despair.'

A great critic has described Mrs Wharton as the Sargent of the modern novel, and it is on her accomplished, rich interiors that it gives me most pleasure to gaze. She has been fortunate enough to belong to a class – the super-rich, the super-philistine, the super-cosmopolitan – that can as a rule be observed only from outside and consequently is misrepresented. Therefore the studies of these jewelled and inaccessible analphabetics by one who is pre-eminently a serious and intelligent writer may become valuable documents. *The Custom of the Country* and *Glimpses of the Moon* are the brightest.

Maurice Baring, semi-complete. *Passing By* and *Daphne Adeane* seem to me his best books, which are all variations on a theme – the rivalry of sacred and profane love. One knows that sacred love will always win, and profane love be always on the point of winning, and the consequent order, regularity, and logic of the treatment, resembling a Greek tragedy, is his greatest power. Like those Spanish *aficionados* who watch a series of dancers repeating the same steps, singing the same song, one resents any alteration in structure as keenly as one derives pleasure from the variations of the performers in tempo, grace, and style. 'It seduces one. And then it seduces one again.'

Aldous Huxley, complete. David Garnett, complete. Lawrence, *passim*. Mr Huxley tells a story of Firbank meeting him in the Café Royal: 'He gave his usual agonized wriggle of embarrassment and said, "Aldous – always my *torture*."' I think I feel the same way about him. At school I borrowed *Limbo* from one master only to have it confiscated by another, while the Frenchman who let me read Mallarmé's *Après-Midi d'un Faune* for extra studies had to turn repeatedly to Huxley's translation to find out what it meant. I bought *Crome Yellow* out of some prize money. After that his novels and stories continued to dominate my horizon, so enormously competent, so clever, sympathetic, and on the spot. During the 'twenties it was almost impossible for the average clever young man not to imitate him – just as he once had imitated Norman Douglas, Firbank, and Eliot. Now that I have been free for a few years I see *Crome Yellow* as his best book, backed up by *Limbo*, *Antic Hay*, and his short stories. His early work had a natural gaiety, his satire lacked the heavy hand of the moralist; Science, with its horrible plausibility, had not yet walked off with Art. The first forty years of Aldous Huxley's literary career have been marred by over-production, for which the present economic system is to blame. Conventionality of thought and diction, fatigue of style result – but his long silence since *Brave New World* is the most hopeful augury for the remaining three score. David Garnett's books remain a standing argument in favour of the short novel, for, though equally bound to his publisher by golden cords, he has resisted Aldous Huxley's temptation to long novels, pamphlets, essays, and philosophical journalism. As for Lawrence, I really believe he is asleep at last, and I think nothing should be done to disturb him. If you must approach him, do it lightly, and by way of his early books, those like *The White Peacock*, with its creamy pastoral descriptions of the English countryside, full of a sentiment that has not yet been muddied by dogma.

Firbank, complete. Every critic, however roughly he may seem to wisecrack away the achievements of his enemies, the creators, will sooner or later shyly unlock his playbox and produce his few treasures. Then woe betide the reader who does not express a proper admiration. For my part, I am secretly a lyricist; the works to which I lose my heart are those that attempt, with a purity and a kind of dewy elegance, to portray the beauty of the moment, the gaiety and sadness, the fugitive distress of hedonism; the poetry of Horace and Tibullus, the plays of Congreve, the paintings of Watteau and Degas, the music of Mozart and the prose of Flaubert affect me like this, and of recent books, the novels of Ronald Firbank. That doesn't mean I think he is as good as Mozart, I hasten to say, but that in him more than in any contemporary writer I find that taste. He and the early Eliot seem to me the pure artists of the 'twenties, Lawrence and Huxley the philosopher-artists, the explainers. His thin black books are incidentally some of the few which it is a pleasure to collect. Of course, it is quite useless to write about Firbank – nobody who doesn't like him is going to like him, and he can be extremely aggravating and silly – but he was a true innovator, and his air of ephemerality is treacherous in the extreme.

Hemingway, complete. Waugh, complete. Powell, complete. Scott

Fitzgerald, complete. Now we are among the Firbank derivatives. Great Hemingway is under a cloudlet, partly owing to the increasing truculence of his subject matter, partly owing to the spate of imitations of him, and his boom. Yet he has created the American style: no other transatlantic novelist so combines native force with mastery of form. Scott Fitzgerald represents a more literary compromise between the American qualities (generosity, courage, open-mindedness, and immoderation) and the English technique. His *The Great Gatsby* and *Tender is the Night* are also, incidentally, two of the novels most typical of the Boom, as is the charming *Gentlemen Prefer Blondes*. Evelyn Waugh, as a novelist, seems also to me to be in a predicament. I regard him as the most naturally gifted novelist of his generation (the round-about-thirty). He has a fresh, crisp style, a gift for creating character, a mastery of dialogue, a melancholy and dramatic sense of life – but his development has taken him steadily from the Left towards the Right, and Right Wing Satire is always weak – and he is a satirist. The anarchist charm of his books (of which *Black Mischief* is the best example) was altered in *A Handful of Dust* to a savage attack on Mayfair from a Tory angle. And though there on safe ground, it is going to be difficult for him to continue, since Tory satire, directed at people on a moving staircase from a stationary one, is doomed to ultimate peevishness [Example, Beachcomber]. *A Handful of Dust* is a very fine novel, but it is the first of Evelyn Waugh's to have a bore for a hero.

The novels of Antony Powell are unaffected monochromes of realism. Anything which might heighten the colouring is scrupulously omitted. They deal in nuances of boredom, seediness, and squalor – 'the artist is recognizable by the particular unpleasantness of his life' is his creed, and since he gaily accepts it his novels have a delightful quality, containing much of the purest comedy that is now being written. I recommend especially *Afternoon Men* and *From a View to a Death* (Duckworth). Then there is that other comedian, Compton Mackenzie, whose *Vestal Fires* and *Extraordinary Women* are among the few modern novels that make the most of that wonderful subject, money, and which bring the Mediterranean lapping round our doors and the smell of cistus through the fog-bound windows. One day I want to do a dossier of the characters in those two books, and their mighty begetter, *South Wind*, with photographs of them all and pictures of their villas. And while still on satirists, there are *Cakes and Ale* and *The Moon and Sixpence* of Maugham. *Cakes and Ale* belongs to that group of satires on literary shop that form one of the most remarkable achievements of the English novel. Max Beerbohm's *Seven Men* belongs also, and Osbert Sitwell's *Dumb Animal* with that admirable short story *Alive, Alive-Oh!*.

It would seem that I do not collect any women writers, but that is not the case. I have the books of Miss Compton-Burnett, though I cannot read them, and Mrs Woolf complete to *The Waves*, which holds one of the key positions of modern novels, inferior only to *Ulysses* (no first edition, alas!), and all Miss Elizabeth Bowen's ironical and delicate studies, and all Rosamund Lehmann, another natural writer, and *Frost in May* by Antonia White, *Orphan Island*, the best novel of Miss Macaulay, *Voyage in the Dark* (Constable) by Jean Rhys, a short and tragic book – and even shorter, *My Mortal Enemy* and *A Lost Lady*, the two best books of Willa Cather, and *Winter Sonata* by Dorothy Edwards. Gay but less haunting are *Country Places*, Christine Longford, and Julia Strachey's *Cheerful Weather for the Wedding*. This leads one on to those novels that one feels are little known or underrated, that are never followed by a successor, or whose effect on people is unpredictable and subversive. Such are Clifford Kitchin's two books, *Mr. Balcony* and *The Sensitive One*. Nathaniel West's *Miss Lonelyhearts* (a defiant masterpiece of futility), George Beaton's *Jack Robinson* and his *Almanack*. Or *How Like a God* by Rex Stout (Kennerley); *Blindness and Living* by Henry Green (who *is* he?), published by Dent; and *Murder, Murder* by Laurence Vail (Peter Davies), which begins so well and ends so badly. And *Arm's Length* by John Metcalfe, *Futility* by Gerhardi, *Some People* by Harold Nicolson (great period interest), and *Café Bar* by Scott Moncrieff (gloomy!). The *Four Just Men* by Edgar Wallace, and that strange sadistic highbrow thriller, and analysis of the Paris Commune, *The Werewolf of Paris* (John Long) by Guy Endore.

And *Extra Passenger* by Oswald Blakeston, and *Tropic of Cancer* (Obelisk Press), a gay, fierce, shocking, profound, sometimes brilliant, sometimes madly irritating first novel, by Henry Miller, the American Céline. Anyone interested in the problem of American genius, whether it can ripen or ever achieve real freedom and honesty in its home surroundings, should try to get this book which would appear completely to justify expectation. Apart from the narrative power, the undulating swell of a style perfectly at ease with its creator, it has a maturity which is quite unlike the bravado, the spiritual ungrown-upness of most American fiction. Miller's writing is more in the nature of a Whitmanesque philosophic optimism which has been deepened and disciplined but never destroyed by his lean years in a city where even to starve is an education. And there are books for the *sottisier*, such as the *Berry* volumes of Dornford Yates. Sometimes, at great garden parties, literary luncheons, or in the quiet of an exclusive gunroom, a laugh rings out. The sad, formal faces for a moment relax and a smaller group is formed within the larger. They are admirers of Dornford Yates who have found out each other. We are badly organized, we know little about ourselves and next to nothing about our hero, but we appreciate fine writing when we come across it, and a wit that is ageless united to a courtesy that is extinct. Or books for collectors which remind one of all the glass cases full of boring limited editions of Coppard, Collier, Hanley, Hampson, Powys, and Potocki de Montalk. And there are parodies like *The Oxford Circus* (Miles and Mortimer) and more American books, Dreiser, Glenway Westcott, Faulkner, O'Hara, Saroyan – and I see I have the complete works of Wyndham Lewis. But that should be enough.

First Edition Fever
(1963)

I don't know when I discovered the Grand Design that was formulating behind the sporadic intensity with which I collected the authors I loved; perhaps it lay always at the back of my activities; certainly it was present by the time I wrote my last article on collecting first editions in January, 1936. My ambition was no less than to possess in their original form all the books which constituted the modern movement in literature; that is to say in the guise in which they first appeared to their contemporaries. The prime necessity was to have a clear picture of the modern movement so as not to be beguiled into the collector's many backwaters, such as the assembling of expensive books from private presses which specialise in fastidious reprints.

Modern books are not always attractive in themselves but in bulk they make a very agreeable picture, a mosaic of human aspiration. A book collector is like a lighthouse keeper who offers sanctuary to buffeted and exhausted migrants as they home towards the friendly beam. Once behind glass they are safe from pollution. If one loves a writer's work the highest form of appreciation is to protect and enjoy his books in the guise in which they first appeared and which illustrates the growth and variation of his talent. The envy, vanity and competitiveness of collectors are a minor phenomenon compared to the satisfaction with which they contemplate 'the precious life-blood of a master-spirit' in its well-cared-for envelope.

There are many other joys in collecting. It sharpens the historical sense. It enhances our encounters with authors and gears us to the land of the living. It also brings us into contact with booksellers, who are a race apart and one and all delightful company, as befits those in whom the ideal and the practical are so nicely blended, and they lead to booksellers' catalogues, favourite reading surpassed only by a good bibliography; and then follows the excitement of the chase, with much opening of parcels and filling up of gaps. Perhaps the relieving of anxiety is a greater satisfaction than any other, for I notice that once a title is crossed off the 'wanted' list one is apt to forget it.

I do not propose to enumerate my rarities, a dull business, or to proclaim my needs, which are really limited to about a dozen books I shall never possess; the earliest works of Joyce, Yeats, Pound and Hemingway, Forster and Lawrence.

I am very lucky however to have backed my own judgment in the 'thirties. For there has been a revolution in favour of the Revolutionaries; the soft-currency minds have been driven out by the hard. Much of the credit for this goes to American critics and professors of literature who have influenced the American university libraries and so created an insatiable demand for the rare books which are seminal to the modern movement and not merely entertaining derivatives. This need has driven up the price of Eliot, Joyce and Yeats to astonishing heights (at least ten times their pre-war value). On the other hand, Pound (all of whose early books were published in this country) has not yet appreciated to the same extent.

The system I advocate is to perceive clearly which are the main peaks in the range, the books by the writers who advance the human spirit further and to go all out for them, afterwards filling in the subsidiaries. Sometimes these books are decorative in themselves, sometimes they are also scarce, occasionally, like *Animal Farm*, they are neither; but in the late 1920's self-consciousness set in and writers began to produce artificial rarities.

Thus Joyce's work opens with two or three almost unobtainable pamphlets, a scarce first book of poems and two expensive but essential works of fiction, *Dubliners* and *The Portrait of the Artist* (New York, 1916), followed by the most important novel of the period (1910–30), *Ulysses*. The first edition of this book (1922) consisted in all of a thousand numbered copies and it is a 'must', in my opinion, to have one of these, which now fetch between £20 and £30 (unsigned). After *Ulysses* the artificial rarities began and various fragments of *Finnegans Wake* came out in expensive limited editions. It affords no proportionate pleasure to acquire all of these, many of them in slip cases, and this also is true of the later work of Lawrence and Norman Douglas. The end of the 'twenties witnessed in fact the inflation of the privately printed book.

Frivolity and monotony are the two aspects of modern first editions which the collector must try to avoid. Some publications are monotonously presented and the result is the Left Book Club or the poets of the 'thirties whose uniform, excellent for each, is the same for all. Only such writers' first books are unusually designed. Here the two rarities are Auden's *Poems* printed (and how!) by the eighteen-year-old Stephen Spender in 1928, of which about a dozen copies exist and Spender's own *Nine Experiments* (Frognal, 1928) which I believe to be even rarer. Evelyn Waugh's privately printed *P.R.B.*, 1926 (on the pre-Raphaelites), of which there has never been a census is also uncommon. Luckily their second books, Spender's *Twenty Poems* (Blackwell) and Auden's *Poems* (Faber, 1930), both in paper covers, are also decorative and contain much better work.

Is this rising market based on an illusion, like the boom of the late 'twenties? It is an illusion only if the modern movement itself turns out to be a momentary fashion or if the driving force (the acquisitiveness of American colleges) becomes spent or changes direction. Or the universities might go all-American. Already they rightly prefer drafts and manuscripts to the printed word and require, above all, documents which their Eng.-Lit. students can exfoliate, extrapolate or just imbricate and explicate.

But something did happen in that crucial period between 1910 and 1930 which cannot be undone by the vicissitudes of fashion. There was a combination of new outlook and new feeling with a new use of words. The outlook was there in Flaubert's *Bouvard et Pécuchet* (1880), the use of words in Hopkins's poems; the process accelerated when Pound became Yeats's secretary and got Eliot and Joyce published in little magazines. I have a feeling that the movement, even if it ended with Dylan Thomas, will outlast our time.

I have noticed that book-collectors tend to go for the item they associate with their own youth (it used to be *The Wind in the Willows*) and so as each generation is written off and boxed, there is a tendency for its sentimental values to die with it. In that case we who welcomed Lawrence, Joyce and the later Yeats as ennoblers and liberators will be deprived of our verdict and they may go the way of Swinburne and Pater, Flecker and Rupert Brooke.

Nothing can replace the excitement of greeting new work by contemporaries when one is young and impressionable; the appearance in the early 1920s of *The Waste Land*, *Ulysses*, *The Sleeping Beauty*, *The Flower Beneath the Foot*, *Antic Hay*, or the Chinese poems translated by Arthur Waley were for me a form of demoniac possession. How can the young experience the same happy desire to enshrine them? They cannot. But they may still uphold Yeats's *Later Poems* of 1922 as proof that he is the greatest poet of the West since Baudelaire. Collectors can gamble that a man who in his middle seventies could write

> Slim adolescent that a nymph has stripped
> Peleus on Thetis stares.
> Her limbs are delicate as an eyelid;
> Love has blinded him with tears. . . .

will not go the way of the other members of the Rhymers Club.

The recent bibliographies of Yeats, Joyce and Eliot are a mine of information. They protect the bookseller against making mistakes and are also an immense help to the collector like those stamp albums which used to have a picture of every stamp in the place for it. Is book-collecting just a deteriorated form of philately? There is that element in it, especially in the filling up of gaps and the emphasis on condition, rarity and such things as dust-wrappers. The Americans are hipped (or should one say squared?) on dust-wrappers, which they regard as an integral part of a book's original appearance. This leads to much painful discrimination and finally to the manufacturing of Cellophane wrappers for the jackets themselves, since these are highly deciduous. Perhaps one should keep the books in the shelves under glass and send the jackets to the bank.

There is no ultimate justification for book-collecting except that it preserves the books for we know deep-down that it is all make-believe; the tenderest inscription, the warmest dedication, the liveliest photograph cannot bring dead authors back to life. The collector has but to fall sick or move house a few times for his possessions to take on a woebegone appearance. It is his own enthusiasm, anxiety and cupidity which maintain order and keep the arrangements alive; without him his books are like a cellar of rare wines buried under an avalanche. How depressing are those roped-up bundles that we see in the auction rooms, how different they will look when they have found a new master.

Let us suppose, however, that some eager youth who reads these words wishes to start a collection. How should he go about it? He will certainly possess some books already. The first thing is to purchase a work like the *Annals of English Literature* (O.U.P.) which gives the year in which most modern books appeared; this acts as a compass which will guide him through the jungle. Then he should get hold of as many booksellers' catalogues as possible to obtain some idea of the prices. *Book Auction Records*, issued annually by Stevens, Son and Stiles, lists all the principal sales under authors and so indicates the 'highs' which exceptional copies have fetched.

A new collector will find he needs many sources. Here are some:

(1) *Local booksellers:* these are always accessible, reliable and not too expensive. They are the joy of provincial towns and many of them keep a couple of shelves for modern first editions.

(2) *London specialist dealers:* these are not cheap but they know much more than we do and so can give good advice. They will in the end discover nearly every rarity but others will also be waiting for it. No one can possibly collect without being on at least one of their mailing lists or calling in to inspect their stock. They always keep a surprising number of cheap books.

(3) *Your friends:* every friend has at least one book which you want and a true friend will part with it, unless he be a collector. This may make him dread your visits but it remains a test of friendship which many survive. Women friends are particularly generous and seldom collect. (Every book-collector's wife rates his obsession slightly below compulsive gambling. A wise collector always gets first to the postman.)

(4) *It is essential* to have one helpful friend or dealer in America as so many modern first editions stem from there. On the other hand it is not nearly so difficult as one would expect to find rare American books in England.

(5) *Swapping with other collectors:* this soon involves a superhuman restraint and delicacy.

(6) *Unsolicited gifts:* delightful, but often unsuitable.

(7) *Treasure trove:* bargain boxes, attics, country auctions, books in antique dealers, etc. Disappointing.

Do not hesitate to ask authors you meet to sign their books for you. It is the only way we can improve them. This should never be done by post or without previous acquaintanceship. No book lent, even if only from one room to another, is ever returned in exactly the same condition. It is less disagreeable to refuse to lend ('I wouldn't even lend it to *myself*', as Jonathan Edax used to say) than to have to pester people to return a book and thus lower their opinion of themselves as well as of you. Conversely a collector does not borrow since it would be intolerable to have to return. He quietly notes the title and sets out to acquire it.

Do not buy books you do not really want because they are cheap nor hesitate to spend more than you intend to obtain a rarity. Rare and even scarce books live up to their name and one may have to wait several years, by which time the price will be much higher. It is not just the famous books which are hard to find. Several million books of 1938, 1939 and 1940 perished in the Blitz, particularly in the fire of Simpkin Marshalls, hence the rarity of Beckett's *Murphy*, Macneice's *Yeats*, McAlmon's *Being Geniuses Together* and so many others. Of all headaches for collectors the amassing of the first editions of Anthony

Powell's five pre-war novels in my opinion brings on the worst. Beside him even Orwell is relatively easy.

If Yeats, Eliot, Joyce and Dylan Thomas are too expensive, whom should the new addict collect? The Edwardians, for a start, for here are to be found many predecessors. Then there are the first books of poets as listed in John Hayward's famous catalogue. Georgian poets are still in very small demand. Of the major poets Edith Sitwell is still undervalued. Only *The Mothers*, her first book (1915), and *Façade* (1922) are above the £10 limit. All her books are delightfully got up and full of variety, several in signed limited editions. Robert Graves was also prolific of slim volumes, many of which are still easy to obtain.

The 'Thirties', as I have said, are unpalatable to collect because of the uniformity of presentation. Nevertheless they are absurdly underpriced and our addict can obtain all Auden (except his American firsts), all Spender, Day Lewis, Macneice and Isherwood (with a little patience) and most of Waugh and Greene. And now is the time to do it.

All collectors tend to live in the past but they should make an effort to buy new books by new authors before they reach the booksellers' catalogue. This, of course, involves reading them. How far should love for favourite authors be carried? Should it extend to collecting all subsequent editions of their books? No. They take up too much room. Should one collect the prose of poets and the poetry of prose writers? Yes; if in book form. Should one collect their contributions to other books? Yes. To periodicals? Only for poets, I think. The test of our devotion to an author is whether we are prepared to collect his journalism. The test of an author's devotion to his collectors is not to provide us with any.

Lastly, should one collect magazines? Yes: they are the undergrowth out of which tower the forest giants and they are never artificial rarities. Nothing else so conveys the *couleur du temps*, the unselfconscious excitement of a particular period. Moreover they are never reprinted. Even so, compared to the true collector our new devotee will probably remain, like myself, hopelessly superficial, possessing only one copy of one edition and confining himself to what he can enjoy reading, his library a memorial to the kind of writer that he would like to have been.

A Collector's Year
(1967)

Tapering off! That is how I answer questions about my book-collecting. The urge is waning: the desperate anxiety to corral all my favourite authors into the Ark where I can gloat on them at leisure even as they gloat on each other is a thing of the past. My want-list gets shorter and shorter.

So 1967 has been a cheap year and I can look my family in the face again. And yet? Is this quite a fair picture? Perhaps more has been going on than I care to admit. Just filling in a few gaps: mostly French. A Cocteau collection came up and I acquired a presentation copy of *Le Grand Ecart*, a beautifully bound *Escales* (brief poems about ports and sailors illustrated by André Lhote, redolent of 1920) and a letter: '*Ma Violette, très chérie . . . j'ai traversé un tunnel . . . Marcel ira dans le Midi avec notre voiture et je vais rejoindre Marie Laure en Suisse . . . Félix a aidé Marcel à se guérir*,' Violette Murat? Violette Leduc? Marcel Khil? Félix Rollo? No date. The names are lost in a cloud of 'opium'.

Then Proust. If there is one key book of the twentieth century it is the first edition of *Swann*, Grasset, 1913. I had only John Hayward's second issue. A friend lent me a French catalogue. There was a presentation copy to the newspaper proprietor Léon Bailby, who had cut only half the pages: '*Souvenir du "temps perdu"*,' Proust had inscribed, '*des jours où a commencé la vive affection . . .*' and three lines more. It seemed to me important because it showed that Proust allowed '*le temps perdu*' to mean 'the good old days' as much as time wasted or rather actually lost through imperfections of memory.

It cost the earth. A gigantic manoeuvre was undertaken, American poets were sacrificed across the Atlantic, the Hayward Proust swapped and a rare Gide, the illustrated *Voyage d'Urien*, flung to the bookseller. Aided by Micky Brand of Marlborough Rare Books *Swann* came to join the Prousts I already owned, including a drawing he made for Reynaldo Hahn.

At the Antiquarian Book Sale I swooped on a china-paper copy of Proust's *Les Plaisirs et Les Jours*, surely the most extraordinary of all first books, given what was to follow; half prophetic, half bathetic, and which I had once owned and given away. I have always found that if one gives away a book one will either find another copy within a week or not at all. This was the first *Plaisirs* I had seen since I parted in the Thirties with the other. It was also in the Thirties that I stripped my Eliot collection of one item, *Shakespeare and the Stoicism of Seneca*, to give to John Hayward who had everything else.

I never saw the pamphlet again till it turned up three years ago in a catalogue of Mr C. G. Baker of Bath. I was in Italy and missed it. This spring he had it again, but now for ten pounds, and I was just in time. Mr Baker died shortly afterwards and this retired bank-clerk with such a flair for modern books will no longer alleviate (he stayed open at weekends) the tedium of the queen of cities. Bertram Rota's death last Christmas was another irreparable loss to all collectors. I had known him nearly all my life and he had corrected the proofs of my article on book-collecting. He was a magnificent proof-reader, in short a scholar, as well as a kind and just man.

From America I obtained a copy of *Poetry*, the magazine which in 1915 first printed 'Prufrock', after sitting on it for so long. I now had the 'Love Song' in magazine state, in Pound's *Catholic Anthology*, and as a slim volume in 1917.

Mr Pound sent me a copy of *If This Be Treason* and another of Canto 110 printed for his eightieth birthday, he also inscribed *Mauberley* for me; one needs three copies of *Mauberley*, one to read, one to re-read and one in dust wrapper to be buried with.

Some writers seem irresistibly drawn to my shelves. They are making their own collections. One is Richard Aldington, nicknamed by Durrell 'Top Grumpy', and now Gordon Bottomley is trying to get in. Another, always welcome, is Valéry. I was given Hayward's copy of the *Cimetière Marin*, and at Sotheby's I bought a page of his manuscript of 'Narcisse' with a drawing on it and two of my favourite lines.

> Fontaine ma fontaine eau froidement présente
> Douce aux purs animaux, aux humains complaisante . . .

From the same sale I also obtained Marianne Moore's little volume, *The Pangolin*, published by the Curwen Press and illustrated by George Plank, a quiet American indeed who lived in a cottage in Kent supporting himself by occasional *Vogue* covers. Plank illustrated that charming and little-known autobiography *English Years* by his friend James Whitall, a kinsman of Logan Pearsall Smith, which includes a vignette of George Moore's shadow as he knocked at the Whitalls' door.

It was to them Moore made his comment on Proust: 'If a man chooses to dig up a field with a pair of knitting needles, is there any reason why I should watch him doing it?'

Moore is another welcome intruder though I can generally read only his autobiographical essays and can't stomach the *Brook Kerith*. This autumn I added *A Story-teller's Holiday* and *Conversations in Ebury Street*, both presentations to his old friend (and Joyce's) William McGee ('John Eglinton'). In *A Story-teller's Holiday* he writes, 'It gives me much pleasure to give you this book though it contains things of which you may (crossed out) will not approve.'

It also contains one of the most Proustian pages in English literature when he gives his reasons for not going back to Moore Hall. 'It is the past that explains everything, I say to myself. It is in our sense of the past that we find our humanity, and there are no moments in life so dear to us as when we lean over the taffrail and watch the waters we have passed through. The past tells us whence we have come and what we are . . .'

'And do you not collect any living authors?' Only poets – and this year I find quite a batch, chiefly from private presses – these include the little Turret Books brought out by Edward Lucie-Smith – Sylvia Plath's

Uncollected Poems, G. Macbeth, William Wantling's *Awakening* (a present from Christopher Logue), Zukovsky's *A14* and Harry Fainlight's *Sussicran* (Narcissus again). Fainlight seems to me to have caught something of the evanescence of promiscuity in his elusive verse. Last exit to Earl's Court.

I have always wanted a signed Hart Crane and when a bookseller catalogued one of *White Buildings* dedicated to 'Allan Tate', I knew it was the rare first issue dedicated to Allen Tate, who wrote the introduction. In the second the misprint was corrected. This copy to a Miss Hughes-Hallett, mentions the Hurricane of 1926. It was in the Isle of Pines, I discovered, and 'many people behaved badly'. How?

I have always had a vow with myself that when I found a copy of Elizabeth Bowen's *The Last September* I would give up collecting or it would be *my* last September. This turned up when I asked Raymond Mortimer for something with Eddy Sackville-West's so typical bookplate. He produced *The Last September* and I had a sudden tussle with my conscience. The vow did not apply to books, I decided, that were already on my want-list and I soon went tearing ahead, for Auden's *Collected Shorter Poems*, perhaps the best produced of all his books, Hemingway's *Spanish Earth* in the anarchist colours, quickly suppressed.

And the one that got away? Lawrence's *Escaped Cock* – pursued for years and lost at auction at £80 – a signed one too. But that remains at the head of my want-list for next year with a letter from Joyce, Auden's *Spain* (Nancy Cunard) and *Sodome et Gomorrhe*.

But I *am* tapering off – although I forgot to mention Lorca's *Romancero Gitano* and Rilke's *Duineser Elegien* among my foreign acquisitions. And only yesterday I discovered a presentation copy of Valéry's *La Jeune Parque*. How slow the Christmas posts are!

POSTSCRIPT: This article produced an offer for the *Escaped Cock* (never give up) and the Middleton Murry copy of *Sodome et Gomorrhe* (dedicated) for a very small sum. I still have no Joyce letter.

The Modern Movement: Introduction to the Exhibition Catalogue (1971)

I suppose this exhibition* makes me one of the few writers who have seen their dream implemented by reality, who have rubbed a magic lamp and beheld a huge djinn turn the contents of an imaginary bookcase into the living word, the word made flesh through photographs, letters, manuscripts, association copies, so that every error of judgement is magnified as well as every correct guess, making clearer every secret influence or unsuspected affinity. Only the University of Texas has had the will and the means and the erudition to raise this memorial to the writers of our time, and I hope it will bring new hope and happiness and inspiration to everyone who loves literature and who owes a debt to these life-enhancing figures.

I would like to say something about how this book, originally titled *One Hundred Key Books in the Modern Movement* and not *The Modern Movement*, which would have been presumptuous in a checklist, nor *The Hundred Best Books*, since a 'best book' implies other criteria than 'key', came into being. One must first go back to my school-days, when, an only child in rebellion against a conventional home and an even more conventional classical education, I first came to awareness. My adolescence, 1918–23, coincided with a larger First-

* This article first appeared as the catalogue introduction to an exhibition held in March–December 1971 at the Humanities Research Center of the University of Texas, Austin, U.S.A., to illustrate the author's book *The Modern Movement: One Hundred Key Books from England, France and America 1880–1950* (New York, 1966).

War phenomenon. I was, without knowing it, in search of a father – or father-replacement. This search for a sympathetic spiritual authority is one of the least understood yet most persistent of the emotional drives, though it is common enough in other gregarious animals. A French teacher at school raised a corner of the curtain on Villon, Verlaine, Mallarmé, Baudelaire, but the cult of Flecker, Housman, and the Georgians still lay heavy. It was not until I got to Oxford in 1922 that I met a young don who shared my love of literature and who introduced me to the contemporary ferment. That is why *One Hundred Key Books* is dedicated to Maurice Bowra, through whom I came to love and appreciate early Eliot, later Yeats, Edith Sitwell, E. M. Forster, Proust, and Valéry. Later on I went to work for Logan Pearsall Smith (another father) who made it possible for me to spend a winter in Paris (1928). There I fell in love with an American girl whom I found reading Ronald Firbank, and there I met Sylvia Beach, who introduced me to Joyce, Gide and Hemingway. I identified with the Paris-American pack and was accepted by them, writing some of the first articles on Hemingway, *Finnegans Wake*, and the Surrealists for *Life and Letters* and *The New Statesman*. Even as I read and got to know these Paris expatriates, I came to see them as part of the explosion of my own emotional life as I wooed and won my American girl, Frances Jean Bakewell of Baltimore, then in her nineteenth year. Joyce and Hemingway, cummings and Fitzgerald, *transition* and Sylvia Beach joined up with Eliot, Yeats, Huxley, the Sitwells and Wyndham Lewis and with the great succession of French writers, Baudelaire, Flaubert, Proust and Valéry, to build the Pantheon from which this book came to be chosen. The one great gap was Pound, whom I did not come upon till Sylvia Beach – once more – introduced me to his *Mauberley* many years later – *mea sola et sera voluptas*, my late and only pleasure. I write of these personal feelings to try to show what an upheaval underlies my passion for poetry, of which this list is merely the aftermath. Many new writers then became my friends; Evelyn Waugh, Elizabeth Bowen, Auden, Spender, Isherwood, Dylan Thomas, but none have been sufficient to obliterate the discoveries or the irrecoverable intensity of the year 1928 and the winter/spring of 1929, of 12 Rue de l'Odéon, 30 Rue de Vaugirard, when I found myself in love at the hub of three cultures.

My book, *The Unquiet Grave*, tried to evoke that profound experience; I rather wished someone had suggested that it should have been included in *The Hundred Books*, particularly in view of its extensive quotations from so many authors in this selection, but there was never a murmur. In fact my *One Hundred Key Books* met with a frigid reception from most reviewers and has had to make its way chiefly through booksellers' catalogues. 'First they'll crab you, then they'll crib you,' as Desmond MacCarthy used to say. This treatment might have been expected for a very idiosyncratic anthology but in fact I have tried very hard to be objective, weighing the claims of country against country, group against group, and allowing for my own weak spots. My worst defect is a blind eye for the grand, an inability to swallow larger than life extravaganzas on a colossal scale. I could reel off a long list but here I will mention some of the most significant. Dreiser, *An American Tragedy*; Gertrude Stein, *The Making of Americans*; Wyndham Lewis, *The Apes of God*; E. E. Cummings, *The Enormous Room*; Claudel, *The Satin Slipper*; St. John Perse, *Anabasis*; Faulkner, Thomas Wolfe, Malcolm Lowry, James Agee, Djuna Barnes, Jules Romains, Roussel, Henry Miller (most regretfully). On the other hand I have included one or two very slight books which should perhaps have made way for some of these titans and twice I fear my judgement has been at fault. I decided on 1880 as the beginning and 1950 as the terminus; even so, 1950, which is marked by the deaths of Shaw and Orwell, with Dylan Thomas's soon to follow, is perhaps too arbitrary.

It has meant excluding several writers whom I should like to have included such as Beckett, Anthony Powell and Robert Lowell. Beckett could have got in on the strength of *Murphy* (1938), with *Watt* on the border-line; *Waiting for Godot* was not yet published. It seemed to me that only the last would have merited his inclusion. Anthony Powell's earlier comic novels, even *From a View to a Death*, are nothing like as important as his novel-sequence, *The Music of Time*, which began with

A Question of Upbringing (1951), and Robert Lowell's *Lord Weary's Castle* is still based on somewhat monotonous versification from which he only escapes in *Life Studies*, a far more significant book (1959).

I do not know if it is due to old age or to the overwhelming tempo of current events, but I form an impression of hurrying flood-waters carrying everything away in a muddy spate of torn trees, huts, hen-roosts rushing past, of monuments of culture now buried and forgotten, even in the few years since this exhibition was planned and the book written. To compile lists and catalogues is an anxious occupation which suggests a morbid preoccupation with the flight of time. Flaubert, Joyce, Thomas Wolfe were dabs at it, Ezra the Scribe (though not the poet) and I feel my list came just in time. Already a hundred new critical works have accumulated round the corpus of Eliot, Joyce, Yeats, Pound, Proust, Lawrence, Hemingway and even Auden, still so very much with the living. And yet literature, never so well taught as now, is perhaps never so little read; I mean that the literary experience, the shock of recognition, the cross-fertilization between minds of which this exhibition gives such wonderful examples, is severely threatened by the distractions of other media and by economic pressures. These writers, many of whom I knew, lived in an emptier world; no one saw Joyce on television or even heard him on the wireless, his voice survives on one gramophone record. Yeats also; and though Eliot received modern coverage, we know nothing about Nathanael West or Hart Crane except from one or two snapshots; even a writer very famous in his time like George Moore is physically elusive, and the only man living who can imitate Proust (Paul Morand) is in his eighties. For this reason the association copy, which plays such a large part here, antedates the radio and television interview as a manifestation of personality, a chain reaction. Before the days of the media, writers were unselfconscious and did not 'sit' to posterity or sign books for collectors. Hardly anyone collected them. They could also be poor and obscure, and there was no campus spread under them to catch them if they fell. Apart from their powers as trail-blazers, as architects of our own sensibility, I think this modest isolation forms part of their beauty, even as Claudel reminded Gide of seeing Verlaine and Villiers 'with destitution in their eyes'.

For visitors who have no time for the introduction to *One Hundred Key Books* or its captions, I would like to repeat that I use the 'modern movement' loosely to mean what we all know, but cannot define, the revolt against nineteenth-century materialism; 'The modern spirit was a combination of certain intellectual qualities inherited from the Enlightenment: lucidity, irony, scepticism, intellectual curiosity, combined with the passionate intensity and enhanced sensibility of the Romantics, their rebellion and sense of technical experiment, their awareness of living in a tragic age.' The word 'modernity' was first used by the Goncourts, then by Gautier. Technical experiment without imagination is not enough, but neither is imagination with an unimaginative attitude to form.

I suspect Robert Frost, Max Beerbohm, Galsworthy, Wilde of being anti-modernists and have left them out with many other traditional writers (Walter de la Mare, Kipling). I have not included translations from languages I do not know – German, Russian, even Italian and Spanish. Exceptions, Waley's *Chinese Poems*, Koestler's *Darkness at Noon* (written in German but first published in English). I have left out philosophical, historical and other subjects whose frontiers march with literature. My method was to go through lists of books under the years they were published, from 1880–1950, and put together all the significant, then slowly weed them out. If some well-known book is not here, there is, I hope, some good reason.

To come back to this exhibition, it is the embodiment of a dream, the incarnation of the dry bones of my catalogue. One would like it to exist in perpetuity like so many side chapels in a great cathedral, each with their images and ex-votos and paintings where the onlooker can meditate and where time stands still. Hemingway's letter to David Garnett – what a treasure that is* – and Hart Crane's message to E. E. Cummings to buy the Graves-Riding *A Survey of Modernist Poetry* –

* He had written the book (*A Farewell to Arms*) so many times trying to get it as he wanted that finally it made no sense to him.

'it has more gunpowder in it'; *The Waste Land* with its eliminated line '(The ivory men make company between us)', and many writers expressing their doubt and despair about books which were to prove seminal. I suppose no critic, bibliophile or maker of a literary litany has had such satisfaction as the summoning to this exhibition of the living genius. As Mallarmé said of Debussy's setting to music of his *Après-midi d'un Faune*: 'Your illustration goes even further *dans la nostalgie et la lumière, avec finesse, avec malaise, avec richesse*' – in nostalgia and light, with subtlety, with inquietude, with luxury. May these books in turn stimulate the visitor to go home and do better.

The Ivory Shelter
(1939)

A controversy has already begun about what people ought to read in wartime. It is more important to know what people ought to write. I know that one cannot advise genius, that it is above the struggle, but most writers are without genius, and it is a function of criticism to hearten them, and help them to avoid mistakes.

As human beings artists are less free now than they have ever been; it is difficult for them to make money and impossible for them to leave the country. Lock-up is earlier every day, and they are concentrated indefinitely on an island from which the sun is hourly receding. As human beings they are no longer emotionally free, for the infection of war induces mental symptoms which indicate the discomforts and torments to follow.

But in the last few weeks two tyrannies have been overthrown, two yokes which many of our artists bore have been thrown off: the burden of anti-Fascist activities, the subtler burden of pro-Communist opinions.

It is a quality of an artist to be more imaginative and more truthful than his fellow-men. For years this greater sensibility and objectivity have wrecked themselves in political causes, and forced political realities on many who would have been stronger exempt from them. The writers with the deepest sense of humanity have expended and often wasted that sense in the hopeless struggle for Manchurians, Abyssinians, Austrians, Spaniards, Chinese and Czechs. What they could say, they have said, what they could feel, they have felt, and no historical change has resulted. Yet there has been one result, a war which was inevitable may have been precipitated, and writers now live in a world no longer political but military. The fight against Fascism is in the hands of the General Staff, and there is no further use for the minor prophet. In short, all artists who are not in the fighting forces, or engaged in active propaganda, are now escapists, their task of making their country conscious of the forces at work in the world is in abeyance. They have made plain what they thought, and, if they were to go on saying it, they would not always find it printed.

Thus one excellent counsel I could give to writers would be: keep off the war. Nothing they can write will do much to win it, and a large collection of second-hand expressions and clichés left over from Spain and Abyssinia forms the vocabulary with which they will have to work. When, two years ago, several hundred writers answered a questionnaire on the side they took in the Spanish war, these terms were already threadbare, and now since anti-Fascism has become the official policy of the Government, its vocabulary is utterly frayed. During the last war the escapists carried on a literary renaissance. Joyce wrote *Ulysses* in Trieste and Zurich, Firbank's novels were written in rooms at Oxford, *South Wind* appeared in 1917, and *Eminent Victorians* a year later. Moore, Yeats, Gide, Eliot, Forster, and Virginia Woolf are other writers in whom it is vain to search for a clear definition of our war-aims, an attack on the Prussian beast, or any reference to the last war whatever. In fact, however writers may serve their country as men, war provides them with the opportunity, as artists, to serve themselves. The best modern war literature is pacifist and escapist, and either ignores the war, or condemns it, with the lapse of time. When the war is, like the present one, a gigantic police operation, the writers who helped in detecting the criminal are often made uncomfortable by the forces called in to apprehend him. Where, for instance, are those two recruiting sergeants of the Left, Auden and Isherwood? At a time when many of those whom they have fired are taking part in 'to-day the struggle', these veterans of Berlin, Barcelona and the Yang-Tse have settled permanently in America, as if our European war were provincial and dowdy. In this they are not to blame; as the pacifist of yesterday becomes the militant of to-day, so the militant tends to become pacifist. The desire to love and understand life replaces the ambition to fight to alter it. And so the central problem for writers to-day is more still to balance the rights and wrongs of pacifism and self-defence, to explore the causes and the cure of war, that troubled frontier where three kingdoms, Marxism, Psycho-analysis, and Biology meet. The watershed is not yet properly mapped, the source of the lust for power investigated. Can violence ever be justified? Yet can pacifists justify permitting, through their own inaction, the slaughter of other pacifists, with the suppression of those ideals for which other idealists are prepared to fight? And the aggressive instinct? Can it be analysed out of us, and would the will to progress then go with it? Should we try gland injections, or have all Europe weaned, like the Eskimos, at the age of twelve? The Eskimos lack the aggressive instinct; on the other hand, their cultural contribution to Europe is inconsiderable. Yes, for thoughtful artists, there seems only one problem: how to reconcile the necessity for this war with the effects of it.

This question of ends and means brings us back to the one event of importance which affects writers since the war has broken out. The Germans, who for political reasons brought Lenin back to Russia, have let Voroshilov out. The aims of the Red Army are not yet known; it may only restore the Russian pre-war frontiers, it may encourage pan-slavism and throw Germany into our arms, it may socialise Germany and throw the two nations against us, or it may bring the millennium, but whatever it builds, it will have destroyed the Infallibility of the Comintern.

The majority of English writers have liberal instincts. These instincts many of us have subordinated before the advocacy of Communist methods. We have felt a sense of inferiority, viewing the uselessness of liberal opinion as compared to that of an organised Communist action, like the International Brigade. This sense of inferiority at 'getting anything done' has extended to other fields, and driven many sympathisers to accept Communist values in literature or theories in art. Now, while Communist energy is unimpeachable, their pretensions to being more right than other people would appear to be shattered. Their leader performs not only acts which they find difficult to justify, but acts which they are unable to predict. They may benefit us in the long run, but the methods are as close to Hitler's as the huge statues on the Russian Pavilion in the Paris Exhibition were to the Colossi on the German one. And it was always the means employed by Communism against which the liberal mind revolted. Their tendency to exalt the will at the expense of the heart, which sets a ruling class apart from its subjects; the aridity of all that obedient thinking; the worship of what is of historical necessity, and the contempt for what might have been; the obstinate intransigence by which Miaja and Azaña were turned into traitors because they gave up a lost war a few days before Negrin and the brawny Pasionaria; the Bogy of the Party Line – all these are discredited, and the sense of relief should generate a new exuberant energy in the creative forces of the Left, more international conception of justice and freedom, and an aesthetic, not a political, approach to art.

For these reasons it would seem that those writers, and they are our best, whose country does not as yet require them, provided they have somewhere to work, and can get enough to eat, are in a wonderful position. 'There will be time to murder and create', without considering the 'flat ephemeral pamphlet, and the boring meeting', or stabbing a Tractor in the back. The censorship will force them back on the abstract, and the esoteric, on pure technique developing the resources of their thought and feeling. Revolutionary movements will be more spontaneous, anarchists no longer be called uncontrollable, liberals ineffectual, or intellectuals bourgeois. Nostalgia will return as one of the soundest creative emotions, whether it is for the sun, or the snow, or the freedom which the democracies have had temporarily to discontinue. War is a tin-can tied to the tail of civilisation, it is also an opportunity for the artist to give us nothing but the best, and to stop his ears.

'Comment'
from *Horizon*, issue one
(1939)

A magazine should be the reflection of its time, and one that ceases to reflect this should come to an end. The moment we live in is archaistic, conservative and irresponsible, for the war is separating culture from life and driving it back on itself, the impetus given by Left Wing politics is for the time exhausted, and however much we should like to have a paper that was revolutionary in opinions or original in technique, it is impossible to do so when there is a certain suspension of judgement and creative activity. The aim of *Horizon* is to give to writers a place to express themselves, and to readers the best writing we can obtain. Our standards are aesthetic; and our politics are in abeyance. This will not always be the case, because as events take shape the policy of artists and intellectuals will become clearer, the policy which leads them to economic security, to the atmosphere in which they can create, and to the audience by whom they will be appreciated. At the moment civilization is on the operating table and we sit in the waiting room. For so far this is a war without the two great emotions which made the Spanish conflict real to so many of us. It is a war which awakens neither Pity nor Hope, and what began as a routine police operation, a military sanction, is now hardening into the grim prehistorical necessity of Keeping Alive.

The original *Life and Letters* which flourished ten years ago had no political aspect. But the change that has come over literature in the last decade is an increased consciousness of its political and economic basis. This is the only Marxist lesson that writers have soundly learnt, and so

Horizon will have political articles, though it will never imitate those journals, in which, like pantomime donkeys, the political front legs kick and entangle the literary hind ones. *Horizon* is concerned with the general issues of peace and war and will consider the origins, ethics, conduct, and conclusion of them in an enquiry open to the most diverse points of view, and for which the articles by Priestley and Read form a starting point.

Mrs Woolf, in her pamphlet on reviewing, published by the Hogarth Press, maintains that the ordinary review is useless to author and reader; that it would be better for the general public if brief synopses of books were given together with a sign to denote approval or disapproval; that if the author wants criticism, he should pay the reviewer a private fee and consult him; and that editors would do better to spend money on a revival of the Essay and Criticism than the Review. *Horizon*, being interested in imaginative writing, has no room for regular features or chronicles of the arts, and there will only be two kinds of review – the critical essay and general discussion of ideas, or the brief short notice. There will be no half-hearted comment on the half-dead.

To those whose lives are tormented by the notion of talent in others a magazine with well-known names appears middlebrow, and without them cliquey. Such critics are implacable, so we address *Horizon* to those who generously enjoy quality in writing, and ask them to help make us known.

Writers and Society (1940–43)

The position of the artist to-day should occasion general concern were it not that the whole human race seems threatened by an interior urge to destruction. He occupies, amid the surrounding dilapidation, a corner even more dilapidated, sitting with his begging bowl in the shadow of the volcano. What can be done to help him? In the event of the defeat of England and France, nothing. We are accustomed to the idea that there is no art worth the name in Germany and Italy (although Italy possesses a high standard of taste – witness her pavilions in recent exhibitions, and a group of interesting young painters), but we are less familiar with the fact that literature and painting are becoming more and more confined to the Western democracies, the countries where wealth and appreciation survive, and where the environment is friendly. A defeat of those countries would mean the extinction of the 'liberal' arts in Western Europe, as much as of liberal opinions.

But in the democracies themselves the artist finds himself tolerated rather than appreciated. Unless he is a purveyor of amusement or a mouthpiece of official cliché he is there on sufferance, and before suggestions for the betterment of his condition can be made, we must consider his ideal status in life. Just as education cannot improve until the world for which children are educated improves, so the artist cannot receive his due until the society in which he lives fundamentally revises its conception of the objects of existence. Many people would accept the idea of a benevolent world Socialism as their political aim, a world in which all the resources were available to its inhabitants, in which heat and fuel and food were as free as air and water, in which Marx's familiar definition of an ultimate civilization, 'to each according to his needs, from each according to his ability', was realized. But this world does nothing for the spiritual life of humanity except to provide for its inhabitants the material comfort and security which has hitherto provided the point of departure only for the spiritual life of the few. The final happiness of humanity must depend on its capacity to evolve, on the use it makes of the capacity – found only in human beings – of getting outside itself, of extending human consciousness to include the perception of non-human phenomena, till it is not only aware of, but able to transcend, the laws by which it is governed. Otherwise to achieve a material Utopia, however difficult and desirable, is still to doom the race to the disintegration of satiety, and to the decay inherent in its own limitations.

There are certain types of human beings who are especially equipped for the extension of human consciousness and for the domination of the in-human world. They are the scientist, the mystic, the philosopher, the creative artist, and the saint. Of these, only the scientist receives the partial appreciation of the world, because by subsidizing his researches the world will grow the richer by such by-products as the aeroplane or the telephone. Einstein and Freud, the physicist and the psycho-analyst whose inventions were of doubtful value, were exiled by their immediate public. These five types, the pure scientist who uses measurement in his investigation of natural laws, the philosopher who uses mind, the saint and the mystic who make use of extra-sensitive emotional machinery, and the artist with his dark lantern, form the aristocracy of a more perfect world, in which the second order is composed of those who, without seeking to expand human possibilities, work at improving their condition. These would include the reformers and administrators, the practical scientists and inventors, the educators, the alleviators, the doctors and nurses, the practical artists, actors, singers, journalists and entertainers, and the men of law. Then would come the middle-men, the keepers of order and the pillars of trade, and then the great mass whose progress towards intelligence and happiness is the concern of the others, and lastly the 'blind mouths', the invincibly ignorant, the obstructive and destructive, the power-grabbers, the back-street Napoleons, the incurable egoists and prima donnas, the gangsters, whether poor or rich.

While the greatest explorations of the world beyond our boundaries have been made by scientists, never have writers been so preoccupied as now with the investigation of spiritual possibilities, and this alone justifies the artist's claim to the respect of mankind. At the moment Wells, Maugham, Joyce, Virginia Woolf, Huxley, Heard, Priestley, Eliot may all be said to be working on it, and, among young writers, a deepening sense of spirituality characterizes the recent poetry of Auden and Spender. There is no escapism from a political present in this, and the best analysis of it is to be found in the opening chapters of Heard's *Pain, Sex and Time*, in which he describes human beings as the prisoners in a submarine who can only escape the fate of the unadaptable species by concentrating all their evolutionary energy on a dangerous and difficult escape by a spiritual Davis apparatus. The value of Picasso's *Guernica*, of the work of Proust, of the landscapes of Cézanne, is to penetrate the darkness which surrounds the human camp-fire, and reveal something of the landscape beyond it. The artist lacks the training and the profound comprehension of a Freud or an Einstein, nor does he make a good philosopher according to academic standards, but his intuitive intensity, his patient obsession, and the quality of his imagination entitle him to rank with the great disappointed Prometheuses of our age, those who are bent on changing the world as inexorably as their rulers appear set on its destruction.

That is the ideal picture. And even there it will be noticed that most of the artist-sages I have mentioned have accumulated their fame and fortune as artist-entertainers. To-day the scientist is subsidized, but the saint is expected to live by his sanctity, the mystic on his mysticism, the artist by his popularity with his sitters, or with the twopenny libraries. Only the entertainer receives his due, which nobody grudges him, but which hardly compensates for the squalor and penury in which the serious poet or painter is permitted to rot. To-day the most precariously situated in any society are that abandoned trio, the writer, the painter, and the liberal intellectual. The intellectual is the most unfortunate, for he has no creative power to absorb him, he is the Cassandra of our age, condemned to foresee the future and to warn, but never to be listened to, nor to be able to profit from his foresight. Without power and without money he has spent the last ten years prophesying a disaster in which he will be the first to perish. For the world has disproved the liberal axiom, that persecution defeats its object; it has been shown that an efficient secret police, a concentration camp, or an invasion with tanks and machine-guns can silence any opposition, can stop the intellect from questioning or the poet from affirming, and thus reduce his historical potency to that of the Redskin or the Carib. In any case, artists are easy to suppress; adaptability and subservience to the powers that be, a happy tropism, characterize them as often as inflexible courage and integrity. They recant more merrily than they burn.

What can be done to improve their position? They must, like every defenceless minority, unite, and learn to help each other, to present their case to the public. They must respect their creative mission more than they do now, and they must force their rulers to respect it, they must understand that their position is desperate, and will become intolerable, that, outside the Western democracies, they are surrounded by enemies, while their friends are dwindling within them. Like the Pet-World, they are the first to feel the rationing and the change in the standard of living; they will be hard hit if the rentier class, on which many of them are remittance men, goes under, nor is there any political party likely to come to power to whom the artist and the intellectual are not at best but means to be exploited.

But it is not easy for artists to help themselves. They are not a class for whom co-operation is pleasant. Besides being envious and bitter, as are the economically under-privileged, many often work better through an inability to appreciate the art and aims of their contemporaries. When success permits them, both writers and painters prefer to barricade themselves deep in bourgeois country, like those birds which we admire for their colour and song but which have divided our woods into well-defined gangster pitches of wormy territory. The artist and intellectual are a kind of life-giving parasite on the non-artist and the non-intellectual, and they are not to be criticized for being slow to combine with each other.

Therefore it is the public who must be educated, and the rulers who must be mollified; and here the artists can combine, for the smug hostility of the English is indiscriminately extended to all forms of art. In a number of *World Review* Sir Thomas Beecham brilliantly attacks the musical apathy of the nation; the attack must be sustained by artists and writers. The public must be asked to distinguish between the serious writer and the potboiling entertainer, between the poet and the prima donna journalist; the ruling class must be seduced into recognizing the importance of the great dollar-producing invisible export of our literature, not only the Mr Chips, Gracie Fields, Peter Wimsey brands, which go wherever a bottle of Worcester sauce can penetrate, but the difficult, conscientious, and experimental work for which England and France are uniquely adapted, the delayed-action art and literature which survives indifference and slowly dominates – as Rimbaud or Hopkins have dominated – the creative minds of a generation. The idea of quality is an Anglo-French obsession; where the quality is not easily apprehended, the judges should be lenient. Here is a black list of some who are not.

Lord Beaverbrook. This nobleman injects into the jaunty philistinism of his papers a breath of the great art-hating, art-fearing open spaces. 'You do not often see a writer mentioned on this page' complacently remarks an article in the proprietor's breezy biblical style. What information about art and literature there is in his papers is intelligently but stealthily purveyed by the younger gossip-writers. The popular press as a whole, when not content to ignore art and literature, fosters such absurd distinctions as that between highbrow and lowbrow, which has done more harm to both serious and popular art than any other false classification.

But there are other circles as much to blame. There are the private and public schools which, under the cloak of a genial obscurantism, do so much to warp the talent that passes through them, and to harden the untalented in their own conceit. Then there is the Government, who, as

Sir Hugh Walpole has recently pointed out, do nothing for literature, except to grant occasionally a miserable pittance for some half-starved veteran. Then there are the increasingly illiterate rich, often the descendants of those patrons who willingly gave a hundred pounds away, not for a picture or for a dedication, but to enable an artist to carry on. This practice is almost extinct, and a poet who was given a sum of money for being a poet rather than for writing copy for underclothes would be regarded as an undesirable. A useful remedy for this would be to let it be known that any benefactions already made to the arts, to the furtherance of research, or to the betterment of conditions in any form would be deducted from tax. But this implies a bureaucracy friendly to the arts, and we are a long way from it. Freud mentions tidiness, parsimoniousness, and obstinacy as the three characteristics of the Anal Type, and it is engaging that they also symbolize what is called the Official Mind.

Then there are the traitors among the artists themselves: the Publisher, with his Cold Feet; those who are ashamed of their vocation, who accept the enemy's estimate of it and become horse-painters or country gentlemen; those who clown for the philistines or who throw away their genuine talent through fear of being unpopular; or those defeatists who enjoy with Oriental relish the ignominy to which they are subjected and pretend that to starve and to be bullied by bank managers and passport authorities is part of the state to which artists are called, and which they must accept without question.

It is true that the artist is drifting into becoming a disreputable member of the lower middle classes waiting, in a borrowed mackintosh, for the pubs to open, but the privations which improve his talent must be imposed not by society but by himself – and any investigation of the artist's circumstances reveals that by far the most favourable conditions for him are neither at the top nor the bottom, but snug in the heart of the bourgeoisie, with a safe middle income, such as nineteenth-century capitalism (the golden age of the remittance man) provided, and such as some other system will now have to be dragooned into paying.

An opponent particularly dangerous in these times is the near-artist, or Pinhead. Pinheads are a race apart, they are generally tall and bony, anal to the *n*th degree, but sometimes small and foxy. They are obsessed by a profound hatred of art and are prepared to devote their lives to gratifying it. To do this they occupy a fortified position, either at a university, or in an advanced political party, or as a publisher, and then proceed to castigate the artist, if from the university, on grounds of faulty taste or scholarship, if from a party, on grounds of political unorthodoxy or loose thinking. Every artist is an exhibitionist. The tragedy of a Pinhead is that he is a repressed exhibitionist, a guilty character whom a too strict censor is punishing for his wicked desire to undress and dance. The Pinhead is consequently attracted to the artist, whose generous immodest antics excite his own, but he is also consumed with envy and disgust for them. The ultimate enemy of art is power. One cannot desire both beauty and power, so the Pinhead, lacking as he does all aesthetic sense, usually obtains power and then becomes one of those Puritan commissars of the arts who see nothing in Picasso, who do not 'understand' modern poetry, who examine art through the wrong end of the scientific telescope and see very little, or find no basis for it in Logical Positivism. They wear their Marxism like a hair-shirt, and their triumph is when they have persuaded a painter to abandon colour for abstraction, or a poet to write a political pamphlet, or to suppress a novel 'for personal reasons.' Fortunate is the artist to-day who is able to follow his invention without one of these poor bald old homo-puritan Pinheads blowing down his neck.

For the time being, the outlook is black. The painter, the writer, the liberal intellectual are in for a bad time; if they can co-operate, if they can assert themselves, if they can survive to the incredible period when nations are not afraid of each other, they will come into their own, for they have powerful allies. The working class, for instance, has not the deep-rooted animosity of the others towards artistic creation. Lawrence was not persecuted by it for his secession, but by his betters. The success of the Penguin library or of *Picture Post* or *The March of Time* show what a great potential benefactor an increasingly educated working class can be. Those who visited Azaña's Spain, our Lost Ally, will recall how pathetically friendly to culture were its masses, and there are many parts of the world where it is still a compliment to call someone an educated man. Even the Court is emerging from two centuries of Hanoverian apathy. Then the technocracies of the future are well disposed, the most powerful of all, the army and navy, show less of that hostility to art which is found in commerce and the Cabinet, and when the war is over they will hardly allow themselves to be quietly deprived of their influence, and handed a gratuity, as before. Revolutions do not happen in this country, but every now and then the public gives a great heave of boredom and impatience and something is done with for ever. When that happens, the artist must be on the crest of the wave, not underneath it, for art occupies in society the equivalent of one of those glands the size of a pea on which the proper functioning of the body depends, and whose removal is as easy as it is fatal.

~

Meanwhile the almond blossom is out, the sun shines, the streets look shabbier and the shops emptier, and the war slowly permeates into our ways of living. It is a war which seems archaic and unreal, a war in which eighty million people are trying to kill us, a war of which we are all ashamed – and yet a war which has to be won, and can only be won by energetic militant extroverted leaders who are immune from the virus of indecision. And the intellectuals recoil from the war as if it were a best-seller. They are enough ahead of their time to despise it, and yet they must realize that they nevertheless represent the culture that is being defended. Abyssinian intellectuals, Albanian intellectuals, Chinese intellectuals, Basque intellectuals, they are hunted like the sea-otter, they are despoiled like the egret. Our own are the last to survive. Granted the whole cumulus of error in the last twenty years, the greedy interlocking directorship of democratic weakness and Cabinet stupidity, then the war is inevitable. It is a war which dissipates energy and disperses friends, which lowers the standard of thinking and feeling, and which sends all those who walk near emotional, mental, or financial precipices toppling over; it is a war which is as obsolete as drawing and quartering; which negatives every reasonable conception of what life is for, every ambition of the mind or delight of the senses; and which inaugurates an era of death, privation, danger, and boredom, guaranteeing the insecurity of projects and the impermanence of personal relations. But there it is. We are in it: for as long as Hitler exists we must stay there. The war is the enemy of creative activity, and writers and painters are wise and right to ignore it and to concentrate their talent on other subjects. Since they are politically impotent, they can use this time to develop at deeper emotional levels, or to improve their weapons by technical experiment, for they have so long been mobilized in various causes that they are losing the intellectual's greatest virtues: the desire to pursue the truth wherever it may lead, and the belief in the human mind as the supreme organ through which life can be apprehended, improved, and intensified.

But they must also understand that their liberty and security are altogether threatened, that Fascism is against *them*. The Anglo-French artist and the intellectual are lucky to be alive. They must celebrate by creating more culture as fast as they can, by flowering like the almond blossom; for if they take a vow of silence till the war is over, or produce as little as do some of our lords of language, they will disappear: and their disappearance will provide further evidence that the human race has outstayed its welcome.

~

Several times a year articles arrive called 'Where are our war poets?' The answer (not usually given) is 'Under your nose.' For war poets are not a new kind of being, they are only peace poets who have assimilated the material of war. As the war lasts, the poetry which is written becomes war poetry, just as inevitably as the lungs of Londoners grow black with soot. It is unfortunate from the military point of view that war poetry is not necessarily patriotic. When the articles ask 'Where are the war poets?' they generally mention Rupert Brooke, because he wrote some stirring sonnets and was killed in action, though his poems were mostly nostalgic or amorous. They want real war poets and a roll of honour. That we lack patriotic poetry at the moment is a healthy sign, for if it were possible to offer any evidence that civilization has progressed in the last twenty years, it would be that which illustrated the decline of the aggressive instinct. This absence of aggressiveness, a danger in the war, is the healthiest of all symptoms for the peace, and makes possible the hope that, once we have had sufficient victories to remove self-confidence from our enemy, the awareness of the whole idiotic archaic process of war, with its boredom, its slaughter, its privations, and its general clumsy uselessness, may sweep over the world and induce people to give it up.

There is another aspect of the war and culture which it is refreshing to notice. Although there is very little new being written, there is a vast amount of old that is being forgotten. Blake told us to 'drive our harrow over the bones of the dead', and such a silent revolution is happening. The vast top-heavy accumulation of learning, criticism, scholarship, *expertise*, the Alexandrian library of nineteenth-century Liberal capitalism, is falling to decay. Human beings have a tendency to over-civilization, they cannot tear up old letters, they collect and catalogue up to the edge of insanity. A burning of the books becomes at times a necessity; it was necessary to think Milton, or Pope, or Tennyson, or Proust, or James, bad writers, if writing was to go on. Before the war the stream of creative writing was choked with the leaves of exegesis; writers were bowed down with their intellectual possessions, with their names and dates, their sense of the past, their collection of unspoilt villages, their knowledge of cheese, beer, wine, sex, first editions, liturgy, detective stories, of Marx and Freud. It was a Footler's Paradise, a world in which, as on a long sea voyage, those came to the top who could best kill time. Culbertson, Torquemada, Wodehouse, Dorothy Sayers, Duke Ellington; the hobby dominated the art, the artists were artists in spite of themselves, or they worked in second-rate and inartistic material. In the realm of criticism the sense of the past dominated, the aunts and uncles of the great were exhumed, the load of material bore down on its inheritors, making them carping and irritable, while the ignorant but talented were forced to suffer for their ignorance, or waste their talent in catching up. The fear of democracy is the fear of being judged for what we are, instead of for what we have. Now that so many of us have no possessions, no houses, or books or cars or notes, we find it less terrible than we thought. Let us also have no theories and no facts, let us forget our great names, who had so much more patience, talent, and leisure than we had, and declare a cultural moratorium. The sooner we accept the Dark Ages the faster they will be over. In the streets round this office, where the exposed green of fourth-floor bathrooms shines against the blue winter sky, an enormous Rolls-Royce often passes. Each time one sees this mammoth of luxury, one wonders to whom it belongs; some fatcat of Bloomsbury? A ground landlord? A member of the Corps Diplomatique? But as it glides past it becomes transparent, and reveals on well-oiled bearings its only passenger, a neat wooden coffin. The limousine belongs to the last people who can afford it: the luxurious dead.

~

Invasion and You! As I write these words I hear on unexceptionable authority that the enemy is on his way, following that route, old as the seasons, by which he has brought off all his most audacious infiltrations. He landed at Europe's extreme south, the sandy scab of the Punto de Tarifa, and at once opened a pincer movement round the Atlantic and the Mediterranean seaboard, with a central thrust up the valley of the Guadalquivir. The cork-woods of Algeciras, the cotton-fields of Estepona, the blue sugar-canes and custard apples of Almuñecar were the first to be penetrated, and in the west he reached that botanist paradise, the Sierra de Aracena and the Sierra de Monchique, at the same time as he encircled, on the east, the Contraviesa and the Gadór. The villages with their Moorish walls, their goats and their aloes, surrendered on the hill-tops. Soon after fell the provincial capitals, Huelva, Cadiz, Seville, Granada, Almeria, Málaga, Jaen, and Córdoba, all of

Andalusia along the river, till the green corn sprouted on the white soil, the Sierra Morena became a creaming waste of cistus, and New Castile and Estremadura were threatened, until even the places with the coldest names, Fregenal, Tembleque, Javalambre, surrendered, and the Duke of Frias betrayed his title. And what has happened in the Peninsula will happen in France: the country is ripe for it, all resistance is undermined, the asphodel blossoms are frothing over the Eastern Pyrenees, the catkins are on the willows, the poplars of the west are covering with new green leaves their balls of mistletoe, the chestnut buds and the outdoor tables have climbed to the Loire. At the longest we have only a fortnight to prepare against the malice and ingenuity of our hereditary enemy, the unsound, unprogressive, uneconomical, unpatriotic, unmechanized, non-belligerent Spring. 'Make no mistake about it,' said a High Official who is in his free time a Military Spokesman, 'Spring will try us hard, but, buttressed in this island bastion, we will withstand him. The enemy will use gas. "Aires, vernal aires," "Banks of violets," "Delicious South." We have a filter for all of them. "April is the cruellest month." Green grass, blue sky, white clouds, primroses; everything will be tried that may distract our attention and sap our resolve. Don't look at 'em. Wear dark glasses. Stay put. What did Gamelin say to Ironside? "Pas bouger!" Stay put!' 'And bacteriological warfare?' 'Ah, yes, Spring fever, glad you mentioned it, very important. When you get that pushover feeling, that false sense of well-being or euphoria, "young man's fancy," desire to receive or bestow affection, to crowd roads and railways, to change domicile; don't give way. If it gets too strong, consult your Mr Sensible. And remember, now as always: win the Spring is win the war. We know what short shrift was meted out to the guzzlers in restaurants, now is the time to punish mental and emotional guzzling. We have got the measure of the food-hog. We must destroy the day-dreamer, the memory-hoarder, the escapist, the beauty-wallah, the reading man. Then and then only, bastioned in this island buttress, will we be totally conditioned to total war, and when victory is ours, when the war has swept the world, when nobody anywhere gets more to eat than the poorest Spaniard or the most starving Chinese, when nobody can read or write, when nobody has anything, nobody wants anything, nobody does anything except work, work, work – when we've got the race war, the class war, the age war, the sex war, going simultaneously, when we look back at to-day as the happiest period of our lives, and when happiness is recognized everywhere for what it is, a dull and dishonest evasion of necessary pain; when we have reduced humanity to its lowest denominator – then the sacrifices we have made in conditioning ourselves against the daffodil and the blackbird will not have been worthless. Good morning. Stay Put.' 'Good morning. Go to it.'

~

It is sad on a spring evening to walk through the bombed streets of Chelsea. There are vast districts of London – Bayswater, for example, or Kensington – which seem to have been created for destruction, where squares and terraces for half a century have invited dilapidation, where fear and hypocrisy have accumulated through interminable Sunday afternoons until one feels, so evil is the atmosphere of unreality and suspense, that had it not been for the bombers, the houses would have been ignited one day of their own accord by spontaneous combustion. Behind the stucco porches and the lace curtains the half-life of decaying Victorian families guttered like marsh-gas. One has no pity for the fate of such houses, and no pity for the spectacular cinemas and fun-places of Leicester Square, whose architecture was a standing appeal to heaven to rain down vengeance on them. But Chelsea in the milky green evening light, where the church where Henry James lies buried is a pile of red rubble, where tall eighteenth-century houses with their insides blown out gape like ruined triumphal arches, is a more tragic spectacle. For here the life that has vanished with the buildings that once housed it was of some consequence: here there existed a fine appreciation of books and pictures, and many quiet work-rooms for the people who made them. Here was one of the last strongholds of the cultivated *haute bourgeoisie* in which leisure, however ill-earned, has seldom been more agreeably and intelligently made use of. Now when the sun shines on these sandy ruins and on the brown and blue men working there one expects to see goats, and a goatherd in a burnous – 'sirenes in delubris voluptatis' – pattering among them.

Meanwhile the bombs, which have emptied so many drawing-rooms, have also been blasting the reputations made in them. Our literary values are rapidly changing. War shrinks everything. It means less time, less tolerance, less imagination, less curiosity, less play. We cannot read the leisurely wasteful masterpieces of the past without being irritated by the amount they take for granted. I have lately been reading both Joyce and Proust with considerable disappointment; they both seem to me very sick men, giant invalids who, in spite of enormous talent, were crippled by the same disease, elephantiasis of the ego. They both attempted titanic tasks, and both failed for lack of that dull but healthy quality without which no masterpiece can be contrived, a sense of proportion. Proust, like Pope, hoaxed his contemporaries; he put himself over on them as a reasonable, intelligent, kind, and sensitive human being, when his personality was in fact diseased and malignant, his nature pathologically cruel and vacillating, his values snobbish and artificial, his mind (like a growth which reproduces itself at the expense of the rest of the body) a riot of alternatives and variations, where both the neurotic horror of decision and the fear of leaving anything out are lurking behind his love of truth.

For Joyce there seems almost less to be said; Proust's endless and repetitive soliloquies are at least the thoughts of an intelligent man, while those of Joyce reflect the vacuous mediocrity of his characters; both relive the past to the point of exhaustion. Both are men of genius whose work is distorted by illness, by the struggle of one to see and of the other to breathe; both seem to us to have lacked all sense of social or political responsibility.

Yet we must remember that the life which many of us are now leading is unfriendly to the appreciation of literature; we are living history, which means that we are living from hand to mouth and reading innumerable editions of the evening paper. In these philistine conditions it is as unfair to judge art as if we were seasick. It is even more unfair to blame writers for their action or inaction in the years before the war, when we still tolerate in office nearly all the old beaming second-rate faces, with their indomitable will to power, and their self-sealing tanks of complacency.

~

It would not be unfair to say that the England of Baldwin, MacDonald, and Chamberlain was a decadent country – 'Cabbage Land', 'Land of lobelias and tennis flannels', 'This England where nobody is well' – its gods were wealth and sport; from any unpleasant decision it flinched in disgust; though assailed by critics from the right and left, it still wallowed supinely in a scented bath of stocks and shares, race-cards and roses, while the persecuted, who believed in the great English traditions of the nineteenth century, knocked in vain at the door.

Since Dunkirk we have seen the end of the political and military decadence of England. Whatever residue of complacency, sloth, and inefficiency there may be left, England is now a great power, and able to stand for something in the world again. When the war is over we shall live in an Anglo-American world. There will be other great powers, but the sanctions on which the West reposes will be the ideas for which England and America have fought and won, and the machines behind them. We had all this in 1918 and made a failure of it. The ideas expired in the impotence of Geneva. The machines spouted Ford cars, Lucky Strike, Mary Pickford, and Coca-Cola. The new masters of the world created Le Touquet and Juan les Pins, fought each other for oil and reparations, blamed each other for the slump, and wandered blandly and ignorantly over Europe with a dark blue suit, letter of credit, set of clean teeth, and stiff white collar. Fascism arose as a religion of disappointment, a spreading nausea at the hypocrisy of the owners of the twentieth century. It is important to see that Fascism is a disease, as catching as influenza; we all when tired and disillusioned have Fascist moments, when belief in human nature vanishes, when we burn with anger and envy like the underdog and the sucker, when we hate the virtuous and despise the weak, when we feel as Goebbels permanently feels, that all fine sentiment is ballyhoo, that we are the dupes of our leaders, and that the masses are evil, to be resisted with the cruelty born of fear. This is the theological sin of despair, a Haw-Haw moment which quickly passes, but which Fascism has made permanent, and built up into a philosophy. In every human being there is a Lear and a fool, a hero and a clown who comes on the stage and burlesques his master. He should never be censored, but neither should he be allowed to rule. In the long run all that Fascism guarantees is a Way of Death; it criticizes the easy life by offering a noisy way of killing and dying. The key philosophies which the world will need after the war are, therefore, those which believe in life, which assert the goodness and sanity of man, and yet which will never again allow those virtues to run to seed and engender their opposites.

The greatest discovery we can make from this war, the one without which no Renaissance is possible, is what human beings are really like; what is good for them, what standard of living, what blend of freedom and responsibility, what mixture of courage and intelligence, heart and head makes for progress and happiness. We find out what we need by having to do without what we think we need. All words and ideas must be tested and built up again from experience. When we have learnt what kind of life we want, what kind of man should live it, a Renaissance becomes possible. Here are some conditions for it.

An artistic Renaissance can only take place where there is a common attitude to life, a new and universal movement. By the time Anglo-American war aims have crystallized from the philosophy behind them, this should be in existence. But no political movement can have the art it deserves until it has learnt to respect the artist. The English mistrust of the intellectual, the brutish aesthetic apathy and contempt for the creative artist must go. Bred of the intolerance of public schoolboys, the infectious illiteracy of the once appreciative gentry, the money-grubbing of the Victorian industrialists and the boorishness of the Hanoverian court, our philistinism (which also expresses the English lack of imagination and fear of life) should be made a criminal offence. There can be no dignity of man without respect for the humanities.

A Renaissance also requires a belief in spiritual values, for materialism distils nothing but a little rare dandyism, an occasional Watteau, and that will not be enough. The most sensible cure for materialism is a surfeit of it, which post-war science and economics should assure us. Yet we cannot get such a spiritual revival until the religious forces and the spiritual humanistic forces come to terms together, as did the Basque priests and the Spanish Republicans, as have Bernanos, Maritain, and the French Left. This is the hardest bridge to erect, but it will have to be done, and should not be impossible; for our civilization is impregnated with Christianity even where it seems unchristian; the foundations of our beliefs are those of Christianity and Greece, however those beliefs may have become distorted.

Regionalism, after the war, must come into its own. There is already a Welsh Renaissance in being; there is activity in Ireland and Scotland. Regionalism is the remedy for provincialism. Only by decentralizing can we avoid that process which ends by confining all art to the capital, and so giving it a purely urban outlook. England is one of those mysterious geographical entities where great art has flourished. We have the racial mixture, the uneven climate, the European tradition, the deep deserted mine-shaft. We must reopen the vein.

The greatest danger, let us hope, to the artist in the England of the future will be his success. He will live through the nightmare to see the new golden age of the West, a world in which no one will be unwanted again, in which the artist will always be in danger of dissipating himself in the service of the State, in broadcasts or lecture tours, in propaganda and pamphlets. As in ancient Rome or China, or modern Russia or U.S.A., the artist will have a sense of responsibility to a world-wide audience, which he must control. But that should be the only temptation for him in what will at last be a serious world, a world in which the new conquerors avoid the mistakes of the old and bring to the opportunities of victory the wisdom and dignity that they learned in defeat.

~

War journalism and war oratory have produced an unchecked inflation in our overdriven and exhausted vocabulary. Dictatorial powers to clean up our language should be given to a Word Controller.

The first act of the Word Controller (Mr Shaw would be a good choice) should be to issue licences (like driving licences) to all journalists, authors, publicists, orators, and military spokesmen. Without such a licence it would be a criminal offence to appear in print or on the platform. The licences of all those found using the words *vital*, *vitally*, *virtual*, *virtually*, *actual*, *actually*, *perhaps*, *probably*, would then be immediately cancelled. This surprise action of the Word Controller would at once eliminate most journalists and politicians, and all military spokesmen. These words should be unmolested, and protected, for several years. The words *democracy*, *liberty*, *justice*, *freedom*, *jackboot*, *serious consideration*, *island fortress*, *love*, *creative*, and *new* should be suspended for six months, and the licence endorsed of anyone found using them. Lists (constantly brought up to date) of forbidden clichés with a scale of fines should be posted on every noticeboard. The Word Controller, at any rate during the few hours of office before his powers turned his head, would be non-political. His aim would be to reshape the English language to its original purpose as an instrument of communication, and an invention for expressing thought. Thus the expression 'The town is virtually surrounded' would become 'The town is, or is not, surrounded,' 'vital necessity' would become 'necessity', and a scientific machine for weighing words would demonstrate that while such terms as 'coronary thrombosis' are as full of content as when first minted, other verbal coins are worn too thin for the public slot-machine and must be withdrawn from circulation. As he became more autocratic and more like other controllers he would find out that there is a connection between the rubbish written, the nonsense talked, and the thoughts of the people, and he would endeavour to use his censorship of words in such a way as to affect the ideas behind them, or, rather, he would give priority to statements of fact over abstractions, and to facts which were accurate rather than incorrect.

Applying himself to art, the Word Controller will remark that no great literature can be made out of the split-mind which is now prevalent. The unadulterated aggressive instinct creates its art; the detached and meditative attitude is also valid, but blended they destroy each other and produce the hotchpotch of standardized, lukewarm, muddled propaganda through which we are floundering. An artist must be in the war or out of it. He must go to America or to Ireland or to prison if he wants to write, or else fight and read the newspapers: the moment he becomes undecided, well-meaning and guilty, he is Hamleted out of service as a writer; however much he concentrates on the Atlantis of the past, or the Utopia of the future, he will be made to suffer in the present. For we live in an imperfect world: history punishes the ignorant and the mistaken: the wicked are left to punish themselves.

In the times in which we live a writer should not be able to put down more than two or three lines without making it obvious whether he has anything to say. The Word Controller, by banning the verbal camouflage of those who doubt, who twist, who are on the make, or who hope for the best, would clarify propaganda and leave literature safely where it belongs, in the hands of the very sane, or the very mad.

We are all prisoners in solitary confinement: when at last we give up trying to escape through mass emotion or sexual union there remains for us only the wall alphabet in which we tap our hopes and thoughts. Nobody should learn this alphabet who can abuse it, who jerry-builds the English language as if it were the English countryside, who wastes the time of his fellow prisoners by tapping out stale rhetoric, false news, or untranslatable messages, and so brings a perfect achievement of civilization into confusion.

~

What are the three characteristics of Puritan verse? Poverty of imagination, poverty of diction, poverty of experience – the characteristics, in fact, of Puritan prose and Puritan painting. If we examine an imaginary poet, for example, John Weaver, 'whose austere verse, eschewing all tricks and facile solutions, so clearly depicts the dilemma of the intellectual in the period of *entre deux guerres*', we find that, of any age between twenty and forty, he is 'the child of professional parents, was educated at a major university and a minor public school, has Marxist sympathies, and is at present trying to reconcile communism with religion, pacifism with war, property with revolution, and homosexuality with marriage'. He will have been published in '*New Verse*, *New Writing*, and *New Directions*, and will have produced one volume of poems [I am quoting from the Introduction] called *The Poet's Thumb*.' 'John Weaver is most actively interested in politics and took part in several processions at the time of the Spanish War. Indeed, his particularly individual imagery discloses an extreme awareness of the contemporary situation.

> Come, Heart, we have been handed our passports,
> Love's visa has expired.
> The consulate of Truth is closed
> And virtue's signature no longer valid,

and many other poems show that he was among the first to await, like MacNeice, "The Gunbutt on the door."'

For an interesting fact about Weaver is that, though several years younger than Auden and MacNeice, he is completely dominated by them. He imitates their scientific eroticism, their Brains Trust omniscience, without the creative energy of the one or the scholarship of the other, just as he assimilates the fervour of Spender and the decorum of Day Lewis into his correct, flat, effortless, passionless verse. And it is Weaver, now at an O.C.T.U. or in the Air Force Intelligence, who is responsible for some of the badness of war poetry, who used to write 'Comrades we have come to a watershed,' and now talks about 'Love's tracer bullets,' even as his brother Paul, who once painted ascetic winter streets for the East London Group, is responsible, with his fossilized landscapes of tanks and hangars, for some of the badness of War Art. An element of Puritanism is always present in a good artist, but in a minute quantity. The Puritan poet of the 'thirties has been all Puritan, he has been afraid of life and repelled by it, and so has acquired no experience to digest; caught in the pincer-movement of the dialectic, he has picked up the modern vice of arrogant over-simplification, nor has he developed his imagination by reading or travel. As a person he is incomplete and therefore as an artist sterile, the possessor of a desiccated vocabulary which is not his own, but which he has timidly inherited from his poetic uncles. Auden and Spender made use of this vocabulary to chasten the Georgians, and, having served its purpose, it should have long been discarded. Such poets as John Weaver, who exist rootless in the present without standards or comparisons, are doomed to swift extinction, for the war has proved a godsend to bad artists, allowing them to make honourably, and for their country's good, that surrender to normality which in peace-time is only accepted after a long and terrible struggle.

There will always be poetry in England: it is the concentrated essence of the English genius, distilled from our temperate climate and intemperate feelings, and there will always be critics who claim that it is dead. But poetry is going through a bad patch. The sophisticated intellectual poetry of the 'twenties is exhausted. Poetry was taken down a cul-de-sac to get away from the Georgians, and now it has to find its way back. The academic socialism of the 'thirties was not strong enough to revive it, we are waiting for a new romanticism to bring it back to life. This will happen when the tide of events sweeps round the lonely stumps on which our cormorants have been sitting and gives them a fishing-ground – for one of the difficulties of John Weaver has been the isolation of his mood from the uneasy fatuity of between-war England, and another, the hitherto sheltered, unwanted, uneventful character of his life. Now that events have caught up with his prognostic and he is no longer out of step with the rest of the population, his work will be deepened and simplified.

This process is only just beginning. As an industrial nation we lag behind: our factories are not the largest, our generals not the wisest, but as an ancient civilization that is not neurotic, where thought once more is correlated with action, and which fights for its beliefs, we should, in those invisible exports like poetry and fine writing, be in a position to lead the world.

The death of Sickert, unhonoured, almost unnoticed, reminds us that we live in a philistine country. Camden Town, Dieppe, Paris, Bath, Brighton, Venice, the places he loved and painted, recall to us that art once was international, that the greatest English painter could yet stem off from the art of France and Italy, could be as English, and as Continental, in the piazza of St Mark's, or a South London music-hall; by the Porte Saint-Denis, or by a brass bedstead off the Tottenham Court Road. Looking at his best pictures, such as the French and Venetian landscapes shown at the Redfern in 1940, or the *Granby Street* shown recently at the National Gallery, we are conscious not only of superb technique, but of the sacred moment, of the absorption of the painter in what he sees, which by talent and patience he is able to communicate. It is the communication of this sacred moment which constitutes a work of art. The vision might be insane, like Van Gogh's, or ponderous with sanity as in Degas or Cézanne, but it existed. Our tragedy is to live at a time when it does not. In a continent which is exterminating itself, a country which is socializing itself, a world that is destroying its standard of living, the existence of the great artist, the free personality, of the solitary smouldering creative figure whose thought and imagination challenge eternity, becomes more and more precarious. If we want great art after the war we must restore the freedom of Europe to our artists, and also guarantee them economic security. The defects of War Art arise through the personality of the artist being shrunken by being fitted in to the military structure, and by his being denied the freedom of Europe, and so cut off from the masterpieces of the past. The sacred moment which the artist is too self-pitiful to communicate or too shallow to perceive has vanished.

As the war goes on, intimations of the kind of world that will come into being after the war become clearer. It will be a world in which the part played by the English will be of supreme importance. In fact, one might say that the whole of English history, tradition, and character will be judged in the future by how we rise to the occasion of the post-war years. England will find itself in the position of one of those fairy-tale princes who drift into a tournament, defeat a dragon or a wicked knight, and then are obliged to marry the king's daughter and take on the cares of a confused, impoverished, and reactionary kindom. That kingdom is Europe, the new dark continent which must perish if it cannot attain peace and unity, and which is yet in a constant eruption of war, economic rivalry, and race-hatred.

England is the weakest of the three great post-war powers: unless it has behind it a strong, united Europe it must be overwhelmed by America, either involuntarily or in a tug-of-war with a Communist Europe and Russia. If England fails to unite Western Europe it fails as a world power, if it succeeds and can hold a balance between American Capitalism and Soviet Communism, defending Western Europe from the reactionary imperialism of one and the oppressive bureaucracy of the other, it will prove itself the greatest and wisest middleman in History. To achieve this, England must resurrect that political wisdom for which it was once famous and produce a scheme for Europe which will incorporate the socialist idealism of Russia with the humanist individualism of America and which will lead towards the gradual atrophy of European race-hatreds and nationalist pretensions. Every European war is a war lost by Europe; each war lost by Europe is a war lost by England. When the struggle for our lives is over, the struggle for our standards of living will have only begun, and our standard includes the liberty to go where we like, stay where we like, do what we like and pay how we like.

To achieve and deserve this leadership will require courage and wisdom, with an appreciation of the complexity of European affairs and a sense of trusteeship for the European spirit which we are still far from possessing. But Europe is more than a political concept, it is still the chief breeding-ground of ideas, the laboratory, the studio, and the reference library of the world's art, science, and imagination. If England is to help Europe, it must assume the cultural as well as the moral and political protection of Europe, it must restore liberty of expression, economic security, and mental audacity to the world of art and ideas.

This is a most difficult task, because England – the only country in

Europe where a man may still paint or write very much what he likes, and find a market for it – is nevertheless a philistine country. Worse still, the philistinism is an essential factor in the national genius, and forms part of the stolid, practical, tolerant, pleasure-loving, responsibility taking English character. There is no other civilization in the world so old, so mellow, so wise, and so polite which can yet so happily dispense with respect for learning, love of art, or intellectual curiosity. The French are saturated in these things; the Americans worship culture even though they are inclined to do so for the wrong reasons; the English, to whom will fall the task of restoring paper and ink and paints and canvases to occupied Europe, dissipate their aesthetic instinct in ball-games, card-games, dart-boards, and foot-ball pools. Even the culture of England in war-time is a most haphazard affair.

A visit to the French Exhibition at the National Gallery (the best picture show since the war started) brings the problem closer. Why is not English painting better? Why do we raise Sargent instead of Renoir, Munnings instead of Degas, Pre-Raphaelites instead of Impressionists? The climate of the Ile de France is hardly different from that of Southern England: many of the scenes chosen by the Impressionists are not in themselves beautiful; their gardens are inferior to English gardens; their tall, red-roofed villas almost as ugly as ours; their magical light is not peculiar to the Seine valley. What have they got that we lack?

Can the question be answered sociologically? The art of the Impressionists and their followers is the supreme flowering of bourgeois society. Many of the Impressionist painters were well-to-do people; they were not only secure in their patrons, they were secure in their investments; all through their lives several of them never had to worry about money. This is not all-important, but it is a great addition to a sense of vocation. They were also secure in their aesthetic philosophy. They believed in devoting a long life to the worship of beauty and the observance of Nature. Politics, society, family were all represented, but they were not the important things. There was a certain Chinese humanism about them; they loved their friends and painted them admirably in their favourite surroundings, they enjoyed, in moderation, the good and simple things of life, they were not ashamed of man's place in Nature, nor of urban civilization with its alcoves and café tables, nor of old age with its arm-chairs and book-shelves. If the highest expression of their art is such a landscape as the Renoir of Argenteuil, a vision of watery paradise, or the Seurat of a wood or the Pissarro of La Roche-Guiyon, there are two smaller pictures which perhaps betray more of their secret. One is a tiny Manet of a dark bistro interior, which reveals all the poetry of city-life; the other is Vuillard's portrait of Tristan Bernard in his garden. The garden is hideous – grass with a flinty rose-bed against the brick of a Normandy villa – and the bearded poet is rocking back in it on a cane chair. The effect is of a civilization as sure of itself as a poem of Li-Po or Po-chüi. One sees immediately that the English could not paint like that because Kipling or Meredith or Henry James would not rock about so irreverently – because the English imperialist bourgeoisie, though just as stable as the French, had that extra moral and mercenary conscience, had too much money, too much sense of duty, and so could never give off such a light and heavenly distillation as Impressionism. Whistler and Sickert succeeded because they were not English, and at the price of a Harlequin defence-mechanism which never left them.

When we restore the arts then to Europe, we can do one of two things: we can attempt to restore to bourgeois civilization sufficient order and stability to enable the cream of art to come to the top, or we can develop a civilization which will permit a new art to arise. If we adopt the second course instead of trying to put back the nineteenth-century Humpty-Deümpty on the wall, then we must radically change our attitude to art here: we must give art a place in our conception of the meaning of life and the artist a place in our conception of the meaning of the State which before they have never known. Never again must our artists be warped by opposition, stunted by neglect, or etiolated by official conformity.

The danger is that the State will take over everything; the State everywhere has discovered its inexhaustible source of wealth – the working hours of the individuals who compose it. In some countries the discovery is a few years old, here it is only two – and woe betide us if we had not made it – but more woe still if we cannot unmake it, if we cannot break the tyranny of State, here and everywhere else, after the war, or never again will we have an hour to call our own. Being a small State-owned country we will have to work twice as hard to compete with the large State-owned countries, like some wretched Cock-house at school whose members never dare break their training. For the State-owned nation will have nothing in common with the dream of international Socialism, since it will always be in total competition with the others, and therefore have to ration and overwork its members while taxing both their work and their earnings. Its weapons will be propaganda, bureaucracy, and a secret police with every man his own informer. For every child born there will be one to spy on it – for life. Our dossiers will open with the first words we say! And this will continue till a revolution is made and world Stakhanovism succumbs to the cry of 'Liberty, Inequality, and Inefficiency'.

The effects of State control are already apparent in art. We are becoming a nation of culture-diffusionists. Culture-diffusion is not art. We are not making a true art. The appreciation of art is spreading everywhere, education has taken wings, we are at last getting a well-informed inquisitive public. But War-Artists are not art, the Brains Trust is not art, journalism is not art, the B.B.C. is not art, all the Penguins, all the C.E.M.A. shows, all the A.B.C.A. lectures, all the discussion groups and M.O.I. films and pamphlets will avail nothing if we deny independence, leisure, and privacy to the artist himself. We are turning all our writers into commentators, until one day there will be nothing left for them to comment on. 'A great work by an Englishman,' wrote Hopkins, 'is like a great battle won by England. It is an unfading bay-tree.' How true that is to-day, and how tragic if *les lauriers sont coupés*.

This year we celebrate the centenary of Henry James, a man who, if he had never written a novel, would be considered the first of short-story writers, and if he had never written a short story, the noblest of letter-writers, and if he had never written anything would by his talk alone be known as a great man. To-day he is more than that, for he has become the symbol of a certain way of life, a way that is threatened not only by the totalitarian enemy but by the philistine friend, and yet a way which is an unpropitious age has helped masterpieces to be created and artists to live; the path of what James called 'the lonely old artist man,' who is so easily destroyed and so quite irreplaceable.

Thirteen years ago Edmund Wilson, in his *Axel's Castle*, attacked this outlook. He criticized all the great individualists – Joyce, Proust, Valery, Yeats, and Mallarmé – on the ground that they had carried the investigation of the ego to a point at which it had become unbearable, and he asserted that the great literature of the future could only arise from a corporate and socialist view of art as the expression not of the individual but of the mass. This literature has not yet arisen, and ten years later, in *The Wound and the Bow*, Edmund Wilson seems to have returned to the conception of the artist as an isolated wounded figure, as different from the social realist as is a huge lightning-stricken oak from a Government conifer plantation.

It is difficult to prove that any age has been propitious for the artist; Socrates was condemned to death, so were Seneca and Petronius, Dante was exiled, the age of Louis XIV was one of both civil and religious persecution; the nineteenth century, as the lawsuits against Flaubert, Baudelaire, Hugo, etc., show, was not much better; and in the twentieth century there are whole tracts of Europe where to be a writer is to invite a firing-squad. 'Silence, exile, and cunning' are the artist's lot, and, exquisite though his happiness will be when his public, educated at last, mobs him like a film-star, we may be wiser to assume that, for our lifetime, 'silence, exile, and cunning' it will remain. For this reason it is necessary to keep the memory of these giants like Henry James and Flaubert, or Baudelaire and Mallarmé, always before us, even if we never read them, for they are the saints of modern bourgeois art, whose virtues – sensibility, intellectual courage, renunciation, and consecrated devotion – emanate even from the mere storing of their books in our rooms. They are sacred relics which we need not too often disturb.

The tragedy of our civilization is that a specialized education has segregated an advanced artistic minority from the main body as with a tourniquet. In the interests of the masses (and therefore by his logic, of art), a Communist may be willing altogether to wash out this 'advanced' literature and, from a level open to all, to make a fresh start which, with an educated proletariat, might lead in fifty or a hundred years to a new and happy art made by artists as integrated in the State as were the builders of medieval cathedrals in the Church. But anyone who does not accept the overriding authority of the proletariat must feel that, since art has advanced so far, even if down the wrong turning, it is too late to turn back. In relation to his public the artist of to-day is like the spelaeologist of the Peak or of the Causses of Southern France; he walks at first with his companions, till one day he falls through a hole in the brambles, and from that moment he is following the dark rapids of an underground river which may sometimes flow so near to the surface that the laughing picnic parties are heard above, only to re-immerse itself in the solitude of the limestone and carry him along its winding tunnel, until it gushes out through the misty creeper-hung cave which he has always believed to exist, and sets him back in the sun.

1940–43

The Cost of Letters
(1946)

The questionnaire which follows was sent out to a selection of writers of various types and ages.

QUESTIONNAIRE:

1. How much do you think a writer needs to live on?
2. Do you think a serious writer can earn this sum by his writing, and if so, how?
3. If not, what do you think is the most suitable second occupation for him?
4. Do you think literature suffers from the diversion of a writer's energy into other employments or is enriched by it?
5. Do you think the State or any other institution should do more for writers?
6. Are you satisfied with your own solution of the problem and have you any specific advice to give to young people who wish to earn their living by writing?

Cyril Connolly

1. If he is to enjoy leisure and privacy, marry, buy books, travel and entertain his friends, a writer needs upwards of five pounds a day net. If he is prepared to die young of syphilis for the sake of an adjective he can make do on under.

2. He can earn the larger sum only if he writes a novel, play, or short story, which is bought by Hollywood and/or chosen by one of the American book societies, but he can add considerably to his income if he tries to publish everything he writes simultaneously in American periodicals, which all pay most handsomely. This is the only dignified way of making more money without giving up more time.

3. A rich wife.

4. If you substitute 'painting' for 'literature', it becomes obvious that no art can be enriched by the diversion of an artist's energy. A good book is the end-product of an obsession; everything which impedes the growth and final exorcism of this obsession is harmful. All writers like to have hobbies and side interests to fill up the interval between obsessions, but this is not the same as having other employment. Compare Pope with Gray, Tennyson with Arnold, Baudelaire with Mérimée, Yeats with Housman. Pope and Yeats *grew*, the two dons, despite their long holidays, remained stationary.

5. The State, in so far as it supplants private enterprise, *must* supplant private patronage. But private patronage was not based on results, and the State should not count on them either. Free gifts of money should be made to those setting out on an artistic career, and at intervals of seven years, to those who persist in one. Most of our good writers need at the moment a year's holiday with pay. Furthermore, pensions to artists and their widows should be trebled, both in value and quantity, and considered an honour, not a disgrace. All State-conferred honours to artists should be accompanied by a cash award. Furthermore, all writers and painters should be allowed a fairly large entertainment allowance, free of tax, and one annual tax-free trip abroad. Books and framed paintings (as opposed to articles, sketches, posters, etc.) should be regarded as capital and the income from them not taxed. This would encourage the production of books rather than the better-paid journalism by which most writers now make their living. Money spent on buying books and works of art by living artists should also be tax-

free. Big Business, too, could do much more for writers and painters. Shell and London Transport before the war were setting the example. Even the general public can send fruit and eggs. The State's attitude towards the artist should be to provide *luxe*, *calme et volupté*, and when it receives *ordre et beauté* in return, to be sure to recognize it.

6. No, certainly not. What a question! As for the young, don't become writers unless you feel you must, and unless you can contemplate the happiness, security and cosiness of respectable State-employed people without loneliness or envy. Otherwise, like most of us, you will resemble the American 'who wanted to be a poet and ended up as a man with seven jobs'.

‘Cannon to Left of Them’
(1946)

‘Horizon – oh no zir!’ The only anagram which the word can produce (collect me if I am light) sums up the comment of our many thousand enemies. For we have enemies, and it is fitting to start a new year by squaring up to them. Here is what Edmund Wilson says in the *New Yorker* about these creatures.

‘*Horizon* has been a remarkable magazine and Mr. Connolly an exceptional editor. It seemed to me a proof of his merit, when I was in London at the end of the war, that, in the political and literary worlds, everybody complained about him and it but that everybody, at the same time, seemed to some degree dependent on them.’

‘Everybody complained’ – but that means *you*, ‘*hypocrite lecteur*’, ungrateful swine! So that is how you talk when our back is turned!

‘People in London used to complain,’ he continues, ‘that Cyril Connolly was out of key with the wartime state of mind’ – complain of the author of ‘Letter from a Civilian’ which reflected the wartime state of mind more closely than a thousand Gallups! Then they will complain of anything.

I put it to you, miserable readers, that complaining has become your second nature, off with your nears! and that the over-indulgence of that dismal faculty has reduced you to a peevish back-biting state in which you are incapable of reacting to any aesthetic or intellectual stimuli, in which you have forfeited your right to happiness and sunk beneath the pleasure principle into a morose and carping esurience.

We will now deal with some particular complaints. ‘*Horizon* has gone off’ – ‘And left you behind, I fear’ – ‘It’s above my head’ – Ah! your head, reader? What recent gains in sensibility have you to register? Do you read or think as much as you used to? You are aware no doubt that your consumption of tobacco and alcohol has practically doubled, you will pay two hundred and fifty pounds for a hideous leather armchair which Ribbentrop may have sat in, you will plank down three quid for a bottle of Scotch, you can't be trusted with a railway towel or a piece of hotel soap, the club nail-scissors have to be kept on a chain, you'll queue a mile for a black-market lipstick, you talk about 'putting the vedge in the fridge', and smoke all through meals, your manners are dreadful, you're full of hate against other countries, you talk of Frogs, and Yanks and Wogs, and write to *The Times* against Picasso; you're more anti-Semitic, even, than before. You think you are a cultivated person yet you don't know who built the house you live in, and can you honestly say that you would rather have your child turn into Baudelaire than Lord Nuffield? You've probably had a manuscript sent back to you recently. I thought so. It might interest you to know that the psychosomatic branch of this paper is making a study of 'Rejectee mentality', and is finding out some interesting things about you. Anything more to say?

Ah, here we have our most fee-rocious critic, Mr Julian Symons, the fox without a tail.

'*Horizon* was born in January 1940. It printed all sorts of work, by writers with all sorts of beliefs: but it avoided conspicuously the two most interesting literary movements of our time – the movement towards methodological criticism represented by Yvor Winters, John Crowe Ransom, Allen Tate and some other American writers, and the movement towards the *literary* left, of those who experimented in the twenties and early thirties in the dangerous medium of *words*. The most notable thing about this bland and cultured magazine, indeed, was the maintenance of its editions at a standard of gentlemanliness hardly approached by any editor of a serious literary paper in the last twenty years. *Horizon* was a neo-Georgian literary paper with modernist overtones: its sire may have been the *Criterion*, but its dam was certainly the *London Mercury*.' (In *Now*, 5.)

'*Horizon*, it may be said, is in England and in wartime the head and shoulders of this movement to keep art going: a movement which to some of us seems today merely banal and disgusting.' (In *Focus one.*)

In *Partisan Review* he tells the Americans even more plainly what he thinks. 'The Editor of the quite frankly belles-lettrist *Horizon*, who prints odd fag-ends of the Twenties . . . bound together by no organized view of Life or Society, no stronger thread than his own erratic intelligence and whimsical Barryesque good taste.'

Mr Julian Symons, brother of the author, and formerly the ardent admirer of Wyndham Lewis, to whom he sacrificed a whole number of his short-lived *Contemporary Poetry and Prose*, is a critic of considerable acumen, driven forward like his master by the spur of envious animosity. I call him a fox without a tail because he is the leader of the art-hating school of Left-wing writers, and always at his best when prophesying the ruin of art, literature, and the 'virtuoso trapeze artists' who practise them. 'The arts are disintegrating,' he exclaims in *Now*. 'The objective of art today is to divert attention from the class struggle,' 'The intelligentsia who try to nurture the coy bloom of art as we know it are tending a dying flower.' In 'Crisis and Dismay', his article in *Focus one*, he attacks the writers of the thirties for failing in their task.

'It was symbolically much, no doubt, that Auden and Isherwood should become ambulance drivers in Spain during the Civil War, that Spender should work at Barcelona radio-station and Day Lewis write a sonnet beginning "Why do we all, seeing a Communist feel small". But practically it was not very much.'

Isherwood never went to Spain, Auden was never an ambulance driver, nor Spender an announcer – even the line of Day Lewis is misquoted – so perhaps the attack on them is not worth very much either. Or am I being methodological?

'The highest kind of creative work likely to be written today,' insinuates the fox, 'will be satiric: taking as a base the visible world and commenting on it with violence and hatred.' There is time for one more quotation before plunging back into the class struggle: a fox's prayer. 'If we stand on the side of "progress" we may find it necessary as William Morris suspected, to resign art altogether. . . . A transition might take place, more or less gradually in individual cases, to a situation in which the writing of creative literature in any way satisfactory to the artist seemed increasingly difficult and even unimportant; that will be the point at which the creative artist who is also an honest man will lay down his pen. This consummation would grieve all artists, and be death to some: but the transition from the bourgeois art of the last three hundred years to any possible socialist art of the future will not be made without such sacrifices.'

May I suggest that Mr Symons, who is, I feel sure, as honest as he is creative, sets us an example, like a good Socialist, and makes that great sacrifice here and now?

Humanists at Bay
(1943)

Horizon was recently the subject of a full-dress attack in a multilingual Moscow magazine called *Soviet Literature*. An unfortunate critic, A. Elistratova, had to read through a lot of back numbers (mostly 1944–5) and tack them on to *The Loved One* for a general blast against our decadent English culture. The Editor, Mr Evelyn Waugh and Mr Herbert Read ('the reactionary decadent clique of *Horizon*') come in for most of the abuse; the Editor is accused of going so far as to simulate anti-Fascism in order to entrap unwary young writers in his reactionary policies. One of the most endearing features of Communism is the charming belief that editors are important: they scheme, they struggle for power, they instigate sweeping reforms and diabolical intrigues. Remove such strong and wicked juggernauts as edit *Horizon*, the *Cornhill*, *New Writing*, *Time and Tide* or the *Times Literary Supplement* and the misguided masses can breathe again. It's all so simple. Evelyn Waugh's sympathies were with the Italians in the war in Abyssinia. Ten years later *Horizon* publishes *The Loved One*. Therefore *Horizon* is Fascist. 'The British citadel of militant decadence in the arts.' One of the objects of the Soviet attack is a list we gave of signs that should mark a civilized community (abolition of death penalty, laws against homosexuality, etc.). This list was also the subject of a violent onslaught from Mr Evelyn Waugh in *The Tablet*. Moscow here joins hands with Rome and causes us once more to reiterate that unless a writer be attacked by both Catholics *and* Communists he is not of his time.

In Jugular Vein
(1947)

GENTLEMEN,

The offensive against Art is developing according to plan. It is too early yet to prophesy total victory, too early even to talk of a break-through or to indulge in wishful thinking about a complete mopping-up of art and artists. We must not underestimate the foe. But it is worth while recapitulating what has been done. A year ago this magazine, under the title of 'The Cost of Letters', published a bundle of documents which revealed that the morale of our enemy was sinking fast. Economic warfare was making itself felt all along the line. Last winter a brilliant exploit deprived the enemy of all paper supplies for more than a month, and another daring fuel raid put their dangerous radio station, Third Programme, out of action for a considerable period. What was particularly encouraging about this brief campaign was the feebleness of the enemy's response. Meanwhile our blockade was not ineffective. We may now proudly claim that, while the steady shipment to America of the entire antique collections of Britain proceeds unhindered, it is almost impossible for a contemporary work of art to pass from one country to another. If it is extremely difficult for a painter to move around the world or export his wares, it is quite impossible for anyone else to go abroad to look at painting. There is only one cause for alarm. We have effectively sealed off the whole civilian population from access to the Continent and its dangers; we have even reimposed a rudimentary censorship. But have we been sufficiently thorough in preventing foreigners from coming here? The autumn has seen the blockade of pictures, tourists, etc., one hundred per cent successful – with films and sheet music added to the list. But the most daring coup was the banning of the import of foreign books; a feat which held that quality of surprise, rapidity and ruthlessness which indicates the born commander. Though the contents can never rival our own, foreign books are – were, I should say – sometimes speciously well printed; the margins immorally wide and the paper indecently thick; the sentiments expressed often well informed and subversive. I don't think we will any of us regret them.

And now I have to pass on to a very unpleasant subject. There exists, as you know, a fifth column in this country. There are artists, writers, poets, crypto-artists and crypto-writers, survivors from the bad old days, over whom the authorities have insufficient powers. There are even one or two publishers or reviewers who compose in their spare time. I blame no one for this; I blame the system. But something must be done. The paper control has just cut the ration of periodicals by ten per cent. That is a step in the right direction, a most salutary step. It will be followed, I hope, by further cuts and by the rationing of fuel to printers and binders in such a way that these very inessential industries are compelled to liberate their manpower for the national effort. It will become increasingly difficult, I am afraid, for gentlemen of the literary and artistic persuasion, when forced out of their Bloomsbury bed-sitting-rooms by cold and hunger, to avoid taking a few tottering steps in the direction of the welcoming sign 'Labour Exchange' where 'guidance' will be freely given to them – with perhaps a shave and a haircut thrown in. But these are slippery creatures – and this is where the public can help. You all hate a spiv (Yes, SIR!) – You all hate an Eel (I'll say we do!) – You know what to do with a Drone, a second-helping wallah, a lipstick lovely, an aesthete (Leave 'em to us); You know the right noise to make when you see a Butterfly (Brrrrerp!) You've been put on your guard against the Gander in his club window – you've been warned against the Royal Turbot, with her French perfume and gigantic hat. I want to warn you against the Artist: I want you to learn to hate him like a whale. We've made short work of the whales lately (cheers); it's no secret that there soon won't be a whale left. (Loud cheers.) Radar, depth charges, blubber bombs – their number's up. Why is it that we all love a journalist, a civil servant, a Public Relations Officer, or a Member of Parliament when we see one? Yet we all hate instinctively an artist! I'm going to call them 'bats' to you, because they squeak, because they have no morals and hang upside down and stink and spend the day in a terrible fug and look revoltingly like human beings. (Laughter.) I'm going to appeal to you to rid our island workshop of our flitter-mice friends – every one of them from the greedy Flying Fox to the dirty little Pipistrelle. *You* don't have to interfere with them. Leave that to *us*. (Laughter.) The public has a perfect weapon ready. Apathy. (A voice – Spell it!) Just don't think about them. That's all. You've got plenty to think about. Rations, the new cuts, the potato shortage, bigamy, the last six murders, the latest currency fine, the long-skirt controversy, the Royal Wedding, the airplane disasters, the Marshall Plan (all aid short of peace), the new combined electric cheater and staggered geyser, holidays with P.A.Y.E. And I'm glad to see that you're reading less. I'm told that books are getting nearly as hard to sell now as before the war. I hope we shall soon live to see the book and periodical entirely superseded by the bulletin and communiqué. (Cheers. For He's a Jolly Good Fellow!)

A word about morale. Morale is good. There is nothing wrong with the people. Their fettle is fine. We are all too busy to read or think; our minds are entirely occupied with material problems; there's nothing so healthy as having to devote all one's energies to the next meal. But sometimes we get a bit blue and then we like to wrap ourselves in the Union Jack and pass moral judgements. Here are a few slogans which I find of great comfort, and which I hope some of you will.

'Thou shalt hate thy neighbour as thyself!' This, I think, is all we really need to know about the bogus modern science of psychology. 'Hatred begins in the home.' Fair enough! That is why we invented the State. 'He preyeth best who hatest best all things both great and small.' 'Hate and it shall be given unto you.' This I take to mean that if we can hate a class and then all other classes, a nation and then all other nationalities, the old and the young, the rich and the poor, the male and the female, then we can end by hating not only the living but life itself. And not until we hate life are we ready to take a creative part in shaping the twentieth century. And remember, Art is the flower of life; it is what is most living. We must cut down the blossom till we have learnt how to uproot the plant.

At present we are passing through a phase of voluntary compulsion. That will fail and be succeeded by a phase of 'guidance' which will restore the controls and penalties of our 'finest hour'. I see one ray of hope: remember, whatever miseries we endure, they are endured to the full by other nations, and among those nations there are rulers so forward-looking as to regret the good old days of war (sound, if not safe) as much as we do. I don't think we shall have to wait long, gentlemen, before I return to my old and treasured post as *Horizon*'s military spokesman.

Decay along with me
The worst is yet to be. (Ovation.)

The Flaws in Commitment (1961)

[John Mander, *The Writer and Commitment* (Secker & Warburg)]

Man is a political animal and so literature is a department of politics. Right? Freedom and justice are political ends and only one party, the socialist party, cares for freedom and justice. Right? Historically, socialism is correct, 100 per cent, *dans le vrai*, and writers are not *dans le vrai* unless they work for socialism 100 per cent. Then they are committed, *engagés*. There have been socialist writers before now but there have been faults in their commitment.

The New Socialism is different. Such faults will not recur. Right? Mr Wesker, author of *Roots*, is the most perfectly committed new socialist: 'It is safe to say that Mr. Wesker's plays are superior to anything by Messrs. Auden, Spender, and Isherwood in that genre in the nineteen-thirties. . . . Mr. Wesker's achievement is certainly relevant also to the assessment of Orwell's work. . . .' (The chapter on Orwell is called 'One step forward, two steps backward.')

'The Socialist is right' concludes Mr Mander:

> in his instinctive assumption that what matters in art is the quality and nature of the artist's commitment. He is right in thinking that art is *about* something, that it has reference to something beyond itself by which it must ultimately be judged. He is right too, in his hunch that the enemies of art are found among those who would isolate it from its human historical context and wish it to refer only to itself. 'Com-

mitment' has become something of a rogue term in recent years; but it deserves to survive its present vogue.

Well, what is to be done? What is a mere 'Sunday reviewer' (Mr Mander's expression) to do when he sees this hoary old fallacy which ruined the Thirties popping up again? 'Wot about the Pyramids?'

'I hear a voice from the back of the hall say "What about the Pyramids?" and I am glad he has asked that question. Comrades, it is no accident that they were pyramidal – with room for only one man to sit on the top. Such was the artefact of tyranny, the useless monument of a slave state. We give you the Cube, the new block of workers' flats, not a tomb but a womb, the womb with a sunshine roof where the Future is born.

'Who will identify himself with that future? The workers – but remember, not every worker is a socialist, so I say the socialist workers – and those intellectuals who have gone over to the workers and refused to allow themselves to be exploited before it is too late. I repeat, before it is too late, for already I see some intellectuals sneaking in to the best seats and trying to look as if they were there when the meeting began; you can't fool the workers, comrades, you can't cheat History!'

Mr Mander is fresh and lively; his book is both interesting and readable. What he has done is to apply a conception which he thinks enlarges criticism but which actively diminishes it; a straitjacket in which no artist can move and which in the end leaves room only for two or three writers whom he happens to like, such as Mr Wesker and Mr Thom Gunn (who is in a state of 'existentialist pre-commitment'). His chapter headings are revealing. 'Must we Burn Auden?' (seventy pages), 'One Step Forward, Two Steps Back' (Orwell, forty pages) – 'A House Divided' (Angus Wilson, divided between socialism and depth-psychology, Arthur Miller, socialist but not socialist enough, forty pages), 'In Search of Commitment' (The Poetry of Thom Gunn) and 'Art and Anger' (John Osborne and Arnold Wesker).

It will be seen that more than half the book is devoted to putting Auden and Orwell in their places, to discussing their failures in commitment (and here Orwell is used against Auden before he himself goes down in the next purge). Mr Gunn is similarly used to deliver a glancing blow at Mr Spender. ('The polemic against him reflects a younger generation's uneasiness in the presence of a commitment felt existentially inauthentic' – a sentence against which there is no appeal.)

The essay on Auden is a typical specimen of denigration. 'Must we burn Auden?' it begins. 'Many people seem to think so. The reputation of W. H. Auden and of the Thirties poets generally is probably as low now as it has ever been.' This creates the appropriate funereal atmosphere and the three executioners are now introduced: the late Professor Joseph Warren Beach, Mr A. Alvarez and George Orwell (taken from the condemned cell).

> George Orwell's attack was the first in print of the time and has been the most widely applauded and accepted. Mr. Auden's brand of immoralism is only possible if you are the kind of person who is always somewhere else when the trigger is pulled.

'The gibe has stuck,' comments Mr Mander (who has 'worked for a time in a Jugoslav youth camp'), 'and there is no doubt that it constitutes for many people a devastating criticism of the Thirties writers.' We are then told that Orwell was wounded 'while Auden (according to Roy Campbell) played ping-pong in an hotel in Malaga.'

We are now ready for Mr Alvarez and Professor Beach. According to the first, Auden is 'not so much a poet as a kind of versifying journalist,' while Professor Beach, who was himself an indifferent poet, has written a whole book about the significant corrections Auden has made in the collected version of his poems.

Mr Mander then announces that 'Look Stranger' is Auden's best book, and proceeds to take us through it. It is his best because he is most assured in it of the loyalty of the clique for whom it was written, his 'we' holds its maximum confidence. But this enthralment to a clique is also his greatest weakness.

> A great deal of ground will have to be given up . . . all the plays written with Isherwood in the Thirties, together with longer works such as 'The

> Orators', 'New Year Letter' and the various travel books. The apologist for Auden must base himself, first of all, on the poems. And even then he must be willing to abandon many poems that have found their way into the anthologies, and into the Auden canon itself. . . . He must drop any claims that Auden is a 'great' poet of the stature of Yeats or Eliot. Such claims have done Auden's reputation great harm in the past.

I hope the technique is becoming apparent. Specific personal attacks are quoted and these are backed up by the invocation of invisible hordes of supporters. 'Many people seem to think so' . . . 'Constitutes for many people' . . . 'Many poems that have *found their way* into anthologies' . . . 'Such claims have done Auden's reputation great harm.' Behind the three Matadors is a vast audience, all thumbs pointed down.

We are not told until the next essay that Orwell's attitude was part of an inferiority complex about all 'university wits,' or that Roy Campbell was a Fascist on the opposite side, that other critics consider 'Another Time' or 'New Year Letter' or 'The Age of Anxiety' or the 'Sea and the Mirror' to be Auden's best book, and that if Orwell is to be dismissed as more conservative than socialist his criticism of Auden is invalid.

Perhaps the best objection to Mr Mander's bright superficiality is simply that Auden is here and unburnt, that it was precisely the spirit of Mr Mander's criticism as exemplified by other polemical commissars which precipitated his search for more spiritual values.

But is it not all a game? People like Eliot and Auden are like ancient landmarks on whom succeeding generations scrawl their names, sometimes with an insult, and then, in a flash, they too are bald and old, and 'many people,' as Mr Mander would put it, wonder who they are and question their commitment. Then another young critic appears. 'Auden is no poet,' he writes, 'his work lacks organic unity' . . . 'Never has his reputation reached such a low ebb' . . . 'Who now reads him or Orwell or Angus Wilson? or Thom Gunn? or even ——.' But before he can say 'John Mander' he has to be fitted with spectacles, false teeth, or is committed to a toupee. The pyramids remain.

'Give Me Back My Youth!'
(1961)

In his editorial for the hundredth number of *Encounter*, Mr Stephen Spender quoted from my comment on the hundredth number of *Horizon*: 'During the eight years I have edited *Horizon* we have witnessed a continuous decline in the arts.' Like a good editor, he goes on to refute this with some optimistic bumbling. 'It may be that there are Rimbauds disguised among the Beatniks, and a D. H. Lawrence just coming from a New Town. I very much hope so, and if that happens we hope that *Encounter* will be the first to publish him.' This brand of hopefulness is something one usually gets through by the time the hundredth number comes round.

'*Horizon*,' I wrote, 'has become aware of the decline of literature through the increasing difficulty of obtaining contributions. If the reader will glance at the present issue he will see that there is a poem by Miss Sitwell. In point of fact, six eminent poets were asked for a contribution to our hundredth number; the other five had nothing ready. Sorry, no eggs.'

~

This was in May, 1947, and Dame Edith's poem was 'The Coat of Fire': it is interesting to see that a poem by her also appears in *Encounter* in January, 1962. In fact it is not on the beatnik Rimbauds and red-brick Lawrences that the number relies, but on the old stalwarts like E. M. Forster, Edith Sitwell, T. S. Eliot, Herbert Read, W. H. Auden, Arnold Toynbee, George Orwell and so on; even as the hundredth number of *Horizon* relied on Edith Sitwell, Bertrand Russell and Lionel Trilling, with a story by a 'new' writer, Angus Wilson (who also appears in

Encounter). The art article was on Balthus by Robin Ironside, while *Encounter* features Henry Moore, Masson, Ghika, Nolan and Eduardo Paolozzi. Only the last two could be considered 'new'.

What really emerges from these special numbers (which are apt to be more conservative than others) is how few writers really carry the burden of English culture. Forster has been doing it since 1905, Eliot and Edith Sitwell since 1915; they have been appearing regularly in magazines for over forty years. In *Encounter* Mr Forster reprints some of his Indian diaries for 1912. Mr Eliot contributes a letter on Harriet Weaver, who printed 'Prufrock' in 1917: even Mr Gregory Corso, the Benjamin of the number, submits a play written back in 1954.

~

I sometimes have a dream in which I have been persuaded to edit *Horizon* again in an atmosphere of widespread expectation – 'now we shall see a real magazine at last'; enthusiasm is general as publication day approaches, until the moment of truth when a blank dummy . . . you can imagine the rest.

I have a small collection of magazines. They teach one a lesson. Thus a complete set of a hundred and twenty numbers of *Horizon* fetches about twenty pounds, while a set of eight numbers of *Personal Landscape*, with many poems by Durrell, went for seventy-five pounds at Sotheby's this month. Some of the earliest magazines are the best, like Ford Madox Ford's *English Review*. Here is a summary for February 1909: three poems by Yeats, five by De la Mare, others by Galsworthy and Hauptmann, 'Isle of Typheus' by Norman Douglas, reminiscences by Joseph Conrad, part of *Tono-Bungay* by H. G. Wells.

Number one of *The Blue Review* (May, 1913) included 'The Soiled Rose', a story about a gamekeeper by D. H. Lawrence, and was edited by Katherine Mansfield and Middleton Murry. 'The Little Review' (Chicago) from about 1915 onwards contains poetry by Eliot and Yeats, and Joyce's *Ulysses*, with stories by Wyndham Lewis and articles by Ezra Pound. Some numbers are still perfectly topical.

Frank Rutter's 'Art and Letters' is another excellent and little-known magazine from the end of the first world war, containing work by the Sitwells, Aldington, Aldous Huxley, Herbert Read, Eliot, Firbank and Wyndham Lewis and modern painting to match: much of it is still contemporary, while 'Wheels' or 'Coterie' have dated. A number of Munro's 'Chapbook' (April, 1923) is devoted to new American poems and contains work by Robert Frost, William Carlos Williams, E. E. Cummings, Wallace Stevens, Marianne Moore and Conrad Aiken, all of whom would have shed lustre on the hundredth number of *Horizon* or *Encounter*: the cover of this 'Chapbook' was by Kauffer.

The first numbers of *Life and Letters* (editor: Desmond MacCarthy, June 1928) included Beerbohm, Hardy, Santayana, and a new writer, A. J. A. Symons, on Corvo: it remained the magazine of the literary establishment – with the *London Mercury* for the sub-establishment – until they were displaced by Mr John Lehmann's *New Writing* and Mr Grigson's *New Verse*.

These two magazines of the Thirties proper sparkle with talent, like the early numbers of *Transition*. Those were the days when one looked forward to the appearance of a new number, for a good magazine has more power than any book to insinuate itself into the imagination by the regularity of its publication, weaving a pattern in and out of the fluctuations of the purchaser's personality. For this reason I cherish particular feelings for the clotted pages of *Transition* and for the shrill polemics of *New Verse*: feelings which one could not have for *Life and Letters*, which was like a jug of home-made lemonade.

~

Sometimes, when people ask me pointedly 'Aren't you ever going to start *Horizon* again?' I know that it has happened also to them and that what they are saying is 'Damn you, give me back my youth.' Hence the nightmare: the sea of expectant faces, the distributors waiting, the vans at the door, the microphones ready to welcome the revival, the critics poised with tolerant pen, 'at last a real magazine,' and – the sweat pouring down his face – the editor beside a silent telephone, an empty in-tray, a blank dummy . . . you can still imagine the rest.

The pieces in this volume originally appeared in the following publications:

'Ninety Years of Novel-Reviewing' *New Statesman* 1929; 'The Movies' *New Statesman* 1939; 'Henry Lamb' *Architectural Review* 1932; 'New Novels' *New Statesman* 1929/35; 'Enemies of Promise, parts I and II' *Enemies of Promise* 1938/49; 'No Peace for Elephants' *Sunday Times* 1953; 'A Cato of the Campus' *Sunday Times* 1957; 'Deductions from Detectives' *New Statesman* 1931; 'The Private Eye' *Sunday Times* 1953/62; 'On Englishmen Who Write American' *New York Times Book Review* 1949; 'The Modern Movement' *The Modern Movement* 1965; 'The Breakthrough in Modern Verse' *London Magazine* 1961; 'The Position of Joyce' *Life and Letters* 1929; 'James Joyce' *New Statesman* 1941; 'Ezra Pound' *Sunday Times* 1969; 'T. S. Eliot' *Sunday Times* 1965; 'e.e. cummings' *Sunday Times* 1962; 'Ernest Hemingway' *Sunday Times* 1961; 'Evelyn Waugh: Was this Journey Really Necessary?' *Sunday Times* 1960; 'Apotheosis in Austin' *Sunday Times* 1971; 'George Orwell' *Sunday Times* 1968; 'Samuel Beckett: *Watt*, *Malone Dies*, *Molloy*' *Sunday Times* 1958; 'W. H. Auden: Some Memories' *W. H. Auden: a Tribute* 1975; 'Albert Camus: Introduction to *The Outsider*' *The Outsider* 1946; 'Albert Camus: Symbol of an Epoch' *Sunday Times* 1961; 'Dylan Thomas' *Sunday Times* 1960; 'The Beats' *Sunday Times* 1960; 'Poetry Today' *Réalités* 1970; 'The Novel-Addict's Cupboard' *New Statesman* 1936; 'First Edition Fever' *Sunday Times* 1963; 'A Collector's Year' *Sunday Times* 1967; 'The Modern Movement: Introduction to the Catalogue' Exhibition catalogue 1971; 'The Ivory Shelter' *New Statesman* 1939; 'Comment' *Horizon* 1939/40; 'Writers and Society, 1940–43' *Horizon* 1940–3; 'The Cost of Letters' *Horizon* 1946; 'Cannon to Left of Them' *Horizon* 1946; 'Humanists at Bay' *Horizon* 1948; 'In Jugular Vein' *Horizon* 1947; 'The Flaws in Commitment' *Sunday Times* 1961; 'Give Me Back My Youth!' *Sunday Times* 1961